UNDERSTANDING AND TEACHING EMOTIONALLY DISTURBED CHILDREN

Phyllis L. Newcomer
Beaver College

ALLYN AND BACON, INC.

Boston   London   Sydney   Toronto

For My Parents
Marguerite and Albert Parker

Copyright © 1980 by Allyn and Bacon, Inc.,
470 Atlantic Avenue, Boston, Massachusetts 02210.
All rights reserved. No part of the material
protected by this copyright notice may be
reproduced or utilized in any form or by any
means, electronic or mechanical, including
photocopying, recording, or by any information
storage and retrieval system, without written
permission from the copyright owner.

Library of Congress Cataloging in Publication Data

Newcomer, Phyllis L.
        Understanding and teaching emotionally disturbed
children.

        Bibliography: p.
        Includes index.
        1.   Mentally ill children—Education.   2.   Mentally
Ill children.   I.   Title.
LC4165.N48   371.9'28   79-21407
ISBN 0-205-06843-X

10 9 8 7 6 5 4 3   85 84 83 82

Printed in the United States of America.

Contents

Appendix

Preface

This book is written primarily for teachers. It presents a broad spectrum of therapies that are useful in varying degrees with children who cannot make healthy adjustments in educational environments. The intent is to arm teachers with information that will change misconceptions of children who are often considered and frequently labeled as "emotionally disturbed." More importantly, the author seeks to acquaint them with intervention methods or approaches that may be used with such children in classrooms or related educational facilities.

This book focuses on the teacher as a therapist. The tenets presented reflect the assumption that the role of teacher involves much more than presenting academic content to children. Successful teaching requires knowledge of individual development and learning styles, awareness of personality characteristics, appreciation of situational stresses and strains, and, most critically, the ability to utilize such information in a manner that facilitates learning for each student. In short, competent teachers must be prepared to recognize and offer solutions to a multitude of problems that may interfere with children's growth. They must act as therapists in the best sense of the word. Actually, teachers have little choice since "the buck stops" within the confines of the classroom. The notion that children's classroom problems can be solved by nonteaching experts has proved to be erroneous. Despite the good offices of a bevy of ancillary personnel such as psychologists, psychiatrists, and counselors, teachers, in the end, must make accommodations for problem children that increase their opportunities for successful experiences in school. Hopefully, this book will help them to do so.

Phyllis L. Newcomer

PART I
HISTORY AND THEORY

1
Overview of Emotional Disturbance

Emotional disturbance is not a new problem. Although the term itself was not used until 1900 (Reinert, 1972), history records human attempts to understand the conditions and behaviors that may currently be subsumed under the label "emotional disturbance" and other labels such as "mental illness," "psychopathology," and "behavioral deviance." Among the earliest explanations of emotional disturbance was the notion that individuals whose behavior marked them as strange, odd, or simply different from their brethren were possessed either by evil or divine spirits. Archeological evidence suggests that primitive man may have used *trephining*, a surgical technique involving chipping a hole in the skull, to release the evil spirits that had invaded individuals and robbed them of control over their behavior. In early Greece epilepsy and psychosis were regarded as signs of possession by divine forces. Afflicted individuals were revered as seers, prophets, or as marked for greatness.

Such ideas prevailed until Hippocrates (circa 460–351 B.C.), the Greek physician known as the father of medicine, recorded detailed descriptions of disturbed states such as melancholia, hysteria, and psychosis and defined them as forms of physical illness. He attributed these conditions to imbalances among the four bodily humors that he deemed responsible for physical health: yellow bile from the earth, black bile from water, blood from fire, and mucus from the air. In so doing, Hippocrates inaugurated a medical approach to understanding these conditions and made the study of emotional disturbance the concern of physicians.

During the Dark Ages, the medical or physical approach to mental illness was lost. As in earlier eras, symptoms of mental illness were thought to be the result of the influence of the devil on the person's spirit or soul. Monks and priests kept voluminous records of the characteristics of various devils that possessed the weak or impious and caused strange

3

or irrational behavior. They were responsible for treating such "possessions" by exorcising the evil spirits. The most benevolent form of treatment involved incantations and pleas for divine forgiveness. Less fortunate sufferers were whipped, stoned, dunked in ponds, and the hard core unrepentant were burned at the stake. The latter treatment was the only known "sure cure," although many miraculous recoveries were attributed to the other approaches.

Little had changed by the middle of the fifteenth century. The idea that disturbed people were evil and a menace to society remained dominant. As a result of the Inquisition, the concept of witchcraft became firmly entrenched and men and women who exhibited strange or deviant behavior were subjected to persecution. Although the clergy continued to bear the primary responsibility for dealing with the problem, the records of several prominent members of the medical profession of the period reveal that their attitudes were similar to that of the clergy. According to Coleman (1972) one physician, Fernel (1497–1558), reported cases of *lycanthropy*, the transformation of a human into a werewolf, and another, Plater (1536–1614), described the devil as the source of all mental illness.

The Renaissance saw the rise of many philosophers whose theories depicted the existence of "mind" as distinct from "soul," thereby directing attention away from the notions of spiritual causation or possession. Thoman Hobbes (1588–1679), John Locke (1632–1704), and George Berkeley (1685–1753) were influential in developing the concept of mental functions. Unfortunately, these theories were of little immediate benefit to the "possessed" members of the population who continued to be purged of their sins in various ways.

Even as the domination of the clergy began to wane in the seventeenth century and the notion of possession weakened, those individuals demonstrating symptoms of "insanity" or "lunacy" were often deprived of their rights and property and locked in institutions. It was not until the eighteenth century that dramatic reforms began to alter these conditions and returned the study of disturbed behavior to the purview of the physician. Philippe Pinel (1745–1826), a French physician who became director of the La Bicêtre hospital after the French revolution, is famous for unchaining the mental patients and advocating more humane forms of treatment.

In the nineteenth century the definition of emotional disturbance as an illness of the mind became firmly entrenched. Physicians began to pay increased attention to conscientious observation of their patients' behavior. They looked for common symptoms as clues to the origins of mental illness and formed schools of psychiatric treatment. Liébault (1823–1904), a French physician, founded the Nancy School and with his colleagues, particularly Bernheim (1837–1919), developed psychotherapy as a form of treatment. This school emphasized the relationship between patients' symptomology and their suggestibility, a premise that provided the foundation for the concept of *functional illness*, which will be described later in this chapter. A rival point of view flourished at the Salpetriere School, which was established by Charcot (1825–1893). These physicians believed that disturbed symptoms were attributable to organic malfunctions or physical disease.

In Germany, Kraepelin (1855–1926) solidified the mental illness concept by developing a classification system of mental diseases according to distinct clusters of symptoms. He identified two major psychoses, *manic-depressive* and *dementia praecox* (in current terminology schizophrenia). He also created two categories of disease, *endogenous* and *exogenous*. Endogenous maladies were of internal origin and were caused by some type of biological malfunction such as brain damage or genetic defects. Exogenous illnesses were of external origin and were unrelated to biological factors.

During this period the scientific method was being applied to the study of behavior in the United States. Empirical research involving hypothesis formation, observation, quantitative measurement, and controlled experimentation was undertaken by men like Fechner (1801–1887) and Galton (1822–1911). The significance of this movement is that it introduced an alternative to medical studies of pathological behavior by investigating normal behavior. It also placed importance on proof through measurement, an idea that was not part of the largely intuitive approach to the study of behavior undertaken in clinical or medical settings.

Finally, the twentieth century saw the study of disturbed conditions revolutionized by the impact of many diverse theoretical perspectives. The work of Freud and his disciples in the psychoanalytic movement, the research into organic or genetic causation of emotional disturbance, the growth of the humanistic movement, the contributions of Sullivan (1953) and the interpersonal theorists, the information gleaned from sociology and social psychology emphasizing cultural influences on behavior, the impact of learning theory, and so forth, all provided pieces of a still-incomplete puzzle. In fact, the very existence of different perspectives on the topic of emotional disturbance has created confusion for those who seek to understand the subject. The days of adherence to one point of view are past. Currently, there is little agreement on the critical issues that pertain to the topic including: *definition*—what is emotional disturbance? *general perspectives*—what criteria establish an individual as emotionally disturbed? and *etiology*—what causes emotional disturbance? Students of emotional disturbance must be familiar with alternate theories pertaining to each of these critical issues if they are to understand the state of the field at this point.

WHAT IS EMOTIONAL DISTURBANCE?

The term *emotional disturbance* is one of many labels used to classify certain abnormal, atypical, or deviant behaviors. Alternate terms sometimes interchanged with emotional disturbance are *emotional maladjustment, mental disorder, psychosocial disorder,* and *mental illness,* among others. Often, the label "emotional disturbance" is used exclusively to refer to children's psychological problems in the same manner that "mental illness" is applied to adults. Although the term has become common parlance, its precise meaning is unclear. To some individuals, it signifies any type of psychological or emotional disorder, including the most severe psychotic conditions. To others it applies only to a variety of less severe disorders. The variance in opinion over the meaning of emotional disturbance is conveyed clearly in various definitions of the term.

Some definitions emphasize the extent to which behavior differs from social norms, for example, "the child who cannot or will not adjust to the socially acceptable norms for behavior and consequently disrupts his own academic progress, the learning of his classmates, and interpersonal relations" (Woody, 1969, p. 7). Other definitions cite typical maladaptive behavioral patterns, for example, "One who because of organic and/or environmental influences, chronically displays: (a) inability to learn at a rate commensurate with his intellectual, sensory-motor and physical development, (b) inability to establish and maintain adequate social relationships, (c) inability to respond appropriately in day to day life situations, and (d) a variety of excessive behavior ranging from hyperactive, impulsive responses to depression and withdrawal" (Haring, 1963, p. 291). Still others focus exclusively on etiology, for example, "a severe behavior disorder that results solely from the effects of the physical-chemical environment. Biological factors may exert their effects prenatally, during labor and birth, and at any subsequent time" (Rimland, 1969).

The common factor in these definitions is that the existence of the condition or state of emotional disturbance *must be inferred from behavior.* Definitions vary because they reflect alternate schools of thought and offer different explanations of behavior. The more specific information a definition contains, the more it reflects a particular theoretical bias and the more disagreement it provokes among those with alternate perspectives. Although no single definition can be completely acceptable to all, one that includes only general statements may be agreeable to most. The following definition is designed to do no more than set boundaries for the ensuing discussion of emotional disturbance.

> *Emotional disturbance* is a state of being marked by aberrations in an individual's feelings about him- or herself and the environment. The existence of emotional disturbance is inferred from behavior. Generally,

if a person acts in a manner that is detrimental to him- or herself and/or others, he or she may be considered in a state of emotional disturbance.

A global definition of this type creates more questions than it answers since it does not delineate the specific behaviors deemed characteristic of emotional disturbance, nor does it reveal information about the causes of emotionally disturbed states. Such a definition does signify that the term will be used as a general descriptor of a broad continuum of abnormal or atypical conditions. The ensuing discussion of general perspectives of emotional disturbance, and that of major schools of thought in Chapter 2, should provide a variety of answers to the questions generated by the definition.

GENERAL PERSPECTIVES OF EMOTIONAL DISTURBANCE

General perspectives of emotional disturbance reflect two major emphases, disability and deviance.

Disability Perspective

This view of emotional disturbance reflects a *medical point of view*. It affirms the existence of an internal pathological condition that generates aberrant behaviors. As is the case with physical illness, where symptoms such as a stomach ache may signify a disease such as an ulcer, certain inappropriate behaviors that are detrimental to self or others are symptomatic of underlying illness. Such behaviors are signals that something is wrong with the person, that is, he or she is sick. By implication, if the individual were not ill then he or she would not behave inappropriately. Therefore, the individual is not directly responsible for his or her behavior.

As disturbed conditions *exist before an individual behaves inappropriately,* and, in fact, cause the inappropriate behavior, *overt behavior per se does not necessarily mark an individual as disturbed.* Two men may demonstrate the same set of behaviors, for example, steal a car, drive at high speeds, and smash into a guardrail. One individual acts in such fashion because he is emotionally disturbed and his reason is clouded by his illness. The other person is emotionally healthy, but simply takes the car for a joy ride. The latter individual is not driven to car theft by underlying pathology, he consciously decides to behave in a manner that he regards as advantageous. Although the behaviors are identical and are regarded as being outside the socially acceptable behavioral norms of any community, they do not establish the condition of disturbance.

Clearly, from the disability perspective the *underlying forces that motivate behavior are critical to the diagnosis of a disturbed condition.*

These forces are the physical and psychological processes that constitute the "persona," the combination of inherent, developmental, and learned factors that characterize the individual and determine behavior. They involve physiological and neural operations as well as the psychological variables of needs, drives, and attitudes. When a state of emotional disturbance exists these forces are diseased or perverted in some manner. In the example cited above, the disturbed individual may be motivated by self-destructive urges that distort his perceptions of the world and cause irrational behavior.

Information about the motivating forces that underlie behavior *cannot be gathered by mere observation of surface acts.* Such basic personal dimensions can be gleaned only through extensive psychiatric and psychoneurological evaluation. This sort of examination is designed not only to establish the condition of emotional disturbance, but, through the measurement of the implicit psychological and neurological operations, to determine the specific etiology of the condition. To return to our example, the emotionally disturbed car thief might be suffering from an organic lesion. His surface behaviors are merely symptoms of his underlying pathology.

To aid in the diagnosis of disturbed conditions, or in the terminology of the disability perspective, mental illnesses, the American Medical Association publishes *The Diagnostic and Statistical Manual of Medical Symptoms* (1968). This manual names and describes hundreds of specific pathological conditions. The sheer number of diagnostic categories included attests to the importance of determining etiology and applying the precise disability label to the "sick" individual. It also reflects the traditional medical belief that specific diagnosis determines the choice of treatment, and that such treatment must focus on the underlying condition causing the behavioral symptoms.

The main categories of diseases or disorders referred to in this manual are psychoses, neuroses, psychopathic or sociopathic conditions, transient situational disorders, and behavioral disorders. Although most of these categories pertain to adult diseases, all of these diagnostic labels are used with children. Consequently, each category will be discussed briefly.

The *Diagnostic and Statistical Manual of Medical Symptoms* contains the following definition of *psychosis:*

> Patients are described as psychotic when their mental functioning is sufficiently impaired to interfere grossly with their capacity to meet the ordinary demands of life. The impairment may result from a serious distortion in their capacity to recognize reality. Hallucinations and delusions, for example, may distort their perceptions. Alterations of mood may be so profound that the patient's capacity to respond appropriately is grossly impaired. Deficits in perception, language and memory may be so severe that the patient's capacity for mental grasp of his situation is lost. (p. 23)

Among the more common psychoses cited in the handbook is schizo-phrenia, a large category of illnesses marked by disturbances of thinking, mood, and behavior. There are four prevalent schizophrenic states. *Simple schizophrenia* is characterized by a reduction of personal attachments and interests as well as apathy and indifference that destroys interpersonal relations and reduces mental functioning. *Hebephrenic schizophrenia* is marked by disorganized thinking, silly behavior, and hypochondriacal complaints. *Catatonic schizophrenia* is manifested either in excessive mo-tor activity or motor inhibition such as rigid body posture, stupor, mutism, or waxy flexibility. *Paranoid schizophrenia* is characterized by the pres-ence of persecutory or grandiose delusions (false beliefs) and often by hallucinations (perceptions with no basis in reality). When schizophrenia occurs in childhood it is manifested by autistic, withdrawn behavior. Among adolescents it may resemble any of the four classic types, although simple schizophrenia is most prevalent.

Another condition, *manic-depressive psychosis,* is characterized by violent shifts in mood ranging from unrealistic excitement and delusions of grandeur to severe debilitating apathy and disinterest in life. Patients may manifest either mania or depression, or both cyclically.

Paranoia is a third psychosis and is marked principally by delusions of persecution. It differs from paranoid schizophrenia because it doesn't involve the other characteristics associated with that disease.

Traditionally, psychoses have been classified as psychogenic or *func-tional* conditions for which there is no apparent physical cause or brain pathology, and *organic* conditions caused by biochemical or neural dis-orders. Recently, there has been increased doubt as to whether any psychosis is a functional disease.

Symptoms of most psychoses are recognized easily, and psychotic individuals usually receive some type of treatment for their condition. According to the American Medical Association, approximately 3 percent of the population suffers from some form of psychosis during some period of their lives. Schizophrenia, depression, and autism, are the principal diseases afflicting children. In 1970, the National Institute for Mental Health estimated that 5,000,000 American children suffer from psychotic or borderline psychotic disorders.

The second major type of major mental disorder, *neuroses,* are de-scribed in the AMA manual as manifesting neither distortions nor mis-interpretations of external reality, nor gross personality disorganization. Anxiety, a feeling akin to fear, is the primary characteristic of neurosis. It may be experienced directly or controlled unconsciously by various psychological defense mechanisms.

An *anxiety neurosis* is an illness where anxiety is experienced directly. The afflicted individual experiences debilitating feelings of tension and fear despite the fact that there is no direct stimulus or obvious reason for fear or apprehension. An elevated state of anxiety causes the individual to be easily upset by ordinary life experiences. Often somatic symptoms appear and the person may develop illnesses ranging from backache to heart disease. Such illnesses are real, not feigned, and are caused by anxiety. Anxiety is not experienced directly in other conditions such as hysterical, phobic, obsessive-compulsive, depressive, neurasthenic, or hypochondriacal neuroses. Instead, the anxiety causes various types of discomforting symptoms.

A *hysterical neurosis* is marked by an involuntary psychogenic loss of function. The individual experiences no fearful feelings, but suddenly is unable to walk, speak, see, or hear. There is no physical reason for the disability. The symptoms characteristically begin and end in emotionally charged situations and often fail to correspond to physiological realities. For instance, a paralysis of the hand may end at the wrist rather than follow neural tracks up the arm.

A *phobic neurosis* involves intense fear of a particular object or situation that the person consciously realizes is not really dangerous. The fear may induce faintness, fatigue, palpitations, perspiration, nausea, tremor, and panic. There are many types of phobias including acrophobia or fear of heights, claustrophobia or fear of closed areas, and so forth. School phobia is a 'common childhood disorder.

An *obsessive-compulsive neurosis* is characterized by the persistent reoccurrence of unwanted thoughts or the involuntary repetition of actions. The thoughts may consist of single words or ideas and the actions may range from simple movements to complex rituals. Lady Macbeth's handwashing is an example of a compulsive ritual. In children, obsessive-compulsive behavior often takes the form of continuous humming, ritualistic rocking, and close adherence to established routines for interacting with the environment. Distress and anger often follow the interruption of a compulsive activity.

In *depressive neurosis,* the individual feels worthless and unable to face the world. Such convictions bear little relationship to reality, since the problem can occur in successful individuals.

In *neurasthenia,* the individual feels too tired to perform everyday functions like going to work or school, bathing, or dressing. *Hypochondriasis* is a preoccupation with body functioning and disease. Sufferers believe that they have a variety of illnesses, although they are actually healthy.

Although the label "neurosis" often is used casually to describe idiosyncratic behavior, the term is more precisely and correctly attached to complex pathological conditions that seriously disrupt the lives of the afflicted. For instance, a child suffering an anxiety neurosis is at a great disadvantage. Anxiety makes concentration difficult and seriously limits ability to function in school. Social interactions also are disrupted, since the individual may be too upset to engage in play activities with peers.

According to the AMA, approximately 10 percent of the population suffers from neuroses. Children experience all forms of the disease

A third major category of mental illness is *sociopathic* or *psychopathic* disorders. These disabilities differ perceptibly from neurotic and psychotic disorders. They are characterized by acting out behavior, exploitation of others, and a lack of guilt or regret over inappropriate behavior. Socio-psychopaths engage in antisocial activities. Their personalities are marked by egocentricity and a lack of true regard, affection, or loyalty for others. Their immediate affect is one of charm, spontaneity, and optimism; however, they do not wear well. Generally, they regard anything they do as justified no matter what social rules they violate. People exist to be exploited, rules are made to be broken, and authority figures beg to be defied. Socio-psychopaths see the world as owing them a living and simply take what they want without regard for consequences. Immediate pleasures far outweigh long-range goals.

Only 1 percent of mental hospital patients are diagnosed as socio-psychopaths. Since these individuals typically run afoul of authority, many of them are confined in penal institutions. Generally, they are extremely resistant to traditional psychotherapeutic treatment.

The last two categories of mental illness to be discussed are *transient situational* disorders and *behavioral* disorders. The former classification pertains to conditions directly precipitated by environmental stress. For example, a child reacting to the death of a parent may display the symptoms of severe depression. Other similar disorders are the "shell shock" experienced by combat soldiers, or the dazed, confused reactions of persons exposed to other catastrophes such as a destructive earthquake. Transient situational disorders are usually alleviated by the passage of time and by support from key persons.

Behavioral disorder is a category that pertains directly to children's problems. Because these conditions are of primary importance, they will be discussed in detail in Chapter 2, which deals specifically with the identification of emotionally disturbed conditions in children.

The classification categories just discussed make it clear that, from the disability perspective, emotional disorders are *fixed conditions*. In other words, an emotionally disturbed individual is always sick, rather than sick on some occasions and normal on others. Social relativity does not affect the existence of internal pathological states. A schizophrenic person is sick regardless of the culture he or she is a member of. Similarly, the existence of an emotional disorder does not depend on displays of deviant behavior. A psychotic individual may be mentally ill for a long period of time without deviating overtly from established social norms. Such is the case, for example, when an upstanding citizen suddenly, for no apparent reason, slaughters his or her friends and neighbors. The illness causing such bizarre behavior probably existed long before the behavior occurred.

From the disability perspective, treatment of emotionally disturbed individuals is *conducted largely by medical personnel.* Psychiatrists, physicians who specialize in mental or psychological disorders, bear primary responsibility for treatment, although they may be assisted by members of ancillary professions such as social workers and clinical psychologists. The principal component of treatment is drug therapy, that is, the use of tranquilizing or sedating drugs to control the symptoms of mental illness. Psychotherapy is often conducted to resolve the underlying causes of the problem.

Treatment facilities include mental hospitals and mental health clinics. For the most part, treatment focuses on curing the individual's internal disability. The forces inside the individual causing the illness must be altered if he or she is to regain mental health. The manipulation or modification of environmental events is a secondary consideration.

To reiterate, the principal points associated with the disability perspective of emotional disturbance are as follows:

1. Emotional disturbance is a disease caused by internal neurological or psychological disorders.
2. The internal disease causes the individual to engage in sick behaviors symptomatic of the underlying illness.
3. Overt behavior per se does not mark an individual as emotionally disturbed.
4. The internal forces motivating overt behavior determine the existence of an emotionally disturbed condition.
5. Diagnosis of disturbance must involve more than observation of overt behavior, it must include measurement of internal functioning.
6. Diagnosis must be conducted by trained medical personnel.
7. The focus of diagnosis must be on etiology, that is, the underlying causes of the behavior.
8. Emotionally disturbed states are fixed conditions, they are not culturally relative.
9. Treatment is conducted primarily by medical personnel in medical facilities.
10. Treatment focuses on curing the individual's underlying pathology.

Deviance Perspective

From the deviance perspective, a state of emotional disturbance is determined by the extent to which an individual breaks social rules. A society establishes rules or standards of appropriate behavior that reflect its values, beliefs, convictions, and traditions. Such rules may be formalized in laws or may be implicit, unspecified criteria for social interaction.

For the most part, each member of the society is expected to conform to such rules or risk negative consequences, since rule breaking is perceived as harmful or threatening to the general welfare. Technically, rules are enforced by the citizenry; the behavior of each citizen is subject to evaluation by every other citizen. When an individual's overt behavior falls outside the limits deemed appropriate by the majority of the community, he or she may be designated as emotionally disturbed. In effect, *emotional disturbance is a label that may be applied to rule breakers.* It represents one of many categories of deviance.

Although an individual's overt behavior may earn him or her the designation of emotional disturbance, as with the disability perspective, *behavior per se,* no matter how extreme or unusual it may appear, does *not signify a state of emotional disturbance.* Behavior deemed deviant in one circumstance may be judged appropriate in another. For instance, a sniper who indiscriminately shoots thirteen strangers appears to be demonstrating deviant behavior. However, as a soldier shooting the enemy, the behavior would be appropriate to the situation. As a soldier, for failing to shoot, the sniper might be regarded as deviant by society. The environmental circumstances affecting an individual—the social milieu—help define the normalcy of behavior. Such variables are part of the criteria that community members use to judge the appropriateness of behavior. Clearly, community opinion is the critical determinant of the existence of an emotionally disturbed state.

A deviance perspective of emotional disturbance might best be termed a *social* or *culturally relative* point of view. A society arbitrarily chooses to regard behaviors as acceptable or deviant. For example, hallucinations and delusions, symptoms of severe emotional disturbance from the disability perspective, are viewed as normal and appropriate occurrences in societies that encourage the use of mind-expanding drugs and regard such experiences as religious events. Also, homicide was sanctified in head-hunting societies but is regarded as extremely deviant under most circumstances in our culture. Ullmann and Krasner (1969, p. 15)[1] note that behavior can never be viewed as pathological if it is normal for a particular society.

> A critical example is whether an obedient Nazi concentration camp commander would be considered normal or abnormal. To the extent that he was responding accurately and successfully to his environment and not breaking its rules, much less coming to the professional attention of psychiatrists, he would not be labeled abnormal. Repulsive as his behavior is to mid-twentieth-century Americans, such repulsion is based

---

[1] Leonard P. Ullmann, Leonard Krasner, *A Psychological Approach to Abnormal Behavior,* 2nd edition, 1975, p. 15. Reprinted by permission of Prentice-Hall, Inc., Englewood Cliffs, New Jersey.

on a particular set of values. Although such a person may be made liable for his acts—as Nazi war criminals were—the concept of abnormality as a special entity does not seem necessary or justified. If it is, the problem arises as to who selects the values, and this, in turn, implies that one group may select values that are applied to others. This situation of one group's values being dominant over others is the fascistic background from which the Nazi camp commander sprang.

From the deviance perspective, emotional disturbance obviously *is not synonymous with mental disease.* The term does not imply that underlying pathological conditions cause atypical or bizarre behavior. The whole question of underlying causation is not critical to determining the existence of a disturbed state. The extent to which behavior is socially inappropriate determines the disturbed classification, not the forces motivating the inappropriate behavior. For example, two individuals might share intense feelings of hatred for their neighbor. One person violates community standards by physically assaulting the neighbor, while the other is content to engage in verbal abuse. The first individual's overt behavior exceeds acceptable social limits and thus is labeled "emotionally disturbed." Although the other person maintains similar internal feelings of hatred, his overt behavior does not violate community norms, and he is not perceived as emotionally disturbed.

The societal norms used to classify disturbed behavior are varied and complex. As noted, the critical variable is not specific behaviors. Many of the antisocial and self-destructive behaviors that characterize emotionally disturbed states are demonstrated by the majority of the population. Adults often violate social rules by driving too fast, telling lies, drinking too much alcohol, and so on. Children often fight, feign illness, cheat on tests, and defy adults, among other things. If disturbance were reflected by deviant behavior alone, then everyone engaging in such behavior would be regarded as disturbed. Yet the designation of emotional disturbance is not applied haphazardly to every person who has a fight or drinks too much alcohol. Society establishes behavioral norms that encompass a range of acceptable deviant acts. Deviant acts indicate disturbance only when they fall outside this range. Generally, this happens when deviant behaviors occur: (1) with excessive frequency, (2) with great consistency, and (3) in unusual abundance. Too many deviant acts displayed too often over too long a time mark the person as different from the norm. In effect, deviant behaviors become typical or characteristic of the individual's personality. They alarm, concern, inconvenience, or irritate others, thereby inviting community intervention and the possible designation of emotional disturbance.

Several examples should illustrate the above point. A person who engages in an occasional heated argument is not unusual, but an individual who consistently quarrels with others is viewed as atypical. An occasional bout of drunkness is perceived by most observers as reflecting nothing more than the frailty of human nature, while frequent over-indulgence in alcohol is viewed as a serious problem. Individuals who drive recklessly probably will not be regarded as disturbed, unless they commit other acts that violate community rules, such as fighting, truancy, and so forth.

Some behaviors deviate so dramatically from societal norms that one act may, under certain circumstances, mark that person as abnormal. The behavioral dimensions of frequency, consistency, and abundance are rela-tively unimportant. Acts such as murder, attempted suicide, and incest are examples of such behavior. However, even these behaviors may occur in circumstances that mark them as normal rather than deviant. A murder may be regarded as justified. An individual who attempts suicide might be construed as engaging in a courageous act if death is chosen over betrayal of comrades. A person engaging in incest might be unaware of the kinship. Regardless of the apparent degree of deviance associated with certain acts, the judgment as to whether it reflects emotional disturbance depends on circumstances and the particular attitudes and values of the community.

Since emotional disturbance is established by socially deviant be-haviors, *it is not a fixed condition.* An individual is not either sick or well. In fact, the same individual might be construed as sick in one community and well in another, since standards vary. Adolf Hitler provides a good example. In a society other than Nazi Germany, he probably would have been regarded as a madman.

The impermanence of the disturbed state is emphasized further by the variance in normalcy criteria among subcommunities of a large com-munity. For example, in various states of the United States, gambling is a deviant behavior, whereas in others it is not. Within each state, cities, towns, boroughs, and neighborhoods form even smaller communities and each establishes unique criteria for deviance. In some cases community values conflict. For example, an individual who stands on the steps of a church oblivious to all around, communing with God, may be accepted and admired by the members of a religious community. However, if that person were to engage in similar behavior on the steps of the Capitol in Washington, D.C., the behavior would undoubtedly elicit a different response from individuals who do not share the values of the small religious community.

Further variation in the criteria of deviance exists within communi-ties. Behaviors may be deemed appropriate or inappropriate depending on variables such as an individual's age, sex, race, social class, and educa-tion. An adolescent boy who fights frequently, uses profanity in public, drives recklessly, and so forth, may be regarded as less deviant than a middle-aged member of the city council who behaves similarly. The latter person's maturity and elevated position produce more stringent behavioral requirements. Similarly, an elderly person may demonstrate a great deal of mental confusion and disorientation without evoking concern. A thirty-year-old person who behaves similarly would incite much more alarm. Even behavior as extreme as homicide may be evaluated differently depending on the prestige and power of the murderer. An individual without influence or status in the community who commits murder is likely to be viewed with less sympathy than a well-connected, "substantial" citizen who commits the same crime.

As a general rule, a designation of deviance tends to be applied more readily to the less mature, less influential, less economically independent members of the community. Thus children, who obviously are controlled by others and are economically dependent, qualify as a population whose behaviors are frequently regarded as deviant. A child who commits an inappropriate act such as cheating on tests in school may be labeled "emotionally disturbed," whereas an adult who cheats on an income tax return may be regarded as clever.

Variation in what constitutes deviant behavior is demonstrated further by the fact that the type of behavior regarded as abnormal fluctuates as societal norms and community attitudes change. Today's deviant act is tomorrow's acceptable behavior. For example, women once prevented by social mores from smoking in public, can now smoke without fear of reprisal.

Obviously, when individuals have internalized the behavioral norms that prevail in one community they may experience difficulty adjusting to the dominant norms of another community. A teenage boy from an innercity ghetto who has learned to regard aggression as appropriate and necessary for survival can be expected to have difficulty in a school setting that regards such behavior as inappropriate.

As the discussion so far has made clear, from a deviance perspective emotional disturbance is a label that may be applied to a vast number of diverse behaviors. The term emotional disturbance has little specific meaning; it simply represents a particular category of deviance. Other, similar categories are criminality or delinquency. In fact, from the deviance perspective, differentiation among the behaviors associated with emotional disturbance and those classified as criminal is done arbitrarily, for the sake of social convenience. Generally, when behavior is self-destructive, the individual is labeled as disturbed. When behavior is harmful to others, the label "criminal" is more likely to be applied. Clearly, however, these categories are not mutually exclusive. Some murderers are committed to mental hospitals rather than to jail. Alcoholics and drug abusers may be treated in jails or in hospitals depending on extraneous circumstances such as age, sex, race, social class, intelligence, and so forth. Suicide, an obvious symptom of emotional disturbance, is a crime.

To reiterate, the principal points associated with the deviance perspective of emotional disturbance are

1. The term "emotional disturbance" is a label that may be assigned to those whose behavior deviates from social norms.
2. The existence of a disturbed condition is inferred.
3. The designation of disturbance is arbitrary, since it depends on community judgments, and communities vary in their views and tolerance of deviance.
4. The etiology of emotionally disturbed states is relatively unimportant. It does not determine who is labeled "disturbed."
5. The diagnostic label "emotionally disturbed" is one of several that may be assigned to deviant persons.
6. Emotional disturbance is not a fixed condition, but a variable state dependent on environmental circumstances.
7. Many behaviors indicative of emotional disturbance are displayed commonly by the general population. Only the frequency, constancy, and abundance of behaviors displayed mark an individual as deviant.
8. Treatment involves teaching individuals socially appropriate behavior so that they can function effectively. It may take place in mental hospitals or in other facilities such as schools or prisons.
9. Treatment is not limited to members of the medical profession, but may be undertaken by teachers, clergymen, psychologists, and other trained individuals.

A Comparative Analysis

Each of the perspectives of emotional disturbance offers a unique answer to the question "What is emotional disturbance?" From the disability perspective it is a disease that exists within an individual regardless of cultural values. From the deviance perspective it is a label assigned to those who break social rules, and therefore is culturally relative.

In modern society, the disability perspective appears to be the prevailing point of view. It has both strengths and weaknesses. One of its principal strengths is that it attempts to establish a culture-free classification system for emotionally disturbed conditions. Thus, individuals may be recognized as ill if they display certain behaviors regardless of who they are and where they are.

The second, related advantage is that the development of an elaborate classification system for pathological conditions provides a frame of reference for understanding unusual or inappropriate behaviors. It is a means of organizing what otherwise would be a mass of fragmented pieces of information. The importance of organizing such information is that it permits the systematic investigation of common conditions that is necessary for the generation and verification of scientific hypotheses. For example, if individuals demonstrate behaviors such as disorientation, bizarre speech, and confused ideation, they might be classified as schizophrenic. Once classified, they might be studied with other schizophrenics in order to isolate the common symptoms of that condition.

The third advantage of the disability perspective lies in the emphasis it places on determining the etiology of disturbed conditions. The isolation of the causes of these conditions paves the way for early intervention and more meaningful treatment. For example, if it were to be proved conclusively that the absence of certain enzymes is responsible for schizophrenia, early diagnosis and treatment would prevent the onset of the disease.

One final advantage is that the disability model is basically a therapeutic approach to the problem of emotional disturbance. It is based on the assumption that kind, compassionate treatment will restore normalcy, and that individuals should not be punished because they are ill.

Unfortunately, several of the advantages of this approach are double-edged swords. First, the disability classification system is often misused. Disability classification categories are primarily descriptive; they describe rather than explain behavior. For instance, schizophrenia is simply a label attached to a category of behaviors. A person who exhibits such behaviors is described as schizophrenic. The term does not explain why such behaviors occur and it cannot be construed as representing the cause of those behaviors. To conclude that an individual's bizarre behavior is caused by schizophrenia is similar to concluding that the bizarre behavior is caused by bizarre behavior, since those specific acts resulted in the application of the descriptive label "schizophrenia."

Second, the emphasis placed on causality is often misleading. It is a relatively easy matter to accurately observe and record samples of an individual's overt behavior. It is far more difficult to measure the internal psychological and/or neurological operations that cause those overt behaviors. It is even more difficult to discern whether or not such internal operations are diseased. Currently the instrumentation used to diagnose disturbed conditions is relatively crude. Most tests and other assessment devices lack the levels of reliability and validity necessary to engender confidence in their results. As a result, the conclusions drawn regarding states of internal mental pathology are often unverifiable speculations. As diagnosis moves away from inferences that refer directly to overt, observable behavior, toward inferences about the inner workings of the psyche or brain, increases the possibility of errors in judgment. This situation is typified in the all-too-frequent occurrence of mental health experts forming diametrically opposite conclusions about the mental state of a particular individual.

Third, the establishment of an elaborate classification system often only results in disability labeling. Unfortunately, any indication that an individual is disabled is stigmatizing. The mere application of a disability label conveys negative characteristics to others. Therefore, when disability labeling does not result in specific treatment, but is done primarily for purposes of classification, the benefits to the labeled individual are questionable. The literature in education is replete with studies of the negative effects of disability labeling on children's self-concepts, teacher's attitudes, parent's opinions, and so forth.

Two final aspects of the disability perspective have solely negative implications. One such limitation stems from the focus on individuals as the major sources of emotional pathology. The notion that emotionally disturbed individuals are ill and that they must be cured, that is, changed internally to regain mental health, de-emphasizes the importance of the social milieu. It leads to the further notion that an individual can be treated in relative isolation, in an environment devoid of the components contributing to the problem. Such a rationale may result in ineffective or inefficient treatment, either because critical environmental components of the problem have been overlooked or because individuals cannot transfer therapeutic benefits to the real world where their problems originate.

The practical implications of this approach can be seen in typical school treatment of emotionally disturbed children. Generally, intervention is focused on diagnosing and remediating the *child's* problem. Diagnostic and remedial procedures are conducted primarily in isolated settings, away from the classroom where the child is experiencing difficulty, a fact that attests to the small importance attributed to environmental events. Such procedures ignore many of the interactive variables present in the classroom situation, such as the effect of teachers and peers upon the child's mental state. Consequently, intervention effects may have limited effect on the child's ability to function in school.

The final disadvantage of the disability approach pertains to the assumption that only highly trained mental health specialists are capable of intervening with emotionally disturbed individuals. This assumption attributes little importance to the ability of key people in the environment, such as parents and teachers, to produce attitudinal and behavioral changes in children with emotional problems. This idea can be challenged, first because research does not support the success of traditional psychiatric practices with children (Levitt, 1957; Levitt, Beiser, and Robertson, 1959; Eysenck, 1967), and second because there are too few mental health experts to provide treatment for emotionally disturbed individuals. Other approaches for dealing with the problem of emotional disturbance must be undertaken.

As opposed to the medical orientation of the disability perspective, the deviance perspective springs from the disciplines of sociology and cultural anthropology. It too has strengths and weaknesses. Its values are inversely related to the problems associated with the disability perspective.

First, the deviance perspective emphasizes the importance of circumstances *outside* the individual to the study of disturbance. Obviously, if emotional disturbance is a culturally relative condition, it cannot be studied in a vacuum. The forces or social milieu that surround the individual must be considered.

Second, the deviance perspective emphasizes the arbitrary nature of disability labeling. Since such labels are assigned because of deviations from community norms, individuals may be designated as emotionally disturbed on the basis of chance. They may engage in particular behaviors in an intolerant rather than a tolerant community. An example of such chance categorization is the relatively common occurrence of a child being considered emotionally disturbed in one classroom, but viewed as normal in another.

Third, the deviance perspective directs attention to overt behaviors in the diagnosis and treatment of emotional disturbance. The advantage of this focus is that it provides direct information about the behaviors that must be altered if the individual's emotional problems are to be lessened.

The principal disadvantage of this perspective is that it equates emotional disturbance with nonconformity. It does not provide for the existence of abnormal conditions unless society labels behavior as abnormal. The validity of this assumption is questionable. Socially accepted behavior may be pathological. For example, the activities of the SS in Nazi Germany can be construed as pathological although they did not violate the norms of that particular society.

A second disadvantage is that normality is not synonymous with conformity. Deviant behaviors do not always signify abnormality. Nonconforming members of society frequently revitalize social custom and engender new growth. Unless there are standards within a society that transcend social acceptability, many creative, forethinking people who engage in deviant behavior would be labeled emotionally disturbed. Obviously, the nonconforming behavior of Thomas Jefferson, George Washington, Benjamin Franklin, and many other revolutionaries, as well as inventors such as the Wright brothers and Thomas Edison, and artists such as da Vinci, Rembrandt, and Michelangelo cannot be viewed as indicative of emotional disturbance.

A third and related problem concerns treatment. If emotional disturbance is synonymous with socially inappropriate behaviors, the therapist is placed in the position of teaching the deviant individual socially acceptable behavior. To do so, the therapist must make a value judgment as to the goodness or badness of behaviors, that is, what is to be taught or extinguished. Under these circumstances the Wright brothers might have been punished for working on their airplane and rewarded for building better bicycles.

In summary, it is clear that these two perspectives of emotional disturbance answer different questions. The deviance point of view attempts to delineate how an individual becomes labeled disturbed. It depicts the labeling process that operates in a particular society.

The disability model attempts to explain what emotional disturbance is. It provides culture-free criteria for establishing the existence of pathological conditions. In one sense, the disability model can be subsumed under the deviance perspective. Members of the medical profession who determine which individuals are mentally ill can be thought of as the social agents responsible for categorizing a deviant individual. In another sense, the disability perspective is broader than the deviance perspective because it provides absolute standards for the determination of mental pathology.

In any event, adherence to either position raises additional questions. If one regards emotionally disturbed persons as inherently different from the normal population, then one must determine whether the individual's sickness is a biological phenomenon due to faulty genes, neural functioning, or biochemistry, or whether the illness was developed because of environmental stress that activated certain predispositions within the individual.

If one accepts the premise that situational circumstances determine who will become emotionally disturbed, then one must decide whether those circumstances are viewed most accurately as a sequence of specific interactions between an individual and varied environmental agents, or as a total or global phenomenon involving a multitude of sociological variables. These issues introduce the discussion of various schools of thought in the next chapter.

STUDY QUESTIONS

1. Discuss why the term "emotional disturbance" is difficult to define. Then define it in your own words and use the information in Chapter 1 to determine what general perspective you hold.
2. Compare and contrast the disability and the deviance perspectives of emotional disturbance. Then decide if Adolf Hitler was emotionally disturbed and justify your conclusions with references to either perspective.
3. Define the terms psychosis, neurosis, schizophrenia, autism, anxiety, phobia, neurasthenia, psychopathic, behavioral disorder, hypochondriasis.
4. Consider the case of "Son of Sam," the man from New York who shot and killed or injured several young women and their dates. He was judged sane and sentenced to life imprisonment. Based on the information in Chapter 1, what perspectives influenced that decision?

REFERENCES

American Medical Association. *The diagnostic and statistical manual of medical symptoms.* New York: AMA, 1968.

Coleman, J. *Abnormal psychology and modern life.* Glenview, Ill.: Scott Foresman, 1972.

Eysenck, H. New ways in psychotherapy. *Psychology Today,* 1967, *1*(2), 39–47.

Haring, N. The emotionally disturbed. In S. Kirk and B. Weiner (eds.). *Behavioral research on exceptional children.* Washington, D.C.: The Council for Exceptional Children, 1963.

Levitt, E. Results of psychotherapy with children: an evaluation. *Journal of Consulting Psychology,* 1957, *21*, 189–196.

Levitt, E.; Beiser, H.; and Robertson, R. A follow-up evaluation of cases treated at a community child guidance clinic. *American Journal of Orthopsychiatry,* 1959, *29*, 337–347.

Reinert, H. The emotionally disturbed. In B. Gearheart (ed.). *Education of the exceptional child.* San Francisco: Intext Educational Publishers, 1972.

Rimland, B. Psychogenesis versus biogenesis: the issues and the evidence. In S.C. Plog and R. B. Edgerton (eds.). *Changing perspectives in mental illness.* New York: Holt, Rinehart and Winston, 1969.

Sullivan, H. *The interpersonal theory of psychiatry.* New York: Norton, 1953.

Ullmann, L., and Krasner, L. *Psychological approach to abnormal behavior.* Englewood Cliffs, N.J.: Prentice-Hall, 1969.

Woody, R. *Behavioral problem children in the schools.* New York: Appleton-Century-Crofts, 1969.

2
Theoretical Models of Emotional Disturbance

Theories of the causes of emotional disturbance vary greatly. Much of their diversity lies in the extent to which they regard forces outside the individual as important causal factors. At one extreme are theories that reflect a *biological orientation*. To a large extent, these theories focus attention exclusively on the human organism and ignore external forces. They attribute the development of emotionally disturbed states to organic pathology, that is, actual physiological malfunctions. Mental illness is viewed as a physical disease. Biological theories reflect a disability perspective, that individuals who become emotionally ill are inherently different from those who do not.

At a more central position are theories adhering to a *psychological orientation*. From this frame of reference, mental illnesses are functional conditions, that is, psychological rather than physical disorders. Causation usually involves a combination of internal and external factors. In some psychological theories, predetermined intraindividual susceptibility and unfavorable environmental forces determine who will become emotionally ill. These perspectives continue to represent mental illness primarily as an inherent disability. Other psychological theories maintain that external stresses distort the emotional development of essentially healthy people. In effect, the individual is not basically different from others but becomes disabled by his or her experiences.

Finally, at the other extreme are the theories that negate the importance of the individual condition or internal state and focus attention exclusively on external variables. Emotional disturbance is a function of certain social, cultural, or environmental phenomena. Individuals designated as emotionally disturbed are deviant, not disabled. Theories advocating this perspective have a *sociological orientation*.

The discussion that follows will present the principal tenets associated with six theoretical models of emotional disturbance beginning with the biological position, progressing through varied psychological viewpoints, and culminating with sociological perspective. The models are, in the order of their presentation: biological, psychoanalytical, behavioristic, phenomenological, existential, and sociological.

THE BIOLOGICAL MODEL

Theories reflecting a biological orientation maintain that emotional disturbance is a form of mental disease, a pathological condition that exists because of deficiencies in the individual. The behaviors characteristic of mental illness are caused by organic malfunctions, that is, actual physical disorders of some type. Such malfunctions may be due to neural, biochemical, genetic, or developmental deficits. The most extreme representation of this position attributes a direct cause and effect relationship between physiological malfunctions and behavioral disorders (Rimland, 1969). More moderate positions hedge against the biological orientation slightly and postulate a biogenetic cause–environmental catalyst–behavioral disorder paradigm (Rosenthal, 1963). The latter position holds to the necessity of biological malfunctions in mental illness, but grants the possibility that such inherent physiological deficits might lie dormant if not triggered by environmental factors. Despite slight variations in these approaches, both agree that biological factors are the key to all types of mental disorders.

From the biological perspective, diagnosis and treatment are focused exclusively on the sick individual. For the most part diagnosis centers on identifying the etiology of the illness. Naturally such efforts focus on physical operations, and particularly on biochemical and neural functions. Little or no attempt is made to examine the social or psychological aspects of disturbance. In fact, those who adhere to this position regard the *in utero* environment as far more important than the environmental events that occur after birth. Treatment consists primarily of the administration of drugs or chemicals to influence the functioning of the central nervous system. In some instances, reeducation to assist the afflicted individuals in adapting to their disabilities is also included. Generally those theorists adhering to this orientation are more interested in research, which they believe will eventually reveal the physical or organic basis for all mental disease, than they are in treatment procedures.

Genetic Research   One of the most important sources of support for the biological model is genetic research (Rhodes and Tracy, 1972). In these studies, investigators attempt to establish a higher incidence of mental illness among persons with common heredity. For instance, identical twins who share the same genetic inheritance would be expected to develop similar conditions if mental illness is transmitted solely through the genes. Other family members would be less vulnerable than identical twins, but more likely to develop the illness than members of the general population. In an early landmark study of the incidence of mental illness in the family backgrounds of psychotic patients, Kallmann (1953, 1958) found for schizophrenics a rate of occurrence or concordance rate of 86.2 percent for identical twins, 14.5 percent for fraternal twins, 14.2 percent for siblings, and 7.1% for half-siblings. Similarly, the concordance rate for manic-depressive psychosis was also significantly higher for identical twins than it was for other family members. When contrasted with the 3 percent incidence figure of mental illness for the general population these results appear to support the inheritability of these two diseases. In fact, Kallman concluded that both diseases are transmitted via recessive genes but are genetically different.

In a review of the schizophrenic research, Buss (1966) reported results similar to Kallmann's. Unfortunately, many of the studies included in his review were clouded by the fact that the psychotic subjects shared a common environment that could have been responsible for the onset of the disease. Studies with better methodological controls report lower concordance rates, but also support the conclusion that genetic factors influence schizophrenia. Kringlen (1967) reported a concordance rate of 38 percent for identical twins and a 10 percent rate for fraternal twins. Hoffer and Pollin (1970) and Pollin et al. (1969) found rates of 15.5 percent for identical twins and 4.4 percent for fraternal twins among 16,000 twin pairs who had been members of the American armed forces.

A similar type of research involves the incidence of mental illness among the children of psychotics. Heston (1970) reviewed the literature pertaining to schizophrenia and reported that about 45 percent of the children who have one schizophrenic parent eventually become either schizoid (mildly schizophrenic) or schizophrenic. Among children with two schizophrenic parents, 66 percent develop the disease. In a study Wender (1969) conducted with children who were separated at birth from one schizophrenic parent, one-third of the children developed schizophrenia. Heston (1966) and Rosenthal et al. (1968) compared the frequency of the disease among two groups of adults—those who had been separated from schizophrenic and from nonschizophrenic parents. They reported that about 9 percent of the children of schizophrenic parents developed the disease as opposed to none of the other group. Similar conclusions have been reported in studies involving manic-depressive disorders; the incidence of the disease is significantly higher among the relatives of patients (Dorzab et al., 1971; Pollin et al., 1969).

Applying the most general interpretation to the data acquired thus far, there appears to be a strong possibility that some types of severe mental illnesses are inherited. However, researchers have been unable to find any characteristic genetic defects among the psychotic samples studied. Apparently the genetic predispositions that exist do not follow Mendel's law of inheritability through a single, dominant gene. Rimland (1969) has noted that deviation from the Mendelian model is not unusual in genetic disorders, citing similar patterns in inherited physical disorders such as tuberculosis and diabetes. The fact remains, however, that the genetic patterns cannot be conclusively demonstrated. Therefore, critics of the biological model cannot be refuted convincingly when they point out that "psychotic" families have inadequate or destructive social relationships that may be the key to high family incidence rates. In fact, as Coleman (1972) notes, the critics of the biological model make a strong case when they note that some physical ailments, such as the vitamin deficiency disease beriberi, appear to run in families. However, they are not inherited illnesses, but are caused by learned patterns of behavior, in this case poor eating habits.

Possibly the most valid objection to the general applicability of the biological model is the scarcity of evidence that most conditions traditionally grouped under the rubric of mental illness are transmitted genetically. For example, researchers have not been able to relate childhood autism to hereditary defects, since the condition does not run in families (Treffert, 1970). Also, Judd and Mandell (1968) have failed to find significant chromosomal abnormalities in autistic children.

The evidence is even less supportive when milder forms of illness are investigated. Pollin et al. (1969) reported that for neurotic disorders, the concordance rate among identical twins was less than 1½ times greater than that found for fraternal twins, an incidence that is readily attributable to environmental factors. They concluded that while some mental disorders may be transmitted genetically, others are not.

Biochemical Research A second line of research (Rhodes and Tracy, 1972) pursued by those who adhere to a biological orientation features investigations into the biochemical causes of emotional disturbance. Essentially these studies focus on the chemical processes that influence interactions among neurons and the metabolic functions involved in energizing nerve cells. The majority of such investigations have been conducted with persons suffering from autism and schizophrenia. Those pursuing this type of research have attempted to identify an endogenous hallucinogen, that is, a body chemical produced under conditions of stress that might cause the hallucinations and disorganization of thought and effect that characterize schizophrenia and other psychotic conditions. There is some evidence that changes in the level of serotonin, a substance found in the brain that has been identified as important in brain metabolism, causes mental disturbance. Shore et al. (1957) found that the antipsychotic drug reserpine caused a significant fall in the level of brain serotonin. Dement (1968) revealed that changes in serotonin levels cause dreamlike and psychoticlike states in nonpsychotic patients.

On a related research effort, Heath et al. (1972, 1958) found that the injection of taraxein, a substance obtained from the blood of schizophrenic patients, produced manifestations of schizophrenia in healthy people. In another study, Heath et al. (1967) concluded that schizophrenia is caused when the body manufactures antibodies against its brain cells. Hypothetically, the antibody taraxein prevents the passage of information from one brain cell to another, thereby interfering with information processing. According to Coleman (1972), Heath's findings have not been replicated by other investigators, but Dearing (1969) cites Russian research that supports Heath's view.

Other recent research has also produced clues regarding the role of biochemical factors in producing psychosis. Gottleib, Frohman, and Beckett (1969) suggest that irregularities in blood protein cause disruption of information processing in the brain. Himwich (1970) concludes that schizophrenics are biologically different and convert certain body chemicals into psychosis-producing agents when subjected to stress. Similarly, both manic and depressive psychoses have been related to the level of catecholamines, a biogenic amine in the blood. Schildkraut (1965) hypothesizes that a deficiency of catecholamines, particularly norepinephrine, causes depression, whereas an overabundance results in mania. Some studies have shown that urinary excretion of norepinephrine is above normal during periods of mania and below normal during periods of depression. Also, a body of research has reported that substances that influence catecholamine metabolism have been used successfully to treat manic-depressive psychosis (Bunney et al., 1971; Goodwin et al., 1969; Van der Velde, 1970).

Other studies have manipulated body chemistry through the administration of vitamins. Theoretically, vitamins act to increase the metabolism of adrenaline and facilitate synaptic transmission of nerve impulses. Rimland (1969) reported that vitamin dosage caused improvement in 80 percent of the severely disturbed children in his study. Cott (1968) reported that he obtained dramatic improvement in 175 children diagnosed as schizophrenic, autistic, or brain damaged after treatment with massive doses of vitamins. Osmond and Smythies (1952) found similar improvement in schizophrenics receiving vitamin treatment.

Despite these optimistic results, this avenue of research remains relatively unexplored. There is no conclusive evidence that vitamin therapy alleviates behavioral disorders or mental disease. In fact, all large-sample treatment studies may be premature. Although investigators are encouraged about the relationship between biochemicals and psychosis, as yet they have not established reliable evidence that biochemical agents are responsible for pathological mental conditions. The relationship between faulty biochemistry and mental illness is similar to that of the chicken and the egg; it is difficult to know which came first. It is possible that psychopathology causes alterations in brain biochemistry rather than vice versa. This possibility is substantiated by the fact that no differences have been found in the brain waves and biochemistry of recovered manic-depressives and control groups of normals. In addition, there is no reason to assume that a relationship exists between biochemical factors and less serious manifestations of emotional disorders such as neurosis.

Neurological Research A third approach (Rhodes and Tracy, 1972) to substantiating the biological basis of mental illness involves the investigation of neurological disorders. From this perspective, mentally ill people have malfunctioning autonomic nervous systems that predispose them to behavioral disorders. One vein of this research involves the investigations of the relationship between schizophrenia and malfunctioning neural excitatory and inhibitory processes.

Pavlov (1941) first suggested that schizophrenics have abnormally excitable nervous systems. Theoretically, they lack protective inhibition, therefore weak stimulation produces cortical excitation. Presumably such malfunctions of the excitatory and inhibitory processes prevent the schizophrenic from distinguishing relevant from irrelevant stimuli. Consequently, thoughts or memories of past experiences have the same arousal force as present events, thereby creating mental confusion. Broen (1968) substantiates the unusual nature of schizophrenic arousal patterns, noting that they overreact to slight stress and underreact to extensive stress in a manner directly opposite to the behavior of normals. Mednick and McNeil (1968) report that schizoid children do not adapt to repeated stress. In addition to a labile and nonhabituating autonomic arousal, they tend to drift away from tasks at hand. In an interesting study of the possibility of early brain injury influencing psychosis, Mednick (1969) reports a relationship between irregularities of the autonomic nervous system and serious pregnancy and birth difficulties. He concluded that damage to the hippocampal region of the brain causes schizophrenia. Delgado (1969) demonstrated a relationship between psychotic behavior and neural reaction by showing that electric stimulation of the brain can bring a schizophrenic patient from catatonic withdrawal to active contact with his or her environment.

A related avenue of investigation into the neurological basis of mental illness focuses on childhood psychoses. Several studies have shown a high incidence of neurological abnormalities such as epilepsy and pathological reflexes in psychotic children (Gittleman and Birch, 1967; Eaton and Menolascino, 1966; Hinton, 1963). Rutter's (1965) investigations of childhood psychoses caused him to conclude that children diagnosed as autistic are mentally retarded and that these conditions are due to abnormality of the brain.

Rimland (1964) related autism to neurological impairment that restricts the child's ability to associate environmental stimuli with previously learned experiences. From his perspective, an autistic child cannot build the reservoir of experiences necessary for cognition. Consequently, a familiar person remains a stranger or a learned task is forgotten. Rimland believes the neurological basis for the disease is proved by the facts that the parents of autistic children do not have autistic personalities, the siblings are normal, the autistic condition is recognizable at birth, there are no gradations of autism, there is a ratio of four autistic boys to each girl, twins usually contract the disease, and the symptomology is highly unusual.

Other investigations of behaviorally disordered children attribute disabilities to "minimal brain injury." The concept of minimal brain injury was popularized originally by Alfred Strauss, a neurologist, to explain the behavior of children experiencing serious learning and adjustment problems. Strauss noted similarities between many of the children's behaviors and those of persons who had suffered obvious cerebral insult. Those common behaviors, called the *Strauss syndrome,* included hyperactivity, distractibility, lability, impulsiveness, and perseveration. Although there was no discernible, objective evidence of brain injury in these children, that is, they had no known damage to their brains, Strauss concluded that their behavior pattern (Strauss syndrome) was sufficient indication of brain injury. Since the children did not display many of the more debilitating symptoms often associated with organic insult, such as spasticity or mental disorientation, the brain pathology was classed as mild or minimal.

In 1947, Strauss and Laura Lehtinen, a teacher, described this condition in their book *Psychopathology and Education of the Brain-Injured Child.* Their ideas have been accepted widely, despite the obvious criticism that the diagnosis of minimal brain injury usually is unconfirmed and is based entirely on the external behaviors presumably symptomatic of the organic pathology. In other words, the display of Strauss syndrome behaviors provides the only evidence of etiology, or brain injury. Confirmation of the diagnosis of minimal brain injury through neurological examination has produced equivocal results. Children regarded as exhibiting the behaviors common to Strauss syndrome do not register abnormal electroencephalograms (EEG's) with any consistency (Money, 1966). On the other hand, many children who exhibit no symptoms of brain damage have abnormal EEG's. Other criteria for neurological evaluation such as reflex testing, eye-hand coordination, balance, gait, posture, and eye-hand dominance, have proved no more reliable as an index of minimal brain injury than the EEG.

At present none of the criteria cited shows conclusively that there is a neurological basis for mental illness. Critics argue that an unloving or rejecting environment can induce signs of extreme pathology in children. Spitz's (1945) famous investigation of the general debilitation resulting from an absence of infant stimulation among institutionalized babies provides an indication of the irreversible damage inflicted by poor environmental conditions.

Developmental Research   The last of the biologically oriented investigations of emotional disturbance emphasizes the importance of development (Rhodes and Tracy, 1972). The underlying basis of this approach is that deficits or lags in early development cause behavioral irregularities throughout life. Newell Kephart (1963), a developmental psychologist, incorporated many of Strauss's concepts into a hierarchical theory of developmental stages. He theorized that early sensorimotor development is a critical determinant of all higher order growth and learning. Deviant development at the sensorimotor stage prevents adequate cognitive and affective development. Therefore, children who have difficulty learning academic content and who have poor social skills may require training to improve underlying, lower level perceptual-motor skills such as balance, movement, and direction.

Another developmental psychologist, William Cruickshank (1961), postulated similar principles. Cruickshank focused attention more directly on perceptual development and attributed behavioral disorders to inadequacies in the ability to take in and organize environmental stimuli, characteristics common to the Strauss syndrome child.

Lauretta Bender (1968) equated childhood psychoses with malfunctions or delays in bodily functions that are integrated by the central nervous system. She suggested that schizophrenic children have not matured beyond an embryonic level, noting that they retain the early embryonic features of the fetal infant. She speculated that such developmental delays are caused by organic conditions. Ritvo and Ornitz (1970) supported her position, noting that children diagnosed as autistic or schizophrenic often respond to external stimuli like infants.

Unfortunately, the notion of developmental deficits as the cause of mental disorders has not been substantiated. Possibly, clear-cut empirical evidence is difficult to obtain because the various avenues pertaining to biological causation are interrelated. Genetic defects impair neurological functioning and cause developmental delays. Organic damage influences biochemical processes or vice versa. Clearly, the biological line of research excites particular interest as a source of eventual solution to the puzzle of psychosis.

Impact on Education

Superficially, it might appear that the biological perspective would have little impact on education. Clearly, the biological model does not attribute great importance to school events. Mental disease is a physical disability and is not dependent on psychosocial forces from the environment. Consequently, school experiences have little or nothing to do with the development of emotionally disturbed states. Not only that, but the physiological basis of emotional disease lies outside the purview of the teacher. Educators can do little either to diagnose or remediate the conditions that underlie emotional problems. Their role involves little more than helping the patients adjust to their conditions. More serious efforts at intervention are reserved primarily for medically trained personnel and their ancillary staff.

Interestingly, it is precisely because of the focus on internal, physical disabilities that the biological model actually has had a great influence on education. The disability perspective of emotional disturbance has permeated many aspects of society, particularly the schools. The principal benefit of embracing such a perspective is obvious: it frees social agencies such as schools from accepting any degree of responsibility for the development of emotionally disturbed conditions. The effect on education has been predictable. First, many educators regard the child displaying symptoms of emotional disorders as sick and therefore in need of treatment they cannot provide. The child is perceived primarily as the responsibility of noneducators such as psychologists, neurologists, or psychiatrists. Although educators may be sympathetic to the child's problems, they often do little to help alleviate them.

Second, as emotionally disturbed children are regarded as disabled and abnormal, it often is considered best to remove them from contact with normal children and to educate them in special facilities. The rationale for this behavior is that disabled children cannot be expected to compete successfully with normal children. Thus, they must be segregated in self-contained special education programs.

Third, since the illness or disorder emanates from within the child, little attention need be given to modification of the classroom environment, as it has little to do with the problem. Instead, a great deal of effort is directed toward isolating the exact nature of the child's disability. The child is administered a large number of diagnostic tests to determine perceptual development, cognitive functioning, affective state, neurological condition, and so forth. The implications are clear; if change is to occur, it must occur within the child. The child must be treated in order to overcome the inherent disability that causes maladaptive behavior.

An additional ramification of the biological model in education warrants discussion. The notion of minimal brain damage has had a particularly significant impact on special programs designed for children who experience academic and behavioral problems in school. To a large extent it has been closely associated with the advent of the learning disabilities movement in special education. *Learning disabilities* is a term used by

Samuel Kirk (1963) to describe children whose academic and behavioral problems were caused presumably by deficits in mental operations. Such deficits include those that affect motor functioning, perceptual processes, and written and spoken language development. These disabilities usually are attributed to some type of neurological impairment such as minimal brain injury or to developmental delay.

Possibly because this adaptation of the biological model in education makes a direct rather than an implicit assertion that the child's problems are caused by malfunctions in his or her autonomic nervous system, it has been accepted widely. A multitude of children have been diagnosed as minimally brain injured, neurologically involved, cerebrally impaired, and so forth. Others have been identified as perceptually handicapped (Frostig, 1963; Cruickshank, 1972), motorically impaired (Doman, Delacato, and Doman, 1964; Kephart, 1963), or psycholinguistically handicapped (Kirk, McCarthy, and Kirk, 1968), with the implication that such conditions reflect underlying neurological or developmental disorders. Programs to train developmental processes such as perception, memory, sensorimotor skills, and so forth also have proliferated (Frostig and Horne, 1964; Kirk and Kirk, 1972; Minskoff, Wiseman, and Minskoff, 1973).

Unfortunately, the efficacy of this approach in education has not been demonstrated. Research suggests that most children receiving mental process training show little or no improvement in the areas trained or in academic learning (Newcomer and Hammill, 1976). Possibly, these remedial efforts were extrapolated for use with too many children, for example, those who in fact suffered no underlying neurological or developmental problems, as Kirk and Elkins (1974) have suggested. In any event, the minimal brain damage concept continues to have an unusually strong impact on many aspects of special education.

Critique and Summary

By and large, the popularity of the biological model has diminished during the past fifty years. The primary criticism has been that, despite intensive investigation, few definitive relationships have been established between biological functions and mental illness. Despite a certain amount of pessimism regarding the dearth of tangible results, those who adhere to this model remain firmly convinced that they will eventually produce the solutions to the dilemma of emotional illnesses. Generally, their position can be summarized in the following statements:

1. Emotional disturbance is an illness or disease.
2. Atypical or deviant behaviors are symptomatic of internal biogenic pathology.
3. The etiology or cause of the behavioral symptoms must be identified if effective treatments are to be developed.

4. Diagnosis and treatment focus exclusively on the human organism.
5. Social or psychological forces have little or nothing to do with the development of the disease.
6. Research into genetic, neurological, biochemical, and developmental factors is the only avenue for understanding the etiology of emotional disturbance.
7. After the onset of mental disease treatment is adaptive, not curative.
8. Treatment often involves drug therapy; psychotherapy is not essential.
9. Treatment facilities are medical centers such as hospitals or clinics.

THE PSYCHOANALYTICAL MODEL

Theories associated with the psychoanalytical school of thought retain the basic premise that disturbed behavioral states are types of mental illness. The most significant variation from the biological perspective is the emphasis placed on psychological processes as the primary determinants of emotionally disturbed behavior. As indicated previously, the biological model attributes all mental illness primarily to physiological malfunctions. The psychoanalytic school opens the door to the study of human behavior as something other than a component of neural synapses or organic lesions. Pathology is due to the functioning of an individual's mind or, more precisely, his or her *psyche*, the reservoir of all psychological functions. Psychological processes or functions involve all aspects of individuals' mental operations, their thoughts, emotions, perceptions, wishes, needs, desires, and so forth. An individual's psychological development is dependent to a certain extent on his or her biological or organic functioning as well as on learned events. Inherited potentialities reach fruition in one way or another depending on the individual's environment. These biological, genetic, or organic factors constitute a predisposition in the individual that, given certain input from the environment, results in the development of particular psychic characteristics. For instance, an individual may display tendencies toward depression throughout life but become seriously depressed when the environmental stresses are untenable. Therefore, it is not the genes or actual neural operations that predicate behavior, but the manner in which an individual thinks, feels, reacts, that is, his or her psychological makeup. Mental illnesses believed to be caused by malfunctioning psychological processes are termed *functional disabilities* as opposed to physiologically based conditions, which are called *organic disabilities*.

Although the notion that most types of mental illness have functional origins has wide acceptance at present, it is a relatively novel point of view. Psychology was still in its infancy in the early 1900's, and clinical psychology, the study of pathological behavior, was not a viable field until much later. With the advent of clinical psychology, greater attention was directed to functional causation of emotional disorders. Previously, disturbed emotional conditions were viewed as physical disorders having an organic basis.

To a large extent, the eventual recognition of the importance of psychological factors in mental disorders can be attributed to Sigmund Freud (1856–1939), the father of psychoanalysis. Freud, a Viennese physician, began his career as a neurologist, specializing in the diagnosis of organic diseases. In 1885 he studied in Paris with the eminent neurologist Charcot at the famous Salpetriere school. During that period, hysterical neuroses were prevalent and there was considerable dispute regarding their etiology. Although many physicians believed that hysterical symptoms such as paralysis must have an organic or physical basis, Freud began to doubt that premise. He was struck by the successful use of hypnosis to treat hysterical patients practiced at the rival Nancy school by the physicians Liébault and Bernheim. He became impressed by the notion that the symptoms of paralysis associated with hysteria were rooted in mental rather than organic malfunctions. On returning to Vienna, he collaborated with Joseph Breuer who was using hypnosis to encourage neurotic patients to speak openly about their feelings. Freud noted that such relaxed, uncensored speech frequently revealed the relationship between the patients' problems and their hysterical symptoms. He realized that his patients lacked conscious awareness of that relationship and from this observation he hypothesized the existence of an unconscious, that is, a body of thoughts and ideas that directly influence behavior despite the patient's ignorance of its existence. In 1893, he and Breuer authored *On the Psychical Mechanisms of Hysterical Phenomena* (1957), a landmark presentation of the constructs that were to serve as cornerstones of the psychoanalytic position.

Freud's perspective of the causes of disturbed behavior can be understood only in the context of his theory of personality. Despite the fact that it is a psychological theory, Freud's concepts have a substantial biological basis and attribute great importance to hereditary factors. Human beings are viewed as the recipients of certain instinctual processes such as a death urge, a life wish and, most important, a sexual instinct that is the primary driving force in the pursuit of life. These instincts provide the underlying base for growth and development. Of equal importance to personality development is the extent to which our inherited predispositions are shaped by early childhood experiences. The occurrences during the first five years of life are critical to development. The inherited or biological components of personality, that is, our urges and instincts, form the portion of the psyche referred to as the *id*. Parental controls and regulations, which are internalized during early development, form the psychic component termed the *superego*. The third psychic component, the *ego*, represents efforts to deal with reality. The ego seeks to compromise between the pleasure-seeking urges of the id and the inhibiting barriers represented by the superego. Thus personality is *dynamic,* not static. Behavior is determined by conflicts between alternte psychic components and their respective needs and wishes. Energy that activates such conflicts emanates from the id and is termed *libido* or *sexual energy.* According to Freud, the gratification of sexual instincts is expressed in stages of development. The first, or *oral,* stage is marked by sucking and biting, and is followed by the *anal* stage, in which the child is preoccupied with its bowel movements. The third, or *phallic,* stage sees the child's interest focus on its sex organs, while in the next stage of latency the child seems to lose all interest in sex. The culminating step in sexual development, the *genital* stage, marks the advent of sexual maturity.

The child frustrated by overcontrolling or repressive parents as he or she attempts to gratify sexual instincts is stymied in growth and remains fixed at an early stage of development despite chronological maturation. For instance, a pathologically dependent and ineffectual adult is fixed at the oral stage and is still attempting to resolve the conflicts induced by the parental rejection that occurred during that period of development. Two variables, *fixation* at an early stage of development, and *regression* to an infantile stage during periods of stress, mark disturbed behavior.

Freudian theory depicts conflict and turmoil as the natural course of events for human beings. The conflict-generating interaction among the intrapsychic subsystems of id, ego, and superego arouses *anxiety,* a critical component in the psychoanalytic model. Anxiety is a form of "psychic pain," an uncomfortable feeling akin to fear, but more pervasive. Freud described three types of anxiety: *reality anxiety,* which arises when a person is threatened by environmental events, *neurotic anxiety,* which occurs when a person's id impulses threaten to overwhelm ego controls, thereby causing socially unacceptable behavior, and *moral anxiety,* which occurs when the person considers engaging in behaviors that conflict with the superego or moral values. Anxiety forces the individual to act to resolve the precipitating conflict if possible and to establish a more tranquil state of psychic equilibrium. Thus, when children encounter predictable and inevitable conflicts with their parents, such as the oedipus situation (when a boy at the phallic stage of development competes with his father for his mother's affections), they must resolve them if mental health is to be retained. The ego either copes with the constant anxiety-evoking stresses of conflicting urges by rational measures or resorts to irrational protective measures termed *defense mechanisms.*

Defense mechanisms are the means by which an individual banishes threatening or anxiety-evoking thoughts from consciousness. *Repression* occurs when a disturbing thought or event is simply forgotten, as when a man forgets being beaten as a child by his father. *Projection* involves the attribution of anxiety-evoking feeling to others, as when an aggressive child attributes aggressive behavior to classmates. *Sublimation* occurs when an urge, such as the desire for forbidden sexual gratification, is channelled to socially acceptable activity, such as high academic achievement. *Displacement* involves altering the object of the feeling, for example, anger at a parent is displaced to a teacher. *Reaction formation* refers to developing feelings that are directly opposite to those that are threatening, as when a mother is overprotective and oversolicitous of a child she dislikes. *Identification* involves assuming the attributes of another individual, usually an aggressor, who is perceived as a threat. For example, a child identifies with the class bully and mimics the bully's behavior.

Defense mechanisms are unconscious psychic events. Individuals usually are not aware of using them. The child who projects aggressive urges onto classmates actually believes that he or she is inoffensive and that others respond aggressively, just as the child who displaces hostility toward a parent onto his or her teacher feels real anger at the teacher. Defense mechanisms are used by people to protect themselves from facing certain unpleasant truths. For example, children who have been taught that it is wrong to be angry at their parents are made anxious by this anger. They release the tension and reduce the anxiety that the conflict induces by using defense mechanisms. Defense mechanisms do not completely block disturbing thoughts, however. Urges that have been denied conscious expression emerge when ego controls are relaxed as in dreaming or in slips of the tongue. Obviously, all people use defense mechanisms. They become indicative of pathology when they prevent individuals from understanding and resolving debilitating problems.

By far the most important aspect of Freudian theory is the notion that human beings are only minimally aware of the causes of their behavior, that is, that they are propelled by unconscious forces that are too threatening to be part of consciousness. These forces cause serious emotional illnesses that are marked by such symptoms as hysterical conversion reactions (paralysis unrelated to physical injury), irrational fears or phobias, compulsive rituals, and so forth. Such pathological reactions may have no obvious relationship to an individual's current environmental circumstances. A child from a seemingly happy family situation suffers from school phobia. An apparently successful career man develops sudden blindness with no physical basis. These individuals are not consciously aware of the source of their problems, nor can they alleviate their symptoms by conscious will. Psychic relief and symptom alleviation can be gained only by psychotherapeutic techniques that free thoughts and emotions that have been trapped in the unconscious behind a wall of defense mechanisms. In other words, patients must be helped to understand the underlying feelings that control their behavior. Therefore, treatment involves encouraging patients to speak in free, unstructured ways about themselves. They must say whatever they think, without the inhibitions that usually characterize social conversation. Termed *free association,* this technique unearths hidden feelings. Patients are helped to accept these feelings without guilt or shame. As patients accept and understand the feelings, anxiety is reduced and pathological symptoms disappear.

Freud's theories are important because they led the way in directing attention to the psychic determinants of behavior. Those who followed him expanded and altered many of his tenets and branched into fields of study that currently have more popular acceptance than do the original Freudian theories. One group of psychoanalysts led by Anna Freud (1937) and Erik Erikson (1947) emphasizes the role of the ego in determining behavior. Erikson's concepts also stress the importance of social interactions, as do the theories of Karen Horney (1945) and Alfred Adler (1963). In fact, Adler's social emphasis led him to depict human beings as creative, active individuals who consciously select a "style of life" that brings self-fulfillment. Obviously, Adler's clearly humanistic position has small resemblance to the Freudian concepts of irrational man driven by socially unacceptable instincts. Nonetheless, Freud's views have had the power to dramatically alter the course of psychological study.

Impact on Education

In many ways the psychoanalytic approach to mental disease has made even greater impact on education than the biological orientation. Both approaches share the underlying influence of disability models, that is, that pathology is rooted in the individual. Although those associated with the psychoanalytic model are more optimistic about the possibilities of curative treatment than are their biologically oriented brethren, such therapeutic intervention is clearly beyond the skill of educators. Treatment is long and tedious and can only be conducted by highly trained psychiatrists. Actually, the psychoanalytic emphasis on the seriousness and intractability of man's emotional dilemmas is in itself enough to encourage educators to adopt a passive demeanor and to confine their efforts with disturbed children to outside referrals and social segregation through special class placement.

In addition to sharing the biological emphasis on inherent pathology, the psychoanalytic model makes several unique contributions to education. The first involves the notion that personality characteristics are largely determined by early childhood events. This premise signifies that the children's personal pathology is developed before they arrive in school. Their emotional disorders are rooted in faulty family relations and have little to do with school events. The problems manifested in school are caused by existing disorders within the child. Therefore, strategies designed to alleviate disturbed emotional conditions focus primarily on the child and its family, rather than on the school environment. School-based intervention that does occur may involve assessing the limitations within the home, and affixing parental responsibility for the child's condition.

A second unique educational influence evolving from psychoanalytic thought is based on the premise that abnormal behaviors are symptoms of unconscious conflict. This premise suggests that children are not consciously aware of the reasons for their behavior and that they have little or no conscious control over their behavior. Further, treatment involving direct manipulation of overt behavior serves no constructive purpose and, in fact, may be harmful. Discouraging one symptomatic behavior may result in the substitution of another, more debilitating symptom. Therefore, educators are encouraged to treat disturbed children carefully, that is, to avoid repressing their behavior. While the idea of a nonrepressive environment has merit, unfortunately it has often been interpreted in education as license to: (1) provide little structure for classroom behavior, (2) avoid clear statement and enforcement of rules, (3) stop teaching academic material until the child is emotionally stable, and (4) reduce expectations for "normal" behaviors. In essence, the resulting philosophy might be summed up in the phrase "Don't bother him, he's sick." Invariably, individuals exposed to this philosophy never behave any way but sick.

In a more positive vein, the psychoanalytic model has assisted educators by popularizing the following ideas: (1) children do not always consciously plan and cannot always consciously control disruptive behaviors, therefore when they misbehave they should not be treated punitively; (2) hostility directed to the teacher should not be viewed as a personal insult since it might stem from a variety of motivations and does not necessarily mean that the child dislikes the teacher; and (3) children respond to internal conflicts, therefore, inconsistencies in behavior should be expected. All three points indicate that the teacher who can maintain reasonable tolerance of human frailty is ahead of the game.

Critique and Summary

Over the years, the psychoanalytic perspective, particularly the Freudian principles, has been strongly criticized on several bases. First, it presents an extremely pessimistic view of human beings as pathetic creatures programmed for strife and unhappiness. Second, its description of human behavior is presented in terms of the hypothetical functioning of hypothetical constructs. Human behavior is reduced to the operations of psychic components of ego, id, and superego, which do not actually exist. Third, it emphasizes the examination of unconscious, underlying motivation as the path to mental health, despite the fact that such awareness, even if it can be assumed to be accurate, has never been shown to alter behavior. Nonetheless, the tenets of this school are influential. They can be summarized as follows:

1. Behaviors that reflect a state of emotional disturbance are caused primarily by internal psychic pathology.
2. Both biological forces and early environmental influences contribute to the pathological condition.
3. Etiology must be identified if effective treatment is to be undertaken.
4. The individual is not consciously aware of the source of the problem.
5. Changing overt behavior is less important than dealing with the underlying conflicts that cause the behavior, since surface treatment only results in symptom substitution.
6. Treatment involves changing the person by providing insight into past conflicts unearthed from the unconscious.
7. Treatment through psychoanalysis can reverse certain pathological behaviors, but the process is long and difficult.
8. Treatment facilities are usually medical centers.
9. Treatment personnel are usually physicians.

THE BEHAVIORISTIC MODEL

Behavioristic theories offer a pronounced contrast to both the biological and psychoanalytical models. Essentially, this approach represents an attempt to make psychology a science, that is, to evolve scientific principles of human behavior through empirical investigation. As in the physical sciences, ideas or tenets must be tested experimentally to determine their validity. Such experimental investigation cannot produce definitive results if the tenets in question are based on interpretations of subjective experiences such as feelings, attitudes, and so on. Therefore, the study of human behavior must be consigned to directly observable behavior, not to subjective experiences. The behavioristic approach focuses on one particularly complex human activity, learning. It provides a basis for formulating scientific principles regarding the stimuli and responses that constitute learning behavior and is often referred to as S-R *learning theory*.

Obviously, the basic assumption of the S-R position is that human behavior is learned. Children are not born speaking, walking or, for that matter, punching classmates. They are exposed to certain stimuli in their environments that generate these responses. Thus, human behavior can be understood only as a function of direct interaction between individuals and their immediate environments.

Although the origins of the behavioristic model can be found in the work of Ivan Pavlov (1849–1936), a Russian physiologist, its development to a position of prominence was due to the contributions of three American psychologists, J. B. Watson (1878–1958), E. L. Thorndike (1874–1949), and B. F. Skinner (1904–   ). Pavlov's monumental contribution to the behavioristic perspective centered on his discovery of the conditioned reflex. He found that a neutral stimulus such as a tone could elicit a response such as salivation if that stimulus had been previously associated with an unconditioned stimulus such as food. Termed *respondent,* or *classical,* conditioning, this type of learning depends on the close association of the conditioned and unconditioned stimuli. Thus food, an unconditioned stimulus eliciting salivation, may be associated with a tone until the tone alone cues the response; then the tone may be associated with another conditioned stimulus such as a light until the latter stimulus elicits the response, and so on. Learning is dependent on the temporal or spatial proximity of the stimuli; they must be contiguous.

J. B. Watson extended Pavlov's principles and maintained that all behavior, including abnormal reactions, could be "conditioned" by external events. He presented his position termed *behaviorism* in his famous book *Psychology from the Standpoint of a Behaviorist* in 1919. The best known demonstration of his viewpoint was the "Albert experiment," in which Watson and Rayner, his associate, proved that they could condition fear in a child. They exposed Albert, an eleven-month-old child who liked animals, to a loud noise every time he reached to play with a white rat. After a brief period of time Albert cried at the sight of the animal even when the noise was discontinued. His fear generalized to all other furry animals and objects. Watson believed that all psychological responses were learned in like fashion.

Although Watson's concepts had a considerable impact on the psychological community, two other major S-R theorists, Thorndike and Skinner, broke and tilled the theoretical ground that make behaviorism more than an interesting compilation of information about human learning. Thorndike (1913) formulated the *law of effect,* demonstrating that rewarded responses are learned, whereas those with negative results are weakened. With this elementary premise he placed the control of learning into human hands through reward and punishment. Skinner (1953) used that information to emphasize the importance of manipulating overt environmental events and the futility of speculating about functions occurring within the individual. Their combined conceptualizations form the bases of *operant conditioning,* the behavioristic model that has had such a penetrating impact on education.

Simply stated, operant conditioning involves a situation in which an individual learns to make a response in order to achieve a particular end. The eliciting stimulus is of small importance, as the response is determined by its contingencies. For instance, a hungry monkey may learn to press a lever if that behavior produces food. Its response has not been directly elicited by a particular stimulus, it has learned to operate or manipulate the environment to gain a satisfying reward. It has undergone operant conditioning.

Both operant and classical conditioning are dependent on reinforcement, or the strengthening of the new response. In classical conditioning, reinforcement occurs by the repeated association of the stimulus and response, thus strengthening the learned response. In operant conditioning, reinforcement may be a positive contingency like a reward. Responses that are not reinforced either do not reoccur or are gradually extinguished.

Currently, the behavioristic position can be divided roughly into two camps. B. F. Skinner is an advocate of the most theoretically pure position. He insists that only observable and measurable events are appropriate for scientific study. He rejects the idea that internal psychological functions are matters of importance, since their existence can never be confirmed empirically. Furthermore, he argues that since the manipulation of reinforcements is the only method of changing behavior, speculation regarding mental functioning serves no purpose. By the proper use of contingencies, learned acts that a person performs can be unlearned and new behavior may be taught. He believes that this is as much as anyone needs to know to alter human behavior.

Other stimulus-response theorists disagree with Skinner's aversion to the study of mental functions. They are interested in intervening variables, that is, the unobservable events occurring between the stimulus and the response. They hypothesize the existence of associations within the brain that account for such mental functions as memory, cognition, perception, and so forth. Included among these theorists are E. R. Guthrie, Clark Hull, R. R. Sears, J. Dollard, N. E. Miller, O. H. Mowrer, D. W. Spence, W. K. Estes.

Despite various theoretical differences among the advocates of behaviorism, they all look at behavior as modifiable through learning. Although they acknowledge the existence of hereditary and developmental components in learning, they regard them as relatively unimportant when compared to environmental influences. Therefore, the essence of their position is that behavior may be shaped, removed, or maintained by changing environmental events.

In the terminology of learning theory, emotional disturbance is *maladaptive behavior* (Ullman and Krasner, 1965). In other words, emotionally disturbed behavior is the result of (1) a failure to learn behaviors that permit a healthy or beneficial adaptation to the environment, (2) learning maladaptive or nonbeneficial behaviors, and (3) developing maladaptive behaviors as a result of exposure to stressful environmental circumstances that force discriminations that are too difficult for decision making (Coleman, 1972). All three of these situations are amenable to treatment through environmental manipulation. The application of S-R learning principles to manipulate the environment and treat disturbed behavior is termed *behavior modification*. Typical behavior modification techniques are (1) using aversive conditioning to eliminate maladaptive behaviors by withholding a reward when a particular behavior occurs, for example, denying dessert to a child who refuses to eat dinner; (2) using positive reinforcement with substitute adaptive behaviors, for example, rewarding a child for stroking a dog rather than pulling its hair; (3) manipulating the environment to remove conditions that may be reinforcing undesirable behaviors, for example, instructing classmates not to pay attention to a child's tantrums; (4) using modeling to teach new responses, for example, demonstrating appropriate social behavior on the playground and reinforcing the child for imitating the behaviors. For behaviorists, the removal of the offending behavior is the basis for treatment. They are not concerned with the premise that the behavior might be symptomatic of an underlying problem, and that the extinction of one symptomatic behavior might result in symptom substitution. Each behavior is evaluated and treated as an independent activity.

Educational Impact

As might be expected, learning theory has made a significant impact on education. First, educators respond to it because it is in one sense an optimistic approach. Although it certainly depicts human beings as mechanistic (behavior determined by previous conditioning), instead of free willed and purposeful, it emphasizes the possibilities of change and growth through environmental manipulation. The biological viewpoint that emotional disturbance is caused by the "bad seed" gives educators few options. A teacher can do little about children's genetic defects or biochemical malfunctions, other than to accept them as irreversible and to help the afflicted children accommodate to their handicaps. In contrast, the learning theory approach emphasizes the role of the teacher, who by using the correct strategies can change behavior. The emotionally disturbed child is not viewed as an inherently pathological creature, but as a victim of inappropriate learning. To some extent this view removes many of the ominous overtones from the notion of emotional disturbance. It is no longer the result of deep destructive unconscious forces. The development of maladaptive behavior can be explained scientifically, just as any other behavior can be explained.

Second, since schools are devoted to learning, they are obvious natural settings for effecting behavioral change. Teachers are logical agents to promote learning in affective areas as well as in the cognitive realm. For example, the classroom is an ideal social environment to apply the notion of learning through modeling the behaviors of others (Bandura, 1965) as both teachers and class members can model constructive behaviors for disturbed children.

Third, the clarity, specificity, and simplicity of behavioristic principles make them very attractive to educators. Specific maladaptive behaviors can be targeted by any diligent observer and the effectiveness of altering the contingency of target behaviors can be charted immediately. Thus, the educator may bring about a fast, efficient remedy to a problem that might otherwise disrupt the learning of the entire class.

Critique and Summary

Despite the popularity and utilitarian aspects of behaviorism some individuals are quick to list what they construe to be serious disadvantages associated with these techniques. Coleman (1972) summarized criticisms that include:

1. Its focus on oversimplified aspects of behavior such as specific responses to specific stimuli and its avoidance of dealing with more elaborate dimensions of human experience such as hate, despair, love, and so forth.
2. Its failure to incorporate subjective experiences into its explanations of behavior.
3. The utilization of conditioning techniques to alter the behavior of others. Such intervention involves decisions regarding the superiority of one person's values over another's.

Regardless of criticism, the behavioristic approach has gained considerable impetus in the treatment of emotional disturbance within the last ten years and its influence shows no signs of diminishing. The basic assumptions of the model may be summarized in the following statements. First, the source of the problem is not specifically within the individual, but is a function of interaction between the person and the environment. Second, the problem is not caused by a pathological condition or illness, but by inappropriate learning. Third, the inappropriate behaviors can be corrected by manipulating the consequences of those behaviors. Fourth, treatment must deal with only overt behaviors. Speculation about non-behavioral factors such as causation, feelings, and motivation is fruitless. Fifth, treatment must include consideration of those environmental components that relate specifically to the maladaptive behavior in question. Other information pertaining to previous experiences is inconsequential. The important events are the specific connections between the child's behavior and its consequences. Sixth, any interested, observant person can intervene to modify maladaptive behavior.

THE PHENOMENOLOGICAL MODEL

The phenomenological model exemplifies a psychological approach stressing the importance of phenomena from all experiential domains as determinants of behavior. Thus it incorporates tenets associated with both the psychoanalytic and behavioral models, but with a totally different effect. Phenomenology shares the behavioristic concern with environmental factors, but does not restrict attention to the immediate relationship between current events and behaviors. This perspective takes a far more global view of environment as the sum total of all events that shape human behavior. These events include the forces that previously shaped personality as well as the pressures of immediate situations. As in the psychoanalytic model, all aspects of human psychological functioning are important. However, unlike the psychoanalysts, phenomenologists pay small regard to a human being's inherited potential, preferring to focus attention on the use made of that potential, that is, the extent to which humans fulfill their heredity. Succinctly, from the phenomenological perspective the behavioristic absorption with stimulus-response associations is an oversimplification. It ignores important components of the individual's internal functioning. On the other hand, the psychoanalytic perspective that incorporates internal variables is found wanting because it is too biologically oriented and overly pessimistic about human potential. The phenomenological approach is probably best described as a conglomerate of theories that reflect a general philosophic perspective of man, rather than as a tight, concise set of behavioral principles. The most unifying tenet is the principle of *self*, which has been an important concept in the work of two representative theorists, Carl Rogers and Abraham Maslow.

Carl Rogers (1951, 1959, 1961) may well be the best known psychologist of the self. His theories of human behavior focus on the development of self-concept, just as ego development is a major component of psychoanalytic theory. From his perspective, self incorporates all subjective experiences including identity and tendencies toward fulfillment of potential. Specifically, Rogers maintains that each individual is an independent entity with a unique identity or self-concept. Individuals' self-concepts determine the manner in which they view or perceive reality. Consequently, reality as an absolute does not exist. Each individual has an idiosyncratic perspective of reality, reflecting his or her self-concept. This notion is akin to depicting each individual as existing in a private world. Each individual's perceptions are unique because all experiences are filtered through the self, which is at the core of his or her world. Reactions toward reality are always consistent with the self-concept. Perceived threats to self arouse defenses that cause increased personal rigidity. Such reactions occur despite the fact that human beings are inherently good, purposeful, and directed toward growth and self-actualization. All else being equal, human beings will act constructively. However, a depressed self-concept can pervert behavior.

From this perspective, it is apparent that behavior cannot be understood from the examination of simple, observable events. An interaction

their behavior if the teacher does not insist on conformity. Second, this viewpoint describes humanity as constantly striving to grow and seek fulfillment. An educational environment conducive to such growth has an important bearing on an individual's life. Since the individual can be expected to make the most of environmental opportunities, the open classrooms that provide a magnitude of diverse opportunities for children to pursue studies of unique interest will effect efficient learning. Third, this approach minimizes the necessity for making value judgments regarding behavior, without negating the importance of guidance. A child who is rude and disruptive is viewed as a person in conflict. Behaviors are not judged negatively, nor are they interpreted as personal insults. The teacher is in a position to alter behavior without rejecting the child. Fourth, the interventionist need not impose societal values on the child. The ethical question of deciding which behaviors to extinguish and which to reinforce is not present. The child is encouraged and supported to draw conclusions and make decisions as to which behaviors are conducive to his or her own general well being.

Critique and Summary

The principal tenet of the phenomenological position makes it unique in the body of theory discussed thus far. For the first time human beings are depicted as purposeful, independent individuals with inherent integrity. Heretofore, theories have adhered to deterministic positions and either described human beings as machines programmed by their experiences, or as inherently pathological creatures. The phenomenological optimism prevails even in their discussion of humanity's disturbed conditions. Not only are human beings consciously aware of their problems, but they have the motivation and the free will to solve them. Such a point of view literally begs for acceptance, yet is subject to certain astute criticisms. First, there is evidence that individuals do not readily understand themselves and their problems. Their self-perceptions and self-reports are colored by their unconscious defenses. Therefore, their insights may be nothing more than acceptance of anxiety-reducing rationalizations. Second, inexperienced or confused persons may not be aware of the best behavior course to pursue. They require firm direction to keep them from harm or to introduce learning experiences that they will eventually come to recognize as advantageous. They are not equipped to make sound judgments before they have those experiences. Third, conscious acknowledgment of problems does not always lead to behavior changes. Fourth, self-actualization is a global concept which, although it synthesizes specific components of human beings' motivational systems into a whole, loses specificity of meaning. In other words, although all behavior may be attributed to humanity's drive for self-actualization, little information about the specific impetus for certain acts is uncovered. To behaviorists like Skinner, self-actualization is simply a metaphysical concept, neither observable nor measurable.

Despite criticism, the phenomenological position appears to be gaining in popularity as an alternate method of approaching the problem of emotional disturbance. The implications of the phenomenological position for the study of disturbed behavior are as follows:

1. Psychopathology is not an inherent disease.
2. Psychopathology stems from threats to the self.
3. Societal restrictions to self-actualization threaten the self.
4. There are no irrational behaviors; reality is perceived differently by every individual and behavior is in accordance with those perceptions.
5. Treatment involves enhancing self-concept and increasing self-awareness.
6. Each person is entitled to select his or her own values and should not be judged or directed to abandon them.
7. Self-understanding is the only means of removing the defense barriers preventing emotional growth.
8. All persons have the will and ability to seek redress from their problems.
9. A warm, accepting, nonthreatening environment is essential for necessary self-awareness and growth.
10. Nondirective psychotherapy will guide the individual in seeking self-truths.

THE EXISTENTIAL MODEL

The collection of ideas and theories of human behavior that may be loosely classified as existential are similar to those associated with the phenomenological position. In both instances the individual is depicted as unique, important, and striving for self-fulfillment. Similarly, emotionally disturbed behavior results from the thwarting of healthy drives toward self-actualization, not from inherent or learned deficits within the individual. To understand one person's emotional condition, one must understand the forces within the society that shape his or her position in life. Theoretical differences between these schools of thought relate to the importance attributed to the effect of society on human beings. In other words, the existential approach moves away, to some extent, from the study of the individual's psychological perspective to the study of the sociological forces that restrict human development and growth.

From the existential perspective, the individual is perverted and tortured, confused by a culture that cannot be understood. The world, particularly the traditional mores and beliefs that provide the foundation for every person's spiritual and emotional well-being, is constantly changing. The individual feels alone and bewildered, unable to pursue the natural tendency toward actualizing his or her potential. Often the person reacts to this situation by abandoning the healthy striving for a free life and accepting a role as an unquestioning, conforming member of society. This decision renders the individual an emotional cripple, living a meaningless, anxiety-evoking life. The alternative, that of continued pursuit of self-fulfillment despite the pressures of society, is the only road to health and satisfaction. Basically the individual alone must take the responsibility and commit her- or himself to making the most of existence. The individual is a free agent, with freedom of will and, therefore, may decide what path to take in life.

One of the principal tenets of the existential position is the "will to meaning" (Coleman, 1972). This principle depicts human beings as choosing agents with the responsibility for selecting healthy values. Human values reflect the essence, or the inner self. Human beings cannot escape selecting the values that underlie their lives. Even a decision to conform to old social patterns reflects a selection of values. Value selection is a difficult matter since it varies with each individual. Values that provide one life with meaning may not be appropriate for another life. In addition, values must be socially constructive since an individual's life cannot be meaningful if it does not fulfill obligation to fellow beings.

The second main tenet of this position is "nonbeing" or "nothingness" (May, 1969). Nonbeing is the opposite of being and ultimately is death. Existential theorists point out that humans are the only creatures aware of the inevitability of death. This awareness or "encounter with nothingness" generates "existential anxiety," the overriding concern about the quality of the life being led (Coleman, 1972). Thus, throughout life we are faced with anxiety-evoking conflicts stemming from decisions over the direction of our lives. For instance, individuals may recognize the need to abandon a current life-style for one providing greater self-fulfillment. Such a path is invariably threatening, since it means less security and greater risk. Inability to take the risk elevates existential anxiety since the individual is aware of the meaninglessness of his or her current life-style and has rejected an opportunity to move toward greater self-fulfillment. Therapy involves individual value clarification. The individual must undergo confrontation, that is, face direct challenges to the meaning of existence. This therapeutic approach is often employed in groups such as encounter groups, where participants demand that members evaluate themselves openly.

The theorists most closely associated with the existential position are Rollo May in America and R. D. Laing in England. May (1969) uncovers a basic principle of the existential position when he writes of existentialists' unwillingness to discuss persons in terms of forces, dynamisms, and energies, as is common in most psychological theories. To the existentialist, such terms are meaningless unless they are used in the context of the living being. To understand and help another person, the therapist must avoid focusing attention on information about the person, for example, on his or her "problem," or the drives that cause the pathological condition, and must respond entirely to the human being as he or she exists in the world. Neurosis must be viewed as an adjustment, not a failure to adjust. Patients' neurotic symptoms represent attempts to protect themselves and maintain their life spaces. Anxiety is to be regarded as an appropriate state for a human being in a struggle against threats to existence. In short, the person must be viewed as a total entity whose behaviors, no matter how bizarre or destructive they appear, signify the will to strive for self-preservation and growth. It is the individual who ceases to struggle and slips into socially conforming roles who surrenders freedom and seeks oblivion.

May's variations from the traditional views of emotional disturbance are obvious. That which the psychoanalysts and behaviorists consider of primary importance, that is, specific symptoms or behaviors, he regards as superficial aspects of pathology.

The unconventional aspects of the existential model are extended by R. D. Laing. Laing (1967) regards typical social interactions as being responsible for the pathological shaping of personality, describing them as nothing more than games persons play to avoid discovering their true selves. From most perspectives, social interactions are viewed as a civilizing process by which innately savage children are taught beneficial social rules and thereby "normalized." From Laing's (1967, p. 58) view, normalcy is society's desire to turn a new human being into a "half-crazed creature, more or less adjusted to a mad world." He sees psychosis as resulting when an individual can no longer maintain a false dichotomy between the false outerself and the true innerself. Such a person no longer attempts to deal with conflicting social demands, irrational social sanctions, and confusing life situations. Clearly, psychotic behavior is not irrational or indicative of illness; it is a meaningful reply to the absurdities of life. As Laing (1965, pp. 99–100) puts it:

> Indeed, what is called psychosis is sometimes simply the sudden removal of the veil of the false self, which had been serving to maintain an outer behavioral normality that may, long ago, have failed to be any reflection of the state of affairs in the secret self. Then the self will pour out accusations of persecution at the hands of that person with whom the false self has been complying for years.

Educational Impact

The impact of this position on education appears more philosophical than practical. Technically, schools should be resources for the selection of values that result in the self-fulfillment of each individual. To establish this type of supportive environment in practice would require a redefinition of the role of the school in society. Certainly today schools are one of the primary institutions encouraging conformity and from Laing's perspective, shaping the half-crazed creatures deemed normal. To reshape education from an existential perspective would involve two shifts in philosophical perspective. First, socialization would have to be redefined. Currently, educators view socializing as a synonym for conforming. That is, they view the socialization process as one that involves teaching conforming behaviors. In so doing, they ignore the fact that truly social behaviors must reflect human nature. Acts that disrupt the status quo such as fighting, dissenting, defying authority, and so forth, are components of human nature and are social behaviors. Disruption is a social process. Therefore, socialization must be dissociated from conformity and disharmonious acts must be recognized as natural social behaviors, not indications of antisocial tendencies.

Second, the concept of normality must be abandoned. From the existential perspective there is no such thing as normalcy. The concept is a totally arbitrary artifact designed for the convenient classification of human beings. Individuals have varying types of skills, aptitudes, and competencies that reflect their uniqueness. There is no norm, no mean or average performance that represents a standard by which people may be judged. Educators must shed the notion of the mean and with it the related belief that deviation from the mean implies some type of deficit or abnormality.

The practical implications of changing prevailing ideas about socialization and normality are clear. First, schools would abandon grading, grouping, testing, and all other related activities that are either indices of expected performance or evaluations based on those expectations. Second, the assignation of disability labels such as "mentally retarded" and "emotionally disturbed" to children who deviate from the norm would be discontinued. The premise underlying labeling is illogical, it reflects the false concept of normality. The labeling procedure has proved to be destructive to children and its continued implementation merely reflects the tendency of institutions such as schools to employ administrative operations that are convenient and do not disrupt their established procedures. Third, educators must provide opportunities for children to pursue unique learning activities by exposing them to a multitude of experiences within the community. School need not be confined to a particular building; the entire community should become part of the school. Fourth, teachers must individualize children's instructional programs, that is, teach children at a level in keeping with their needs. Finally, schools must expand the curriculum to include affective materials. Children must be encouraged to recognize and freely examine the forces that really shape their behavior.

Critique and Summary

The existential position is a conglomeration of philosophical principles, but the primary message is clear. Human beings are constantly striving to find a meaning for existence, a means by which they can counter their alienation from society and their fear of death. Human beings are responsible for their behavior and capable of going to any lengths to sustain their principles and values. As is true of all other perspectives, the existential position is subject to certain criticisms. The first point involves the tenet that society dehumanizes and alienates humanity. It is argued that human beings create their society. If we are inherently programmed for self-fulfillment, why do our social systems remain so detrimental to our welfare? The second criticism involves the sense of pessimism that permeates this model. The overwhelming nature of the forces that repress human beings, as well as our obsessive preoccupation with death, constitute a picture not significantly less negative and depressing than the psychoanalytic approach, despite the existential acceptance of human beings as purposeful and self-directed. Third, many of the actual techniques for psychotherapeutic intervention advocated by the existential psychologists, particularly the group-encounter experiences, are novel only to the extent that they confront the subject and forcefully strip away defenses. As with other therapies that recommend the exploration of inner motivational forces, the existentialists accept the assumption that people can recognize their "true" underlying motivation, and that dropping socially acceptable roles will aid them in discovering these underlying truths. Some behavioral scientists question the validity of those assumptions.

Although there is no uniform existential theory regarding the problem of emotional disturbance, the following statements probably represent an acceptable summary of underlying premises.

1. Human beings become disturbed because they have problems leading fulfilling lives.
2. Behaviors labeled "emotionally disturbed" or "mentally ill" may simply be appropriate indications of people's alienation from society.
3. Many healthy, nonconforming, or deviant behaviors are typically labeled as "ill" by the existing social institutions.
4. Man is not inherently disabled and deviant behaviors are not symptomatic of mental illness.

5. Treatment of emotionally disturbed states is a misnomer reflecting an inaccurate disability or medical perspective. An individual's condition is a social problem. Emphasis must be placed on social reorganization to solve such problems.

6. Social reorganization can be accomplished by breaking down the social façades that encourage people to play deceitful, dishonest games with each other in the name of social interaction. Honest communication with emphasis on the real values of living is the means by which true understanding of self and others can be gained.

THE SOCIOLOGICAL MODEL

The sociological approach to the study of emotional disturbance is perhaps the most encompassing of all the perspectives presented here. Thus far, with the exception of the biological model, we have drawn our theoretical positions from branches of psychology. Social theory, however, largely emanates from another discipline, sociology, the systematic study of man's collective behavior, the development, structure, and interaction of groups of human beings. In other words, this perspective does not emphasize the individual and is less concerned with personal characteristics than with the social forces that act on us. One of the most "psychological" explanations of man as a social being is the interpersonal theory developed by Harry Stack Sullivan (1953). In the same vein as Sullivan's work, but with less emphasis on personality development, are other broad positions that depict emotional disturbance as a *role* assigned to certain individuals for a variety of reasons. From one such point of view, labeling theory, deviant roles are assigned to those who break society's rules (Jarlais, 1972). Other perspectives emphasize the importance of cultural transmission (Sutherland and Cressey, 1966) and social disorganization (Park and Burgess, 1924) in determining values and roles. Still another point of view depicts the interaction between individual needs and social norms as the source of the strife that creates deviant roles within a society (Durkheim, 1951). Although these perspectives of the critical forces influencing human behavior differ to some extent, they uniformly view emotional disturbance as a social phenomenon. The understanding of emotional disturbance is dependent on investigations of the social forces that produce it. Thus, the study of human beings must involve the study of the social milieu or it cannot produce meaningful results.

From the perspective of Harry Stack Sullivan, interpersonal relationships determine personality development. From early childhood, parents are concerned with the socialization of the child and repeatedly communicate society's expectations of behavior. The child's self-concept is developed from these communications and actually depends on the appraisals of parents and other significant persons. In other words, the child's internalized views of others comprise the self. The essential component of the interpersonal relationship is the act of communication among people. In the absence of supportive, constructive communication, self-concept is inadequate. Communication must be subject to "consensual validation," that is, to the confirmation or negation of others, if it is to be effective in molding the self. Individuals, for some reason closed off from consensual validation and consequently who do not receive valid feedback about their behavior, develop distorted perceptions of reality and become maladjusted.

In addition to self-concept development, communication facilitates successful role playing. Children learn role reciprocity, that is, to behave in a manner expected of a person in a certain role. They learn to expect the same behavior of others. Group functioning is based on correct role playing; consequently, such interactive skills are rewarded when performed successfully and censored when they are not. For instance, a football team could not operate successfully if every player assumed the role of quarterback.

Without open communication and knowledge of social roles, the individual cannot achieve interpersonal accommodations, that is, healthy interpersonal relationships. Interpersonal accommodation is a reciprocal process involving the fulfillment of complementary needs. Emotional security is dependent on such relationships. Social relationships that are not mutually satisfactory are generally not sustained, or, if they do persist, are unhealthy, since one person's needs remain unfulfilled.

Sullivan's position draws heavily from social role-playing theory as introduced by George Herbert Mead in 1934. Mead believed that mental illness was the direct result of an inability to play the roles required for successful social interaction. Faulty role playing prevented effective communication and isolated the "sick" person. In addition to Sullivan's work, Mead's theories inspired a vast amount of investigation into "taking the role of others." One offshoot of his principles was the development of the concept of deviance and the evolution of labeling theory in the 1960's.

As previously discussed, society's agents ostracize rule breakers by designating them as deviant and assigning some type of label to them that demonstrates their deviance. The essence of labeling theory is that the label itself carries social *consequences*. Theoretically, once an individual is labeled, she or he is characterized by that label in the eyes of society. Consequently, the behavior of an individual labeled psychotic, for example, takes on the characteristics of psychosis. Actually, the labeled individual is under social pressure to assume the deviant role. In other words, society expects the individual's behavior to conform to the deviant identity. For instance, a girl may be assigned to a teacher who dislikes her and be labeled emotionally disturbed as a result of that situation. Once labeled she is under intense social pressure to behave in a manner appropriate to her label. Peers and authority figures expect it and their expectations are quickly communicated to the child. She is expected to disrupt the class, act like a clown, and start fights. To some extent, her normal behaviors are ignored. That is, other people tend to remember the behavior that confirms their expectations and to overlook those that do not. From this perspective, those labeled deviant actually may differ little from their normal brethren. Social factors, such as influence and power, community values, and so forth, all determine who is tapped for the deviant role.

Cultural transmission theory, which grew out of studies of juvenile delinquency and crime, presents a slightly different concept of deviance. The major tenet is that all individuals are basically alike in their needs and aspirations. The behaviors they select to fulfill themselves depend largely on the social interactions to which they have been exposed. Thus traditions in high crime areas are toward criminal activity and such behaviors receive social support. Breaking the law is a socially acceptable behavior. Sutherland and Cressey (1966) termed this type of social learning *differential association*. Presumably, the behavior an individual regards as socially appropriate is that learned from his or her closest associates. From this perspective, mental illness may actually be construed as conforming behavior. Deviance is perceived only with regard to the values of a larger community.

An alternate explanation of the high rates of deviance in certain geographic areas is called *social disorganization theory*. This relatively old perspective (Park and Burgess, 1924) sees deviant behaviors as increasing as community institutions break down and no longer meet the needs of the citizens. Such disorganization occurs when individuals must acculturate to a new society, thus giving up old customs (Faris and Dunham, 1939). Presumably, once acculturated the deviant behaviors reduce.

Finally, Emile Durkheim (1951) developed the concept of *anomie* to account for deviant behavior. He saw deviance as the inevitable result of conflict between group norms that represent social and individual needs. When individual needs expand beyond the point where they can be met in a society, a state of perpetual frustration, discontent, or anomie results. Thus deviance is more pronounced in times of rapid social change, when society cannot develop new norms quickly enough to keep pace with varied individual needs.

From this perspective individuals who violate social norms have pathological needs. The causes of such inappropriate needs are both innate and learned. Any society, regardless of its norms, will have a proportion of deviant members. A high rate of deviants suggests that the norms are no longer appropriate and is an indication of social pathology.

Impact on Education

The sociological model has had a considerable impact on education, particularly within the past ten years. First and foremost has been the revolution within special education regarding the legitimacy of disability

labeling. Cogent arguments describing the stigmatizing effects of designating children mentally retarded, emotionally disturbed, brain injured,
and so on, have been advanced by Iano (1972), Christoplos and Renz
(1969), and others. The emphasis has switched in schools from the segregation of children who share common disability labels to mainstreaming,
which emphasizes integration in regular education classrooms. Efforts are
made to avoid useless labeling and to provide for specific educational
needs in an environment close to the mainstream of educational services.

The second area of the influence of the sociological model on education can be seen in the increased awareness of the variation between the
concepts of deviance and disability. Children who do not display "typical"
behaviors are no longer automatically thought of as impaired. For instance, children who speak dialects that vary from standard English are
not construed as linguistically disabled, but simply as deviating from a
traditional norm.

The third point involves the increasing emphasis on the social milieu
as a significant variable in helping children develop and learn. Theorists
such as Fritz Redl (1959) have developed popular interpretations of the
implications of such sociological concepts within the classroom. William
Rhodes (1967) has gone a shade further and has developed an ecological
perspective that incorporates sociological concepts into the educational
community. From his perspective a child's emotional reactions cannot be
separated from the entire constellation of environmental events.

These indications of the influence of the sociological model on education do not mean that it is a dominant theory in education. Such is not the
case. Currently sociological theory, particularly the concepts of deviance
and labeling, represents an alternative point of view to the dominant
disability model.

Critique and Summary

The sociological perspective shares its emphasis on the social milieu
with both the existential and phenomenological models. Its variation lies
in the focus on group behavior and its emphasis on interpersonal relationships in shaping behavior. All three models put human beings first and
attack rather than explain the social forces that label them as deviant.

The principal criticism leveled at the sociological perspective is that
it fails to discriminate among emotional disorders, classifying socially deviant behaviors such as psychosociopathic acts with the bizarre, irrational activities associated with psychosis. Critics argue that these types
of disorders may have different roots and that, whereas the former classification may be generated by social factors, the latter category is not.

In addition, the sociological perspective provides a less comprehensive portrait of human beings than the other perspectives discussed. It

does not illuminate the individual attitudes, traits, drives, needs, emotions, and so on that determine behavior.

The basic tenets of the sociological model may be summarized as follows:

1. Emotional disturbance is not a pathological condition existing within the child.
2. Emotionally disturbed behaviors are those that deviate from established norms.
3. Any individual, given certain community-based conditions, may become labeled emotionally disturbed.
4. Deviant behaviors reflect social roles, and social pressure to conform to those roles.
5. Faulty communication and inappropriate role playing lead to deviant behavior.
6. Problem behavior is interactive and cannot be studied in isolation.
7. The child's social milieu contains the significant forces that influence his or her behavior.
8. Effective treatment must incorporate aspects of the social milieu.

CONCLUSION

In our discussion of the sociological model we have come full circle in the various perspectives of human beings. We began with the theoretical school that depicted human beings as passive creatures whose development is predetermined by their biological processes and genetic inheritance. We moved to the psychoanalytic position, where our fate is only slightly less determined by biology and by the fixed stages of sexual development that shape our personalities. We progressed to the behavioristic position that depicts humanity as the product of conditioning, no better or worse than any animal whose behavior is determined by its learning experiences. We described the phenomenological school of thought, and for the first time were exposed to positions that view humans as something more than will-less creatures whose behaviors are shaped by forces neither recognized nor understood. Human beings are represented as active agents who plan and direct the course of their existence. Optimism is short-lived, however, and as we moved from the phenomenological to the existential position we were again confronted with the view of human beings as victims. In this instance, it is not our inherent weaknesses nor our faulty learning experiences that do us in. Our downfall is precipitated by the overwhelming dehumanizing forces of a mechanistic, callous society that neutralizes our drive toward self-actualization. Finally, we arrive at the sociological position and find that the emphasis on human beings as actors who may select the values that underlie their lives, has disappeared. Instead, we are again acted on by the forces of society that assign us the roles that we play throughout life.

As we review these six positions we cannot fail to notice that each point of view resembles a piece in a puzzle. Each focuses on a unique aspect of human beings and each makes a valid contribution to our understanding of emotional disturbance. It is trite but true to say that each position has some answers but not *the* answer. The causes of emotional disturbance are myriad. Common sense tells us that some disturbed behaviors are due to biological or genetic deficits, others to maladaptive learning, while still others are the products of sociological forces. When all is said and done, it is not in our best interest to select and adhere to one theoretical position exclusively. To the extent that we can understand and make practical applications of all theoretical perspectives our efficiency in dealing with emotionally disturbed children is increased.

STUDY QUESTIONS

1. Select two theoretical models of emotional disturbance that primarily reflect a disability perspective. Discuss each, noting their similarities and differences.
2. Discuss in detail the theoretical model of emotional disturbance that is based on learning theory.
3. Discuss the theoretical model that depicts human beings optimistically and regards self-actualization as a basic, intrinsic motivating force. Note the impact of this model on education.
4. Discuss the various types of social forces that are components of the sociological model.
5. Select the model that you find most appealing. Compare and contrast it to the model you find least appealing.

REFERENCES

Adler, A. *The problem child.* New York: Capricorn Books, 1963.

Bandura, A. Behavior modification through modeling procedures. In L. Krasner and L. Ullmann (eds.). *Research in behavior modification.* New York: Holt, 1965.

Bender, L. Childhood schizophrenia: a review. *International Journal of Psychiatry,* 1968, 5, 123–129.

Breuer, J., and Freud, S. On the psychical mechanism of hysterical phenomena. In J. Strachey (ed.). *Studies on hysteria.* New York: Basic Books, 1957.

Broen, W. *Schizophrenia: research and theory.* New York: Academic Press, 1968.

Bunney, W.; Brodie, H.; Murphy, D.; and Goodwin, F. Studies of alphe-methl-paratyrosine, L-dopa, and L. trypitophan in depression and mania. *American Journal of Psychiatry*, 1971, *127*(7), 48–56.

Buss, A. *Psychopathology*. New York: Wiley, 1966.

Christoplos, E., and Renz, P. A critical examination of special education programs. *Journal of Special Education*, 1969, *3*, 317–379.

Coleman, J. *Abnormal psychology and modern life*. Glenview, Ill.: Scott Foresman, 1972.

Cott, A. Orthomolecular treatment: a biochemical approach to the treatment of schizophrenia. Unpublished manuscript, 1968.

Cruickshank, W. Some issues facing the field of learning disability. *Journal of Learning Disabilities*, 1972, *5*, 380–388.

Cruickshank, W.; Bentzen, F.; Ratzeburg, F.; and Tannhauser, T. *A teaching method for brain-injured and hyperactive children*. Syracuse, N.Y.: Syracuse University Press, 1961.

Dearing, G. Russians support genetic basis for schizophrenia. *Psychiatric News*, 1969, *4*(8), 18.

Delgado, J. Electronic pacing of behavior: brain research, treatment tool. *Roche Reports*, 1969, *6*(7), 8.

Dement, W. A new look at the third stage of existence. *Stanford Report*, 1968–1969, *8*, 208.

Dorzab, J.; Baker, M.; Cadoret, R.; and Winokur, C. Depressive disease: familial psychiatric illness. *American Journal of Psychiatry*, 1971, *127*(9), 48–60.

Doman, G.; Delacato, C.; and Doman, R. *The Doman-Delacato Developmental Profile*. Philadelphia: Institutes for the Achievement of Human Potential, 1964.

Durkheim, E. *Suicide, a study in sociology*. Glencoe, Ill.: The Free Press, 1951.

Eaton, L., and Menolascino, F. Psychotic reactions of childhood: experiences of a mental retardation pilot project. *Journal of Nervous and Mental Disorders*, 1966, *143*, 55–67.

Erikson, E. Ego development and historic change. *Psychoanalytic Study of the Child*, 1947, *2*, 359–397.

Faris, R., and Dunham, H. *Mental disorders in urban areas*. Chicago: University Press, 1939.

Freud, A. *The ego and the mechanisms of defense*. London: Hogarth Press, 1937.

Frostig, M. Visual perception in the brain-injury child. *American Journal of Orthopsychiatry*, 1962, *32*, 279–280.

Frostig, M., and Horne, D. *The Frostig program for the development of visual perception: teacher's guide*. Chicago: Follett, 1964.

Gittleman, M., and Birch, G. Childhood schizophrenia, intellect, neurologic status, perinatal risk, prognosis, and family pathology. *Archives of General Psychiatry*, 1967, *17*, 16–25.

Goodwin, F.; Murphy, D.; and Bunney, W. Lithium-carbonate treatment in depression and mania. *Archives of General Psychiatry*, 1969, *21*(4), 486–496.

Gottlieb, J.; Frohman, C.; and Beckett, P. A theory of neuronal malfunction in schizophrenia. *American Journal of Psychiatry*, 1969, *126*(2), 149–156.

Heath, R.; Krupp, I.; Byers, L.; and Liljekvist, J. Schizophrenia as an immunologic disorder. *Archives of General Psychiatry*, 1967. *16*(1), 1–33.

Heath, R.; Martens, S.; Leach, B.; Cohen, M.; and Angel, C. Effect on behavior in humans with the administration of taraxein. *American Journal of Psychiatry*, 1957, *114*, 14–24.

Heath, R.; Martens, S.; Leach, B.; Cohen, M.; and Feigley, C. Behavioral changes in nonpsychotic volunteers following the administration of taraxein, the substance obtained from serum of schizophrenic patients. *American Journal of Psychiatry*, 1958, *114*, 917–920.

Heston, L. Psychiatric disorders in foster home reared children of schizophrenic mothers. *British Journal of Psychiatry*, 1966, *112*, 819–825.

Heston, L. The genetics of schizophrenic disease. *Science*, 1970, *167*, 249–256.

Himwich, H. Study backs biochemical etiology in schizophrenia. *Psychiatric News*, 1970, 5(10), 15.

Hinton, G. Childhood psychosis or mental retardation: a diagnostic dilemma. Pediatric and neurological aspects. *Canadian Medical Association Journal*, 1963, *89*, 1020–1024.

Hoffer, A., and Pollin, W. Schizophrenia in the NAS-NRC panel of 15,909 veteran twin pairs. *Archives of General Psychiatry*, 1970, 23(5), 469–477.

Horney, K. *Our inner conflicts*. New York: Norton, 1945.

Iano, R. Shall we disband our special classes. *Journal of Special Education*, 1972, *6*, 167–177.

Jarlais, D. Mental illness as social deviance. In W. Rhodes and M. Tracey (eds.), *A study of child variance*. Ann Arbor, Mich.: University of Michigan Press, 1972.

Judd, L., and Mandell, A. Chromosome studies in early infantile autism. *Archives of General Psychiatry*, 1968, *18*(4), 450–457.

Kallmann, F. *Heredity in health and mental disorder*. New York: Norton, 1953.

Kallmann, F. The use of genetics in psychiatry. *Journal of Mental Science*, 1958, *104*, 542–549.

Kephart, N. *The brain injured child in the classroom*. Chicago: National Society for Crippled Children and Adults, 1963.

Kirk, S. Behavioral diagnosis and remediation of learning disabilities. *Proceedings of the Annual Meeting of the Conference on Exploration into the Problems of the Perceptually Handicapped Child*. Vol. 1, 1963.

Kirk, S., and Elkins, J. Characteristics of children in resource rooms. Unpublished manuscript, Leadership Training Institute in Learning Disabilities, University of Arizona, Tucson, 1974.

Kirk, S., and Kirk, W. *Psycholinguistic learning disabilities: diagnosis and remediation*. Urbana, Ill.: University of Illinois Press, 1971.

Kirk, S.; McCarthy, J.; and Kirk, W. *The Illinois test of psycholinguistic abilities*. Rev. ed. Urbana, Ill.: University of Illinois Press, 1968.

Kringlen, E. *Heredity and environment in the functional psychosis: an epidemiological–clinical twin study*. Oslo: Universitsforlaget, 1967.

Laing, R. *The divided self: an existential study in sanity and madness*. Baltimore: Penguin Books, 1965.

Laing, R. *The politics of experience*. New York: Ballantine, 1967.

Maslow, A. *Toward a psychology of being*. Princeton, N.J.: Van Nostrand, 1962.

Maslow, A. Self-actualization and beyond. In J. Bugental (ed.). *Challenges of humanistic psychology*. New York: McGraw-Hill, 1967.

Maslow, A. Toward a humanistic biology. *American Psychologist*, 1969, *24*(8), 734–735.

May, R. *Love and will*. New York: Norton, 1969.

Mead, G. *Mind, self and society*. Chicago: The University of Chicago Press, 1934.

Mednick, S. Birth defects and schizophrenia. *Psychology Today*, 1971, *4*(11), 48–50.

Mednick, S., and McNeil, T. Current methodology in research on the etiology of schizophrenia: serious difficulties which suggest the use of the high risk group method. *Psychological Bulletin*, 1968, *70*, 681–693.

Minskoff, E.; Wiseman, D.; and Minskoff, J. *The MWM program for developing language abilities*. Ridgefield, N.J.: Educational Performance Associates, 1972.

Money, J. Dyslexia: a postconference review. In J. Money (ed.). *Reading disability*. Baltimore: Johns Hopkins, 1966, 9–33.

Newcomer, P., and Hammill, D. *Psycholinguistics in the schools*. Columbus, Ohio: Merrill, 1976.

Osmond, H., and Smythies, J. Schizophrenia: a new approach. *Journal of Mental Science*, 1952, *98*, 309–315.

Park, R., and Burgess, E. *The city*. Chicago: University of Chicago Press, 1924.

Pavlov, I. *Conditioned reflexes and psychiatry*. New York: International, 1941.

Pollin, W.; Allen, M.; Hoffer, A.; Stabenau, J.; and Hrubec, Z. Psychopathology in 15,909 pairs of veteran twins: Evidence for a genetic factor in the pathogenesis of schizophrenia and its relative absence in psychoneurosis. *American Journal of Psychiatry*, 1969, *126*(5), 43–56.

Redl, F. The concept of a therapeutic milieu. *American Journal of Orthopsychiatry*, 1959, *29*, 721–734.

Redl, F. The concept of the life space interview. *American Journal of Orthopsychiatry*, 1959, *29*, 1–18.

Rhodes, W. The disturbing child, a problem in ecological management. *Exceptional Children*, 1967, *39*, 449–455.

Rhodes, W., and Tracy, M. *A study of child variance*. Ann Arbor, Mich.: University of Michigan Press, 1972.

Rimland, B. *Infantile autism: the syndrome and its implications for a neural theory of behavior*. New York: Appleton-Century-Crofts, 1964.

Rimland, B. Psychogenesis versus biogenesis: the issues and the evidence. In S. C. Plog and R. B. Edgerton (eds.). *Changing perspectives in mental illness*. New York: Holt, Rinehart and Winston, 1969.

Ritvo, E.; Ornitz, E.; Tanguay, P.; and Lee, J. Neurophysiologic and biochemical abnormalities in infantile autism and childhood schizophrenia. Unpublished manuscript, 1970.

Rogers, C. *Client centered therapy*. Boston: Houghton-Mifflin, 1951.

Rogers, C. A theory of therapy, personality and interpersonal relationships, as developed in the client-centered framework. In S. Kock (ed.). *Psychology, a study of science*. New York: McGraw-Hill, 1959.

Rogers, C. *On becoming a person*. Boston: Houghton-Mifflin, 1961.

Rogers, C. *Freedom to learn*. Columbus, Ohio: Merrill, 1969.

Rosenthal, D. *The Genain quadruplets: a case study and theoretical analysis of heredity and environment in schizophrenia*. New York: Basic Books, 1963.

Rosenthal, D.; Wender, P.; Kety, S.; Schulsinger, F.; Welner, J.; and Ostergaard, L. Schizophrenics' offspring reared in adoptive homes. In D. Rosenthal and S. Kety (eds.). *The transmission of schizophrenia*. Elmsford, N.J.: Pergamon Press, 1968.

Rutter, M. The influence of organic and emotional factors on the origins, nature, and outcome of childhood psychosis. *Developmental Medicine and Child Neurology*, 1965, 7, 518–528.

Schildkraut, J. The catecholamine hypothesis of affective disorders: a review of supporting evidence. *American Journal of Psychiatry*, 1965, *122*(5), 509–522.

Shore, P.; Pletscher, A.; Tomich, E.; Carlsson, A.; Kuntzman, R.; and Brodie, B. Role of brain serotonin in reserpine action. *Academic Science*, 1957, *66* 609–615.

Skinner, B. *Science and human behavior*. New York: Macmillan, 1953.

Skinner, B. *Beyond freedom and dignity*. New York: Knopf, 1975.

Spitz, R. The role of ecological factors in emotional development in infancy. *Child Development*, 1949, *20*, 145–156.

Strauss, A., and Lehtinin, L. *Psychopathology and education of the brain injured child*. New York: Grune & Stratton, 1947.

Sullivan, H. *The interpersonal theory of psychiatry*. New York: Norton, 1953.

Sutherland, E., and Cressey, D. *Principles of criminology*. Philadelphia: Lippincott, 1960.

Thorndike, E. *The psychology of learning*. New York: Teachers College, 1913.

Treffert, D. Epidemiology of infantile autism. *Archives of General Psychiatry*, 1970. *22*, 431–438.

Ullmann, L., and Krasner, L. (eds.). *Case studies in behavior modification*. New York: Holt, Rinehart and Winston, 1965.

Van der Velde, C. Effectiveness of lithium carbonate in the treatment of manic-depressive illness. *American Journal of Psychiatry*, 1970, *127*(3), 345–351.

Watson, J. *Psychology from the standpoint of a behaviorist*. New York: 1919.

Wender, P. The role of genetics in the etiology of the schizophrenias. *American Journal of Orthopsychiatry*, 1969, *39*, 447–458.

PART II

IDENTIFICATION OF EMOTIONAL DISORDERS IN CHILDREN

3
Emotional Problems
in Children

The disability classification system of the AMA reported in Chapter 1 describes adult conditions but may also be applied to children. According to NIMH (1970), an estimated 10–20 percent of the elementary school children in the United States suffer moderate to severe emotional problems requiring some kind of mental health care. An estimated 500,000 American children are afflicted with psychoses and borderline psychotic conditions. Others experience a range of pathological conditions similar to those experienced by adults. However, the following points, adapted in part from Coleman (1972, 1964),[1] illustrate how the variations in development that separate adults from adolescents and adolescents from children produce variations in the manifestations of illness among these groups.

First, there is variation in the clinical patterns for specific disorders according to age. For instance, childhood schizophrenia is a relatively prevalent disease and, like the adult form, is characterized by withdrawal and the inability to relate to others. It is not until adolescence, however, that delusions and hallucinations become characteristic of schizophrenia (Fish et al., 1968). Another psychosis, pathological depression, is found in all age groups. However, the suicidal impulses commonly associated with adolescent and adult depression usually are not present in childhood depression (Poznanski and Zrull, 1970).

A second variation is that some conditions are found exclusively, or often have onset in childhood and adolescence. These include: (1) autism; (2) behavioral disorder syndromes such as hyperactivity, unsocial-

---

[1] From *Abnormal Psychology and Modern Life*, Fourth Edition by James C. Coleman, Copyright 1972, 1964 by Scott, Foresman and Company. Reprinted by permission.

ized aggressive reaction, overanxious and withdrawn reactions, runaway reaction, group delinquency, and significant single behaviors such as stuttering, sleep disorders, feeding disturbances, enuresis, and tics; and (3) transient adjustment reactions of childhood and adolescence. Each of these conditions, as well as other childhood psychoses, will be discussed in detail later in this chapter.

The third variation between childhood diseases and those exhibited later in life involves the more transitory nature of children's illnesses. Children lack the rigid personality structure characteristic of adults. Their self-concepts are less firm, and they have had fewer experiences with the realities of living. Consequently, they are more susceptible to situational stress. They tend to react disproportionately to immediate incidents and are easily upset by minor problems. They also tend to recover from emotional upheavals more readily than adults. Therefore, what appears to be a major emotional problem may respond readily to treatment and have a relatively short duration.

Finally, it is frequently easier to identify the pattern of psychopathology among adults than it is to discern specific illnesses in children. Children lack the verbal skills necessary to communicate information that would lead to effective diagnosis of their conditions. Also, they tend to mask reactions such as depression through acting-out behaviors such as disobedience and running away (Leese, 1968). As children mature, their emotional responses become more differentiated and more consistent.

The most convenient method of approaching the variety of conditions affecting children is to discuss each of the classification categories listed by the American Psychiatric Association (1968), since this system is applied most often. These categories include childhood psychosis, behavioral disorders, significant independent disorders, and transient situational disturbances. Many persons interested in childhood mental disorders find this classification system inadequate (Menninger, 1969; Fish, 1969) and prefer a system that provides additional categories such as developmental deviations, psychophysiological disorders, psychoneurotic disorders and personality disorders.

CHILDHOOD PSYCHOSES

Autism

Autism means absorption in fantasy as an escape from reality. As indicated elsewhere, it is a prevailing symptom of schizophrenia. Kanner (1943) was the first person to characterize infantile autism as a distinct syndrome, as differentiated from other syndromes associated with childhood schizophrenia. According to Kanner, autism is manifested at birth. The child seems aloof and unresponsive to the presence or absence of other people. As the child matures, other common characteristics are absence or severely restricted development of speech, aversion to noise, and repetitive or stereotyped movements. Attention is often fixed on the manipulation of an object to the exclusion of all other interests. Although this condition appears to be clinically similar to childhood schizophrenia, and many regard it as the earliest form of that disease, there are others who regard autism as a separate disease. These individuals note variations in the manifestations of symptoms. The schizophrenic child undergoes what appears to be normal development before displaying withdrawn behavior and thought disturbances. Also, schizophrenic children retain interest in their personal relationships, although they may be unable to pursue them satisfactorily. Autistic children are oblivious to their social environment. Bettelheim (1967) has illustrated the difference by stating that the schizophrenic child withdraws from the world, but the autistic child fails to ever enter it.

Clancy and McBride (1969) present an alternate view, minimizing the basis for differentiating between autism and schizophrenia. After studying fifty-three autistic children, they concluded that some autistic children experienced normal language development that disappeared as they became increasingly autistic. They also concluded that autistic children are actively involved with their environment. They noted that autistics structure the environment to suit themselves when they avoid interaction with others and maintain rigid routines. They are as adept at manipulating people toward these ends as normal children are at arranging more typical types of interactions.

Perhaps some of the children labeled autistic in the Clancy-McBride study might have been more accurately diagnosed as schizophrenic. If autism is, as it appears to be, arbitrarily defined as a disease that occurs during infancy, whereas childhood schizophrenia is defined as occurring somewhere after the first several years of life, then obviously differential diagnosis can be made on the basis of the onset of the disease.

Etiology   The cause of autism is unknown and is the subject of some controversy. The conflicting causation theories that have been advanced can be grouped into three major categories: nurture, nature, and nature-nurture interaction.

The nurture position attributes autism to adverse parental influences. Bettleheim (1959) cites angry, rejecting parents as causal agents, while Szurek (1956) reports that the parents of autistic children have disordered personalities. Clerk (1961), Pavenstedt (1955), and Knight (1963) attribute primary responsibility to mothers who are described as aggressive, unresponsive, unemotional, and cold. In all of these theories, the infant is viewed as biologically normal. Parental deficiency causes social withdrawal, thus preventing the normal acquisition of speech and language, as well as cognitive and social skills. Therefore, autistic children have the potential for normal intellectual, linguistic, and social development if they receive prompt and effective treatment.

The nature-nurture interaction position regards autism as a product of biological inferiority and faulty parental influences. Anthony (1958), Eisenberg and Kanner (1956), Garcia and Sarvis (1964), Rank (1955), Mahler (1955), and Clancy and McBride (1969) support this position, although there is disagreement about the kind of biological dysfunction involved or the precise type of parental inadequacy that exacerbates the condition. Generally, the biological deficiency is not viewed as causing irreversible cognitive and linguistic damage. For example, autistic children are not regarded as mentally retarded despite their consistently poor performance on intelligence tests. Their low intellectual functioning is attributed to their affective disorder. When autistic behavior is modified, intelligence improves. Also, parents of autistic children have been described most often as highly intelligent, overly serious persons who provide their children with physical necessities but are unresponsive to their emotional needs. Rank used the term "the frigidaire atmosphere" to describe the emotional climate of the home.

The nature point of view attributes the disease solely to biological disorders. Parents are exonerated from responsibility. Fish (1960, 1961) and Pollack and Krieger (1958) regard the deficiency as a general neurological dysfunction that affects perceptual-motor, cognitive, and linguistic development. Other, more specific neural dysfunctions cited involve the vestibular pathway (Colbert, et al., 1959), the limbic lobe (Schain and Yannet, 1960), and the reticular formation (Rimland, 1964). Rutter (1968) concluded that the innate disorder affected the ability to filter, integrate, categorize, and understand the sounds of language. The noncomprehension of stimuli forces social withdrawal and the development of compensatory ritualistic and compulsive behavior. His position that central language disability may explain the major autistic symptoms is supported by DeMyer (1976) who also offers evidence that autistic children, like other neurologically impaired children, have general intelligence in the moderately to profoundly retarded ranges.

Generally, the nature theorists regard any signs of parental maladjustment as reactions to the stress of coping with biologically impaired children. Wolff and Morris (1971) failed to find evidence that parents of autistic chldren were cold, unfeeling, overintellectualized people. DeMyer et al. (1972) found that autistic parents had no greater incidence of psychopathology than parents of normal children. Also, supporters of the nature position believe the effects of the disease to be generally pervasive and largely irreversible. For example, many regard autistic children as mentally retarded. They recommend an adaptive rather than a curative approach to treatment.

Treatment Approaches to treatment vary. Bettelheim (1967) advocates the establishment of a warm, accepting environment. The therapist must attempt to break through the child's autistic defenses by communicating love and respect to him or her. Other therapists, such as Silver (1955) and Axline (1947), use play therapy techniques with such children, while Clancy and McBride (1969) report some success with family therapy. The most popular form of treatment involves some form of educational and behavioral therapy (Bandura, 1969; Lovass, 1967; Schopler, et al., 1971; Fischer and Glanville, 1970). Lovass has been able to demonstrate that behavioral modification techniques may be used to teach language to autistic children. The progress, however, is slow and tedious, requiring round-the-clock efforts of teams of highly trained teachers.

Coleman (1972) reports that, regardless of the treatment used, the prognosis in infantile autism is unfavorable. As is the case with childhood schizophrenia, less than one-fourth of the afflicted children attain marginal adjustments in later life. Hingtgen and Churchill (1969) report that even with high motivation most autistic children do not overcome their specific and general learning disorders. According to DeMyer (1976), IQ is the best predictor of the level of functioning the autistic child will be able to obtain. Brighter children show the most improvement. Another important component affecting improvement is the development of language skills (Lovass et al., 1972). Autistic children who learn to use and to understand speech make far better adjustments than those who remain mute and uncomprehending.

Schizophrenia

Schizophrenia is the most common form of childhood psychosis, encompassing several syndromes of symptoms. As noted earlier, infantile autism, one such syndrome, is regarded by some as the earliest form of schizophrenia. Another syndrome, generally referred to as *process schizophrenia* (Garmezy and Rodnick, 1959), manifests a gradual, insidious onset of symptoms. The most pronounced characteristic is an increasing disinterest in the realities of daily life. Children begin to ignore friends, parents, toys, and so forth. They may also stop performing routine activities such as dressing and undressing, bathing, eating, and so forth. As withdrawal progresses, autistic behavior increases and the child appears to spend an inordinate amount of time daydreaming. Affect becomes flat; the child's face often is unexpressive. Verbalizations become inappropriate and increasingly infrequent. Motor activity decreases or becomes purposeless, repetitive, and rhythmic. Typical activities are restless pacing, body rocking, whirling, or bizarre hand movements. Symptoms abate slowly, if at all, and the child's disorder may become permanent.

A second major syndrome, termed *reactive schizophrenia* (Phillips, 1953), has a sudden onset. The principal symptoms are severe panic and mental confusion. The child displays emotional outbursts such as severe temper tantrums. The thoughts, language, and motor behavior of the child are often bizarre. The reactive syndrome is generally triggered by a stressful situation such as illness, hospitalization, or sudden death in the family. Symptoms appear to abate rapidly, although in some cases, a more chronic pattern of illness emerges (Ullmann and Eck, 1965).

Wolman (1972) considers the reactive–process distinction inaccurate, arguing that so-called reactive conditions often involve long periods of inner turmoil, and that the prognosis for this type of condition is not necessarily better than for so-called process conditions. He prefers to categorize schizophrenia in a reverse order of decreasing severity as *pseudo-amentive*—the most severe condition involving mental retardation and no language development; *autistic*—a childhood condition that corresponds to the hebephrenic and simple syndromes in adults; *symbiotic*—a condition marked by a peculiar dependence on the mother and corresponding to catatonia in adults; and *aretic*—the mildest form, corresponding to paranoid schizophrenia in adults.

Clearly, many specific symptoms have been associated with childhood schizophrenia. Apparently symptoms vary from one case to another and change over a period of time. Most of the symptoms that have been observed can be classified in five general categories (adapted in part from Coleman, 1972).[2]

The first category involves *malfunctioning of perceptual filtering*. Normal children selectively filter incoming sensory information to perceive the world in an orderly and meaningful way. Schizophrenics are apparently unable to discriminate between relevant and irrelevant stimuli. Their perceptual world, therefore, is disordered and meaningless. Thus, children might be aware of so many sights and sounds in the environment that they are incapable of attending to or concentrating on those that are important. The perceptual effect might be akin to a kaleidoscope of color devoid of form or pattern.

The second category involves *disorganization of thought processes*. In effect, the child is unable to keep ideas sequenced and focus on the topic at hand. Therefore, his or her verbalizations appear unassociated— a conglomeration of jumbled, senseless remarks. For example, when asked to define the word *ball*, the child might say "A ball is on the head. It's green and she has one too." The ideas that the child has associated to produce this definition are obviously not apparent to the listener.

Category three involves *intense anxiety*. The inability to control perceptions and thoughts apparently induces intense anxiety and a corre-

---

[2] From *Abnormal Psychology and Modern Life*, Fourth Edition by James C. Coleman. Copyright 1972, 1964 by Scott, Foresman and Company. Reprinted by permission.

sponding panic. The child is understandably afraid of what is happening to him or her. Severe anxiety is a particularly common symptom in young schizophrenic children. As they mature they learn to cope with their inner feelings without showing panic. Typical defense or coping mechanisms are the obsessive-compulsive or ritualistic behaviors that begin to consume more and more of the child's time. For example, a schizophrenic child might require 3 to 4 hours to dress because of elaborate ritualistic procedures that he or she feels compelled to repeat during each small step of dressing. Efforts to interfere with these compulsions produce anger and are often resisted with violent, aggressive outbursts.

Category four involves *language disorders.* The speech and language disorders of schizophrenic children vary. Disturbances may include mutism, neologisms (newly created words), ecolalia (parrotlike repetition of speech), fragmented speech, immature speech patterns, and bizarre speech. In some instances speech does not develop. In other cases, speech develops but regresses as the child matures. On rare occasions, schizophrenic children develop their own language system that they use to speak to imaginary playmates in fantasy worlds. Among older children whose speech and language are well developed before the obvious onset of the disease, language usage may be fluent, but so abstract that it ceases to be meaningful to listeners.

The fifth category is *withdrawal from reality.* The schizophrenic child is unable to formulate any reliable concepts regarding the organization of the environment or his or her position within that environment. Discriminations as basic as separating self from others are apparently affected, and the fact that the child often cannot distinguish "you" from "I" is shown in confused use of pronouns. Since the external world is unfathomable, the schizophrenic child becomes progressively preoccupied with inner fantasies and private thoughts. The child may become hostile and negative when aroused from such autistic behavior.

Etiology   There has undoubtedly been more written about the causes of schizophrenia than about all the other psychopathological conditions put together. Investigations have been conducted to demonstrate that schizophrenia results from genetic factors, neurological disabilities, biochemical disorders, faulty family dynamics, and an interaction between inherited predispositions and environmental stress. Despite the plethora of literature, or perhaps because of it, the issue remains unresolved. Possibly the fact that schizophrenia is a label applied to a variety of symptomatic behaviors contributes to the elusiveness of conclusive data about its causes. In any event, the following discussion will include only a representative sample of the studies supporting each position.

Evidence of a genetic cause of schizophrenia is produced in the famous twin studies by Kallmann (1953, 1956, 1958). He found a concordance rate of 86.2 percent for identical twins, 14.5 percent for fraternal twins, and 7.1 percent for half-siblings. These findings contrast with an incidence figure of approximately 1 percent for the general population. A similar study (Kringlen, 1967) using more stringent methodological controls reports substantially lower concordance rates—38 percent for identical twins and 10 percent for fraternal twins—but still substantiates the genetic relationship.

Much research has been done on the role of neurophysiological disturbances in causing schizophrenia. The results suggest that schizophrenics suffer from malfunctions in excitatory and inhibitory neural processes (Delgado, 1969), irregularities in the autonomic nervous system that predispose an individual to overarousal or underarousal in stressful situations (Fenz and Velner, 1970, Broen, 1968, Mednick and McNeil, 1968), and the presence of unusual chemical agents in the bloodstream (Akerfeldt, 1957; Shore et al., 1957).

The other side of the coin, the set of environmental causation theories, is advanced by Laing (1969), who regards the disease as an adaptive strategy for living in a sick society; Wahl (1956), who notes the importance of early psychic trauma and deprivation, such as the death of a parent; and a variety of others who point to the following as causal agents (after Coleman, 1972): (1) pathogenic family patterns, including faulty parent personalities, marital stress, and unhealthy family communication patterns, (2) faulty learning, (3) excessive stress, and (4) sick social roles.

The majority of research into pathogenic family patterns has involved aspects of parent personality. Many have concluded that the disease is caused by the "schizophrenogenic mother," a cold, dominating, unfeeling individual who rejects her child (Bettelheim, 1955, 1959; Rank, 1955; Bowen, 1960). Kaufman et al. (1960) divides the blame by concluding that both parents of schizophrenic children demonstrate the classic schizophrenogenic personality pattern.

Among those interested in studies of marital stress, Gerard and Siegel (1950) report a high incidence of parental fighting and other problems in 87 percent of the cases they investigated. Lidz et al. (1968) found similar marital difficulties in all families of schizophrenic children they studied. A pronounced family characteristic in these cases was an absence of respect between the parents.

Bateson (1959) used the term "double bind" to describe the communication patterns in schizophrenic-producing home environments. The child is given mixed messages, that is, told one thing but treated in a manner that belies what he or she is told. For example, parents may assure a child of their love but then treat him or her in a rejecting, unloving way.

Studies in the second environmental category, faulty learning, reveal that children learn inadequate interpersonal relationships from rigid parents who reward only dependent, "good child" behaviors and punish normal assertiveness (Ruesch, Brodsky, and Fischer, 1963; Wolman, 1970).

Investigations of the role of stress in schizophrenia suggest that the schizophrenic breakdown is directly precipitated by increased stress (Will, 1959; Aronson and Polgar 1962; Glover, 1956; Becker, 1962). From this perspective, the schizophrenic has no means of dealing with the typical conflicts that develop in life situations, such as interpersonal relationships, and achievement demands.

Finally, Cameron and Margaret (1951), Laing and Esterson (1964), and Carson (1969) attribute schizophrenia to the child's failure to learn appropriate role behaviors from parents. The child does not understand the social roles played by others, is unsure of his or her own position, and therefore cannot interact with others.

Treatment   The outlook for schizophrenic children is not generally favorable. Bender (1955) investigated 120 children fourteen years after treatment and found that over 50 percent were in state mental hospitals still suffering from schizophrenia. Most of the others had various other types of emotional disorders.

Drug therapy in the form of both tranquilizers and energizers has been used with indifferent success. The main benefit of the utilization of these drugs is the reduction of agitation and bizarre behavior patterns. The underlying schizophrenic condition remains unaffected.

Electroshock has been used with schizophrenic children but not to a great extent. Bender (1955) reports that it relieves anxiety and makes management easier. Since drugs are capable of the same effect, however, electroshock is generally not recommended.

Psychotherapy is practiced with schizophrenic children, also with limited success. Silver (1955) recommends that therapists attempt to reduce anxiety and help the child strengthen coping behavior or defense mechanisms. For example, compulsive ritualistic behaviors that a child may use to minimize anxiety may be structured so that they are less interfering with his or her life and less inconvenient to others. This approach makes no attempt to treat the underlying disease.

Milieu therapy (Paul, 1960) has gained popularity as a technique for use with hospitalized schizophrenics. The entire environment is therapeutically structured to strengthen the child's self-reliance in daily living situations. Token economy programs also have been implemented with some success. These programs require the child to perform certain self-help skills to gain tokens that may be used to buy treats or privileges (Atthowe and Krasner, 1968).

Finally, group therapy, which forces the child to interact with others, has been recommended as having beneficial effects (Peck, Rabinovitch, and Cramer, 1949). However, despite all treatment methods, Eisenberg

(1968) has revealed that only approximately 25 percent of the children will make moderately good adjustments in later life. One-third will deteriorate and require institutional care. The remainder will function on a marginal level.

Manic-Depressive Psychosis

Manic-depressive psychosis does not occur frequently in children. It is most pronounced in persons between the ages of twenty-five and sixty-five. However, the disease, particularly the depressive aspects, has been observed in children as young as three years of age (Poznanski and Zrull, 1970); thus it warrants discussion here.[3]

The clinical picture is one of mood variation, ranging from elation to depression. Manic reactions involve wild, unrealistic optimism. The individual appears to have unlimited energy that is expended in jumping from one activity to another. Little perseverance is displayed, however, and most projects are left incomplete. Manic individuals experience difficulty concentrating and often show poor judgment. Accomplishments never support their grandiose attitudes.

In depressive reactions, the individual experiences feelings of sadness, loneliness, and despair. Thought, speech, and other behaviors slow down. The individual appears too listless to interact with others. He or she generally avoids social encounters and is unable to meet minimal responsibilities. Children are reported to engage in self-injurious behavior (Malmquist, 1972). They may have an inordinate number of accidents. For example, one 10-year-old boy had a history of cuts, bruises, and broken bones brought about by a rough style of play where he showed himself no mercy. He had been struck by automobiles twice. Other injuries can be inflicted deliberately, as when a child burns or cuts himself or herself.

Older manic-depressives often express suicidal urges and are high suicide risks. Unfortunately, this characteristic is becoming progressively more prevalent among children and adolescents. Epidemiologic studies reveal a steady increase in suicide in the fifteen to nineteen age group (Malmquist, 1972), despite the fact that the true incidence probably is underreported. Schrut (1964) found that in New York City there were fifty known attempts for every successful suicide among persons under

---

[3] Psychoanalytically oriented therapists write of "infantile depressions," but those reports are based on retrospective data taken from disturbed adults (Malmquist, 1972). Also, Spitz (1946) used the term "anaclitic depression" to describe institutionalized infants but this syndrome has never been substantiated.

twenty years of age, and that 3 percent of the successful suicides were committed by persons in that age category.

Generally, both manic and depressive reactions are episodic and of relatively brief duration. The depressive episodes usually last longer than the manic periods on about a 3-to-1 ratio. In twelve of eighteen cases of this psychosis studied by Campbell (1953) only the depressive phase was present. Campbell reports further that these children were generally liked by their peers and teachers. They were extremely anxious about succeeding and, therefore, usually attempted to do well in their school pursuits. As their feelings of depression increased, they evidenced somatic complaints such as nausea and headaches.

Etiology   The cause of manic-depressive psychosis has been attributed to biological, psychosocial, and sociocultural factors. Adhering to the notion of biological causation are those who attribute the disease to a hereditary predisposition (Slater, 1944; Kallmann, 1952; Dorzab et al., 1971; Pollin, et al., 1964), faulty neurophysiological processes (Goldstein, 1965; Whybrow and Mendels, 1969), and deviant biochemical factors (Greenspan et al., 1969; Schildkraut, 1965). All of these individuals agree that familial relationships or experiential factors have little to do with the onset of the disease.

The psychosocial position attributes the disease to abnormal reactions to stressful life situations. The child is born with a weakness that is manifested in manic-depressive reactions if the stress produced in the environment becomes too pronounced. Some of those supporting this position are Gibson (1958), Becker (1960), Becker and Altrocchi (1968), Katkin, Sasmor, and Tan (1966).

Finally, the notion that sociocultural factors cause the disease reflects the fact that the incidence seems to vary among different societies (Coleman, 1972). For example, manic-depressive reactions are low in Finland and Israel and high in New Zealand and Switzerland (Gold, 1951; Hes, 1960; Murphy, Wittkower, and Chance, 1967). Whereas depressive states are prominent in America, Kendell (1970) reports that manic reactions predominate over depressive states in Formosa and Africa. The implication of this research is that the disease is a response to cultural factors.

Treatment   Among children, symptoms of manic-depressive conditions may abate without treatment (Harms, 1945; Sadler, 1952). Malmquist (1972) reports cases of successful treatment with psychoanalytically oriented therapy, while Craighead, Kazdin, and Mahoney (1976) regard behavioral therapy as a promising approach. In older persons, antidepressant drugs have been used successfully (Heller, Zahourek, and Whittington, 1971).

BEHAVIORAL DISORDERS

Hyperactive Reaction

The hyperactive or hyperkinetic reaction is a condition characterized by excessive muscular activity. In other words, it describes children who appear to be constantly in motion. Symptoms of hyperactivity are short attention span, distractibility, poor motor coordination, impulsiveness, low frustration tolerance, inhibition, and general emotional instability. The hyperactive reaction is the primary syndrome associated with the group of children Kirk (1963) designated as learning disabled. These children frequently fail to learn adequately in school despite good intellectual potential. However, hyperactivity and many of the related behaviors are also common symptoms associated with other types of conditions, such as autism or schizophrenia.

A typical case of hyperactive reaction is that of Billy, a six-year-old first grader. Billy's teachers complained that he "hit the room like a tornado on the first day of school and has been moving ever since." He was a friendly child with an engaging smile, but that did not prevent him from disrupting the class. From the beginning, he had difficulty attending to the teacher's instructions and directions. Instead, he attended to almost anything else—a piece of string, his pencil, and so on. Independent seat work was impossible for him. He would always attempt the assignment, but quickly became frustrated and visibly upset. He reacted by complaining vocally that tasks were too difficult, destroying his papers, and so forth. As he became upset, his activity level increased. He seemed unable to remain in his seat longer than several consecutive minutes. In one furious 15-minute period of activity, he played with the cords of the curtains, raised and lowered the curtains, knocked over a plant on the window sill, and threw a pencil at a classmate, in that order.

Attempts to control Billy had limited success. He responded briefly to the teacher's efforts when he was taken aside and spoken to quietly but soon returned to his disruptive behaviors. He reacted adversely when openly corrected or scolded in front of classmates and often responded by crying, screaming, and striking out at the teacher, his classmates, or any objects in his way. He needed time away from the classroom to calm down. After he had regained control of himself, he always regretted his reactions. He wanted in his words, "to be good." When evaluated by the school psychologist, he had a verbal IQ of 117 and a performance IQ of 91 on the *Weschler Intelligence Scale for Children*. During the individual evaluation, he had the same problems with attention, frustration, and hyperactive behavior that he demonstrated in the classroom. He showed that he was not the least bit intimidated by the psychological evaluation by asking if he might play the psychologist's role and give the tests. According to the report he role played perfectly, mimicking voice, mannerism, and generally having a good time.

Etiology   There has been a great deal of speculation that the hyperactivity is caused by the immature functioning of the central nervous system or "minimal brain dysfunction" (Jenkins, 1970). Some theorists point to so-called poor perceptual-motor coordination as evidence of "soft neurological signs" or neural pathology (Caputo and Mandell, 1970; Strauss and Kephart, 1955; Wikler, Dixon, and Parker, 1970). However, the concept of minimal brain dysfunction has never been satisfactorily validated, and at present there is no hard evidence that hyperactive behavior is caused by irregularities in brain processes (Myers and Hammill, 1976; Edwards, Alley, and Snider, 1971).

Treatment   Typically the hyperactive condition is manifested before age 8 and disappears before the middle teens. Residual symptoms persist, however, and may include serious learning deficits as well as negative attitudes toward school. Such secondary symptoms are usually treated through modified educational programs, including remedial instruction and career-vocational education.

The primary hyperactive syndrome has been treated successfully with drug therapy (Freedman et al., 1971). Tranquilizers have been used to slow down the functioning of the autonomic nervous system. More effective drugs are the cerebral stimulants such as amphetamines or methylphenidatehydrochloride (Ritalin), which frequently decrease muscular activity and distractibility while increasing attention span. In a study of drug therapy, NIMH (1971) reported that medication does not affect intelligence and enables children to function in a classroom situation.

Critics have pointed out, however, that the use of drugs with hyperactive children is potentially dangerous. They fear overprescription of medication to children whose symptoms are too slight to warrant such treatment. They also fear the side effects of drugs, such as dizziness or headache, and, more importantly, the unknown long-term effects of prolonged usage. These persons regard treatment with behavioral, psychological, and educational therapy as superior to any form of drug therapy. Even the advocates of drug therapy agree that it must be used with caution and that most hyperactive children benefit more from environmental adjustments that accommodate their condition.

Unsocialized-Aggressive Reaction

The unsocialized-aggressive reaction in children is similar to the sociopathic or psychopathic category described for adults. Characteristic behaviors include disobedience, lying, stealing, vandalism, truancy, physical and verbal aggressiveness, temper tantrums, and assorted destructive ness such as setting fires, killing animals, and slashing furniture. In addition, such children tend to be sexually uninhibited and often sexually aggressive (Coleman, 1972).

Many of the children demonstrating this reaction evidence a total disregard for the rights or welfare of others. Their aggressive behaviors are displayed in blatant, defiant fashion, and they are relatively unfazed by the possibility of punishment. They are braggadocios and seem to enjoy the attention they receive as a consequence of their behaviors. Others of these children are less obvious in their overt behavior and appear less interested in winning the attention of others. These children appear to have little conscious control over themselves, however, and display certain of the above behaviors despite efforts to avoid them. Finally, some of these children closely resemble adult psychopaths in that they often attempt to use superficial charm to get what they want, or to escape responsibility for their actions. They may con adult authority figures with smiles and socially appropriate remarks, while engaging in sneaky anti-social behaviors. Often they are more obvious in their relationships with other children, particularly those they perceive as weak. They are deceptive, exploitive, manipulative, and apparently unable either to accept responsibility for their actions or to experience feelings of remorse.

A typical case of unsocialized-aggressive reaction is represented by the following description. John, a nine-year-old boy, was considered a serious problem in school where he had a history of truancy, vandalism, fire setting, and various other destructive activities such as stopping up toilets and setting off the fire alarm. When caught in the act, John typically denied guilt or told what he regarded as a plausible story to justify his behavior. For example, the toilet stuffing resulted from accidentally dropping a roll of toilet paper down the hopper, the fire alarm incident occurred because he didn't realize the alarm was connected, setting fires occurred when he accidentally dropped a match, and so forth.

In class, John typically did little work. He "finished" assignments as quickly as possible with little regard for accuracy and apparently was unconcerned about grades. He enjoyed drawing pictures with war themes and spent as much of his class time as possible on that activity. He frequently provoked fights among his classmates by telling one that he was disliked by another. When the battle erupted, he usually managed to remain on the sidelines, and when the teacher was present, he even played the role of peacemaker. He often complimented the teacher on her appearance but made ridiculing statements about her to his classmates.

Etiology   Unsocialized-aggressive reactions constitute a large proportion of children's diagnosed mental health disorders. Jenkins (1968) found that approximately one-third of 1,500 children seen at the Institute for Juvenile Research bore this label. Three of four of these children were male. Females so labeled tended to engage more in sexual delinquency than in other behaviors.

The preponderance of opinion suggests that this reaction pattern results from pathogenic family relationships. Investigators have found evidence that the nuclear family is disorganized (Bratfos, 1967; Shamsie, 1968). Often parents are divorced or separated. The family dynamics are such that the children are usually rejected and subjected to harsh, inconsistent punishment (Lippman, 1951; Sullivan, 1953).

Treatment   The success of treating children with unsocialized-aggressive reaction depends on two key variables: the age of the child and the extent to which the home situation can be modified. According to Ginott (1961), once children who display these behaviors pass the age of 8, they generally become very resistant to therapy. They are too hostile toward adult authority figures to relate to a therapist in individual therapy, and they victimize other children in group therapy. Before age 8, they are more pliable and less skillful at manipulating or conning behaviors. They can more readily be brought to accept responsibility for their behaviors.

Modification of the home situation that contributes to these types of problems is possibly more difficult than working directly with the children. Parents who establish disorganized and rejecting family environments are either unreceptive to therapeutic suggestions for change or lack the emotional stability to institute such change. Coleman (1972) is so pessimistic about the success of attempted interventions unless the home situation is changed dramatically, that he recommends removing children from homes where such change is impossible and placing them in foster homes. Of course, such an alternative is far from ideal. Children who demonstrate these types of behavior would be difficult for foster parents to deal with. Even well-intentioned persons might resort to punitive methods of control. A change of environment can only be effective if it ensures that the child will be exposed to warm, accepting adults who know how to be firm without being punitive. Robins (1968) indicated the importance of helping these children when he revealed that their behavior is highly predictive of antisocial activities in adulthood.

Overanxious Reaction

Overanxious reaction describes children who display the following characteristics: oversensitivity, unrealistic fears (including fear of school), shyness and timidity, pervasive feelings of inadequacy, obsessive-compulsive behavior, and somatic symptoms. These characteristics in adults would be classified as neurosis. As is true of neurosis, overanxious reactions are attributed to excessive anxiety (Wolman, 1972).

Overanxious children suffer from an inordinate tendency to worry. They are apprehensive about activities that other children undertake enthusiastically. Examples of their numerous fears and typical reactions include fear of injury that causes avoidance of normal play activity, fear of the dark that causes requests to sleep with parents or requests for a night light, fear of animals that causes avoidance of even the most benign creatures, fear of school that causes panic at the thought of attending or refusal to attend despite a history of excellent achievement, fear of new experiences that prevents normal exploration of the environment and causes excessive dependency on adults.

Typically overanxious children encounter social problems because their dependence on adults and their own apprehensions make them appear infantile to their peers. Also, they cry easily and complain frequently about numerous physical ailments, additional immature characteristics. Ginott (1961) describes them as "too good," noting that they lack normal assertiveness and aggression and are afraid of authority, so they tend to engage in activities that they believe will please adult authority figures.

The overanxious syndrome is typified in this representative case. Joan is a large, attractive third-grade student whose behavior belies her size and appearance. At the beginning of the school year, Joan was skipping lunch because she disliked going through the cafeteria line. Her teacher's attempts to solve the problem by accompanying her in the lunch line and reassuring her were of no avail. She remained unwilling to purchase lunch when unaccompanied by an adult. The problem was circumvented when her mother began packing her lunch and a classmate purchased milk for her.

Joan's attitude toward her school work also reflected her lack of self-confidence and dependence on adults for support. She became noticeably upset when new instructional information was presented. Typically, she cried and put her head on the desk. She attempted written assignments only when given individual attention by her teacher, including frequent reassurance that she was proceeding correctly. Even under these circumstances, her achievement was generally below average. She labored extensively over each item and erased frequently. She worked so slowly that she rarely completed an assignment in the time allotted. As she fell behind her classmates, she became increasingly upset, often reverting to tears or complaining of illness.

Etiology   Currently, there is no simple, confirmed cause of overanxious reactions. Coleman (1972) cites a possible causal factor, that these children appear to have "unusual constitutional sensitivity," thus they may be "easily conditioned by aversive stimuli," and build up "surplus fear reactions." In other words, such children may be constitutionally predisposed to develop these conditions.

Environmental circumstances that appear to contribute to the development of overanxious reactions often include an overprotective, over-solicitous parent. Such a parent teaches the child that he is inadequate by restricting and otherwise controlling all activities, not assigning any responsibility, and emphasizing the difficulties and dangers connected with life.

Another contributing environmental condition involves a perfection-istic, demanding parent. This parent regards the child as a miniature adult and holds unrealistic expectations. In this circumstance, the child quickly learns that he or she is incompetent. Few efforts are perfect enough to win parent approval. Some children react by striving to earn parental love through perfection. This type of child becomes hypercritical of his or her own efforts and overreacts to failure or minor setbacks. Regardless of the level of achievement, the child is never satisfied. Unrealistic standards prevent the child from attempting to learn many new activities. The necessity of being perfect is emotionally exhausting, and he or she cannot cope with the slow progress involved in new learning. Other children respond by refusing to make whole-hearted attempts at achievement. These children avoid committing themselves to any project since such commitment entails risking failure once again. Failure that results from a lack of effort can always be rationalized with "I don't care about it" or "I didn't really try."

Occasionally, children become overanxious because of unfortuitous circumstances. Early hospitalization is often a traumatizing experience affecting emotional development. Not only does this type of circumstance imply that the child experienced early suffering because of illness or acci-dent, but it also suggests that the child was suddenly separated from his or her parents at a time of suffering.

Another traumatic event is the death or serious illness of a parent. In these circumstances, children may find their lives dramatically altered by the sudden disappearance of a parent and by the emotional upheaval affecting the survivors.

Finally, the child simply may be reared in an environment that is not conducive to healthy interaction with others. For example, an only child living in a remote area may develop few social skills until reaching school. By that time, the child may be overwhelmed by the social demands sud-denly thrust on him or her and withdraw from interaction. Similarly, a child whose values and attitudes differ drastically from those of his or her peers may experience rejection and respond by withdrawing.

Treatment   Overanxious children generally respond well to treatment. In fact, typical school experiences can be therapeutic if the teacher is sensi-tive to the child's needs. Such children require encouragement, success experiences, and carefully planned interpersonal arrangements. Montenegro (1968) reports that behavioral therapy supplemented with parental counseling is an effective treatment for children with these reactions.

In some instances, particularly when the child's early overprotective or overperfectionistic experiences are continued in school, the child maintains neurotic symptoms throughout life.

Withdrawn Reaction

Withdrawn reaction encompasses many of the characteristics discussed under overanxious reactions. The primary difference is that these children tend to avoid interactions with others, as opposed to becoming excessively dependent on others. Generally, withdrawn children view the world as hostile or threatening, and other persons as potentially harmful. In addition to their suspicion and mistrust of others, they are characterized by a fear of failure so pronounced that the simplest task is difficult to undertake. The preferred response to many daily activities, such as school assignments, is to "give up" and withdraw to the comfortable world of daydreaming. Because these children do not usually try to complete tasks, they tend to have more pronounced academic deficits. Also, since they demand little attention, adults are often likely to ignore or overlook their problems.

The withdrawn syndrome is typified by Bill, a child who, beyond answering an occasional question, never speaks in class. He makes little or no effort to attempt academic assignments and avoids participating in class activities such as parties or recess. He has no known friends outside of school, preferring to spend his time in his room where he plays with toy dinosaurs.

The etiology and treatment of this reaction are similar to that presented for the overanxious reaction.

Runaway Reaction

The runaway reaction, once treated with somewhat tolerant indulgence as a trip around the block for a temporarily perturbed child, no longer is treated so casually. Within the last ten years, the number of children fleeing their homes has risen alarmingly. According to *Newsweek* (1971), there are an estimated 600,000 runaway children in the United States during any given year. Approximately 50 percent of arrests of adolescent girls involve running away.

The runaway reaction is displayed by Jeff, a fourteen-year-old who has been picked up by the juvenile authorities three times in the last two years because he has run away from his home. Jeff is described by his teachers and fellow students as a nice boy who gets along well with others and who appears to abide by school rules. His obvious problems are that he often seems unhappy and has a history of underachievement in school.

His current teacher reports that he has good intellectual potential but usually appears distracted and unable to concentrate in class. His work is marred by many careless errors caused by a lack of real effort. He appears distressed by poor grades, but his work habits remain unchanged. Lately, he has begun to spend more time in the company of students with similar achievement problems.

Jeff's parents describe him as well behaved at home. They note that he is generally uncommunicative and relatively indifferent to family interactions, but they attribute those attitudes to his age. Although school authorities suspect that Jeff takes drugs, his parents deny it.

Jeff's attempts to run away have always followed the same pattern. He leaves in the morning as though he were going to school, and hitchhikes to a nearby large city. Once he arrives, he apparently wanders around aimlessly, sleeping on the street. He continues this pattern until he runs out of food money. He then finds some reason to call himself to the attention of the police. Usually, he simply identifies himself and appears to have no objection to returning home. His parents are becoming increasingly annoyed with his behavior, which they consider to be willfulness because he does not always "get his own way." Jeff's only explanation is that he "just feels like taking off."

Etiology Generally, adolescents who run away from home have histories of conflict with their parents. Often parents are rejecting, overrestrictive, or in conflict themselves. In some instances, however, the parents are loving and supportive but have not enforced behavioral limits consistently. As the child matures, parents become more alarmed by the adolescent's behavior. Their sudden attempts to enforce discipline are met with predictable rebellion. In other cases, children love their parents but believe they have failed them in some way. Finally, most adolescents are highly suggestible and susceptible to the attitudes of friends. Running away has become an "in" behavior. Consequently, certain children are only too eager to give it a try when they encounter some superficial disagreement with their parents.

To demonstrate the importance of peer-group support for this reaction, runaways usually join up together in large cities or in communes where they live on a share-and-share alike basis. They often become involved in drug abuse and sexual activity, behaviors that are also the "norm" among their peers. In some cases, they steal or engage in prostitution, usually to make money for their group of fellow runaways.

Treatment The runaway reaction decreases as persons mature. As adolescents begin to assume greater responsibility for their own welfare, their need to flee from interactions that displease them diminishes. Some return to their homes voluntarily, possibly because a first-hand view of the realities of communal living is disenchanting. In cases where the runaway child is extremely maladjusted emotionally, individual and family therapy is often necessary to effect a reunion with the family.

Group Delinquent Reaction

The group delinquent reaction describes children who have acquired the values, behaviors, and skills of a delinquent peer group or gang to whom they are loyal. Identification with the gang sets them at odds with society as a whole, and they consistently violate rules. They are truant from school, steal, engage in physical assault, and even kill, not for personal gain, but to maintain the ascendancy of their gang and their status within the gang.

Although individuals who display this reaction violate society's rules, they strictly abide by the rules of their gang. In fact, they will discontinue personal activities such as taking drugs, if they are disapproved of by the gang. The gang serves a realistic purpose of protecting them from harm at the hands of outsiders, and it provides emotional security as well. Individuals feel accepted and have a sense of purpose. They identify with strong individuals within the gang and model their behavior.

The group delinquent reaction is demonstrated by Jim, a fifteen-year-old, ninth-grade student. Jim has been a member of a neighborhood gang for two years. He says that he was eager to join because the gang controlled the "turf" he lived on. Since his induction, he is always in the company of several fellow gang members which, he says, provides protection from rival gangs. He wears the official gang uniform—jeans, T-shirt, boots, and a wide belt. His hair is also styled according to specifications—long with pronounced sideburns. He walks with an exaggerated swagger, and his face is programmed to slide into a contemptuous grin whenever he encounters authority figures from outside the gang. He is defiant and disrespectful to both his parents and school personnel. He openly carries weapons on the street, usually a knife or a chain. On several occasions he has gone to school armed. When questioned about his weapons by the school principal, he remarked that they were none of the principal's business.

Jim considers school a waste of time. He admits that he attends only because he is too young to quit. He is often truant, and when he is present does little academic work. He is severely retarded in oral language skills and reading. His mathematic ability is slightly better but is still considerably below that of most ninth-grade students. Despite his inadequacies, he considers himself "good" in math and "OK" in his other subjects. He complains, however, that school is too much work.

Jim's nonacademic school behaviors are aggressive and antisocial. He often swears at students and teachers alike and will not hesitate to physically assault another person. Outside of school, he has been involved in several "rumbles" with rival gangs. He is very proud of these activities and boasts of them to others. Thus far he has a history of two arrests, one for assault and battery and one for car theft. He has never been convicted.

Etiology   All children make strong identifications with peer groups. The group delinquent reaction reflects peer associations of youths in environments where violence, threat, and failure are the norm. These children have little security within their families. In many cases, their parents are divorced, the father has never been present in the family, or both parents are absent and grandparents have full responsibility for their rearing. Even when parents are present, the child is often one of a multitude of poorly cared for children in homes racked by poverty. They lack models with status at home and cannot identify with the standards of behavior established in the schools. They are not equipped to compete academically with more fortunate peers. Therefore, they make their identification with others similar to themselves and obtain their status through antisocial acts.

Treatment   Gang control has become a very serious problem, particularly in the large Northeastern cities such as New York and Philadelphia. Gang warfare fatality statistics have risen steadily throughout the years, and in the inner-city, large neighborhoods have become unsafe for nongang members. So-called treatment intervention has run the gamut from imprisonment of juvenile offenders to programs of vocational and psychological counseling. Efforts have been made to redirect gang activity, to give them alternatives to antisocial acts. For example, groups have been funded to establish car-washing businesses to make money legitimately. Gang leaders have also been encouraged to negotiate differences with rival gangs rather than resorting to violence. Unfortunately, such solutions have only a temporary effect. The membership of the gangs changes often as older members leave and younger ones enter. Leadership changes quickly and gang commitment to socially acceptable activities lessens. Also, gang members are usually immature individuals who feel hostile toward others. They obtain much more gratification from antisocial activities than from the mundane drudgery of working for pay.

Efforts to work with children exhibiting this reaction on an individual basis have met with discouraging results. Best results occur when the child is removed from his or her environment and housed in a home with greater stability that provides him or her with more constructive behavioral models. Once again, younger children are more amenable to treatment than older children.

SIGNIFICANT INDEPENDENT DISORDERS

Significant independent disorders that may indicate emotional disturbance are stuttering, enuresis, feeding disturbances, tics, and sleep disorders (Coleman, 1972). Children who engage in any of these behaviors on a consistent basis may be reflecting accelerated states of tension. Frequently these symptoms appear in children who demonstrate more pervasive behavioral reactions. For example, an unsocialized-aggressive child may be enuretic and may have a tic. An overanxious child may stutter and may sleep walk. Occasionally, however, these symptoms appear in relative isolation and serve as warnings of underlying anxiety.

Stuttering

Stuttering is a speech dysfluency that involves blocking, hesitations, or repetitions of speech sounds. In its primary form, stuttering is a normal developmental phenomenon. All children stutter during a certain period of their speech development. They cease stuttering as they mature. Some children, however, continue to stutter, and the condition becomes a speech problem termed *secondary stuttering* (Johnson, 1961). At this point the stutterer is extremely self-conscious about his or her speech. Attempts to speak are accompanied by tension-induced behaviors such as grimacing and foot stamping. Hesitations and blockages become more frequent and prolonged. A vicious circle develops as increased dysfluency in turn causes increased loss of confidence and self-devaluation. Thus the child who stutters risks lasting damage to his or her self-concept.

Etiology   Although there is some evidence that stuttering may have a genetic basis because it runs in families (Johnson, 1961) and may result from faulty auditory feedback (Dinnan, McGuiness, and Perrin, 1970) or a malfunctioning larynx (Perkins, 1978) many investigators currently believe that stuttering, at least in part, is a learned behavior. Johnson (1961) attributes secondary stuttering to parents' undue concern about primary stuttering. Parental attempts to correct normal dysfluency cause the child to become anxious about his or her ability to speak fluently. Sheehan and Martyn (1970) support a reinforcement theory to describe how stuttering is learned. They believe that the act of completing a stuttered utterance relieves the tension built up in making the utterance and is therefore reinforcing to the individual.

Even those who disagree about the etiology of stuttering agree that stress has an extreme effect on the condition. There is extensive evidence revealing that speech dysfluency increases as feelings of stress increase. In fact, many stutterers are able to articulate normally in situations where they feel no tension. For instance, they can sing or recite a memorized poem or speech without stuttering.

Treatment   Two important points pertain to the treatment of stuttering. First, primary stuttering should be ignored. The child should not be made conscious of the speech dysfluency if no signs of tension are displayed when attempting to speak. The majority of experts believe that if a child does not perceive himself or herself as having a speech problem, then self-consciousness or anxiety about the dysfluency will not result, and it will disappear.

Second, stuttering accompanied by tension-induced symptoms such as grimacing should be regarded as a problem. The individual must be encouraged to accept the stuttering and to concentrate on control techniques. Treatments vary and include aversive conditioning, desensitization, rhythm exercise, voice masking, delay of auditory feedback, assertion training, and social reinforcement of fluency.

Sheehan and Martyn (1970) report that four out of five cases of stuttering clear up spontaneously. These statistics provide support for Johnson's primary-secondary stuttering dichotomy and for his recommendation that primary stuttering be ignored.

Enuresis

Enuresis is a term used to describe the involuntary discharge of urine after age three. The condition is common, occurring in approximately five million children in the United States (Linde, 1966). Although it may occur during the day, it most often occurs at night.

Etiology   Enuresis may be caused by a variety of organic conditions. Consequently, a thorough physical examination is the first step in attempting to help an enuretic child. Most often, however, enuresis is caused by underlying stress or tension and signifies a maladaptive emotional pattern. For example, it may reflect the child's anxiety over meeting new challenges in school or feelings of hostility toward parents.

Treatment   The most prevalent methods of treating enuresis are drug therapy and behavioral therapy. Drug therapy, which usually involves tranquilizers and drugs that inhibit reflex bladder emptying, has met with limited success. Behavioral therapy involves the use of an electrified mattress that rings an alarm at the first drop of urine and awakens the child. This method also has had limited success, but although it appears to work initially, the relapse rate is quite high.

Although there is disagreement on what works best, most experts agree that punishment is an unsatisfactory method of treating enuresis. In most instances, the child is greatly embarrassed by the condition. Efforts to curb the behavior through punishment only heighten anxiety and increase the probability that the behavior will occur.

Feeding Disturbances

Feeding disturbances constitute another indication of possible emotional pathology in children. Many children engage in feeding games with adults. They may refuse to eat at mealtime or agree to eat only certain foods. Adults who attempt to insist that children eat are met with either overt or passive resistance. The child may become agitated, cry, pick at food listlessly, chew without swallowing, gag, vomit, and so on, until each meal becomes chaotic. Generally, children who behave in this way have learned how to frustrate overly concerned parents. Increased parental indifference to the child's eating habits, plus withholding of preferred foods such as desserts and candy, soon alleviate the symptoms.

Other feeding problems involve excessive eating that results in obesity. This pattern of feeding reflects conditions in the home. The child may copy familiar parental eating habits or the child may eat to reduce anxiety produced by an unstable home situation. Often this condition eases as the child matures and becomes more concerned about physical appearance. In other cases, however, the eating habit becomes so deeply entrenched that therapeutic intervention is necessary.

In rare cases, feeding disturbances reflect a more serious emotional patholgy. Anorexia nervosa is a prolonged loss of appetite resulting from psychological stress. The afflicted individual refuses to eat and eventually may die of starvation (Stunkard, 1972).

Etiology   Currently, anorexia nervosa is increasing among adolescents, particularly females, many of whom, before their refusal to eat, have shown no other overt symptoms of emotional disturbance. The condition appears to be related to deep feelings of self-loathing learned in pathogenic family situations.

Treatment   Those suffering from anorexia nervosa are very resistant to conventional therapy. There is little time available for in-depth psychotherapeutic sessions, and surface appeals to reason are futile. Apparently, eating has become an aversive activity that elevates anxiety. Anxiety remains reduced only when the individual fails to eat. In effect, not eating is reinforcing because anxiety is not activated. Thus, the individual may consciously resolve to eat but after the first bite of food be unable to continue. Behavioral therapy that decreases the aversiveness associated with eating appears to be a viable option (Kauffman, 1977).

Tic

Tic is a term referring to a wide variety of persistent involuntary muscle twitches or spasms. It includes facial movements such as blinking the eye, twitching the mouth, grimacing, licking the lips; sounds such as clearing the throat, blowing through the nostrils; and bodily movements such as twisting the neck and shrugging the shoulders. Often individuals are not aware of tics when they occur. They either do not know they have a tic or they demonstrate the tic so habitually that they are not aware of it. Although tics usually occur between the ages of 6 and 14, they persist in some adults. In fact, an interesting example of a tic in an adult occurred in a major league baseball player. When at bat, this player rotated his neck and head until he was looking away from the pitcher. However, he always recovered before the pitch was thrown.

Etiology   Apparently, tics may have an organic basis but are most frequently caused by psychological stress and tension. As with other tension-induced behaviors, tics frequently increase self-consciousness in the individual, thereby increasing the likelihood that the tic will persist.

Occasionally, tics occur as reactions to a specific fatiguing or stressful situation and disappear when the situation alters. For example, an extremely tired person who must continue working might develop a tic that disappears after sufficient rest is obtained.

Treatment   Frequently tics occurring in young children are best ignored. In instances where the child is upset by the tic, however, he or she may be helped with psychotherapy or behavioral therapy. Generally, in instances where the presence of the tic is symptomatic of a general state of psychological disturbance, the emphasis is not on eliminating the tic but on solving the problem causing the tic.

Sleep Disorders

Sleep disorders are quite common in children. The most common disorder is nightmares, followed by sleeptalking and by the relatively rare sleepwalking. As nightmares are not unusual, they are a problem only when they occur persistently. At such times, they may signify psychological stress. Occasionally, nightmares generate sleeptalking. Typically, the child talks, cries, or screams when sleeping because he or she is frightened by the dream.

Taves (1969) has studied sleepwalking and reports that sleepwalkers roam around with eyes open, avoiding obstacles, and usually responding when spoken to. If they are awakened they are surprised at being out of bed, and if they return unawakened to bed, they do not remember the episode.

Etiology   Other than the fact that sleep disorders appear to be caused by stress, little information is available. Kales et al. (1966) have measured sleep states and have found that sleepwalking occurs during non-rapid-eye-movement (NREM) sleep, whereas dreams occur during rapid-eye-movement (REM) states. They concluded that sleepwalking is not caused by bad dreams as was previously believed.

Treatment   Little information is known about treating these conditions. Generally, parents are advised to awaken and reassure children. Clement (1970) reports the successful use of behavioral therapy with a seven-year-old sleepwalker.

TRANSIENT SITUATIONAL DISTURBANCES

Transient situational disturbances that produce adjustment problems of childhood and adolescence provide another category of disorders unique to childhood. This category encompasses the problems that occur in individuals who evidence no underlying emotional problems. Such persons are reacting to overwhelming environmental stress. Their symptoms usually disappear as the stress diminishes. For example, a child might react adversely to the birth of a new sibling by regressing to bed wetting, baby talk, and an unwillingness to go to school. If treated with kindness and affection and assured that his or her parents still regard the child as highly as they regard the baby, the symptoms will quickly disappear.

An adolescent might be extremely upset over failure to gain acceptance to college. Behavior might be characterized by temper tantrums, brooding, and discouragement. He or she should be helped to find an alternative activity that will lead to an interesting career or perhaps be encouraged to apply to less-demanding college programs. As the adolescent becomes interested in new options, disturbed behaviors disappear.

SUMMARY

The psychiatric clinical syndromes presented in this chapter offer a helpful system for putting children's emotional disorders in perspective. Classifying children's conditions as psychoses, behavioral disorders, or transient disturbances provides important information about etiology and prognosis for recovery and suggests possible alternatives for treatment. However, the APA classification system has several obvious limitations.

First, it provides no criteria for identifying the extent to which a child must engage in deviant behaviors before being regarded as maladjusted. In fact, the collection of pathological conditions seems to include some aspect of behavior displayed by every child every day. Children have bad dreams, wet their beds, fight, have temper outbursts, act fearful, cry easily, and so forth, on a more or less regular basis. A practical distinction must be made between the normal display of maladaptive behaviors and the disturbed reactions of troubled children.

Second, the APA system does not provide an index of the severity of a child's condition once he or she has been diagnosed as having an emotional problem. Even psychosis, an indisputably serious condition, occurs in varying degrees of severity. Behavioral syndromes and adjustment reactions may also be manifested as mild, moderate, or severe conditions. Obviously, knowledge of the severity of a child's condition is extremely important since it predicates the type of treatment strategy devised. A severely disturbed child, regardless of the particular diagnostic label, might require drug therapy, individual psychotherapy, as well as special education programs that encompass alternate therapeutic interventions. A mild or even a moderately disturbed child might be able to benefit from therapeutic group settings conducted as part of or in conjunction with classroom intervention programs. In short, a classification system delineating the major components that might be used to categorize emotionally disturbed states as mild, moderate, or severe would be a valuable asset to those individuals responsible for identifying and treating emotionally disturbed children. The following chapter discusses various approaches to identifying emotionally disturbed children and to judging the severity of their conditions.

STUDY QUESTIONS

1. Discuss two childhood reactions that are similar to neurotic reactions in adults.
2. Consider autism and the runaway reaction. Discuss them in terms of the disability–deviance perspectives of emotional disturbance.
3. Discuss the five categories of symptoms that indicate schizophrenia.
4. Discuss how children's emotional disorders differ from those of adults.

REFERENCES

Akerfeldt, S. Oxidation of N, N-Dimethyl-p-phenylenediamine by serum from patients with mental disease. *Science,* 1957, *125*(1), 117–119.

American Psychiatric Association. *Diagnostic and statistical manual of mental disorders.* 2nd ed., Washington, D.C. 1968.

Anthony, J. An experimental approach to the psychopathology of childhood. *British Journal of Medical Psychology,* 1958, *31*, 311.

Aronson, J., and Polgar, S. Pathogenic relationships in schizophrenia. *American Journal of Psychiatry,* 1962, *119*, 222–227.

Atthowe, J., and Krasner, L. Preliminary report on the application of contingent reinforcement procedures (token economy) on a "chronic" psychiatric ward. *Journal of Abnormal Psychology,* 1968, *73*, 37–43.

Axline, V. *Play therapy.* Boston: Houghton Mifflin, 1947.

Bandura, A. *Principles of behavior modification.* New York: Holt, Rinehart and Winston, 1969.

Bateson, G. Cultural problems posed by a study of schizophrenic process. In A. Auerbach (ed.), *Schizophrenia: an integrated approach.* New York: Ronald, 1959.

Becker, J. Achievement related characteristics of manic-depressives. *Journal of Abnormal and Social Psychology,* 1960, *60*, 334–339.

Becker, J., and Altrocchi, J. Peer conformity and achievement in female manic-depressives. *Journal of Abnormal Psychology,* 1968, *73*(6), 585–589.

Bender, L. Twenty years of clinical research on schizophrenic children with special reference to those under six years of age. In G. Caplan (ed.). *Emotional problems of early childhood.* New York: Basic Books, 1955.

Bettelheim, B. *Truants from life.* Glencoe, Ill.: Free Press, 1955.

Bettelheim, B. Joey: a mechanical boy. *Scientific American,* 1959, *200,* 116–127.

Bettelheim, B. *The empty fortress.* New York: Free Press, 1967.

Bowen, M. A family concept of schizophrenia. In D. D. Jackson (ed.). *The etiology of schizophrenia.* New York: Basic Books, 1960.

Bratfos, O. Parental deprivation in childhood and types of future mental disease. *Acta-Psychiatria Scandinavia,* 1967, *43*(4), 453–461.

Broen, W. *Schizophrenia: research and theory.* New York: Academic Press, 1968.

Cameron, N., and Margaret, A. *Behavioral pathology.* Boston: Houghton Mifflin, 1951.

Campbell, J. *Manic-depressive disease.* Philadelphia: Lippincott, 1953.

Caputo, D., and Mandell, D. Consequences of low birth weight. *Developmental Psychology,* 1970, *3*(3), 363–383.

Carson, R. *Interaction concepts of personality.* Chicago: Aldine, 1969.

Clancy, H., and McBride, G. The autistic process and its treatment. *Journal of Child Psychology and Psychiatry,* 1969, *10*(4), 233–244.

Clement, P. Elimination of sleepwalking in a seven-year-old boy. *Journal of Counseling and Clinical Psychology,* 1970, *34*(1), 22–26.

Clerk, G. Reflections on the role of the mother in the development of language in the schizophrenic child. *Canadian Psychiatric Association Journal,* 1961, *6,* 252.

Colbert, E.; Koegler, R.; and Markham, C. Vestibular dysfunction in childhood schizophrenia. *Archives of General Psychiatry,* 1959, *1,* 600–617.

Coleman, J. *Abnormal psychology and modern life.* Glenview, Ill.: Scott, Foresman, 1972.

Craighead, W.; Kazdin, A.; and Mahoney, M. *Behavior modification.* Boston: Houghton Mifflin, 1976.

DeMyer, M. Research in infantile autism: a strategy and its results. In S. Chess and A. Thomas (eds.). *Annual progress in child psychiatry and child development.* New York: Brunner/Mazel, 1976.

DeMyer, M.; Pontius, W.; Norton, J., Barton, S.; Allen, J.; and Steele, R. Parental practice and innate activity in normal, autistic, and brain-injured infants. *Journal of Autism and Child Schizophrenia,* 1972, *2,* 49–54.

Delgado, J. Electronic pacing of behavior: brain research, treatment, tool. *Roche Reports,* 1969, *6*(7), 1–8.

Dinnan, J.; McGuiness, E.; and Perrin, L. Auditory feedback—stutterers versus nonstutterers. *Journal of Learning Disabilities,* 1970, *3*(4), 30–34.

Dorzab, J.; Baker, M.; Cadoret, R.; and Winokur, G. Depressive disease: familial psychiatric illness. *American Journal of Psychiatry,* 1971, *127*(9), 48–60.

Edwards, R.; Alley, G.; and Snider, W. Academic achievement and minimal brain dysfunction. *Journal of Learning Disabilities,* 1971, *4*(3), 134–138.

Eisenberg, L. The interaction of biological and experiential factors in schizophrenia. In D. Rosenthal and S. Kety (eds.). *The transmission of schizophrenia.* Elmsford, N.Y.: Pergamon Press, 1968.

Eisenberg, L., and Kanner, L. Early autism—childhood schizophrenia symposium. *American Journal of Orthopsychiatry,* 1956, *26,* 556.

Fenz, W., and Velner, J. Physiological concomitants of behavior indexes in schizophrenia. *Journal of Abnormal Psychology*, 1970, 76(1), 27–35.

Fischer, I., and Glanville, B. Programmed teaching of autistic children. *Archives of General Psychiatry*, 1970, 23(1), 90–94.

Fish, B. Involvement of the central nervous system in infants with schizophrenia. *American Medical Association Archives of Neurology*, 1960, 2, 115.

Fish, B. Limitations of new nomenclature for children's disorders. *International Journal of Psychiatry*, 1969, 6(7), 393–399.

Fish, B. The study of motor development in infancy and its relationship to psychological functioning. *American Journal of Psychiatry*, 1958, 79(1), 720.

Fish, B.; Shapiro, T.; Campbell, M.; and Wile, R. A classification of schizophrenic children under five years. *American Journal of Psychiatry*, 1968, 124(10), 109–117.

Freedman, D., and members of drug panel. The use of stimulant drugs in treating hyperactive children. *Children*, 1971, 18(3), 111.

Garcia, B., and Sarvis, M. Evaluation and treatment planning for autistic children. *Archives of General Psychiatry*, 1964, 10, 530.

Garmezy, N., and Rodnick, E. Premorbid adjustment and performance in schizophrenia. *Journal of Nervous and Mental Diseases*, 1959, 129, 450–466.

Gerald, D., and Siegel, J. The family background of schizophrenia. *Psychiatric Quarterly*, 1950, 24, 47–73.

Gibson, R. The family background and early life experience of the manic-depressive patient. *Psychiatry*, 1958, 21, 71–90.

Ginott, H. *Group psychotherapy with children.* New York: McGraw-Hill, 1961.

Glover, E. *On the early development of mind.* New York: International, 1956.

Gold, H. Observations on cultural psychiatry during a world tour of mental hospitals. *American Journal of Psychiatry*, 1951, 108, 462–468.

Goldstein, I. The relationship of muscle tension and autonomic activity of psychiatric disorders. *Psychosomatic Medicine*, 1965, 27, 39–52.

Greenspan, K.; Schildkraut, J.; Gordon, E.; Levy, B.; and Durell, J. Catecholamine metabolism in affective disorders. *Archives of General Psychiatry*, 1969, 21(6), 710–716.

Harms, E. Childhood schizophrenia and childhood hysteria. *Psychiatric Quarterly*, 1945, 19, 243–247.

Heller, A.; Zahourek, R.; and Whittington, H. Effectiveness of antidepressant drugs: a triple blind study comparing impramine, desipramine, and placebo. *American Journal of Psychiatry*, 1971, 127(8), 132–135.

Hes, J. Manic-depressive illness in Israel. *American Journal of Psychiatry*, 1960, 116, 1082–1086.

Hingtgen, J., and Churchill, D. Identification of perceptual limitations in mute autistic children. *Archives of General Psychiatry*, 1969, 21, 68–72.

Jenkins, R. The varieties of children's behavior problems and family dynamics. *American Journal of Psychiatry*, 1968, 124(10), 134–139.

Jenkins, R. Diagnostic classification in child psychiatry. *American Journal of Psychiatry*, 1970, 127(5), 140–141.

Johnson, W. *Stuttering and what you can do about it.* Minneapolis: University of Minnesota Press, 1961.

Kales, A.; Paulson, M.; Jacobson, A.; and Kales, J. Somnambulism: psychophysiological correlates. *Archives of General Psychiatry*, 1966, 14(6), 594–604.

Kallmann, F. *Genetic aspects of psychoses.* New York: Harper, 1952.

Kallmann, F. The genetics of human behavior. *American Journal of Psychiatry,* 1956, *113,* 496–501.

Kallmann, F. The use of genetics in psychiatry. *Journal of Mental Science,* 1958, *104,* 542–549.

Kallmann, F. *Heredity in health and mental disorder.* New York: Norton, 1953.

Kanner, L. Autistic disturbances of affective content. *Nervous Child,* 1943, *2,* 217–240.

Katkin, E.; Sasmor, D.; and Tan, R. Conformity and achievement-related characteristics of depressed patients. *Journal of Abnormal Psychology,* 1966, *71* (6), 407–412.

Kauffman, J. *Characteristics of children's behavior disorders.* Columbus, Ohio: Merrill, 1977.

Kaufman, I.; Frank, T.; Heims, L.; Herrick, J.; Reiser, D.; and Willer, L. Treatment implications of a new classification of parents of schizophrenic children. *American Journal of Psychiatry,* 1960, *116,* 920–924.

Kendell, R. Relationship between aggression and depression. *Archives of General Psychiatry,* 1970, *22,* 308–318.

Kirk, S. Behavioral diagnosis and remediation of learning disabilities. *Proceedings of the Annual Meeting of the Conference on Exploration into the Problems of the Perceptually Handicapped Child.* Vol. 1, 1963.

Knight, E. Some considerations regarding the concept of "autism." *Diseases of the Nervous System,* 1963, *24,* 224.

Kringlen, E. *Heredity and environment in the functional psychosis: an epidemiological-clinical twin study.* Oslo: Universitsforlaget, 1967.

Laing, R. D. *The divided self.* New York: Pantheon, 1969.

Laing, R., and Esterson, A. *Sanity, madness, and the family.* London: Tavistock, 1964.

Leese, S. The multivariant masks of depression. *American Journal of Psychiatry,* 1968, *124* (11), 35–40.

Lidz, T. The family, language, and the transmission of schizophrenia. In D. Rosenthal and S. Kety (eds.). *The transmission of schizophrenia.* Elmsford, N.Y.: Pergamon Press, 1968.

Linde, S. What parents need to know about bed-wetting. *Today's Health,* 1966, *75,* 50–51.

Lippman, H. Psychopathic reactions in children. *American Journal of Orthopsychiatry,* 1951, *21,* 227–231.

Lovass, O. Behavior therapy approaches to treating childhood schizophrenia. In J. Hill (ed.). *Minnesota Symposium on Child Development.* Minneapolis: University of Minnesota Press, 1967.

Lovass, O.; Koegel, R.; Simmon, J.; and Steven, J. Some generalizations and follow up measures on autistic children in behavior therapy. *Journal of Applied Behavioral Analysis,* 1972, *34,* 17–23.

Mahler, M. On symbiotic child psychosis: genetic, dynamic and restitution aspects. *Psychoanalytic Study of the Child,* 1955, *10,* 195.

Malmquist, C. Depressive phenomena in children. In B. Wolman (ed.). *Manual of child psychopathology.* New York: McGraw-Hill, 1972.

Mednick, S., and McNeil, T. Current methodology in research on the etiology of schizophrenia. *Psychological Bulletin,* 1968, *70,* 681–693.

Menninger, K. Sheer verbal mickey mouse. *International Journal of Psychiatry,* 1969, *7* (6), 415.

Montenegro, H. Severe separation anxiety in two preschool children: successfully treated by reciprocal inhibition. *Journal of Child Psychology and Psychiatry*, 1968, *9*(2), 93–103.

Murphy, H.; Wittkower, E.; and Chance, N. Crosscultural inquiry into the symptomatology of depression: a preliminary report. *International Journal of Psychiatry*, 1967, *3*(1), 6–15.

Myers, P., and Hammill, D. *Methods for learning disabilities.* New York: Wiley, 1976.

National Institute of Mental Health. Amphetamines approved for children. *Science News*, 1971, *99*(4), 240.

Newsweek. Prostitutes: the new breed. July 12, 1971, p. 78.

Paul, G. Chronic mental patients: current status—future directions. *Psychological Bulletin*, 1969, *71*, 81–94.

Pavenstedt, E. History of a child with an atypical development and some vicissitudes of his treatment. In G. Capland (ed.). *Emotional problems of early childhood.* New New: Basic Books, 1955.

Peck, H.; Rabinovitch, R.; and Cramer, J. A treatment program for parents of schizophrenic children. *American Journal of Orthopsychiatry*, 1949, *19*, 592–614.

Perkins, D. *Human perspectives in speech and language disorders.* Saint Louis: Mosby, 1978.

Phillips, L. Case history data and prognosis in schizophrenia. *Journal of Nervous and Mental Diseases*, 1953, *117*, 515–525.

Pollack, M., and Krieger, H. Oculomotor and postural patterns in schizophrenic children. *Archives of Neurology and Psychiatry*, 1958, *79*(1), 720.

Pollin, W.; Allen, M.; Hoffer, A.; Stabenau, J.; and Hrubec, Z. Psychopathology in 15,909 pairs of veteran twins. *American Journal of Psychiatry*, 1969, *126*(5), 43–56.

Poznanski, E., and Zrull, J. Childhood depression. *Archives of General Psychiatry*, 1970, *23*(1), 8–11.

Rank, B. Intensive study and treatment of preschool children who show marked personality deviations or "atypical development," and their parents. In G. Caplan (ed.). *Emotional problems of early childhood.* New York: Basic Books, 1955.

Rimland, B. *Infantile autism.* New York: Appleton-Century-Crofts, 1964.

Robins, L. *Deviant children grown up: a sociological and psychiatric study of sociopathic personality.* Baltimore: Williams & Wilkins, 1968.

Ruesch, J.; Brodsky, C.; and Fischer, A. The acute nervous breakdown. *Archives of General Psychiatry*, 1963, *8*, 197–207.

Rutter, M. Concepts of autism: a review of the research. *Journal of Child Psychology*, 1968, *9*, 1–25.

Sadler, W. S. Juvenile manic activity. *The Nervous Child*, 1952, *9*, 303–309.

Schain, R. and Yannet, H. Infantile autism: an analysis of 50 cases and a consideration of certain relevant neurophysiological concepts. *Journal of Pediatrics*, 1960, *57*, 560–567.

Schildkraut, J. The catecholamine hypothesis of affective disorders: a review of supporting evidence. *American Journal of Psychiatry*, 1965, *122*(5), 509–522.

Schopler, E.; Brehm, S.; Kinsbowine, M.; and Reichler, R. Effect of treatment structure on development in autistic children. *Archives of General Psychiatry*, 1971, *24*(5), 415–421.

Schrut, A. Suicidal adolescents and children. *Journal of the American Medical Association*, 1964, *188*, 1102–1107.

Shamsie, S. (ed.). *Adolescent psychiatry*. Pointe Claire, Quebec: Schering Corp., 1968.

Sheehan, J. (ed.). *Stuttering: research and therapy*. New York: Harper & Row, 1970.

Sheehan, J., and Martyn, M. Stuttering and its disappearance. *Journal of Speech and Hearing Disorders*, 1970, *13*(2), 279–289.

Shore, P.; Pletscher, A.; Tomich, E.; Carlsson, A.; Kuntzman, R.; and Brodie, B. Role of brain serotonin in reserpine action. *Academic Science*, 1957, *66*, 609–615.

Silver, A. Management of children with schizophrenia. *American Journal of Psychotherapy*, 1955, *9*, 196–205.

Slater, E. Genetics in psychiatry. *Journal of Mental Science*, 1944, *90*, 17–35.

Spitz, R. Anaclitic Depression. In *The psychoanalytic study of the child*. Vol. 2. New York: International, 1946, 113–117.

Strauss, A. and Kephart, N. *Psychopathology and education of the brain-injured child*. Vol. II. New York: Grune and Stratton, 1955.

Stunkard, A. New therapies for eating disorders. *Archives of General Psychiatry*, 1972, *26*, 391–398.

Sullivan, H. *The interpersonal theory of psychiatry*. New York: Norton, 1953.

Szurek, S. Childhood schizophrenia symposium: psychotic episodes and psychotic maldevelopment. *American Journal of Orthopsychiatry*, 1956, *25*, 519.

Taves, I. Is there a sleepwalker in the house? *Today's Health*, 1969, *47*(5), 41.

Ullmann, L., and Eck, R. Inkblot perception and process-reactive distinction. *Journal of Clinical Psychology*, 1965, *21*, 311–313.

Wahl, C. Some antecedent factors in the family histories of 568 male schizophrenics of the United States Navy. *American Journal of Psychiatry*, 1956, *113*, 201–210.

Whybrow, P., and Mendels, J. Toward a biology of depression: some suggestions from neurophysiology. *American Journal of Psychiatry*, 1969, *125*(11), 45–54.

Wikler, A.; Dixon, J.; and Parker, J. Brain function in problem children and controls. *American Journal of Psychiatry*, 1970, *127*(5), 94–105.

Will, O. Human relatedness and the schizophrenic reaction. *Psychiatry*, 1959, *22*, 205–223.

Wolff, W., and Morris, L. Intellectual personality characteristics of parents of autistic children. *Journal of Abnormal Psychology*, 1971, *77*(2), 155–161.

Wolman, B. *Children without childhood: a study in childhood schizophrenia*. New York: Grune and Stratton, 1970.

Wolman, B. Prevention of mental disorders in childhood. In B. Wolman (ed.). *Handbook of child psychoanalysis*. New York: VanNostrand Reinhold, 1972.

4
Identification Procedures

The approach used by educators to identify emotionally disturbed children has traditionally been determined by varied philosophical and pragmatic considerations. In cases where legal classification of disturbance is sought to secure state funds for special education programs, identification procedures usually are specified in state laws. Usually mental health professionals such as psychologists or psychiatrists are given the responsibility for identification. Where legal classification is less important and services are not dependent on categorical labeling, identification procedures might depend largely on teacher reports of classroom behaviors, perhaps supplemented by additional diagnostic input from counselors, psychologists, or psychiatrists if those professional services are available.

Some educators have made a philosophic commitment to avoid extensive diagnostic assessment by noneducators, which, they argue, culminates in disability labeling. They believe that children's maladaptive behaviors can be identified by teacher observations and that they can be changed without subjecting the child to the stigmatizing effects associated with labels such as psychopathic, neurotic, or aggressive.

Other educators feel differently, believing that differential diagnosis of emotionally disturbed states by an expert in psychopathology is required to plan appropriate treatment. They believe that the identification of an infinite number of emotionally disturbed behaviors is of little use unless the child's behavioral syndrome, for example, psychosis, behavioral disorder, or adjustment reaction, is identified.

From these alternate attitudes and procedures, four approaches to the identification of emotional disturbance appear to emerge. They are the psychiatric, psychological, educational, and behavioral approaches. With the exception of the behavioral approach, the method of identification is named for the professional bearing primary responsibility for the implementation of treatment. The behavioral approach represents a distinct methodology that may be applied by varied professionals. Obviously, the specific techniques associated with each of these approaches are not limited exclusively to that approach. For example, the clinical interview, discussed under the psychiatric approach, might be used by a psychologist. Also, many school identification programs incorporate more than one of these approaches. They are presented as distinct entities here to delineate different perspectives toward the problem of identifying emotionally disturbed children.

PSYCHIATRIC APPROACH

Clearly an application of the disability model in education, the psychiatric approach emphasizes the discovery of the underlying etiology as necessary for determining the existence of emotional disturbance. Overt behavior alone is not a sufficient indicator. The psychic factors that cause overt behavior determine whether or not a child is emotionally disturbed. For instance, a child might be withdrawn and uncooperative in school because of physical illness or because others appear menacing. Only the latter state indicates emotional disturbance. It is also important to make a differential diagnosis of the specific type of disturbed condition. The child's perceptions of others as menacing might signify psychotic delusions or an aggressive reaction to rejecting parents.

The identification of emotional disturbance is the function of psychiatrists. The preferred diagnostic methods are subjective, usually involving *informal observation* and the *clinical interview*.

Informal observation consists of watching an individual exhibit typical behaviors during ordinary daily activities. It can be conducted in a contrived situation where the individual is unaware of the observation, as when a child is observed at play through a one-way mirror. It also can be conducted in a more natural situation, as when the professional openly observes the child in a group meeting or in the classroom. Informal observation is a relatively unstructured procedure designed to provide an impression of the child's general behavior. Therefore, it involves neither precise counting of specific maladaptive behaviors nor elaborate record keeping. Records that are kept are anecdotal. Hypothetically, the observer draws on clinical experience to formulate opinions about the appropriateness or inappropriateness of the child's behavior.

The clinical interview is another informal means of obtaining information about a child's psychological condition. With older children who have adequate cognitive and linguistic development, it may consist solely of verbal discussion. The child is encouraged to talk about himself or herself and his or her problems. Particular emphasis is placed on eliciting the child's fantasies and free associations to discover his or her underlying personality structure. In some cases, various techniques can be used to stimulate discussion. For example, the child may be asked to draw and describe pictures, to give three wishes, or to discuss a favorite television show.

Younger children are interviewed less directly since they lack the linguistic competence necessary for elaborate verbal discussions. In these cases, the child is encouraged to engage in symbolic play activities and is asked about the play. For example, if a child, while playing with a doll, remarks that it hates school, the interviewer asks questions about that topic. Leading statements such as "I guess school can really be tough" are more effective than direct questions such as "Do you have trouble in school?"

Another component of the clinical interview involves parents. Parental input regarding the family dynamics, as well as the child's developmental history, interpersonal relationships, school experiences, and behavior at home contributes greatly to the general clinical picture.

For the most part, the psychiatric approach occurs in clinical settings removed from the school, such as hospitals or mental health clinics. Teacher input about the child's behavior is at best used to provide a small part of the child's case history. Diagnosis of the type and severity of the child's condition is based on clinical judgment.

PSYCHOLOGICAL APPROACH

This approach to the identification of emotional disturbance also adheres to a disability perspective. As with the psychiatric approach, the primary goal is to determine whether emotional disturbance is an underlying cause of maladaptive behavior and to make a differential diagnosis among disturbed conditions.

The most important differentiation between the psychiatric and psychological approaches is that the latter places greater emphasis on the use of objective criteria for diagnosis. Psychologists are trained to administer and interpret psychoeducational tests. Thus, the identification of a disturbed state is dependent largely on the child's performance on a standardized test battery. Typically, the test battery includes measures of

1. Intelligence
2. Perceptual-motor development
3. Auditory sensitivity and visual acuity
4. Oral language development
5. Academic achievement
6. Personality development

For the most part, psychologists use performance on measures of intelligence, perceptual-motor skill, auditory and visual acuity, and oral language to ensure that a child's odd or inappropriate behaviors are not caused primarily by conditions other than emotional disturbance, such as mental retardation, brain damage, visual impairment, or aphasia.

In addition, however, these tests are used to gather clinical data pertaining directly to emotional disturbance. For example, a child's performance on an individual intelligence test such as the WISC (Wechsler, 1949) may reveal a pattern of subtest strengths and weaknesses that suggests emotional pathology. Scatter, or significant inconsistency in subtest performance, is generally interpreted as indicating emotional instability. Also, depressed scores in specific subtests such as arithmetic and digit span are viewed as indicative of extreme anxiety. These are subjective clinical interpretations of subtest scores, they are not substantiated with empirical evidence.

Clinical interpretations are also made from perceptual motor, oral language, and academic achievement tests. For example, the *Bender Visual-Motor Gestalt Test* (1938), a perceptual-motor instrument that measures a child's ability to draw geometric designs depicted on nine cards, may be scored for psychodynamic constructs such as aggression, hostility, and passivity. Unusually small drawings are associated with constricted, fearful personalities, whereas excessively large figures are indicative of a tendency toward mania. A careless, slap-dash reproduction of each symbol suggests impulsiveness, whereas a slow, laborious rendering is typical of obsessive-compulsive tendencies. Heavy, dark pencil lines may be regarded as representing hostility, whereas a light drawing suggests passivity and indecisiveness.

Objective oral language scales, such as the TOLD (Newcomer and Hammill, 1977), may be analyzed informally for bizarre responses, infantile language usage, senseless syntax, and inconsistent language comprehension. Academic achievement tests may show inconsistencies in performance that are inexplicable in the light of good intellectual potential.

Obviously, personality tests constitute the most important diagnostic index of emotional disturbance. These instruments are generally placed in two principal categories: nonprojective and projective. Nonprojective tests have objective formats. They usually involve a number of items that elicit specific responses. For example, the child might be required to answer "yes" or "no" to a series of questions or statements such as "Do you like school?" or "I have trouble making friends." Scoring and interpreting these tests are standardized, for example, a positive response on a certain number of items suggests that the respondent has certain types of personality problems. These instruments are usually paper-and-pencil tests and may be administered to groups as well as to individuals. Relatively well-known instruments of this type are the following:

The California Test of Personality—California Test Bureau

The Thomas Self-Concept Values Test—Educational Service Company

The Mooney Problem Checklist—Psychological Corporation

Edwards Personal Preference Schedule—Psychological Corporation

Eysenck Personality Inventory—Educational Testing Service

Gordon Personal Inventory—Harcourt, Brace and World

Guildford-Zimmerman Temperament Survey—Sheridan Psychological Services

Bernreuter Personality Inventory—Consulting Psychologists Press

Sixteen Personality Factor Questionnaire—Institute for Personality and Ability Testing

Jr.–Sr. High School Personality Questionnaire—Institute for Personality and Ability Testing

Myers-Briggs Type Indicator—Educational Testing Service

Critical reviews of these instruments and others of this type are available in the *Mental Measurements Yearbook* (Buros, 1978). The addresses of major test publishers also are available in that source.

Projective tests have a subjective format. They involve ambiguous stimuli that can be interpreted in a variety of ways. They do not elicit responses that are easily recognized as correct or incorrect. Instead they tap the child's opinions, beliefs, attitudes, and feelings that typify his or her conscious and unconscious personality characteristics. The following are popular projective devices:

Sentence Completion (Ronde, 1957; Rotter, 1950)

The format requires the child to finish incomplete sentence stems. For example: "My brother . . ." or "My trouble is . . ." Presumably, the child will reveal information that pertains to his or her feelings about himself or herself and his or her life. This test generally elicits conscious attitudes and problems rather than unconscious personality traits. Unfortunately, the results are not always useful, as it is easy for a child to disguise or conceal real feelings by providing socially acceptable responses.

Figure Drawings

The most popular method, *Draw-A-Person*, involves asking the child first to draw a person, then to draw a person of the opposite sex. Hypothetically, the figure drawn provides an index of the child's self-perceptions. Clinical interpretations are based on variables such as the sex of the first figure drawn, the size of the figures, the facial expressions, omission of parts, elaboration of parts, position of the figures, location of figures on the paper, and so forth. For example, children typically draw like-sex figures first. Failure to do so may indicate a problem with sexual identification. Also, a small figure in relationship to the opposite sex figure may indicate a poor self-concept. Machover (1949) has provided guidelines for clinical interpretations. Other similar techniques are *House-Tree-Person* and *Family Drawings*.

Thematic Apperception Test (Murray, 1943)

This test consists of thirty pictures, most of which depict people in various situations. Some of the pictures are designed specifically for males, others for females. The child is shown a series of ten pictures and asked to make up a story about each one. Each story should include the events that lead up to the pictured scene, what is happening in the scene, and what the outcome will be. Hypothetically, the child identifies with the central figure in the picture and creates a story that projects his or her feelings about the events. For example, one picture shows a boy staring at a violin. The child's story describes the boy as depressed because he must practice. Presumably, the child has identified with the boy, and the events in the story represent the child's attitude toward tasks that require practice or hard work.

Bakwin and Bakwin (1960) report five criteria for analyzing each story. They are

1. The types of individuals the child identifies with, for example, happy, sad, rejected
2. The needs the key figure or hero manifests, such as high achievement, rebellion, love
3. The environmental influences, for example, economic deprivation, hostile forces, unhappy home
4. The interaction between the hero's needs and external pressures, such as rebellion against unsympathetic authority figures, lack of opportunity that restricts achievement
5. The outcome, such as victory, defeat, withdrawal.

Child's Apperception Test (Bellak, 1954)

This is a modification of the *Thematic Apperception Test* that uses ten animal pictures as stimulus cards for children aged 3–10. Hypothetically, children identify readily with animals and have less difficulty generating stories when pictures of this type are used.

The Blacky Test (Blum, 1950)

This format is similar to the *Child's Apperception Test* but features a puppy named Blacky. Twelve cards with cartoon drawings depict Blacky and his dog family in a variety of situations.

Rorschach (1942)

This test consists of ten symmetrical inkblots printed on a white background. Five blots are achromatic, two are black and red, and three are multicolored. The child must describe everything seen on each card. Scoring is based on criteria such as: (1) the area of the blot used in each response, for example, the whole blot, large details of the blot, small details, the white area, (2) the aspects of the blot that generated the response, such as the form, shading, color, and (3) the content of the response, for example, human beings, animals, movement. Extensive data regarding the clinical interpretations of responses is provided by Klopfer and Kelly (1942) and Bochner and Halpern (1945).

The projective techniques that have been discussed are but a few of those available to psychologists. They are among the most popular, however, particularly in clinical settings. Apparently, clinical psychologists find them useful for making differential diagnoses of underlying pathological conditions despite the fact that their validity has been questioned (Kleinmantz, 1967; Anastasi, 1968).

School psychologists, on the other hand, use projective techniques infrequently, often assessing personality with objective instruments exclusively. They are less concerned with uncovering specific personality dynamics than their clinical colleagues. Their diagnostic efforts are conducted at the request of teachers concerned about children's behavior. Thus their orientation is toward finding the general disability causing children's problems achieving or adjusting in school, rather than uncovering information that may influence psychotherapeutic treatment. Both clinical and school psychologists use test results and clinical judgment to determine whether the child's behavior is severe enough to warrant the label "emotionally disturbed" and to formulate treatment plans.

BEHAVIORAL APPROACH

This approach to identification reflects a deviance perspective of emotional disturbance in that it is based on measuring the extent to which a child's behavior deviates from established norms. Thus, the emphasis is on the specific maladaptive behaviors a child displays, not on the emotional conditions that may or may not cause such behaviors. As maladaptive behaviors are the important consideration, their measurement must take place in the child's natural environment, in the place where the problems are occurring. In school, the environment is often the classroom. Therefore, teachers or teacher's aides are usually the individuals who undertake these identification procedures, although any other interested professional, such as the counselor, psychologist, or school principal, may do so as well.

The techniques involved in the behavioral approach are based on formal observation and detailed record keeping. The child is observed in class on a daily basis for a fixed period of time. An incidence record is kept of the maladaptive behaviors displayed during that period. The precise information regarding the type and frequency of a child's behavior is direct, objective evidence of his or her deviance. Although the child might be described as emotionally disturbed on the basis of that evidence, the categorical label is far less important than the direct information regarding the behaviors that cause the child trouble and that, therefore, must be modified.

To simplify the interpretation of the information that is gathered, data are plotted on a graph such as the one depicted in Figure 4.1. This graph plots John's maladaptive behaviors during morning and afternoon recess over a period of two weeks. Three behaviors were targeted for attention: swearing at others, fighting, and making rude remarks. The graph shows that John often resorted to swearing and rude remarks but did not usually fight. The incidence of the two verbal behaviors was greater in the afternoon and increased as each week progressed. The information gathered has isolated two behaviors that require attention and will provide a baseline to determine if John improves once treatment is begun.

Obviously this approach focuses directly on the child's activities in his or her everyday world. It has great attractiveness for teachers who seek to eliminate behaviors that deviate from group standards. It reflects the assumption that if the child's deviant behaviors are extinguished, and he or she learns more adaptive behaviors, then the child will be better ad-

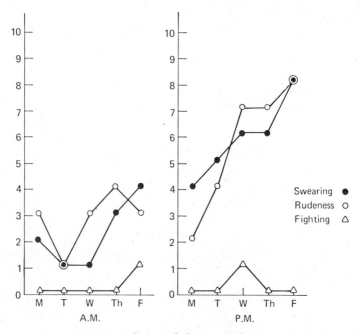

Fig. 4.1. *John's Maladaptive Behavior*

justed. The severity of the child's problem is reflected objectively in the number of maladaptive behaviors exhibited and in the frequency of the behavior.

EDUCATIONAL APPROACH

This approach primarily reflects a deviance model of emotional disturbance. For the most part, an emotionally disturbed state is signified by deviant, overt behaviors although some estimation of underlying emotions may be included. The teacher is the principal identifying agent. In addition to teacher opinion, however, peer attitude and self-ratings contribute alternate identification criteria.

Teacher Ratings

One of the basic differences between the educational and the behavioral models lies in the objectivity of the data-gathering techniques. In the educational approach, the teacher generally gets to know the students for 1 to 2 months, then judges whether or not they display specific problem behaviors. The teacher usually does not observe and record specific data on each pupil. Instead, he or she formulates impressions about each child in the class.

The teacher's evaluative criteria may be highly informal and represent nothing more than subjective opinions and attitudes. There is reason to believe, however, that teachers' subjective opinions are an extremely useful index of emotional disturbance. Teachers are exposed to their students for long periods of time on a daily basis. With the exception of the children's parents, they learn to know their charges better than anyone else. Their judgments may even be more reliable than the parent's. Teachers can view the child's behaviors with relative objectivity. They see the child as a group member, and they have the opportunity to evaluate the child on an implicit set of norms that is a culmination of their experiences with countless children.

In addition to teachers' informal criteria for judging when children's deviant behaviors are sufficiently persistent, intense, and/or bizarre as to indicate emotional disturbance, various formal criteria have been proposed as indices for teacher identification of emotional disturbance. Bower (1969) lists five characteristics that must be displayed to a *marked* extent over a period of time:

1. An inability to learn that cannot be explained by intellectual, sensory, or health factors
2. An inability to maintain satisfactory interpersonal relationships with peers and teachers
3. Inappropriate types of behaviors or feelings under normal conditions

4. A general pervasive mood of unhappiness or depression
5. A tendency to develop physical symptoms, pains, or fears associated with personal or school problems.

Bower's criteria are of sufficient interest to warrant further discussion. He regards an inability to learn as the single most significant characteristic of emotional disturbance. Certainly, it is one that teachers do not fail to notice. Obviously, not all emotionally disturbed children fail to learn. Some of the most seriously maladjusted individuals still function well academically. However, the high levels of anxiety associated with many disturbed conditions often depress learning efficiency. Attention, concentration, and retention are impaired. Also, a child may be consciously preoccupied with his or her problems to the extent that instruction is useless. Thought disturbances such as those associated with psychosis also interfere with learning.

Occasionally learning patterns are bizarre. Some emotionally disturbed children become absorbed in one specific area of interest that apparently is anxiety reducing. That particular interest becomes an obsession and blocks most other learning. For example, a child may become an authority on dinosaurs. He or she reads, writes, and talks about the subject almost exclusively. The level of learning about that subject far exceeds the child's general level of learning. He or she may be able to spell *tyrannosaurus,* but not his or her name. Lest there be some confusion, this preoccupation is not similar to a healthy interest in certain specific areas that many children display. It is an all-consuming, unhealthy adjustment to anxiety that is debilitating to the child.

Satisfactory interpersonal relationships are defined by Bower as the ability to demonstrate warmth toward others, have close friends, work and play with others, and stand alone when necessary. Many emotionally disturbed children are isolates. Some are afraid of social interactions; others are inept; still others are indifferent. A significant number of disturbed children show a superficial regard for others and have no difficulty forming friendships. Their relationships are short lived, however, as they are unable to demonstrate real social warmth and attempt to manipulate and exploit others. These children have many acquaintances, but few friends. Often children are more astute than their teachers in recognizing classmates who have problems with interpersonal relationships.

Inappropriate types of behavior describe children who react atypically to situations. For example, such a child might laugh when a classmate is severely injured on the playground. Another child might begin to cry hysterically because the school assembly is cancelled. These atypical reactions invariably strike the other children as odd. They often respond with amazement, indignation, or embarrassed silence.

A pervasive mood of unhappiness is self-explanatory. Disturbed children rarely smile and gain little enjoyment from their activities. Even events that are calculated to bring pleasure to children, such as the class Christmas party, have little or no effect on them. They remain troubled and depressed.

Finally, a tendency to develop physical symptoms includes children who are often absent because of illness, those who visit the nurse regularly, or those who constantly complain of illness. Although these illnesses have no physical cause, they are not feigned or imaginary. They are a response to stress. The incidence of these behaviors increases in direct proportion to the stressfulness of a given situation. For example, test-taking produces many such symptoms.

Alternate and more specific identification criteria are supplied by Gropper et al. (1968). These include thirteen principal areas that teachers consider as sources of potential problems. They are:

1. Attention to classroom activities (inattention, daydreaming, withdrawal)
2. Physical activity (restlessness, hyperactivity, noisemaking)
3. Reaction to tension (emotional upsets)
4. Appropriateness of behavior (telling tales, collecting objects)
5. Meeting work requirements (self-criticism, giving up, not working)
6. Interest in work (playing, doodling, drawing)
7. Getting along with others (name-calling, fighting, passivity)
8. Consideration for group needs (impatient with others, interrupting others, talking out loud)
9. Response to teacher requirements or instructions (arguments, rudeness, disobedience)
10. Degree of independence (seeking praise, attention, support, currying favor)
11. Regard for school rules and conventions (swearing, smoking)
12. Regard for general rules (truancy, tardiness, destroying property)
13. Integrity (cheating, tattling, stealing)

These behavioral areas appear to cover the gamut of activities indicative of emotional disturbance in children. However, as noted before, all children engage in some of these behaviors at some time. How does the teacher determine whether or not the child is emotionally disturbed? Bower notes that it is a question of degree. Disturbed children consistently display deviant behaviors. R. Newcomer (1977) regards conscious control of behavior as a critical index. Emotionally disturbed children appear driven to engage in certain activities despite conscious efforts to avoid them. For instance, a child may punch and harm children he or she wants to play with.

Gropper et al. provide multiple criteria by which teachers may judge the severity of each child's problem. They include:

1. Intensity—does the activity disrupt the child's other activities?
2. Appropriateness—Is the behavior a reasonable response to the situation?
3. Assessability of circumstances—Is there an obvious reason for the behavior?
4. Comparison with maturity level of the class—Is the behavior commonly exhibited in class?
5. Duration—How long does it last?
6. Frequency—How often does it occur?
7. Manageability—Is the behavior influenced by management efforts?
8. Contagion—do other children copy the behavior.

Utilizing these criteria, the teacher can make an objective determination of the significance of a child's behavior, that is, whether it is normal, a problem that can be handled in the classroom, or a condition so serious as to warrant referral to mental health experts for treatment. Table 4.1 demonstrates the criteria for classifying behavior as normal, problem, or referable.

A classification system designed solely for judging the relative severity of children's problems has been developed by Newcomer (1977). This system is designed for use by teachers after they have determined

Table 4.1. *Summary of Criteria for Classifying Problem Behavior*

Description of Criteria	Normal	Problem	Referable
A. *Intensity* How disruptive of the child's other activities is the problem behavior?	NON-DISRUPTIVE Behavior does *not* interfere with the child's other activities	DISRUPTIVE Behavior interferes with the child's other activities	EXTREMELY DISRUPTIVE Behavior completely disrupts child's other activities
B. *Appropriateness* Is the behavior a reasonable response to the situation?	REASONABLE Response is acceptable or expected for the situation	INAPPROPRIATE Response is undesirable for the situation	EXCESSIVE Response is out of proportion to the situation
C. *Duration* How long does the behavior episode last?	SHORT-LIVED Episode lasts only a short time (short time within a class period)	MODERATELY LONG Episode extends over a longer period (some carryover from one class to the next)	LONG-LASTING Episodes are long-lasting (greater part of a day)

Description of Criteria	Normal	Problem	Referable
D. Frequency How often does the behavior occur?	INFREQUENT Behavior usually is not repeated (rarely repeated in a day; rarely repeated on other days)	FREQUENT Behavior is repeated (may be repeated several times a day; may be repeated on several days)	HABITUAL Behavior happens all the time (repeated often during day; repeated on many days)
E. Specificity/ Generality In how many types of situations does the behavior occur?	OCCURS IN SPECIFIC SITUATION Behavior occurs in specific type of situation	OCCURS IN SEVERAL SITUATIONS Behavior occurs in more than one type of situation	OCCURS IN MANY SITUATIONS Behavior occurs in many types of situations
F. Manageability How easily does the behavior respond to management efforts?	EASILY MANAGED Responds readily to management efforts	DIFFICULT TO MANAGE Inconsistent or slow response to management efforts	CANNOT BE MANAGED Does not respond to management efforts
G. Assessability of Circumstances How easily can the circumstances that produced the behavior be identified?	EASILY ASSESSED Easy to identify situation or condition producing behavior	DIFFICULT TO ASSESS Situation or condition producing behavior difficult to identify	CANNOT BE ASSESSED Cannot identify situation or condition producing behavior
H. Comparison with Maturity Level of Class How close to the norm of the class is the problem behavior?	NO DEVIATION FROM LEVEL OF CLASS Behavior is par for the group	BELOW LEVEL OF CLASS Behavior is below the group level	CONSIDERABLY BELOW LEVEL OF CLASS Behavior is considerably below the group level
I. Number of Problem Behaviors Exhibited	Rarely more than one	Usually more than one	Usually many and varied
J. Acceptance by Peers Does the child have difficulty being accepted by peers?	ACCEPTED Is accepted by peers	HAS DIFFICULTY GETTING ALONG May have difficulty with particular individuals	NOT ACCEPTED Unaccepted by group

Table 4.1. *Continued*

Description of Criteria	Normal	Problem	Referable
K. *Recovery Time* How quickly is the situation leading to the episode forgotten?	RAPID Gets over episode quickly	SLOW Gets over episode more slowly	DELAYED Does not get over episode
L. *Contagion* 1. Does the behavior disrupt the activities of others? 2. Do others copy the problem behavior?	LITTLE OR NO EFFECT ON OTHERS Behavior does not disturb or does not serve as a model for others	CONSIDER-ABLE EFFECT ON OTHERS Behavior disturbs immediate neighbors or neighbors copy behavior	EXCESSIVE EFFECT ON OTHERS Behavior disturbs whole class or whole class copies behavior
M. *Degree of Contact with Reality* Does the behavior represent a loss of contact with reality?	NO CONFU-SION BE-TWEEN REAL/UNREAL	SOME CON-FUSION BE-TWEEN REAL/UNREAL	CONFUSES REAL/UNREAL
N. *Response to Learning Opportunities* How readily does the child respond when learning opportunities are provided?	RESPONDS POSI-TIVELY TO ENRICHMENT/REMEDIAL WORK	RESPONDS SLOWLY OR WEAKLY TO ENRICHMENT/REMEDIAL WORK	DOES NOT RESPOND TO ENRICHMENT/REMEDIAL WORK

Source: Gropper, G., Kress, G., Hughes, R., and Pekich, J. Training teachers to recognize and manage social and emotional problems in the classroom. *Journal of Teacher Education*, 1968, *19*, 477–485. Reprinted by permission of the publisher.

that a child has displayed sufficient maladaptive behaviors to be judged emotionally disturbed. Table 4.2 contains the nine criteria that constitute the basis of the classification system. A child rated in the third or severe column on all or most of these criteria clearly is a severely disturbed individual regardless of the diagnostic label he or she may bear. Similarly, a child rated in the severe column on the first two criteria but in the mild column on the remaining criteria presents a far less bleak picture, despite the fact that he or she might appear initially to be equally disturbed and might bear the same label as the first child.

Table 4.2. *Criteria for Determining the Degree of Disturbance*

Criteria	Degree of Disturbance		
	Mild	*Moderate*	*Severe*
Precipitating Events	Highly Stressful	Moderately Stressful	Not Stressful
Destructiveness	Not Destructive	Occasionally Destructive	Usually Destructive
Maturational Appropriateness	Behavior typical for age	Some behavior untypical for age	Behavior too young or too old
Personal Functioning	Cares for own needs	Usually cares for own needs	Unable to care for own needs
Social Functioning	Usually able to relate to others	Usually unable to relate to others	Not able to relate to others
Reality Index	Usually sees events as they are	Occasionally sees events as they are	Little contact with reality
Insight Index	Aware of behavior	Usually aware of behavior	Usually not aware of behavior
Conscious Control	Usually can control behavior	Occasionally can control behavior	Little control over behavior
Social Responsiveness	Usually acts appropriately	Occasionally acts appropriately	Rarely acts appropriately

1. *Precipitating Events*

This component refers to the extent to which the child's behavior, however undesirable or maladaptive it may be, is directly related to precipitating environmental conditions. The more obvious the relationship between the precipitating event and the child's behavior appears, the less serious the implications for emotional disturbance. For example, when teased by classmates a child may typically respond by fighting. Another child who fights frequently may attack classmates without apparent motivation. Although the first child's response may not be desirable in a classroom and may cause him or her difficulties among peers, it is at least a plausible reaction to causal factors, in this case, the ridicule. It is a relatively easy task to help the child recognize that fighting does little good and to help him or her respond better. The second situation involving unprovoked assault is not appropriate to the environmental circumstances. The child's behavior is irrational—he or she may not know why he or she attacks others. Such behavior is far more difficult to alter.

2. Destructiveness

This component reflects the extent to which the child's behavior is harmful to others or to himself or herself. High destructiveness correlates with severe disturbance. Children who engage in sadistic activities, such as killing animals or deliberately injuring other children, have serious emotional problems. Children who engage in a great deal of bombast or threat without actually becoming destructive are less disturbed.

Another equally predictive type of destructiveness involves self-injury. Highly disturbed children frequently attempt to hurt themselves. They might have many injuries from "accidents," or they might engage in direct masochism by slashing themselves with knives, burning themselves with matches, raking their fingernails over their flesh until they have large sores, tearing out their hair, and so forth. Mildly maladjusted children may complain often about physical suffering or even threaten to hurt themselves, but they rarely carry out their threats.

3. Maturational Appropriateness

This component reflects the extent to which a child's behaviors are generally considered appropriate for his or her age group. Severely disturbed children frequently show highly regressed behaviors characteristic of younger children. For example, the language of a five-year-old psychotic child may regress to a one-year-old level. Other infantile behaviors such as enuresis may occur.

On the other end of the scale, disturbed children may display behaviors that appear "too old" for them. For example, an eleven-year-old girl might dress and act as though she were ten years older. The greater the age gap between the child's real and acted age, and the more numerous the behaviors that reflect this over- or undermaturity, the more severe the disturbance.

4. Personal Functioning

This component refers to the child's capacity to take care of personal needs, including cleaning, dressing, eating properly, finding his or her way from one place to another, and so forth. A child who seems unaware or unconcerned about such routines of daily living may be severely disturbed.

5. Social Functioning

There are two aspects to this component: The extent to which the child's behaviors prevent the making of friends and the quality of the behaviors displayed in a group. The more severe an individual's emotional problems, the more isolated from peers the child will be. The child either ignores peers or rejects them. On occasion, severely disturbed children may relate satisfactorily to few select peers but demonstrate poor social functioning by a total inability to contribute to a large-group activity. They either withdraw from participation or engage in disruptive behaviors.

6. Reality Index

This component refers to the extent that a child's view of the events that affect his or her life correspond with objective reality. The greater the gap between what is believed and reality, the greater the severity of the emotional problem. For example, a severely disturbed child with a low reality index might feel persecuted and be suspicious of all other persons, including those who consistently treat him or her with kindness. A less disturbed person is less oblivious to the specific events in each environmental situation. Thus, he or she may tend to respond to people with suspicion but abandon or alter the suspicious behavior when treated with kindness.

7. Insight Index

Insight pertains to the child's level of understanding about his or her problems. High insight suggests that the child at least recognizes which behaviors may cause problems. Insight does not imply that the child can change the behavior, but it is often regarded as a first step toward that goal. Severely disturbed children often have little understanding of their symptoms and behaviors.

8. Conscious Control

This component reflects the extent to which the child can control emotions and maladaptive behaviors. Mildly disturbed children often exert conscious efforts to stop maladaptive behaviors. For example, the child who fights recognizes that it is a problem and tries to control his or her temper. Severely disturbed children often act as if they were driven by forces they cannot recognize or control.

9. Social Responsiveness

The final component indicates the extent to which the child values others. The child lacking social responsiveness is unwilling to delay the gratification of his or her own impulses for any reason. Therefore, the child has difficulty coexisting with others. He or she is indifferent or contemptuous of others, seeking neither their love nor their acceptance. Thus there is no external social force that can influence behavior. Severely disturbed children demonstrate limited responsiveness to social forces. In fact, they may structure their environments to avoid dealing with such forces, as when they live in fantasy worlds. Mildly or moderately disturbed children, however, may have difficulties with social functions but retain their desire for acceptance.

Walker (1969) proposes a still more elaborate system in a multidimensional teacher identification model. He uses three scales that represent increasingly refined levels of observation and assessment. They consist of (1) a fifty-item behavioral checklist that serves as an initial screening device, (2) a seventy-five-item behavior rating scale that provides frequency measures on individual items as well as indices of teacher response and reaction to each behavior, and (3) a behavioral observation form that records task-oriented behaviors in cumulative 10-second intervals for 10-minute observation periods.

The first step, the fifty-item checklist, contains representative behaviors typically associated with disturbed states such as: Displays temper tantrums and uses profane language in the classroom. Teachers rate the behavior as absent or present.

The second step, the seventy-five item scale, is completed for children who make high scores on the first scale. These behavior items also depict emotionally disturbed states. The teacher evaluates the rate of occurrence on a 0 to 5 scale as in: Displays temper tantrums—0= never, 1=once every two months, 2=once a month, 3=once a week, 4=once a day, 5=at a constant or near constant rate.

Next, for each of the seventy-five behaviors, the teacher rates his or her response on a 1 to 5 scale as in: When the behavior occurs, do you, 1=ignore it, 2=give a warning glance, 3=interact verbally or physically, 4=temporarily remove the child from class, 5=refer the child to an outside source such as the counselor or psychologist.

For the final portion of step 2, the teacher rates his or her own reaction to each behavior on a 1 to 5 scale as in: 1=the behavior does not disturb you, 2=the behavior disturbs you to a slight extent, 3=the behavior disturbs you to a moderate extent, 4=the behavior disturbs you to a great extent, 5=the behavior disturbs you to a very great extent.

The third step, the behavioral observation form, involves direct observation and recording of a behavior sample. This step is performed to verify the teacher's ratings of behavior by an independent observer.

There are other, less complex techniques available to aid in teacher identification of emotionally disturbed children. A sample of the most popular standardized behavioral checklists is presented in Table 4.3. Generally, these checklists contain behaviors considered by clinical experts to be most indicative of emotional disturbance. The child exhibiting a large number of these behaviors is considered to be emotionally disturbed.

Peer Ratings

As noted previously, the educational approach is not entirely dependent on teacher opinion to identify emotionally disturbed children in school. Peer perceptions constitute an equally important source of data

Table 4.3. *Behavioral Checklists*

Walker Problem Behavior Identification Checklist (1970)
Hill Walker, Western Psychological Services
12031 Wilshire Boulevard, Los Angeles, CA 90025

Devereux Elementary School Behavior Rating Scale Manual (1967)
George Spivack and Marshall Swift, The Devereux Foundation
Devon, PA 19333

Ottawa School Behavior Checklist
J. B. Pimm and G. McClure, Pimm Consultants Limited
85 Spanks Street, Suite 211, Ottawa 4, Ontario, Canada

Behavior Problem Checklist (1967)
H. Quay and D. Peterson, University of Illinois Press
Champaign, IL 61820

Delinquency Proneness Scale (1966)
W. Koaraceus, Charles E. Merrill Publishing Company
Columbus, OH 43216

Pupil Behavior Inventory (1966)
R. Vinter, C. Saari, D. Vorwaller, and W. Schafer, Campus Publishing
Ann Arbor, MI 48106

Classroom Behavior Inventory, Jr. and Sr. H.S.
E. Schaefer, L. Droppleman, and A. Kalvenboer
Earl Schaefer, National Institute of Mental Health
5454 Wisconsin Ave., Chevy Chase, MD 20015

Minnesota Personality Profile II
University of Minnesota Institute of Child Development and Welfare
Dale B. Harris, Pennsylvania State University
Burrows Building, University Park, PA 16802

Peterson Problem Checklist
Donald Peterson
American Documentation Institute, No. 6632, AID Auxiliary Publications
    Project
Library of Congress, Washington, D.C. 20540

School Observation Schedule
S. Cooper, W. Ryan, and B. Hutcheson
S. Cooper, Community Mental Health Center
220 E. Huron, Ann Arbor, MI 48108

Rating-Ranking Scales for Child Behavior
R. Cromwell, D. Davis, & J. Held
Rae Cromwell, Lafayette Clinic
915 E. Lafayette, Detroit, MI 48207

Behavior Rating Profile (1978)
L. Brown and D. Hammill, Pro. Ed.
333 Perry Brooks Building
Austin, TX 78701

---

and have been shown to be highly accurate predictors of emotional disturbance (Bower, 1969). Moreno (1953) popularized the notion of formally measuring students' attitudes toward their peers through socio-metrics. The simple but effective sociometric procedures he developed evaluate each child's social position and provide a graphic representation of the class social structure through the sociogram. Also, Bower and Lambert (1971) have developed several useful sociometric peer rating techniques: *The Class Pictures, A Class Play,* and *Student Survey.* The Bower and Lambert techniques[1] and the Moreno sociogram will be discussed below.

1. *The Class Pictures*   (Kindergarten to Grade 3)

This test is administered individually, requiring 15–20 minutes per child. It consists of twelve picture cards containing twenty scorable items. Ten items depict emotionally maladjusted behavior, five involving boys and five involving girls. The other ten items show five boys and five girls engaging in positive or neutral behaviors. The child to whom the test is being administered is asked to consider which of his or her classmates is most like the child in each situation. Scoring is done by counting the number of times a child is picked. The total score for any given child selected indicates how the child is "seen" by his or her peers. The number of negative selections for a child shows negative perceptions. A ratio of negative perceptions for each child is obtained by dividing the number of negative selections by the total number of times the child is picked for all twenty pictures. The resulting percentage is used as the screening index.

2. *A Class Play* (Grades 3 to 7)

This device is similar to *Class Pictures,* but useful with older children. It may be administered to a group and requires 35–40 minutes to complete. Section 1 contains descriptions of twenty hypothetical roles (ten positive and ten negative) in a play. Each pupil must choose a classmate to play each role. Section II measures self-perceptions. The pupil must select roles he or she would prefer and roles he or she thinks others would assign to him or her. The scoring involves the computation of negative percentages for each section.

3. *Student Survey* (Grades 7 to 12)

This paper-and-pencil test is group-administered and requires 35–40 minutes to complete. Section I contains twenty statements, ten illustrating negative behaviors and ten illustrating positive behaviors. A typical posi-

---

[1] The Bower and Lambert screening techniques are used with the authors' permission. Revised materials may be obtained from the California Test Bureau, Monterey, California.

tive statement is "A student who is good in school work," whereas "A student who gets into fights or quarrels with other students" depicts a negative item. Students must write the name of the classmate who best exhibits the behavior described in each item.

Section II of the *Student Survey* contains the same twenty items randomly arranged in thirty groups of four statements each. The student selects one of the four statements in each group which he or she believes might apply to him or her on the basis of three criteria: the student's opinion, classmates' opinions, and teacher's opinion. Typical items are:

Which one of these four students would your classmates think is *least* like you?"

_____ 1. One who sometimes behaves in ways which are dangerous to self or others.
_____ 2. One who has difficulty learning.
_____ 3. One who gets upset when faced with a difficult school problem.
_____ 4. One who has lots of common sense.

Which one of these four students would your teacher think is *most* like you?

_____ 1. One who is respected by other students.
_____ 2. One who makes unusual or odd remarks in class.
_____ 3. Someone who will probably be a success in life.
_____ 4. One who has difficulty learning.

Which one of these four students is *least* like you?

_____ 1. One who makes unusual or odd remarks in class.
_____ 2. A student who is good in school work.
_____ 3. Someone who is interested in things he can do alone.
_____ 4. Someone who will probably be a success in life.

Once again scoring involves computation of separate negative percentages for Sections I and II.

Bower points out that peer ratings inform the teacher of children who have little or no visibility within the class. Among these children are those who are slow learners, those who are nonintrusive and prefer solitary activities, and a small core of children who are withdrawn from the group because of emotional problems.

The teacher also learns which children are perceived negatively by the class. On some occasions, peer perceptions differ dramatically from teacher perceptions, and the teacher may become aware of class attitudes for the first time. Children viewed negatively by their peers often have emotional problems.

These types of ratings are also useful because they provide the teacher with the means to compare peer ratings with self-ratings. More will be said about self-ratings and their usefulness later.

4. *Moreno's Sociometric Techniques* (All Grades)

These techniques may be administered to a group in 5 to 10 minutes. Each class member is asked to choose one or two classmates with whom he or she would most like to share an experience, for example, play, work, or go to the zoo. An alternate approach involves assessing one or two classmates each child would least like to play with, work with, and so forth.

After obtaining the children's ratings, the teacher plots the results graphically. In this way, the number of times each child was selected, whom each child selected, and who selected each child can be illustrated. The social stars of the class as well as the isolates or near isolates can be identified.

Figure 4.2 illustrates a typical sociogram. It shows that Tommy, the star, was selected by five other children as one of two classmates they

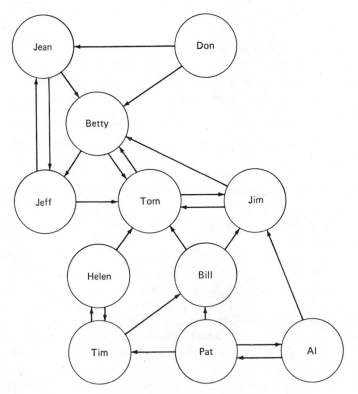

Fig. 4.2. *Moreno's Sociogram*

would most like to invite to their birthday party; Betty, the runner-up, was the choice of four children; whereas Don, the isolate, was chosen by no one.

Repeated administration of sociometric measures throughout the school year enables the teacher to assess the stability of children's attitudes. Sudden dramatic variations in class opinion toward a particular child may indicate the onset of problems that were not active previously.

Self-Ratings

The third useful predictor of disturbance in the educational approach is self-ratings. These indices provide information about an individual's self-concept. Since self-concept is a nebulous construct and may be operationally defined in many ways, there are different types of self-rating scales. Two of the most popular types of self-concept scales measure ideal self, or the characteristics one would have if one were perfect, and the real self, or the individual with all flaws exposed. Hypothetically, the discrepancy between these indices shows the gaps between what an individual wants to be and what he or she perceives as the truth.

It is difficult to assess the value of instruments measuring self-perceptions. Their results are easily contaminated. First, they are invalidated by deliberate distortion. The individual simply may choose to lie. For example, children who habitually steal from others may describe themselves as honest. Second, they may reflect an individual's sincere convictions, but those convictions may be erroneous. For instance, the most flagrant class gossip may perceive himself or herself as a discreet, closed-mouthed person, capable of keeping even the most shocking secrets. Third, self-perceptions vary and are susceptible to situational pressures. Thus, an individual may depict himself or herself as depressed, withdrawn, and unhappy on a self-rating scale administered one day and project a significantly different profile the following day. Finally, self-evaluation may be so threatening to an individual that he or she unconsciously resorts to denial. In other words, the person projects himself or herself in a manner obviously inconsistent with reality. For example, a student who has steadily failed in school and is currently repeating fifth grade may insist that he or she is a high achiever despite the fact that he or she is neither unaware of academic problems nor deliberately lying.

Possibly the safest conclusion regarding self-ratings is that persons who display a negative self-concept usually have problems of some type. They may be severe adjustment problems, or they may be temporary reactions that exist at the time of the rating. Positive self-ratings, however, do not imply mental health since they may be distorted by conscious or unconscious interference. Such distortions are obvious when positive self-ratings conflict with negative peer ratings. When positive self-ratings coincide with positive peer ratings, the probability is that the individual is psychologically healthy.

To some extent, positive self-ratings may be a critical factor in determining peer evaluation. Individuals with good self-concepts generally have positive perceptions of others and interact with them successfully, whereas those with negative self-concepts usually devalue others and have predictable problems with social relationships (Sheerer, 1949; Stock, 1949). Also, positive self-concept is highly correlated with good academic achievement, another variable often influencing peer perceptions (Woolner, 1966; Combs and Soper, 1963; Brookover et al., 1962).

Bower (1969) suggests that self-concept scores are most useful when compared with peer ratings. This comparison reveals the reality level of each child's self-perceptions, that is, the extent to which the ratings coincide with the perceptions of others. Studies by Sears (1940); Rogers, Kill, and McNeil (1948); and Davids and White (1958) all suggest that children with histories of success in school activities generally had accurate perceptions of reality. On the other hand, many emotionally disturbed children have faulty reality perceptions, that is, they see themselves in a positive light but are viewed negatively by their peers.

Measures of self-concept abound and may be obtained rather inexpensively from any of the major test publishing houses. Table 4.4 contains a representative sample of the most popular standardized instruments. The interested teacher who wishes to examine reviews of such scales should consult the most current edition of *The Mental Measurement Yearbook* (Buros, 1978).

Bower (1969)[2] has developed several relatively simple self-rating scales that will serve to illustrate such instruments:

1. *A Picture Game* (Kindergarten to Grade 3)

This is a group test requiring approximately thirty minutes to administer. The test consists of sixty-six pictures that illustrate normal home and school relationships and events. The first ten pictures depict obviously happy or sad situations. The remaining fifty-six pictures depict neutral events. The child is asked to sort each picture into happy or sad categories. Theoretically, the children's evaluations of neutral events as either sad or happy depicts their attitudes toward themselves and their life situations. Scoring is done by counting the number of happy cards. Children who score 37 or higher or 20 or lower are included in future screening procedures.

---

[2] From Bower, E., *Early Identification of Emotionally Handicapped Children in School,* 2nd ed., 1969, courtesy of Charles C Thomas, Publisher, Springfield, Illinois.

Table 4.4. *Measures of Self-Concept*

Thomas Self-Concept Values Test—Age 3–9 (1967)
    Author: W. Thomas
    Obtain from: Educational Publishing Service Co., 75 Moulton Street, Cambridge, MA 02138

Adjective Check List—Gds. 4, 5, 6 and Jr. H.S., (1960)
    Authors: H. Davidson and G. Lang
    Obtain from: Davidson, H., and Lang, G. Children's perceptions of their teachers' feelings toward them related to self-perception, school achievement and behavior. *Journal of Experimental Education*, 1960, 29, 107–118. HELDREF Publications, 4000 Albemarle Street, N.W. Washington, D.C. 20016

Children's Self-Conception—Age 6–11 (1955)
    Author: M. B. Creelman
    Obtain from: University of Michigan Microfilm, Ann Arbor, MI 48106

Elementary School Index of Adjustment and Values—Gds. 3, 4, and 5 (1963)
    Author: R. E. Bills
    Obtain from: R. E. Bills, College of Education, University of Alabama, Tuscaloosa, AL 35486

Lipsitt Self-Concept Scale for Children—Gds. 4, 5, 6 (1958)
    Author: L. P. Lipsitt
    Obtain from: Lipsitt, L. A self-concept scale for children and its relationship to children's form of the Manifest Anxiety Scale. *Child Development*, 1958. Child Development Publications, Society for Research in Child Development, Inc., Purdue University, Lafayette, IN 47907

Perception Score Sheet—K and 1 grd. (1963)
    Author: A. Combs and D. Soper
    Obtain from: Combs, A., and Soper, D. The relationship of child perceptions to achievement and behavior in early school years. Cooperative Research Project No. 814, University of Florida, 1963. Gainesville, FL 32601

Self-Concept Inventory—Gds. 3, 4, 5, and 6 (1966)
    Author: P. Sears
    Obtain from: P. Sears, 110 Golden Oak Drive, Portola Valley, CA 94026.

Self-Concept–Self-Report Scale—6th grd. (1963)
    Author: A. Combs, D. Soper, and C. Courson
    Obtain from: Combs, A., Soper, D., and Courson, C. The measurement of self-concept and self-report. *Educational and Psychological Measurement*, 1963. 2121 Cheek Road, Durham, N.C. 27704.

Self-Social Symbols Tasks—Age 10 and over (1965)
    Authors: R. Ziller: B. Long, and E. Henderson
    Obtain from: Henderson, E., Long, B., and Ziller, R. Self and social constructs of achieving and non-achieving readers. *The Reading Teacher*, 1965, 19, 114–118. A publication of the International Reading Association, 800 Barksdale Road, Newark, DL 19711.

---

2. *Thinking About Yourself* (Grades 3 to 7)

This paper-and-pencil test is group administered in about 45–60 minutes. It has two sections: Section I measures ideal self, and Section II measures real self. The test contains forty statements describing people behaving in a variety of ways. In Section I, the students must indicate to what extent they would or would not like to be the person described. A sample item is: "This boy has many dreams. Would you like to be him?" Possible responses range from emphatic "yes" to emphatic "no" as in: YES, yes, no, NO. In Section II, the forty items are repeated, but to measure real self. A sample item is: "This boy has many dreams. Are you like him?" Again, responses are YES, yes, no, NO.

The test is scored by attributing numerical scores 1, 2, 3, 4 to YES, yes, no, NO, respectively. Numerical quantities are obtained on both scales for each item. The smaller number is subtracted from the larger number, and the item difference is recorded. In the example given, the student might select "no" on the ideal scale and obtain three points. On the real scale he or she might circle "YES" and obtain 1 point. Subtracting 1 from 3 produces a discrepancy of 2 points for the item. The total score is the cumulation of differences between the two scales on each of the forty items. This score indicates the divergence between the pupil's ideal and real selves. A high score indicates that the pupil sees himself or herself differently from what he or she would like to be. Such discrepancy is an indication of emotional problems.

3. *A Self Test* (Grades 7 to 12)

This instrument also measures the difference between real and ideal selves. It may be administered to a group in 45–60 minutes. The test format is identical to *Thinking About Yourself*. The only variation lies in the items that reflect the problems and concerns of more mature individuals.

The educational approach incorporates multiple components from the school environment. Although it focuses largely on behavior rather than emotions, it emphasizes teacher and student impressions rather than focusing on precise behavioral counts. Thus, a child's specific behaviors are put into a more global perspective as to whether or not they are indicative of emotional disturbance. This type of perspective is necessary because a child's maladaptive classroom behaviors per se do not automatically cause him or her to be judged emotionally disturbed by teachers and peers. Other factors must be considered. For instance, two children may talk out frequently, thereby irritating their teacher and classmates. Both may be relatively disinterested in school work and underachievers. However, one person may be so enthusiastic and engaging that few remain annoyed with him or her for long, and, in fact, she is admired for the social skills represented in her excessive talking. The

revealed that there was a zero correlation between teacher and mental hygienist ratings of the seriousness of fifty behavioral traits. Such an outcome was not particularly surprising because Wickman had designed the study to obtain diverse professional perspectives, that is, teachers were instructed to define the seriousness of the problem by the amount of difficulty it produced in the classroom, while the mental hygienists were to rate problem behavior on the basis of its effect on the child's future life. Nonetheless, Schrupp and Gjerde (1953) reviewed references to this study in twelve psychology textbooks and, in all but two cases, found the results interpreted to imply that the mental health experts were correct in their ratings while the teachers were incorrect.

Those supporting the educational and behavioral positions advance contrasting statements. First, they note that children's classroom activities are the most important source of information regarding their emotional adjustment. As with adults, children's problems are most obvious in the life situations that are most important and most demanding. School is children's major concern and occupation. Problems may be caused, precipitated, or worsened by children's inability to interact well with teachers and peers, learn readily, conform to behavioral standards, and function as group members. Such problems might not be apparent when children are in alternate, less demanding situations. Thus diagnosis and remediation of children's emotional problems in isolated, clinical settings have proved less than helpful to many children. Such procedures often do not provide sufficient attention to the child's behavior in the world outside the clinic. Observations of children's classroom behaviors provide an operational view of mental health—a perspective of the children's ability to function that cannot be obtained through other procedures, including psychometric evaluation. The teacher is therefore in the best position to recognize children's emotional problems.

Second, subsequent studies of teachers' accuracy in identifying emotionally disturbed children present empirical evidence that generally refutes the conclusions based on the Wickman study and suggests that (1) teachers accurately identify emotionally disturbed children, (2) children accurately identify the emotionally disturbed among them, and (3) for the most part, teachers and mental health experts agree about the characteristics of emotional disturbance.

Bower (1969) conducted a rather extensive study of teachers' abilities to identify emotionally disturbed children. He reported that teachers selected as poorly adjusted 87 percent of the children clinically diagnosed as emotionally disturbed. He also found that children consistently attributed hostile or negative characteristics to classmates later clinically diagnosed as emotionally disturbed. Other studies (Lambert, 1963; Maes, 1966; Stennett, 1966) support Bower's conclusions: Teacher and peer ratings are highly accurate indices of children's emotional adjustment.

Schrupp and Gjerde (1953) and Hunter (1957) reviewed and summarized the literature and concluded that, for the most part, teachers and mental health experts agree in their perceptions of emotional disturbance.

Some studies in this area compared the accuracy of teacher ratings with other school-related indices. Rogers (1942) considered nine variables, including achievement measures, intelligence, paper-and-pencil personality tests, school attendance, and self, peer, and teacher rating scales, and found them highly predictive of poor mental health. Ullmann (1952, 1957) used six indexes including teacher, peer, and self-ratings. He found that teacher ratings were the best predictors for children who act out their problems. Self-ratings had the poorest predictive power when compared to teacher and peer ratings, but they were useful for total appraisal.

Third, the differential diagnosis of emotional states by clinical personnel has not been particularly beneficial to children. It has resulted primarily in disability labeling that stigmatizes children but does not directly bring about treatment. Consequently, the efficacy of undertaking assessment to isolate the cause of children's maladaptive behaviors must be substantiated if it is to be continued in education.

Fourth, the treatment of emotionally disturbed states must involve the teacher. Since children's emotional states cannot be separated from their cognitive functioning and are key variables in determining school behavior, the teacher must be concerned not only with the identification of emotional problems but with treatment procedures as well. The "cure" cannot be left exclusively to others; it must be effected in the environment where the problem is demonstrated.

All the rhetoric and firmly held convictions presented in this essentially pro-con discussion do little to alter one perfectly obvious conclusion: Teachers must play a crucial role in the treatment and diagnosis of children's emotional problems. The difficulties associated with the identification and treatment of emotionally disturbed children illustrate the teacher's importance. First, unlike troubled adults, children do not refer themselves directly for diagnosis and treatment. Even if children recognize they are unhappy and are motivated to seek help, they are dependent on parents to know where to turn. Second, the parents of children with problems are often less than eager to have their children identified as emotionally disturbed. Problems at home may often be hidden or denied. Third, there are too few mental health experts available for work with children. Public resources such as child guidance clinics are so overwhelmed with potential clients that relatively few of the many children who have emotional problems receive service. Fourth, the expense of private treatment limits its availability to those who can afford it.

Thus, the responsibility for helping emotionally disturbed children must fall on qualified professionals with access to large numbers of children for substantial periods of time. Teachers have such exposure. They are in a position to know each class member as an individual and as a member of a group. They see each child cope with the demands of academic achievement and social interaction.

It is reasonable to assume that the teacher's role might encompass all or any of three hierarchical dimensions of screening, diagnosis, and therapy.

Screening

The role of the teacher in screening emotionally disturbed children has been advocated by Bower and Lambert (1971) and Reinert (1976). As the individual responsible for screening, the teacher need only identify a child as different from his or her peers by recognizing the maladaptive behaviors displayed. The teacher need not be concerned with the reasons for the child's behavior, nor with diagnosing the type or severity of the child's condition. Formal identification of disturbance and diagnosis of the type and severity of the disturbed state is the function of mental health experts. The teacher simply refers children suspected of having such problems to these specialists. The teacher's suspicions may reflect subjective impressions or the results of objective rating scales. The crux of the screening position is presented by Bower and Lambert (1971, p. 144):

1. It should be possible to complete the screening procedure with only such information as the teacher could obtain without outside technical or professional assistance.
2. The procedure should be sufficiently simple and straightforward for the average teacher to undertake without long training or daily supervision.
3. The results of the procedure should be *tentative identification* of children with emotional problems—leading the teacher to *refer* to competent specialists those children who could benefit most from thorough diagnosis.
4. As a corollary to number 3 above, the procedure should not encourage the teacher to diagnose emotional problems, nor to draw conclusions about their causes, nor to label or categorize children; in fact, the procedure should actively discourage the teacher from undertaking any of these highly technical interpretations.
5. The procedure should be one which neither invades the privacy of individuals nor violates good taste.
6. The procedure should be one which does not offer a threat to any child.
7. The procedure should be inexpensive to use.

Notably, the screening level of teacher participation still places the responsibility for children's emotional problems squarely on the shoulders of the mental health experts. It may help to alleviate certain of the identification difficulties discussed previously, but it does not affect treatment.

Diagnosis

The teacher undertaking to diagnose emotional disturbance may function at any of three levels. The first level is *diagnostic decision making*. It involves determining whether or not a child has an emotional problem. This level varies from screening procedures in that the teacher's identification is not tentative and does not depend on corroboration from mental health specialists. The teacher may use any of the identification procedures referred to in the educational approach to identification—behavioral checklists, peer ratings, and self-ratings—to conclude that certain children have emotional problems. Research indicating that teachers and mental health experts largely agree about the emotionally disturbed children tends to support the teacher assuming this role. Arguments that the teacher does in fact know more about children's behavior than ancillary professionals also provide support.

The second level of diagnosis, *assessment of severity*, involves determining the seriousness of the child's problem. The teacher must judge whether the child is mildly, moderately, or severely disturbed. The Gropper et al. (1968) and Newcomer (1977) criteria presented previously may be used to accomplish this level of diagnosis. At this level of diagnosis the teacher is able to estimate the treatment procedures.

Mildly disturbed children might be helped within the regular classroom by the teacher and available school resource personnel, such as the school counselor or the resource teacher. Referral to mental health specialists for further diagnosis and treatment is not necessary unless the child's problems grow worse.

Moderately disturbed children might remain in the regular classroom and gain help from an integrated therapeutic program conducted by the teacher and by available mental health specialists. Referral to outside experts is usually made to elicit further diagnosis and to develop an integrated plan for treatment that is conducted in private clinical settings as well as in the classroom.

Severely disturbed children might require intensive therapy from mental health specialists and a therapeutic special education placement. These children are always referred for further diagnosis, treatment, and official classification as emotionally disturbed, which will result in special education placement.

The third diagnostic level, *differential diagnosis,* leads specifically to determination of clinical conditions. The teacher undertaking this level of diagnosis must have extensive training in abnormal psychology and must be qualified to administer and interpret psychometric instruments such as projective tests. Since few teachers meet these qualifications, this level of diagnosis is wisely left to mental health specialists. The most efficient procedure involves referring severely and, in some cases, moderately disturbed children for this level of diagnosis. This procedure benefits the mildly disturbed children who usually can be helped without such elaborate diagnosis, the severely disturbed children who receive needed help from members of the mental health profession, the mental health experts whose case loads are reduced so they can focus on the children who most need their attention, and the teachers who obtain clinical information about the children who are the most puzzling and most difficult to assist.

Therapy

Clearly, the levels of diagnosis discussed offer implications for treatment decisions and identify the teacher as a therapeutic agent. The highest level of teacher involvement in the problem of emotional disturbance involves the *teacher as therapist*. Teachers choosing this level of intervention accept the notion that the era of separating therapy from ongoing classroom activities is in the past. One major and significant contribution of the behaviorist model (Whelan, 1976) has been its emphasis on the teacher as a therapeutic agent. Teachers have become increasingly aware that the resolution of children's emotional problems may lie within the classroom. In effect, teaching effectiveness may depend on the teacher's ability to help children resolve the affective problems that limit their productivity and make them unhappy.

The designation of the teacher as a therapist does not imply that he or she is expected or recommended to take on the role of the psychiatrist or psychologist in treating emotionally disturbed children. Those professionals are trained to provide in-depth psychotherapy to moderately and severely disturbed individuals. However, those children require extensive educational support in addition to the therapy provided by the mental health personnel. Also, there are a multitude of other children whose mild problems may not warrant the intervention of mental health professionals, but who require some type of therapeutic assistance during the course of their school careers. Many of these children might never be officially labeled emotionally disturbed. It is hoped that effective teacher intervention will render such labeling superfluous, since it is the treatment that children receive, and not the label assigned to them, that determines their future course of development.

To aid the teacher in developing strategies to function as a classroom therapist, Part III of this book contains discussions of a variety of therapeutic methods, techniques, and procedures that are useful in educational settings.

STUDY QUESTIONS

1. Discuss the four different approaches to the identification of emotionally disturbed children. Designate the teacher's role in each approach.
2. Compare Bower's criteria for identifying emotionally disturbed children with those developed by Gropper et al.
3. Discuss two types of peer ratings that can aid in identifying emotionally disturbed children. Apply one type with a group of children, or, if none is available, a group of friends.
4. Take a position on the question of whether teachers are qualified to identify emotionally disturbed children. Support your position with information from the chapter.
5. Discuss the three hierarchical dimensions of a teacher's role pertaining to emotionally disturbed children: screening, diagnosis, and therapy.

REFERENCES

Anastasi, A. *Psychological testing.* New York: Macmillan, 1968.

Bakwin, H., and Bakwin, R. *Behavior disorders in children.* Philadelphia: Saunders, 1960.

Bellak, L. *The thematic apperception test and the child's apperception test in clinical use.* New York: Grune and Stratton, 1954.

Bender, L. *Visual-motor gestalt test and its clinical use.* Research Monog. No. 3, New York: American Orthopsychiatric Association, 1938.

Blum, G. *The Blacky pictures: manual of instructions,* New York: The Psychological Corp., 1950.

Bochner, R., and Halpern, F. *Clinical application of the rorschach test.* 2nd ed. New York: Grune and Stratton, 1945.

Bower, E. *Early identification of emotionally handicapped children in school.* Springfield, Ill.: Thomas, 1969.

Bower, E., and Lambert, N. In-school screening of children with emotional handicaps. In N. Long, W. Morse, and R. Newman (eds.). *Conflict in the classroom.* 2nd ed. Belmont, Calif.: Wadsworth, 1971.

Brookover, W., Paterson, A., and Thomas, S. Self concept and school achievement. Cooperative Research Project, Office of Research and Publications, Lansing: Michigan State University, 1962.

Buros, O. (ed.). *The mental measurements year book.* Highland Park, N.J.: Gryphon Press, 1978.

Combs, A., and Soper, D. The relationship of child perception to achievement and behavior in the early school years. Washington, D.C.: U.S. Government Printing Office, 1963.

Davids, A., and White, A. Effects of success, failure and social facilitation on level of aspiration in emotionally disturbed and normal children. *Journal of Personality*, 1958, *26*, 77–83.

Gropper, G.; Kress, G.; Hughes, R.; and Pekich, J. Training teachers to recognize and manage social and emotional problems in the classroom. *Journal of Teacher Education*, 1968, *19*, 477–485.

Hunter, E. Changes in teachers' attitudes toward children's behavior over the last thirty years. *Mental Hygiene*, 1957, *41*, 3–10.

Kleinmantz, B. *Personality measurement.* Homewood, Ill.: Dorsey, 1967.

Klopfer, R., and Kelly, D. The Rorschach technique. Yonkers, N.Y.: World Book, 1942.

Lambert, N. The development and validation of a process for screening emotionally handicapped children in school. Cooperative Research Project 1186, U.S. Office of Education, 1963.

Machover, K. *Personality projection in the drawing of the human figure.* Springfield, Ill.: Thomas, 1949.

Maes, W. The identification of emotionally disturbed elementary school children. *Exceptional Children*, 1966, 33, 607–611.

Moreno, J. *Who shall survive? Foundations of sociometry, group psychotherapy, and sociodrama.* 2nd. ed. New York: Beacon House, 1953.

Murray, H. A. *Thematic apperception test.* Cambridge, Mass.: Harvard University Press, 1943.

Newcomer, P. L. A classification system for judging the severity of emotional disturbance. Unpublished manuscript, Glenside, Pa.: Beaver College, 1977.

Newcomer, P. L., and Hammill, D. D. *The test of language development.* Austin, Texas: Empiric Press, 1977.

Newcomer, R. A. The relationship between anxiety and emotional disorders. Unpublished manuscript, Glenside, Pa.: Beaver College, 1977.

Reinert, H. *Children in conflict.* Saint Louis: Mosby, 1976.

Rogers, C. Mental health findings in three elementary schools. Educational Research Bulletin. Ohio State University, *21* (3), 1942.

Rogers, C.; Kill, P.; and McNeil, D. The role of self-understanding in the prediction of behavior. *Journal of Consulting Psychology*, 1948, *3*, 174–180.

Ronde, A. *The sentence completion method.* New York: Ronald, 1957.

Rorschach, H. *Psychodiagnostics.* New York: Grune and Stratton, 1942.

Rotter, J. Manual for the Rotter incomplete sentence blank, college form. New York: Macmillan, 1968.

Schrupp, M., and Gjerde, C. Teacher growth in attitudes toward behavioral problems in children. *Journal of Educational Psychology*, 1953, *44*, 203–206.

Sears, P. Level of aspiration in academically successful and unsuccessful children. *Journal of Abnormal and Social Psychology*, 1940, 35, 498–506.

Sheerer, E. An analysis of the relationship between acceptance of self and respect for others in ten counseling cases. *Journal of Consulting Psychology*, 1949, *13*, 169–179.

Stennett, L. Emotional handicap in the elementary years: phase or disease. *American Journal of Orthopsychiatry*, 1966, *36*, 444–451.

Stock, D. An investigation into the interrelationships between the self-concept and feelings directed toward other persons and groups. *Journal of Consulting Psychology*, 1949, *13*, 179–185.

Ullmann, C. Identification of maladjusted school children. Monograph No. 7, Washington, D.C.: U. S. Public Health Service, 1952.

Ullmann, C. Teachers, peers and tests as predictors of adjustment. *Journal of Educational Psychology*, 1957, *48*, 257–264.

Walker, H. *Walker problem behavior checklist manual*. Los Angeles: Western Psychological Services, 1970.

Wechsler, D. *The Wechsler intelligence scale for children*. New York: Psychological Corporation, 1949.

Whelan, R. Human understanding of human behavior. In A. J. Pappanikou and J. L. Paul (eds.). *Mainstreaming emotionally disturbed children*. Syracuse, N.Y.: Syracuse University Press, 1977.

Whelan, R. The emotionally disturbed. In E. Meyen (ed.). *Exceptional children and youth*. Denver, Co.: Love, 1978.

Wickman, E. *Children's behavior and teachers' attitudes*. New York: Commonwealth Fund, 1928.

Woolner, R. Kindergarten children's self-concept in relation to their kindergarten experiences. *Dissertation Abstracts*, 1966, *27*, 2761-A.

PART III
THERAPIES

As noted in the preceding sections of this book, the teacher may serve as a therapist in the classroom. Familiarity with and the trust of the students make the teacher an ideal agent to

1. Incorporate affective components into the curriculum to teach children about their emotions and the effect that emotional disorders have on others.
2. Remediate relatively mild emotional problems through the use of alternate therapeutic procedures.
3. Identify and refer severely disturbed children to mental health personnel so that the children might receive appropriate treatment.
4. Cooperate with mental health experts in planning and implementing treatments for severely disturbed children within the classroom.

The tasks listed above are difficult ones. Teachers accept primary responsibility for instructing children in basic learning and that alone is a challenging job. Yet, most teachers would agree that shaping children's growth in nonacademic areas is an equally important and an even more difficult task. The therapeutic approaches presented in the following chapters will provide the teacher with a variety of techniques and methods that may be useful in accomplishing that latter task.

5
Group Therapy

Group therapy is the term applied to a therapeutic relationship involving more than two persons. In the past ten years, group therapy has become an increasingly popular technique. Several reasons for its popularity are:

1. Individual therapy often has proved too costly to be practical.
2. There is a scarcity of trained therapists, therefore it is more efficient for those available to see more than one person during the same time.
3. The notion of obtaining help for emotional problems from a group of lay persons, as well as from a professional expert has interested many people.
4. Group therapy has evolved a methodology, body of research, and descriptive literature independent of individual therapy.

Group therapy methods reflect a variety of psychological orientations, for example, psychoanalytical, behavioral, phenomenological and cognitive. To some extent, the theoretical orientation of the therapist influences the therapeutic process. For example, therapy conducted by a psychoanalytically oriented leader might dwell on childhood experiences and the emotions those experiences generated. A phenomenologically oriented therapist might emphasize the development of feelings of self-acceptance and improved interpersonal relationships. A more detailed discussion of various theoretical approaches to group therapy will be presented later in this chapter.

Group therapy also may involve varied techniques and strategies depending on the characteristics of the participants and the preferences of the leader. For example, group therapy may use a play format if the participants are very young children, or a dance or music format if the leader is trained in those therapeutic modes. In this chapter the group methodology presented will pertain primarily to discussion formats. Alternate techniques such as art, music, or play therapy will be discussed in separate chapters. First, the principles and methods pertaining specifically to group dynamics will be explored. Second, techniques associated with various theoretical schools will be discussed. Third, methods that may be used by teachers in school settings will be presented.

PRINCIPLES OF GROUP DYNAMICS

The principles of modern group dynamics have many of their roots in the work of Wilfred Bion (1962). Bion stressed the importance of studying group processes as phenomena distinct from individual behaviors. His ideas contributed greatly to the theoretical underpinnings of the Institute of Group Relations at The Tavistock Institute in England and at the A. K. Rice Institute for Human Relations in America. These institutes were established for the sole purpose of investigating group processes. Through the analysis of actual group experiences, they have shed light on critical principles of group dynamics including the dimensions of leadership, group roles, authority distribution, and communication barriers. Their contributions have demonstrated the importance of examining the group process as a whole, that is, as more than a sum of the individuals who comprise the group.

An equally important source of group study is the National Training Laboratory in Washington, D.C. This organization is best known for developing the concepts of sensitivity groups and training or T-groups. The idea behind sensitivity group training, that of helping individuals become more aware of themselves in relationship to others, has had a significant impact on the study of human relationships. It has spawned a variety of groups with varied formats, such as consciousness raising, family interaction, nonverbal contact, bioenergetic and encounter.

The literature produced by these sources and other independent sources pertaining to group dymanics suggests that groups may be functionally categorized in three ways: task oriented, developmental, and remedial.

Task-oriented groups are formed to accomplish specific purposes such as problem solving, leadership development, and fund raising. For example, a group such as the President's Committee on Mental Retardation is a task-oriented group charged with brain storming the problems associated with retardation and with providing a comprehensive plan for national action. All committees are task-oriented groups with specific agendas. Obviously, groups of this type can be of great use to educators. However, they are not oriented toward affective growth or the resolution of emotional problems, consequently they shall not be discussed further in this chapter.

Developmental groups focus on improving interpersonal skills and developing open communication patterns. Their goal is to promote growth for relatively well adjusted persons who seek increased self-awareness, better communicative skills, or the resolution of relatively minor adjustment problems. Developmental groups are not designed for the severely disturbed. Members are not encouraged to divulge intense personal problems, express deep emotion, or probe one another about their underlying feelings.

The discussions conducted in developmental groups may involve topics of general interest and explore common problems. For example, adolescents in a group might communicate their feelings and attitudes about dating, or might explore their mutual difficulties relating to their parents. Often the name applied to the group reflects its purpose— assertiveness training, consciousness raising, sensitivity training, family interactions, life planning, and so forth. Although formats vary, developmental groups often incorporate didactic presentations about topics of interest with experiential exercises.

Scheduling in developmental group sessions is flexible. Sessions may be held for relatively brief periods of time such as one- or two-day workshops, or they may be planned to conform to a more traditional weekly meeting schedule. Developmental groups are extremely useful in educational settings.

Remedial groups involve group psychotherapy. These groups are designed to help seriously disturbed individuals solve personal problems. Participants are expected to discover and reveal inner feelings. The methodology employed is designed to direct attention to personal crises or to long-standing personality disorders. The therapeutic techniques and strategies used are similar to those employed in individual therapy and reflect the theoretical orientation of the therapist.

The differences between developmental and remedial groups are of degree, not of kind. Both deal with affective adjustment. Developmental groups seek to keep the emotional intensity level reduced while the group members explore better ways of coping with stress or of interacting with others. Remedial groups attempt to raise the level of emotional intensity through the analysis of deep personal feelings. Both types of groups involve many of the same group processes or group dynamics. These include *leadership principles, the therapeutic process, and therapeutic techniques.*

Leadership Principles

The role of the group leader evokes considerable interest and debate among those interested in group dynamics. Mental health professionals, many of whom view group techniques as extensions of individual psychotherapy, assume that the leader must be a highly trained expert in psychopathology. Other professionals more interested in the interactive social processes associated exclusively with group dynamics (Brammer and Shostrom, 1977; Berzon and Solomon, 1966) argue that groups may function effectively with lay leaders or without a specified leader. Obviously, both points of view are correct. The qualifications required of the group leader depend on the type of group being established. Remedial groups require experts in psychopathology as leaders, whereas developmental groups may function well with other persons serving as leaders including classroom teachers, guidance counselors, or members of the clergy. Regardless of their professional backgrounds, Yalom et al. (1971) have revealed that leaders who are extremely active or passive during group sessions are less effective than leaders who are actively interested but relatively nondirective. The most important characteristic of an effective leader is that he or she not attempt to dominate the group. In other words, the successful leader must not act as an advice-giving paragon who has all the answers. Instead he or she must be a facilitator who oversees the formulation, development, and progress of the group by (1) carefully selecting each group member, (2) identifying group patterns, and (3) promoting group growth.

Group Formation   The initial responsibility of the group leader, the composition of the group, may be the most important task. In forming a group for developmental or remedial purposes, the therapist must consider both the needs of each individual and the needs of the group, and select members with great care. The inclusion of an inappropriate individual in a group might cause interactions that are so threatening that that member's personal discomfort is increased. Also, an individual might benefit from inclusion in a group, but his or her presence might seriously limit the therapeutic value of the sessions for all other members. Remedial groups provide the greatest challenge to effective group formation since each member has relatively serious emotional problems and can be expected to cope less effectively with a disruptive or disturbing member. Developmental groups present fewer problems, but even their effectiveness can be reduced by careless grouping.

Unfortunately, despite the emphasis on the importance of careful group formation, actual criteria for the selection of group members vary. Some experts recommend that developmental groups consist of individuals who share common characteristics, such as all rebellious adolescents or academic underachievers. Joel and Shapiro (1950) recommend that individuals have common emotional problems, for example, all withdrawn. Coffey (1948) and Winder (1945) believe that members should have fairly homogeneous backgrounds, such as all middle class or all well educated.

Other theorists have concluded that groups should include persons with varied personality structures and alternate types of problems (Ginott,

1961; Cohen, 1945; Glatzer, 1956). For example, aggressive, volatile persons should be mixed with overly anxious, controlled individuals and depressed persons. Slavson (1947) recommends mixed-sex groups to generate greater therapeutic action.

Powdermaker and Frank (1953) take a middle position when they conclude that common attributes for grouping such as age, sex, intelligence, education, or clinical diagnosis are important, but that their significance varies with each group. In other words, it might be important that one group include only members of like sex, whereas another group might be hampered by such a restriction. Consequently, the importance of each attribute can not be generalized to all group sessions.

Bach (1954) offers a technique to minimize the difficulties of group formation that he calls *nuclear expansion theory*. He recommends starting the group with two or three members and expanding it as the needs of those individuals become obvious. Thus, if an original member appears to require the steadying influence of an older more experienced person, one is added. If, on the other hand, the original group is focused exclusively on the problems of adolescence, only adolescents are added.

Brammer and Shostrom (1977) support Bach's theory but opt for a "balanced" approach. They recommend meeting the needs of the nucleus members by adding individuals who have opposite personality characteristics. For example, an extremely dominant, aggressive group member is balanced by the inclusion of a submissive, passive individual. The "opposite" submissive personality type is expected to provide a model of the behaviors that must be developed by the overly aggressive member. An alternate means of balancing a group is to select persons to fulfill role needs. For example, a group might be structured to include a father figure, a mother figure, a sex object, a delinquent, a moralizer, a self-punisher, a male hater, a female hater, and so forth.

Possibly it is less difficult to isolate persons who should be excluded from groups than it is to determine who should be included. Hobbs (1951) has found several types of persons who tend to disrupt or hinder group progress. They are

1. Psychologically sophisticated persons who use their knowledge to defend themselves from genuine interaction with the group or to dominate other members.
2. Extremely aggressive or hostile people who prevent the other group members from developing the feelings of acceptance and security necessary for the success of the group.
3. People who are in close contact with each other outside of the group.

Bach (1954) cites four personality criteria for exclusion of individuals from group therapy. He recommends excluding persons who

1. Have insufficient reality contact.
2. Demonstrate extremes of culturally taboo or illegal behavior.
3. Tend to chronically monopolize discussion.
4. Have impenetrable psychopathic or sociopathic characteristics.

Identifying Group Patterns   The second main part of the leader's responsibility is to identify the patterns of action and reaction demonstrated by each group member. Schutz (1975) has identified three types of patterns that reflect basic interpersonal needs. He calls them *inclusion, control,* and *affection* needs.

Inclusion is the need to be accepted as a worthwhile group member. During this stage in therapy, individuals demonstrate attention-seeking behaviors such as making too many remarks, making pompous statements, withdrawing, being an exhibitionist in dress or behavior, and making self-aggrandizing statements. Often the individual's concern about inclusion is voiced directly as feelings that he or she does not fit in with the other group members. Inclusion needs and fears are most obvious during the early stages of group therapy when each member is seeking to define his or her relationship with the other members.

Control needs involve the search for power and influence. Dominant, assertive individuals seek to extend their influence over less dominant, passive persons. They use manipulative techniques and strategies that range from positive offers of support and concern to negative expressions of contempt. Efforts to manipulate the group leader also occur. The control needs become apparent after the inclusion needs have been resolved. Once the members begin to feel comfortable about their positions in the group, they begin to develop concerns about those in charge and about their own relative power.

Affection needs become apparent after control needs are resolved. Both positive and negative feelings become pronounced and are openly expressed. Generally, dyads form as individuals ally themselves with some members and establish hostile interaction with others.

Other interactive patterns that the leader must recognize are various communication techniques used by group members to establish their position in the group. The most easily identified are verbal ploys. Brammer and Shostrom [1] (1977, p. 328) list typical examples.

> Appeal to reason and logic . . . "it seems only reasonable"
> Appeal to interest . . . "should be interesting"
> Appeal to sanity . . . "don't be foolish"

---

[1] Source: Lawrence M. Brammer, Everett L. Shostrom, *Therapeutic Psychology: Fundamentals of Counseling and Psychotherapy*, 1977. Reprinted by permission of Prentice-Hall, Inc., Englewood Cliffs, New Jersey.

Appeal to decorum and good taste . . . "not in mixed company"
Appeal to enjoyment . . . "might be fun to"
Appeal to need . . . "would help you to"

In addition to direct overt verbal approaches, individuals attempt to influence fellow members with indirect methods. For example, they might exploit personal characteristics such as differences in age, sex, or physical size. They also use status characteristics, such as vocation, education, or experience, to gain influence.

The final interactive patterns that the leader must be alert for involve nonverbal methods of communicating. These include *eye signals*—opening and closing eyes, staring; *body position*—slouching, rigidity, nonchalance; *head movements*—looking away, nodding, grimacing; and *physical actions*—fidgeting, hand clenching, foot tapping, table pounding. All aspects of the individual's physical bearing must be evaluated to glean his or her feelings about each topic under discussion.

The importance of the indirect message is illustrated by Satir (1966) who points out that group communication is always at two levels: the literal and the metacommunicative. It is the metacommunicative level that the leader must recognize, since that communication represents the speaker's feelings. Satir classifies communication patterns as:

1. literal message is agreement—affective message is placating
2. literal message is disagreement—affective message is blaming
3. literal message is changing the subject—affective message is withdrawing
4. literal message is being reasonable—affective message is conniving
5. literal message is reporting oneself—affective message is making a place for others.

These mixed messages or verbal games are often the basis for inadequate, unrewarding social relationships.

Promoting Group Growth The third important aspect of leadership is the extent to which the leader can help each member of the group reach new levels of personal understanding and develop more constructive methods of dealing with life situations. To facilitate group growth, the leader must help each member explore and solve problems without attempting to dominate the group. Brammer and Shostrom [2] (1977) present fifteen general leadership techniques that the effective leader can use. They are problem setting, process moderating, sentiment testing, idea developing, monitoring, energizing, group serving, content par-

---

[2] Source: Adapted from Lawrence M. Brammer, Everett L. Shostrom, *Therapeutic Psychology: Fundamentals of Counseling and Psychotherapy*, 1977. Reprinted by permission of Prentice-Hall, Inc., Englewood Cliffs, New Jersey.

ticipating, initiating, amending, supporting, opposing, summarizing, controlling, and informing.

Problem setting   The leader states and clarifies a problem to which the group might address itself. No attempt is made to suggest a solution. Problem setting may occur at the beginning of a session when the leader uses it as an impetus for the upcoming discussion. It may also occur during a session when an issue has become clouded or lost in discussion.

Process moderating   The leader attempts to structure the group proceedings by a series of procedural techniques. For example, he or she might influence the participation of respective group members by directing questions to some or by asking for an opinion. Other procedural techniques might be a call for order or a suggested recess. Process moderating structure pertains to the process of the meeting, not the content of the discussion.

Sentiment testing   The leader seeks to gauge group opinion on various issues. She or he may ask for a vote on an issue or state an impression and ask for group confirmation. For example, several members of the group may be interested in discussing the issue of racial prejudice. The leader may sense the group's interest in this topic and seek to confirm that impression.

Idea developing   The leader aids the group in clarifying its ideas about an issue. She or he may restate or summarize the remarks that have been made previously. Where conflict or disagreement exist, the leader may contrast the opposing positions. When developing ideas, the leader does not correct, alter, or add to the group's ideas. Nor does he or she express an opinion in cases of conflicting ideas. The leader's goal is to increase group understanding.

Monitoring   The leader ensures that the group observes the rules or limits under which it operates. For example, ground rules may have been set delineating time limits, barring profanity, assigning authority solely to the leader, and so forth. The leader must remind group members when they violate regulations.

Energizing   The leader attempts to motivate the group to further activity. She or he simply may remark on inactivity or may attempt to stimulate members into more productive lines of discussion with questions or remarks.

Group serving   The leader performs service functions such as record keeping, note taking, and so forth.

Content participation   The leader joins the discussion, giving opinions and impressions as another group member. She or he does not exercise leadership functions during this period of time.

Initiating The leader may propose new topics for discussion by stating new ideas or by extending old discussions. She or he seeks to stimulate further activity. This procedure is particularly valid when the group has become inactive.

Amending The leader develops ideas that the group is discussing. She or he does not initiate the idea, but modifies the group's statement. For example, the group might agree that parental overcontrol causes children to feel angry and hostile toward their parents. The leader might point out that their anger often is directed toward all authority figures, not just toward parents.

Supporting The leader acknowledges the validity of an idea being discussed by the group and seeks to accelerate its acceptance. She or he may, for instance, emphasize the relationship between parental overcontrol and children's anger by citing further examples or by giving additional reasons why this occurs.

Opposing The leader challenges or questions a group opinion, usually to persuade them to reconsider their ideas. For example, the group may be attributing all delinquent behavior to parental overcontrol and the leader may wish to change their attitudes.

Summarizing The leader discusses the main ideas brought forth during the group session.

Controlling The leader tries to insure that all group members get an opportunity to participate in the discussion. The more reticent members may be invited to join in.

Informing The leader gives the group factual information.

The Therapeutic Process

The discussion of leadership principles above makes it clear that group therapy is not simply a collection of individuals haphazardly discussing problems and concerns. Effective group sessions involve a clearly defined process through which each participant proceeds, step by step. Brammer and Shostrom [3] (1977, p. 101) identify seven steps in the therapeutic process:

1. Stating concerns and establishing a need.
2. Establishing the relationship.
3. Determining goals and structure.
4. Working on problems and goals.

---

[3] Source: Lawrence M. Brammer, Everett L. Shostrom, *Therapeutic Psychology: Fundamentals of Counseling and Psychotherapy*, 1977. Reprinted by permission of Prentice-Hall, Inc., Englewood Cliffs, New Jersey.

5. Facilitating awareness.
6. Planning a course of action.
7. Evaluating outcomes and terminating.

Step 1 *Stating concerns and establishing a need for help.* Individuals who are newly exposed to a therapeutic group are often confused or defensive about their reasons for joining. Even when they are self-referred, they may resist talking about their problems and question their real need for therapy. Their defenses include blaming others for their situations, "the teacher picks on me," or making general statements about problems that they expect someone else to solve for them. The leader's first goal is to help the individual establish his or her reason for attending. The second goal is to help the individual understand that a successful therapeutic situation requires that each group member take responsibility for his or her own welfare and make a commitment to hard work. Both goals reflect the fact that the individual must recognize a need to change.

Step 2 *Establishing a relationship.* There is increasing evidence (Barak and LaCrosse, 1975) that the success of therapeutic situations depends on the leader's credibility as a helpful, trustworthy person. Group members must perceive the leader as fair, objective, and concerned if the most constructive therapeutic relationship is to develop. The extent that they gain such perceptions depends largely on the leader's success in overcoming typical resistances to therapy.

The primary resistance reflects a cultural bias against seeking emotional support. Most persons are taught that they should be strong enough to solve their own problems through logic or rational thinking. Failure to do so suggests personal weakness, inferiority, or immaturity.

A second resistance involves concerns about privacy. On one level the individual may fear that the leader will elicit statements from him or her that are too revealing and which he or she may later regret. Another level involves fear of the unfamiliar. The individual may feel uneasy in a strange room with unfamiliar people.

A third resistance reflects the individual's lack of familiarity with group proceedings. The new participant may have little factual information about the operation of therapeutic groups, and therefore may be unsure of what to expect and how to behave.

The leader may help the individual overcome these resistances by acquainting him or her with the goals of group therapy, that is, what the participant can hope to accomplish. The leader may also explain the therapeutic process or the means of accomplishing goals, including the leader's role, the group rules, and each member's responsibilities. Such *structuring* of the group process usually makes the new member feel more secure about participating. There is evidence (Crider, 1964) that better informed individuals have more successful therapeutic experiences.

Another advantage to providing factual information about the group process is that it clarifies limitations. For example, a new participant who has unrealistic expectations about the leader's role should have these erroneous notions corrected to be spared the resulting disappointment when the leader does not meet these expectations. The leader should immediately project him- or herself as knowledgeable and honest about the process being undertaken. The new participant gains the type of impression about the leader's competence that is necessary for a trusting leader–client relationship.

Step 3 *Determining goals and structure.* At this step the individual is ready to decide what specific goals she or he wants to accomplish. The leader stimulates thought and discussion on this topic and helps the individual identify the specific behaviors that will lead to goal attainment. For example, a teenager may be concerned with increasing his or her popularity among his peers. One specific related goal may be to work harder at team sports, which he or she enjoys. Specific behaviors may involve attending each team practice, eating high-protein foods, and stopping smoking. To demonstrate a commitment toward self-help, the individual makes a *contract* with the group delineating all responsibilities. The contract is a key structural component of the group sessions.

Step 4 *Working on problems and goals.* This step of therapy signifies the beginning of hard work. The individual has begun to focus on obtaining specific goals and encounters predictable problems. She or he learns that goals are not easily attained and is often depressed by that information. For example, the person who decided to improve his or her popularity by joining an athletic team may find that practice sessions are difficult and may begin to doubt that persistence will allow the goal to be reached.

Also, at this step, another level of problem exploration may be uncovered as the individual thinks about his or her life situation and discovers information that had previously been ignored. For instance, the teenager may begin to examine his or her peer relationships more closely and discover that his or her inadequate social skills antagonize others. The definition of the problem may thus be altered and the teenager's goals may change accordingly. He or she may begin to focus on behaviors that will help build better relationships with others. Throughout this step, the leader must be responsive to the individual's changes in perceptions and attitudes. Once again, therapeutic goals and the process of obtaining them must be clarified.

Step 5 *Facilitating awareness.* This step in the therapeutic process is critical and the most difficult to attain. Often group members feel discouraged at step 4, when they begin to realize that personal change and growth depends on their own efforts. Thus, they may be defeated by the very dawning of the awareness necessary for successful therapy. The leader must reassure and prepare each person for those negative emotions if sessions are to continue. The individual must be encouraged to continue self-examination and to increase awareness.

In this context, awareness refers to gaining insight or understanding of one's problems. Although awareness of problems does not automatically result in their solution, most experts regard it as a necessary first step. Ellis (1963) distinguishes between two types of insight or awareness, "intellectual" and "emotional." Intellectual understanding of a problem occurs first when the individual begins to see previously hidden facts. Emotional insight, which is developed through increased understanding, is the process that really conveys a new view of life experiences. The individual recognizes that previous patterns of behavior were based on false assumptions and is now prepared to alter those behaviors.

Many traditional approaches to psychotherapy, particularly the psychoanalytic approach, have assumed that the development of insight or awareness was sufficient to reduce the symptoms of a problem. However, cognitive and behavioral theorists such as Ellis (1958) and London (1964) suggest that self-knowledge alone will not change behavior. Strategies for action or behavioral change must follow.

Step 6 *Planning a course of action.* At this point the individual is ready to apply new levels of awareness to life situations. The leader's responsibility is to help the individual to plan action that will result in successful, reinforcing life experiences. For example, the teenage boy with the social problem is ready to establish liaisons with others. He may select an individual and try out new social behaviors. If he experiences success and the person is responsive to his overtures, his need for therapeutic support lessens. Successful life experiences constitute the best possible reinforcement for his changed behavior.

Step 7 *Evaluating outcomes and termininating.* This step is more difficult than it may appear to be. Often successful therapy is prolonged needlessly because the client may fear regression if he or she leaves the group. The leader must be sensitive to this fear and encourage termination when the individual's goals for therapy have been met. In other cases the client may have made as much progress as possible and, although goals may not be met, there is little probability that further group involvement will alter that situation.

The greatest difficulty in recommending termination is related directly to the lack of criteria for judging progress. Internal feelings and personality change are difficult to measure, therefore improvement may not always be apparent. Simulation techniques that place the individual under stress in a clinical laboratory setting and charting reactions offer some promise as an evaluation tool, but they are still highly experimental. Currently, the leader's opinion and clinical judgment still remain the most used criteria for termination.

Therapeutic Techniques

The success with which the group proceeds through the steps of the therapeutic process just discussed depends primarily on the leader's skillful use of therapeutic techniques. As noted, leaders may operate from varied theoretical orientations that, to some extent, determine the techniques used to conduct therapy. However, many approaches to group therapy incorporate certain common procedures. These include leading techniques, listening techniques, reflecting techniques, structuring techniques, and reassurance methods (Brammer and Shostrom, 1977).

Leading Techniques These techniques involve the leader's attempts to direct the client's thinking. Leads may be direct, as in the form of a specific statement, such as "Tell me more about your mother!" or indirect, as in "What do you mean?" To apply these techniques properly, the therapist must lead the client into topics that he or she is ready to discuss. The skillful therapist never probes too far ahead of the client's previous remarks, but always moves in logical sequence from one point to the following point.

Listening Techniques These techniques involve the leader's ability to withhold comments and to permit the client to remain silent. Generally, group leaders feel under intense pressure to speak when there is a brief lull in conversation. Hypothetically, in a therapeutic situation silence serves an important function. The client can mull over an important thought, deal with painful feelings, generate the next point for discussion, cover embarrassment, and so forth, during silent periods. Should the client's silence reflect shyness or negativism, the leader's answering silence forces him or her to speak, since the client also is made uneasy by lags in the discussion. Since there is evidence (Carnes and Robinson, 1948) that a positive correlation exists between the proportion of client talk and the extent of client responsibility for the discussion, leader silence appears to be an important component to the success of therapy.

Reflecting Techniques These techniques use the leader's ability to paraphrase the ideas, attitudes, and opinions expressed by the client. The leader uses reflection to pinpoint or clarify the underlying feeling in the client's statements. For example, when the client remarks: "The kids in this school aren't as nice as my friends in my old school," the leader might reflect: "You miss your old friends and feel that you might not make new friends in this school." In this reflection, the leader has focused on the feelings that he or she perceives to be underlying the client's statement. The actual content of the statement, the relative niceness of the children attending both schools, is not the critical component. In fact, reflecting content is considered to be an error in therapeutic technique, since the idea is to convey understanding of the client's communication, not simply to parrot his or her remarks.

According to Brammer and Shostrom (1977), key aspects of reflecting techniques are depth, meaning, and language. *Depth* refers to the degree of feeling conveyed in reflection. Ideally, the depth of the reflection should correspond to the depth of the client's remarks. If, for instance, the leader in responding to the remark illustrated above said "You have difficulty making friends," his reflection would be "too deep." If she or he said "The kids in the new school aren't nice," the reflection would be "too shallow."

Meaning refers to the fact that a reflection should convey the same message represented in the client's statement. The reflection "You have difficulty making friends," not only violates the depth rule, but it interjects a meaning not implied in the client's statement.

Finally, the language used in the reflection must be appropriate to the situation. Clearly, a reflection to our example remark such as "Your social interactions in your current educational environment are less than gratifying," would serve only to confound the client and to stifle further remarks.

Reflecting techniques may be used immediately after the client's remarks or as a summary. The immediate reflection has been demonstrated in the examples given previously. The summary reflection involves formulating one statement that incorporates the underlying feelings in many of the client's statements. For example, after listening to a client talk about social relationships and school experiences, the leader might reflect: "Your comments today all seem to convey your feelings of doubt and depression over attending your new school."

Structuring Techniques   Structuring techniques provide a framework for the therapeutic situation. Most experts (May, 1939; Bixler, 1949; Curran, 1944) believe that the leader must reduce ambiguity in therapy by clearly defining the goals, establishing the limits, and clarifying the conditions of the therapeutic process. Lack of structure creates unrealistic expectations about therapy, tending to perpetuate naive beliefs in magical cures and therapist infallibility. Also, ambiguous situations, where an individual does not know what to expect and cannot see an overall pattern to his or her activities, tend to produce anxiety and insecurity. Methods for structuring therapeutic situations include contracts, time limits, action limits, role limits, and procedural limits (Brammer and Shostrom, 1977).

Contracts are formal agreements between client and leader that document the specific, feasible goals of therapy. The client's responsibilities are delineated clearly and criteria for goal attainment are decided. For instance, the client may decide to control excess drinking that both she or he and the leader view as a serious obstacle to healthy personal and social adjustment. A criterion for goal attainment may be that the client drink no more than one 4-ounce glass of wine daily. The advantage of the contract is that the burden for personal change and growth is placed squarely on the client. The therapist may facilitate growth but the client must do the hard work. Also, establishing clear criteria for behavioral change allows the client to recognize when the goal has been met.

Time limits are usually established during the initial meeting. The leader specifies how much time may be spent in each session. The leader also may estimate the number of sessions that may prove necessary.

Action limits refer to control of physical behavior. Clients in permissive group situations usually are permitted great freedom to verbalize attitudes or emotions, but they are not permitted to act out at will. For example, breaking furniture or assaulting another person are taboo, regardless of the level of emotional intensity being experienced.

Role limits pertain to clarification of the client's expectations when one individual functions as leader and in other roles. For example, the client must be aware that a teacher functioning as a therapist may accept behaviors in the therapeutic situation that are not acceptable in the classroom.

Procedural limits refer to the general operation of the therapeutic process. The therapist must reinforce consistently the principles that successful therapy is possible only if the client accepts the notions that (1) self-study is valuable and necessary for change, (2) self-study is not designed to affix blame, but to increase understanding, (3) the demonstration of emotion is not a sign of weakness, and (4) values and attitudes can change.

Reassurance methods are designed to convey support to the individual as he or she grapples with issues and feelings that may induce anxiety. Reassurance tells the individual that she or he is capable of solving personal problems. It also assures the client that, in therapy, his or her attitudes are accepted. Finally, it reinforces the client's efforts to display newer, more constructive behavior patterns. Typical reassurance techniques include approving remarks, predictive statements, factual input, and affiliative gestures.

Approving remarks are self-explanatory. The leader simply tells the client that his or her judgment is good, that he or she is on the right track, and so forth. Predictive statements refer to projections about upcoming experiences such as "You may feel upset after you leave today." They also may be references to experiences that the leader assumes the client has undergone, such as "Last week probably was a tough one for you." Factual input involves statements such as "People generally feel depressed when they grapple with an issue like this one." Affiliative gestures include touching, patting, nodding, smiling, or any nonverbal activity that gives support to the client.

SPECIFIC APPROACHES TO GROUP THERAPY

The three topics that have been discussed, leadership principles, the therapeutic process, and therapeutic techniques, represent an analysis of general group dynamics. As noted, specific group therapeutic procedures have emanated from a variety of psychological orientations. Some of the more popular approaches will be discussed in this section of the chapter.

The Psychoanalytic Approach

Freudian Therapy   This approach to group therapy reflects the principles of Freud (1935) and his disciples. The most important psychoanalytic notion is that behavior is motivated by unconscious, dynamic forces. To use Freud's analogy, personality structure is like an iceberg. By far the largest proportion is submerged below a readily perceptible level. These submerged dimensions, unconscious, irrational, pleasure-seeking, and sexual drives, are the essence of personality. They are far more important than the superficial characteristics that are easily observed. Successful therapy depends on the extent to which an individual's unconscious motivation can be brought to light and understood. To accomplish this task, an individual's feelings must be analyzed to discover their foundations, rooted somewhere in the past. Discussions of an individual's early history, particularly parent-child interactions, are perceived as the key to understanding problems. The individual must be helped to recognize feelings that were repressed long ago. It is these repressed feelings, blocked from conscious awareness, that evoke debilitating anxiety or generate psychological defense mechanisms. In effect, these emotions drive the individual to act in ways she or he doesn't understand. Once they are recognized openly and the individual develops insight into the causes of the problems, the behaviors symptomatic of emotional disturbance will disappear or be alleviated.

The therapeutic techniques used to help the individual uncover deeply hidden emotions involve interpretation of past and present behaviors, as well as analysis of dreams and fantasies. Through the principal procedure, free association, the person is encouraged to allow his or her mind to travel back to earlier periods of life and to reexperience the feelings generated during that time. The process of psychoanalysis is quite lengthy and treatments typically take between two and five years.

Freud has noted in *Group Psychology and the Analysis of the Ego* (1921) the unique processes of group therapy. He equated the leader's role as the symbolic father figure—stern, disapproving, and correcting, while the group assumes the mother figure role—accepting and approving. Thus, the original family constellation is reestablished in groups. Through the critical process of transference, the leader becomes the target of the love and hate emotions that each member originally felt for his or her parents.

Freud also believed that a second unique component of group therapy involved identification. He isolated three types of identification: first, an emotional tie with someone; second, the introjection of someone into the ego, and third, the perception of a common quality shared with someone. The types of identification operating within the group are indicative of each participant's ego ideal, that is, the characteristics she or he would most like to display.

In an analytic group the leader gives direct suggestions and offers interpretations of the client's behaviors. Particular attention is devoted to the interpretation of transference feelings and to the analysis of the client's resistances to the proceedings. In effect, the leader *tells* the client what she or he has observed in the therapy sessions and suggests the reasons underlying the observed behaviors.

Adler's Social-Ecological Approach   Although much psychoanalysis follows the stream of classic Freudian therapy, the approach is not without its varied branches. Several of Freud's contemporaries modified his emphasis on children's early sexual development, therefore their approaches to psychoanalysis have varied thrusts. Possibly, the most important modifications of Freudian theory are represented in the work of Alfred Adler and his social-ecological approach to group therapy.

Adler emphasized that we are social beings. He saw human behavior as goal directed and purposive, as opposed to the Freudian instinctual-biological premise. His key principles are *status or power motives, style of life,* and the *unity of personality.* Deemphasizing sexual drives, Adler believed that the need for status or power motivated human behavior. He perceived human beings as striving to compensate for inferiority feelings that were developed through unsatisfactory early social relationships. In effect, our choice of life goals is determined by our inferiority complexes. Life goals, in turn, reflect an individual's style of life, that is, the individual's unique way of perceiving and behaving in the social environment. A vast difference exists between an individual's stated or conscious life goals and the unconscious goals that are the real determinants of behavior.

Adler's emphasis on the unity of personality reflected his belief that a person must be considered as a whole. To understand an individual as a totality, it is necessary to adopt a phenomenological perspective, to view the individual as a self-determined force pursuing personal goals in a unique fashion.

The thrust of Adlerian therapy is to determine the individual's real goals, and to substitute them for the fictitious goals she or he might profess. Real or basic goals are reflected by the individual's past. A person consistently engages in behaviors that meet psychological needs regardless of how unrewarding they may appear to be. For example, a woman marries three different men, all of whom beat her. She attributes her behavior to fictitious goals—the desire for financial security, the desire for a stable married life, and soon. Her consistent selection of unsuitable mates, however, suggests that she is driven by alternate, self-destructive goals.

An additional clue to an individual's real goals are early recollections. Early recollections are events that fit into a person's concept of life. They are "biased" recollections that permit the individual to maintain basic convictions regardless of how incorrect they may be. For example, an individual may remember his or her parents as being harsh and unloving. The individual recollects only events that support this conviction despite the fact that she or he may have experienced many happy family interactions. Primary among "biased" recollections are those that lead to the development of inferiority feelings.

According to Brammer and Shostrom (1977) the basic dimensions of Adlerian group therapy are (1) establishment of a therapeutic relationship, (2) exploration of the client's underlying dynamics, (3) promotion of insight through the communication of these dynamics to the client, and (4) a reorientation. Adlerians believe that the client's therapeutic relationship to the therapist is enhanced by the group. The cornerstones of the relationship, confidence and trust, are contagious. They spread from one participant to another.

The exploration of the client's underlying dynamics also is made easier in a group because the leader can observe the client's interaction with others. Similarly the group facilitates the third dimension, the development of insight. At this step, the therapist's interpretation of dynamics to a client often evokes resistance. The client does not believe or accept the interpretation. In the group setting, each person observes the resistant behavior of others. Group members aid the therapist in pointing out the resistance and in supporting the validity of the dynamic interpretation.

Reorientation involves relinquishing faulty premises that have dominated the individual's life-style. This is accomplished when inferiority feelings are removed and self-respect is increased. The group aids in this process not only by helping the individual recognize faulty premises, but also by communicating their support for efforts to select new life goals.

Jung and Rank   Other deviations from Freud's approach to psycho-analysis by his disciples include the work of Jung (1933) and Rank (1947). Jung focused on the paradoxical nature of human personality, such as the masculinity–femininity components of every individual. In addition to human personality paradoxes, he saw problems arising from denial or repression of archetypes that he defined as collections of primordial universal motives. Jungian therapy stresses the development of the self through a mystical or religious like acceptance of human importance in the universe.

Rank advanced the notion that birth trauma or loss of security over separation from the mother is the basic precipitator of ongoing personality problems. His major deviation from Freud's perspective was his positive view of human beings as possessing a will to select their paths through life. Rankian therapy involves helping the individual recognize his or her true values and beliefs. In so doing, the current events of the client's life assume far more importance than past history. As the person is perceived as being capable of assuming responsibility for his or her own welfare, the Rankian therapist is less directive than the strictly Freudian therapist.

Neo-Analysis

Sullivan's Interpersonal Theory   Freud's ideas influenced not only his contemporaries but many other modern theorists. Sullivan (1953) modified the psychoanalytic position to emphasize *interpersonal relationships.* Borrowing from sociology, he developed the idea of cultural roles determining individual behavior. He noted that individuals can be understood only when their behavior is viewed in particular social situations, such as family, work, and school. Each life situation requires a unique type of social role. Individuals may succeed at some and fail at others.

Sullivan's second key principle is the *self system,* which evolves through interaction with others throughout life. When an individual's inherent needs for acceptance and security are not fulfilled in social contacts, the self system is disturbed. Anxiety is generated and the person develops specific dynamisms or characteristic patterns of behavior that signify his or her unique self system. In other words, the nature of the specific dynamisms displayed, obsessionalism, aggression, passivity, and so forth, characterize the individual.

Sullivan's interpersonal therapy involves acquainting the person with the processes and techniques that she or he uses to avoid anxiety. She or he must be brought to see that anxiety responses evolve from historical events in life as one interacts with significant persons. An individual's anxiety responses make sense only when they are viewed as products of interactions with others. To alleviate the anxiety, an individual must reexperience significant interactions. She or he must symbolically relive the experiences that contributed to the development of the problem. To help the person accomplish this goal the therapist must understand the need for social acceptance that underlies most negative or maladaptive behavior. She or he must provide such acceptance to the individual by establishing a warm, supportive therapeutic environment. A primary therapeutic goal is to help the individual increase his or her feelings of self-worth. Therefore a client's behaviors or attitudes that typically have contaminated interpersonal relationships do not result in rejection from the therapy group. The therapist remains cognizant that those behaviors are not novel to the therapeutic situation, but reflect the client's displaced feeling from previous social interactions. The therapist strives to maintain open communication, which is the key to understanding the client.

Horney's Sociocultural Approach   Another analytically oriented theorist, Horney (1939, 1950) also stresses the sociocultural determinants of behavior. Faulty human relationships are the source of personal disturbances. These relationships, which are encountered throughout childhood, cause the individual to develop a unique personality that predisposes him or her to later difficulties. Many of the early tensions and frustrations encountered by an individual are induced by contradicting cultural forces. For example, there is great social emphasis upon competition, yet children are also expected to be cooperative. Such cultural conflicts are internalized. An individual may become torn between the appropriateness of aggression versus submissive behaviors, or between self-aggrandizement and self-sacrifice. Normal anxiety, which is realistic fear of concrete events such as death, is replaced by neurotic anxiety, which reflects fear of a world perceived as hostile and confusing. In turn, neurotic anxiety generates neurotic hostility, as the anger caused by social pressures is expressed inappropriately.

From Horney's point of view, therapy is designed to help the individual recognize the cultural conflicts that induce personal problems. Neurotic anxiety that causes the individual to experience, in Horney's words, "alienation from self" and the "tyranny of the shoulds," must be uncovered. The individual alienated from self feels dissociated from his or her thoughts and feelings. The individual feels powerless to direct or control behavior. The tyranny of the shoulds reflects the individual's neurotic perceptions that life should be perfect, that one should never make errors, one should be liked by everyone, and so forth. The therapist seeks to promote self-acceptance, by increasing the individual's responsibility for self-welfare and emphasizing the realities of the world we live in.

Fromm and Menninger   Like Sullivan and Horney, Fromm (1947) stresses social influences on individual behavior. Fromm's principal contribution was to apply the concept of "self-realization" to the therapeutic situation. The purpose of therapy is to promote personal growth through the recognition of strengths and assets. The individual is viewed as a victim of social inconsistencies and contradictions that are manifested in social interactions. She or he has the power to recognize the debilitating effects of social experiences and to restructure his or her social behaviors. The therapist's ultimate goal is to help the individual experience "mature love," which transcends the infantile, dependent social relationships that may have previously passed for love.

Another neo-analyst, Karl Menninger (1958) also incorporates social forces into the motives that underlie human behavior. His theory is of interest because he delineates the steps of interpretation in therapy that enable the patient to develop insight into his or her problems. Menninger notes that the first step is *preparation for interpretation*. This step involves identifying common elements occurring throughout the individual's life, for example, the way the client typically handles stress, or the feelings the client usually evokes in others.

The next step involves *content interpretation*. The therapist tells the patient about the key behaviors that cause personal difficulties. The therapist also points out the probable reasons for the behaviors. Usually, this stage of interpretation evokes resistance from the person in the form of misunderstanding, justifications, depressions, and so on.

The advent of resistances indicates the necessity for the third step, the *interpretation of resistances*. At this stage the therapist points out that the individual is resisting, indicates how she or he is resisting, and speculates about the purpose of the resistance.

The fourth step focuses on *transference interpretation*. The individual's attempts to manipulate the therapist through flattery, bribery, negativism, seduction, and the like are discussed.

Finally, the last step, *repeat interpretations,* is reached. The client's resistances, which occur periodically throughout the sessions, are pointed out as they occur. The therapist must repeat interpretations until they are internalized by the client.

Transactional Analysis   Eric Berne's (1961) neo-analytic contributions are represented in a therapeutic approach called *transactional analysis*. His principal postulate is that every individual is a combination of three basic ego states: parent, adult, and child. The parent ego is akin to the Freudian superego, encompassing the person's internalization of parental morality. The child ego resembles the Freudian id, or the person's basic desires for need gratification. The adult ego is similar to the Freudian ego and generates rational, adaptive, realistic behaviors. Any of these ego states may be used in social interactions. For instance, persons who typically respond to criticism with tantrums may be using their child ego to reply to another person's parent ego.

Berne calls these typical response patterns *games*, which are used either to manipulate others or to defend against others. The goal of therapy is to help individuals reconstruct their life styles, that is, to change the types of games that they play under certain social conditions. Individuals are brought to understand their use of ego states by analyzing personal communications with others. After individuals learn to recognize the situations that trigger child or parent behaviors, they are helped to substitute adult behaviors.

In summation, it can be noted that the neo-analysts differ from the traditional psychoanalysts in placing greater emphasis on sociocultural events, deemphasizing the past and emphasizing the present, placing greater stress on the client's ability to take responsibility for his or her life, deemphasizing sexual needs as the cause of maladjustment, and stressing cognitive rather than emotional approaches to problem solving. In fact, many aspects of their theoretical positions are shared by the next group of theorists to be discussed, those embracing a phenomenological or "self" approach.

The Phenomenological Approach

The phenomenological or self approaches to group therapy emanate from a variety of theoretical perspectives. Actually, the historical backgrounds of this school of therapy are so diverse that the inclusion of the theorists in this section was based entirely on the emphasis they gave to the concepts of phenomenology and self. Clearly, they differ on many other theoretical and operational points.

Phenomenology reflects the notion that a person's reality is that which is perceived. The significance of events is determined by the individual's view of them. For example, if three persons see an accident, their views or perceptions of reality, what actually happened, may differ dramatically. Thus, the emphasis in the phenomenological approach to therapy is on discerning an individual's internal frame of reference—the manner in which the client views himself or herself and the environment. The bond of understanding established between the therapist and the client must exceed intellectual awareness. It must be based upon empathy, or the ability to feel as the client does. In other words, the therapist must "walk in the client's shoes." To reach this level of understanding, the therapist must accept the client's perception of events without attempting to correct them or to substitute personal perceptions.

Client-Centered Therapy A key tenet of the phenomenological approach is "self-concept." Although the concept of a self did not originate with the phenomenological theorists, it gained prominence in the 1940's with the advent of Carl Rogers's client-centered or nondirective therapy. Rogers (1942, 1951) viewed the self as a dynamic organization of concepts, values, goals, and ideals that determine behavior. In simpler terms, self is the individual's inner portrait, the totality of I or me.

From Rogers's perspective, the concept of self is learned from direct experiences throughout life. A child's early experiences are particularly important, since parental perceptions contribute directly to the development of self-perceptions. As the individual matures the self-portrait becomes more clearly defined. The self is seen as unique, with individual needs, capacities, values, and aspirations. The individual develops an internal sense of self, which determines behavior.

According to Rogers, emotional disturbance results when the individual behaves in a manner not in accord with self-concept. The knowledge that behavior is not in accordance with values and ideals causes the individual to feel insecure and anxious. To alleviate anxiety or the threat to self-perceptions caused by the conflict, the individual uses defense mechanisms. For example, a young man who regards himself as an independent, self-sufficient person, yet behaves in a dependent manner when he interacts with his parents, for example, takes money from them, permits them to solve his problems, and so on, may use the defense mechanism of rationalization; "I'll only take their money until I find a better job" to alleviate anxiety.

A related concept that pertains to emotional disturbance is *congruence*. Rogers defined congruence as a close matching of awareness and experience. Congruent individuals will communicate accurately their feelings about life events because they are aware of those feelings. Incongruent persons will communicate feelings that they are not really experiencing because their "self" defenses prevent an accurate perception of true emotions.

According to Rogers, the therapist's role is to establish a relationship with the client that is so nonthreatening and secure that the client can penetrate his or her own defenses and gain levels of awareness that were previously blocked. The therapist is nondirective. Also, the therapist does not dispute the client's interpretations of life situations, nor attempt to provide solutions to the client's problems. Such directive activity tends only to evoke further defensiveness as the client attempts to protect his or her self. Instead of attempting to provide the answers, the therapist must encourage the client to probe further into his or her self, gain fresh insights, and, in so doing, discover new answers to old problems.

Rogers's emphasis on the client's ability to increase awareness without overt direction by the therapist illustrates another tenet associated with the phenomenological approach, the self-actualization motive. The phenomenologists believe that all individuals have an inherent drive toward self-improvement. Human beings seek to live the fullest, most rewarding life possible. Deviations from the path of self-fulfillment to avenues of behavior that are detrimental or destructive to self, reflect a distortion of this innately determined developmental process. Given the opportunity, in a constructive, supportive therapeutic environment, the individual will abandon self-destructive behavior and return to a life-style that will lead to self-actualization.

Clearly, phenomenological therapy focuses on the uniqueness of each individual. A person's symptomatic behaviors are not viewed in terms of categories of maladjustment, for example, obsessive-compulsive or un-socialized-aggressive conditions. The therapist attempts to explore the client's specific phenomenological field, assuming that his or her percep-tions cannot be the same as another person's perceptions.

Also, the responsibility for growth lies with the client. The therapist's role is to help the client clarify feelings, gain new insights, and plan new behavior that will reflect a new outlook on life. However, the client must make a commitment to change. Without that commitment therapy can-not possibly succeed. The therapist facilitates this commitment by com-municating concern and regard for the client, and by establishing a trust-ing relationship.

Maslow's Theory of Needs   Many of the phenomenological theorists have adopted approaches that closely parallel Rogers's. Others hold similar ideas but add unique contributions. In the latter category is Abraham Maslow (1954), who incorporates the concept of basic human needs to his phenomenological theory. Maslow sees all human behavior as need fulfilling. At the most basic level are survival needs such as the need for food and water. In hierarchical fashion, needs become progressively more social. Thus, for the mature individual the need for love and accep-tance assumes major importance. When needs are not gratified, the individual is barred from the ultimate goal of life, self-actualization. The unfulfilled individual becomes despondent and alienated.

From Maslow's perspective, therapy involves helping the person to recognize ungratified needs and to plan steps that will lead to their ful-fillment. An additional therapeutic goal is to determine what type of life situation will lead each person to self-actualization and to direct behavior toward that life situation. For example, the successful executive who is despondent despite financial success, may need to recognize that his or her striving for self-actualization will be satisfied only when he or she resigns and becomes a farmer. As in Rogerian therapy, the relationship between the therapist and the individual is of primary importance to the success of the endeavor. Acceptance, trust, and understanding of the client's phenomenological space are all keystones in the therapeutic process.

Gestalt Therapy   Gestalt therapy, formulated by Perls, Goodman, and Hefferline (1951) also encompasses many key phenomenological constructs. Once again, the importance of the individual's unique perceptual field is stressed. The therapist must see through the client's eyes. Also, the focus of therapy is to provide opportunities for self-discovery, not to interpret the individual's behavior. Increased awareness or insight is a necessary ingredient in the development of more adaptive behavior. Although a system of needs culminating in self-actualization is not given the emphasis it receives in Maslow's theory, a similar notion is drawn from Gestalt psychology, the principle of the "good gestalt."

The *good gestalt principle* states that an individual is innately driven to move toward the most orderly, adaptive, rewarding life-style possible. In other words, an individual will instinctively attempt to structure the environment in a manner that is most beneficial to him-/herself. Thus, as environmental experiences produce conflicts and generate tension, the person acts to alleviate tension by reorganizing the forces causing it.

As for therapeutic techniques, Levitshy and Perls (1969) have developed rules for therapy which include: (1) the principle of the "now," (2) I and thou, (3) "It" language and "I" language, (4) the "awareness continuum" or the "how" of experience, (5) no gossiping, and (6) on asking questions.

The principle of "now" refers to the emphasis in Gestalt theory on immediate behaviors and current events, feelings, attitudes, and so on. To promote now awareness, communication is usually in the present tense. The idea is to explore present awareness and to discourage intellectualizations about past events. In therapy, even events of yesterday or last week must be referred to in present terms.

I and thou illustrates the belief that true communication involves both the sender and the receiver. The client is forced to realize that what she or he says reaches another person. The client must consider how far she or he is willing to touch the other person with words, whether the client is willing to make genuine contact as opposed to engaging in the usual impersonal conversations that mark most social interaction.

The "it" language and "I" language rule deals with the semantics of involvement. The Gestaltists maintain that most persons erect barriers between themselves and others by avoiding references to I. For example, an individual might say "That's a nice tie," rather than, "I like your tie." In therapy clients are encouraged to use the I form on the assumption that it forces them to be less impersonal and to become more involved with others. Also, the client is more likely to see him- or herself as an active agent who does things rather than as a passive person to whom things happen.

The use of the awareness continuum is a basic Gestalt rule. It is designed to lead the client away from emphasis on the "why" of behavior, toward the "what" and "how" of behavior. The client is asked: "What are you aware of?" or "How do you feel?" According to Perls, the idea behind such questions is to help the client "lose his mind and come to his senses." The client must distinguish between reality and his or her fear-evoking fantasies.

The no gossiping rule is designed to force group members to talk to each other rather than about each other. For instance, a person may not say: "The trouble with Bill is . . . ," but must say "Bill, your trouble is . . . ." The premise behind this rule is that people often gossip about an individual when they cannot cope with the feelings that individual evokes in them. The no gossiping rule facilitates direct confrontation of feelings.

On asking questions refers to the client's defensive use of questions. Gestalt therapists point out that many questions are not formulated to seek information, but are used to avoid making definitive statements.

Perls (1969) sums up the emphasis in Gestalt therapy. A critical component is the *here and now*, the individual's immediate behaviors rather than the possible historic cause for those behaviors. The second major premise involves the notion of *personal encounter*. In Gestalt therapy, the individual is not permitted to hide behind defenses. Defense mechanisms such as rationalization, denial, and intellectualizations, or manipulative techniques such as flattery, seductiveness, helplessness, and boasting are recognized and challenged by the group and/or therapist. Thus, the client is permitted no escape from self-examination. She or he must face certain realities that have been previously avoided.

The Gestalt use of encounter as a therapeutic technique is obviously quite different from the Rogers's or Maslow's emphasis on a warm, accepting therapeutic environment. Far from feeling comfortable in Gestalt therapy, the individual is deliberately made to feel uncomfortable. Theoretically, the client benefits from this treatment because she or he is prevented from wasting time and is forced to deal with the problems that brought him or her to therapy.

In summary, the phenomenological approach generally emphasizes

1. The here and now rather than the past,
2. The uniqueness of the client,
3. The client's responsibility and ability to solve his or her problems,
4. The importance of the client's unique perceptions,
5. A warm, intimate client-therapist relationship,
6. Little direct interpretation of client behaviors by the therapist,
7. Insight learning that underlies new behaviors and personal growth.

Behavioral Approach

The behavioral approach to group therapy is based on the notion that symptoms of emotional disturbance are simply maladaptive learned behaviors. They are responses to direct or implicit stimuli. Since maladaptive behaviors are learned as any other response is learned, they can be altered.

The goals of behavioral therapy are stated only in objective terms, that is, as overt, measurable behaviors. There is no attempt to draw inferences about conscious or unconscious personality dynamics. The emphasis is on cognitive processes and how they can be altered to produce behavioral change, rather than on emotions or feelings.

Behavior Modification   The application of learning theory as a therapeutic tool has traditionally been along two avenues: behavior modification and behavior therapy. Behavior modification, an application of Skinner's operant conditioning principles, is based on the premise that the overt behaviors or responses that an individual demonstrates are determined by reinforcement. A behavior that is positively reinforced or rewarded occurs again, whereas those that are not reinforced extinguish or disappear. Reinforced responses associated with one stimuli generalize to similar stimuli.

Goal-Oriented Behavior   Similarly, most behavioral therapies also stress principles of reinforcement. Dollard and Miller (1950) have theorized that behavior is goal-oriented. Individuals have basic physiological drives and secondary social motives that cause them to act. An environmental stimuli or cue provokes a response that gratifies or rewards the individual by reducing the drive or satisfying the social motive. The response is maintained. Successful therapy depends on identifying environmental cues and substituting adaptive responses for maladaptive responses.

Desensitization   Wolpe (1958) has popularized a distinctive method of behavioral therapy which he terms *desensitization*. This technique involves exposing the individual to increasing amounts of anxiety-evoking stimuli until the client no longer emits the maladaptive response. Simultaneously, the individual undergoes training in relaxation methods. The goal involves substitution of a relaxation response for the maladaptive response. For example, an individual who has a pathological fear of animals is exposed to associated stimuli that are below his or her anxiety threshold, such as pictures of animals. In response to the pictures the client consciously practices relaxation. The stimulus gradually is made more similar to that which evokes anxiety. A stuffed animal might be introduced, then a small baby animal such as a kitten. The sequenced introduction of stimuli desensitizes the individual to the stimulus that formerly evoked a fear response.

Interference Therapy Phillips (1956) has evolved another adaptation of learning principles called *interference therapy*. This approach establishes conditions that interfere with the individual's customary maladaptive behavior, thereby forcing him or her to develop new ways of responding to the environment. For example, an individual who typically withdraws from an unpleasant task by physically leaving the premises is placed in a situation where she or he cannot leave. No effort is made to uncover the individual's deep feelings or to examine defense mechanisms. The individual simply must display a new response in the situation.

The behavioral approach differs significantly from both the psychoanalytical and phenomenological models. Behavioral therapists

1. Focus on current behavior, not past events,
2. Establish new learning in place of old maladaptive responses,
3. Emphasize learning, not emotions or feelings,
4. Are directive rather than permissive and accepting,
5. Have highly structured systematic procedures for altering behavior,
6. Are unconcerned with underlying motivation or defense mechanisms,
7. Are action-oriented in that the client must engage in behaviors other than verbal discussion.

Rational Approach

The rational approach to group therapy bears some resemblance to behaviorism in its emphasis on cognitive processes. The guiding principle is that human beings are rational, capable of controlling their behaviors by changing their thought processes. This approach is best illustrated by Albert Ellis's rational-emotive system of psychotherapy.

Ellis's Rational-Emotive System Ellis (1958) bases his approach on the notion that people become emotionally disturbed because they acquire irrational thoughts or attitudes. These distorted or irrational thoughts actually constitute the feelings or sensations referred to as *emotion*. The therapist's task is to show the person that his or her emotions arise from irrational thinking, not from past events or external pressures. In effect, disturbance is not caused by the behavior of others, but by the individual's thoughts about his or her behavior. The solution is to attack the person's irrational beliefs and show how emotional problems are maintained by continuing to believe them. Discussions of possible historic causes of disturbed thoughts are deemphasized. Instead, the client must examine his or her illogical thoughts and identify the self-talk that is tension-evoking. Verbalizations in therapy help clarify those thoughts.

As Ellis sees it, successful therapy depends on the client's willingness to replace his or her illogical thoughts and ideas with healthy, rational substitutes, then to engage in behaviors or activities that test the validity of his or her new assumptions about life.

Grossman's Hyperbolic Approach   A less encompassing approach that also focuses on cognitive processes is Grossman's hyperbolic approach (1964). Grossman attempts to reorient the client's values by exaggerating his or her typical defenses. He recommends strategies such as humor, sarcasm, and ridicule to induce the client to see the absurdities of his or her behavior. For example, a client who typically responds to mild criticism with pouting and silence is teased about his or her behavior or is exposed to exaggerated pouting by others in the group. The individual is helped to see that his or her behavior is irrational and is encouraged to develop a more rational attitude toward criticism.

Reality Therapy   Another rational approach to therapy, William Glasser's reality therapy, is quite well known in educational settings. Reality therapy is based on the premise that in the early, formative years, the individual develops a basic sense of right and wrong that serves as the foundation of his or her value system throughout life. Emotional difficulties occur when the individual's behavior runs contrary to this basic sense of right and wrong.

The thrust of therapy is to help the individual clarify basic values, examine behavior, recognize the inconsistencies between values and behavior, and plan future actions to eliminate the conflict. In Glasser's terminology, the individual must learn to do what is *realistic, responsible,* and *right.*

Right or correct behaviors are those reflecting the therapist's value judgments. High moral standards are an integral part of correct behavior. The therapist must convey those standards to the client confused about his or her values.

Responsibility refers to the individual's ability to meet life's demands without evasion or excuses. The individual must be responsible for all his or her acts. Only responsible behavior will lead to the fulfillment of needs. In effect, the individual gets from life what he or she earns or deserves. According to Glasser, "People do not act irresponsibly because they are ill; they are ill because they act irresponsibly." The therapist must always emphasize responsibility by helping the client examine his or her behavior in the "here and now," pointing out the relationship between irresponsible acts and unfavorable life situations, and refusing to accept excuses, rationalizations, or justifications for behavior.

Realism refers to awareness of the consequences of behavior that are facts of life. For example, individual may break laws, offend neighbors, or make rude remarks. Such behavior is unrealistic because she or he ignores its consequences. The therapist must help the client recognize the cost of maladaptive acts by emphasizing their realistic outcomes— the trouble they cause the perpetrator.

In summary, the rational approach to therapy

1. Focuses on current events in the individual's life,
2. Emphasizes cognitive control over self,
3. Attributes emotional disturbance to faulty thought processes,
4. Places the responsibility for improvement on the individual,
5. Emphasizes reality rather than acceptance of an individual's unique perceptions.

Bioenergetic Approach

The therapeutic approaches discussed thus far have, for the most part, used a verbal format. An alternate approach that de-emphasizes discussion or verbal exchanges in favor of movement or physical behaviors also warrants inclusion in this section of the chapter. The bioenergetic approach to group therapy as described by Lowen (1969) is based on the direct involvement of the body in the therapeutic process. The body is involved to the extent that (1) it is sufficiently visible so that it's form and movement can be observed, (2) control of breathing and movement can facilitate the expression of feeling, and (3) direct physical contact between client and therapist can occur.

One rationale for this approach is to obviate the dichotomy between mind and body that dominates many verbal psychotherapeutic approaches. Although verbal dialogue is part of the bioenergetic approach, it is not the sole mode of interaction. Another rationale is that the active involvement of the body in therapy adds an experience that is more meaningful than that gained in simple verbal therapy. It generates a psychic sensation of reliving significant experiences that in theory helps to ensure that the client gains more than an intellectual comprehension of his or her problems.

A third rationale is that one gains immediate access to the emotions through the body. Theoretically, the body has self-regulatory processes that, if unimpeded by artificial intellectual controls, will direct the client toward health and happiness. Bioenergetic exercises release these self-healing properties.

In a typical group situation the participants wear only leotards so that most "material facades" that conceal true identity are removed. Bodies are studied with regard to form and degree of flexibility or rigidity. Form involves proportion, height, weight, facial features, harmony of body parts, posture, and carriage. Rigidity involves chronic muscle tenseness that produces an unbending back and a stiff neck. Exaggerated flexibility is marked by spasticities in the small muscles surrounding the vertebrae and or loss of tone in the larger longitudinal muscles of the back.

The physical properties of the body, including rigidity and flexibility, are interpreted as indications of personality characteristics. For example, rigidity denotes a rigid personality, whereas exaggerated flexibility denotes an impulsive, immature personality. As a first step in treatment the individual must be made aware of his or her bodily difficulties. These problems may be revealed through bioenergetic exercises such as placing the body in a hyperextended arc, then reversing the arc by bending forward until fingertips touch the ground. Involuntary leg vibrations will occur unless the muscles are so tense that feeling does not develop in them. Such tenseness reflects personality tension.

Other treatment techniques involve the release of feeling through physical activity. Clients are required to kick or pound pillows while shouting "No." Should an individual be unconvincing in his or her emotional release, the group confronts him or her and encourages a greater degree of self-assertion. From this perspective mental health develops from the feeling of respect for one's unique body. Physical respect generates self-respect.

Clearly, the bioenergetic approach to group therapy differs dramatically from all the verbal therapies discussed thus far. Great emphasis is placed on tension release through physical movement rather than discussion of problems.

Marathon Approach

The marathon approach to group therapy reflects a process rather than an underlying theoretical frame of reference. However, the process of marathon therapy has become so well established that it has developed a unique set of premises that justify its inclusion as a separate category. As described by Bach (1966) a principal premise of the marathon technique is the use of encounter to motivate behavioral change. In effect, group pressure strips an individual of his or her defenses, thus forcing the recognition of certain facts about self. Group pressure is seen as the most effective vehicle available to force "honest leveling."

The second major premise is that therapy is a whole. To be successful a therapeutic experience must encompass five components of the therapeutic process: (1) identification of personality components, (2) honest leveling about those components, (3) group pressure and influence, (4) commitment to behavioral change, and (5) practicing new behaviors.

Therapy that does not encompass all five aspects is neither long nor intense enough to reach the goal of behavioral change. Thus, traditional weekly, hour-long therapy sessions are perceived as fragmented and inadequate. The marathon group overcomes this problem by bringing individuals together for three or four days and by forcing continuous meetings without interruption. Sessions may be held all night so that participants go without sleep twenty-four hours or longer to maintain the continuity of the group. Hypothetically fatigue and personal discomfort help break down typical defenses and expedite insight.

The third major premise of the marathon approach is that the real self only can be uncovered through psychological intimacy within the group. To accomplish the necessary degree of intimacy, the group remains together in the same place until the therapy session ends. Rules are established for eating and bathroom breaks to avoid disrupting the group. Group rules state that each participant must communicate his or her true feelings, absorb the group's frank reaction, and react to the group. Communications must be frank, not tactful, although threats and physical violence are forbidden. The goal is to strip defenses and block the use of evasion or psychiatric game playing, not to make people "feel better." Conciliatory remarks are not permitted.

As for the actual group process, participants must display their emotions on the spot, not talk about how they typically behave. For example, a person who feels angry when criticized must respond to a critical remark with anger, not discuss the fact that criticism makes him or her angry. Theoretically, the group is a microcosm of the real world of social and personal interactions. Although group members have no secrets from each other, all information revealed during the session is confidential.

It can be noted that the marathon approach is basically an extention of two key premises from Gestalt therapy, the idea of encounter and the emphasis on the here and now. The approach varies from Gestaltist principles because it de-emphasizes the importance of self and the uniqueness of the client's perceptual field. One of the most popular of the marathon approaches is EST training developed by Werner Erhard in 1971. This training involves prolonged periods of lecture and discussion that focus on the individual's ability to control his or her life. It makes marathon procedures available to all persons, not just those with emotional problems.

GROUP TECHNIQUES IN EDUCATION

Many scattered references have been made throughout this chapter to the feasibility of applying group techniques in school situations. However, certain points require clarification and elaboration. First, the information on group dynamics discussed in the first section of this chapter was designed to present a methodology for the practitioner. Discussions of the leadership role, group processes, and therapeutic techniques all provide tools for the implementation of group sessions. They may be used in school settings if the practitioner observes these sensible guidelines

1. *Establish only developmental-level groups.* As noted previously, developmental groups are designed to improve children's communication skills, increase their self-awareness, increase their sensitivity to others, and

alleviate mild emotional problems. Each of these goals is compatible with the teaching role in the schools. The teacher who uses group work for these purposes does not exceed his or her level of competence.

2. *Do not involve seriously disturbed children in verbal discussion groups.* The inclusion of children with serious emotional problems in teacher-directed groups introduces an element of risk to all the children involved. Obviously, the teacher is not qualified to deal with the emotions associated with serious disturbance and ineffectual efforts to do so may increase a child's unhappiness and upset the group. Brammer and Shostrom (1977)[4] have developed a set of criteria that the teacher can use as a guide for determining which children to exclude from developmental group activities.

Criteria 1 *The nature and severity of symptoms.* Some behavior is so indicative of severe disturbance that there is little question that the individual requires a remedial therapy placement. For example, delusional thinking and uncontrollable hostility are severe symptoms that indicate the inappropriateness of a developmental group placement.

Criteria 2 *Length and persistence of symptoms.* An individual who consistently engages in relatively serious behaviors, such as stealing or setting fires, for a long period of time probably needs remedial treatment.

Criteria 3 *The nature of the predisposing and precipitating experiences.* An individual may have undergone a series of severe traumas such as death in the family or hospitalization that make him or her too labile for developmental-group experiences.

Criteria 4 *Past stability and defensive functioning.* Individuals with a history of stable behavior may be permitted occasionally to ventilate intense feelings in a developmental group since they are unlikely to lose control of themselves. Persons who are obviously fragile and unstable, however, are very poor risks to handle any elevated degree of emotional probing.

Criteria 5 *Resistance to psychotherapy.* It is typically true that seriously disturbed persons have poor defenses against pressure. In contrast, normal or mildly disturbed individuals defend themselves vigorously against attacks from the outside world. In group discussions they will resist or resent probing into areas that are their private reserve and back off from further interaction. Individuals who cannot defend themselves from probing require remedial placement.

---

[4] Source: Lawrence M. Brammer, Everett L. Shostrom, *Therapeutic Psychology: Fundamentals of Counseling and Psychotherapy*, 1977. Reprinted by permission of Prentice-Hall, Inc., Englewood Cliffs, N.J.

In addition to these five criteria several other operational criteria may prove helpful. The teacher should exclude from discussion group sessions children who find some means of consistently disrupting the group, who become visibly agitated or upset in group sessions, who express reluctance about participating, and who are caustic, cruel, or otherwise unpleasant to group members.

3. *Gear discussions toward cognitive solutions to problems.* This rule is in keeping with the first two guidelines. Teacher-led groups are not designed to explore great depths of feeling or emotion. Group discussion should be focused on thoughts and actions rather than feelings. For example, an individual whose problem pertains to excessive fighting might be helped to think of alternative activities to substitute for fighting.

Brammer and Shostrom point out that there is a direct relationship between the therapist's training, including experience in psychotherapy, and the depth of feeling that should be explored in group sessions. Relatively untrained leaders are advised to use their own sensitivities to recognize when a situation is becoming too emotionally charged. When the leader becomes uncomfortable with the discussion, the topic should be changed.

4. *Set clear, realistic goals for group activities.* The teacher may use discussion-group sessions to accomplish any of a multitude of good, sound objectives. For example, she or he may want to relate to students in a nonteaching role, involve shy or withdrawn individuals in nonthreatening discussions, provide students with an outlet for discussion of problems or concerns, demonstrate or model communication skills, explore a particular problem that has arisen between students, or try to open communication with a particular unhappy individual.

The important aspect of goal setting is that it be done before the implementation of the therapeutic sessions. Before engaging in the group sessions, the leader must be aware of what she or he wants to accomplish, develop a tentative plan for goal accomplishment, and develop criteria for recognizing goal attainment. For example, the leader who establishes as a primary goal the involvement of a shy, withdrawn child in open discussion, uses therapeutic techniques such as leading, listening, reflection, and reassurance to draw that individual into the group's discussion and achieves success if the individual participates freely.

An equally important aspect of goal setting pertains to the feasibility of attaining the goals. Goals must be realistic. They must pertain to outcomes that *can* be obtained in developmental-group sessions. Often the extent to which goals are realistic is a function of the leader's experience. Inexperienced persons tend to have grandiose expectations about the outcomes of group sessions. They often set goals that are too ambitious and become pessimistic when they fail to reach them. For example, the teacher who expects group sessions to turn a shy, withdrawn child into a gregarious, social butterfly is prone to failure.

A related point about realistic expectations pertains to too much enthusiasm. The inexperienced leader tends to overgeneralize from the satisfactory aspects of group experiences. Indeed, it is discouraging to discover that an aggressive child, who, during the course of group therapy, vows never to fight again, within the next fifteen minutes engages in a fight. Unfortunately, dramatic personality upheavals rarely materialize in group therapy. Progress is slow and often depends on the extent to which the leader can help the group members set behavioral goals for activities that are part of their daily living. Discussion in group sessions usually is simply the first step in the establishment of new behavioral patterns.

The final point about realistic goals may help the new practitioner avoid the problems associated with inexperience. Goals should be modest, relatively specific, and, so far as possible, measurable. In other words, the teacher's goals should not be global generalizations like curing Jane of her shy, withdrawn behavior. A realistic goal for Jane would be to involve her in a nonthreatening group discussion. This is a modest goal in that it refers to a first step for working with Jane, specific in that it denotes a particular activity, and measurable in that she either does or does not become involved.

5. *Secure parental and administrative support for group activities.* The notion of a teacher conducting group sessions with children might prove to be extremely threatening to individuals who associate group work only with depth therapy. Often such persons have visions of "head shrinking," which must be faced directly or the teacher's program may never get off the ground. The most effective means of overcoming ignorance or misunderstanding is to plan and refer to group sessions as part of the affective education program. The teacher must make clear that she or he is not assuming the role of psychotherapist, that group sessions do not involve depth therapy, and that group activities are not restricted to problem children, but are used with the entire class.

The best means of familiarizing both administrators and parents with the developmental group program is to prepare a plan of program goals and objectives. These may be discussed with the school principal before the group sessions are begun. The plan should include such details as scheduling. For example, on the elementary level, group sessions may be integrated into the school day, whereas at the secondary level they may be established on a voluntary basis after school or during free periods. Having secured administrative approval for the program, the teacher may communicate with parents of the children who will be involved. In most cases, advance information prevents misunderstanding and parental opposition based upon misinformation.

The second major point regarding the educational application of the information presented in this chapter pertains to the discussion of the specific approaches to therapy. Much of the information provided in that section of the chapter was to familiarize the reader with the principal perspectives that currently underlie group psychotherapeutic operations. The intent in discussing each theorist's specific approach was not to provide models for direct application. Many of the techniques and procedures discussed would not be readily adaptable to school settings with children who are not seriously disturbed. Other techniques are adaptable, but require further elaboration if they are to be used effectively. The remainder of this chapter will be devoted to discussing techniques that are and are not applicable to school-based developmental groups. Approaches and procedures not useful in school situations are those that

1. Have a classic psychoanalytic orientation. Psychoanalysis is designed exclusively for depth therapy. The principles that behavior is controlled by unconscious forces and that maladjustment is due to early sexual fixations, have little relevance for educators. Useful psychoanalytic concepts, such as Sullivan's emphasis on interpersonal relationships, Adler's ideas about self-concept, and Horney's interest in the social forces causing emotional maladjustment, have been incorporated into theories associated with the phenomenological school. Their importance to educational operations will be evaluated from that perspective.

2. Place major emphasis on underlying emotions and personality dynamics. The teacher acting as therapist is not qualified to expound on the personality dynamics that underlie a child's attitude or behavior. Such emphasis is not consistent with the goals of developmental group work.

3. Stress leader interpretations of behavior. The teacher goals do not include telling children what's wrong with them.

4. Emphasize encounter or confrontation as a major tool. Although the principle of encounter may be useful with adults, it should not be attempted with children. Personal confrontation evokes intense emotional outbursts and, as has been stated repeatedly, the teacher's goals do not include the probing of deep emotion.

5. Involve prolonged marathon sessions. Prolonged group sessions are far too intense for children and may jeopardize their physical and emotional well being.

6. Delve into children's past histories. The focus of school-based group sessions should be on current events and behaviors.

Approaches and procedures that are adaptable in school settings are those that draw from aspects of the phenomenological, behavioral, and rational perspectives. These three approaches appear to be most useful for developmental group work because they

1. Place the responsibility for emotional health on the individual.

2. Emphasize conscious control over behavior.

3. Attribute the development of adaptive behavior to new learning.

4. Focus on current behaviors or life events rather than on the past.

5. Use methods that may be implemented by persons not trained primarily in psychopathology.

The first common attribute, the individual's responsibility for self-improvement, is particularly appropriate for school-based developmental group procedures, where the teacher's primary goal is to provide opportunities for affective growth. Children who are not seriously disturbed can be expected to benefit from opportunities to learn about their affective behavior, much as they benefit from opportunities to learn academic information. Even when the emphasis is on solving a particular child's problems, the notion that the successful solution depends primarily on the child's efforts to improve is valid. The lesson in assuming responsibility for self is perhaps one of the most valuable a child can learn.

The second attribute, the emphasis on conscious control over behavior is also important in school settings. The idea of teachers conducting group sessions with children is predicated on the notion that changes in feelings, attitudes, ideas, and behaviors will result. If children are viewed as nothing more than the pawns of their unconscious motivation, then it would be unrealistic and impractical to conclude that teacher-directed developmental groups could produce such changes. On the other hand, if children are perceived as having conscious control over their beliefs and feelings, it is probable that developmental group work will help them learn to behave more cooperatively, be more tolerant of others, accept deviance, and, in short, become more concerned about human relations.

In addition, focusing attention on children's conscious attitudes about themselves is in keeping with the limitations of their cognitive and emotional development. Children, even many adolescents, are not equipped intellectually or emotionally to explore the underlying motivation behind their behavior. Speculations along those lines either are not understood or evoke undesirable emotional reactions.

The third common attribute, the relationship between affect and new learning is particularly important for teachers. Most teachers find it relatively easy to respond to the idea that new learning is the key to changing undesirable behaviors and attitudes, because learning is their primary area of professional interest. In effect, discussing affective development in terms of learning removes much of the trepidation that may accompany the idea of a teacher acting as a therapist.

The behavioral notion that children's attitudes, emotions, and opinions are learned responses to stimuli is particularly familiar in education since many teachers have applied behavior modification to promote academic learning. There is no reason to assume that teachers cannot become equally comfortable applying similar principles in group sessions.

The rational school's emphasis on faulty learning and self-defeating thoughts as the precipitators of emotional problems is equally attractive to educators. It is relatively easy for teachers to understand the idea of helping children develop constructive thought processes. For example, a young boy who thinks of himself as a stupid person may be helped greatly by being brought to recognize that such thoughts are self-defeating and that to feel better he must substitute thoughts of competence for self-derogatory thoughts.

The phenomenological focus on insight learning is perhaps less directly associated with the typical teaching role than the other two learning concepts. However, insight or self-awareness is an obvious goal of affective education. The critical factor in insight learning is the association between newly learned assumptions about self and actual behaviors that test the validity of those assumptions. For example, the child referred to above must have life experiences that attest to his competence if he is to believe in the truth of those assumptions.

The fourth common attribute, the emphasis on current behaviors rather than past events, signifies the importance of dealing with that which can be altered. A child's past, no matter how traumatic, is history and cannot be changed. Current behaviors and attitudes can be altered. If fact, children's personality flexibility makes it comparatively easy for them to forget past events and develop new feelings and ideas about life. In general, children who persist in displaying disturbed behaviors do so because the components of their current environments support those behaviors. The teacher's interest in emotional problems must focus on what is occurring, what environmental factors cause the occurrence, and what other interventions might alter the occurrence.

The last common attribute, methodology that can be implemented by persons not previously trained in psychopathology, is reflected in part by the other points discussed. Aspects of these three approaches to emotional disturbance may be used by relatively inexperienced persons without risking adverse consequences to the children they desire to help.

The common characteristics of the phenomenological, behavioral, and rational approaches to therapy make it feasible to integrate them into an eclectic approach useful in school settings. Obviously, however, these three major perspectives encompass many contradictory and conflicting premises about group techniques. For example, the phenomenological approach places emphasis on nondirective leadership, whereas the behavioral approach involves directive leadership. Therefore, the school practitioner must be prepared to adapt unique characteristics from each approach to meet the specific demands of developmental group activities. Of course, there is no single or correct method of doing so. In fact, the strength of an eclectic approach is that it permits the practitioner to select techniques for specific purposes. Thus, the approach used in group sessions may depend on variables such as the goals of the group, the group size, the characteristics of the children involved, and the methodology the leader feels most comfortable using. The following discussion should serve to illustrate the aspects from each major approach that can be used in developmental group activities.

The key contributions of the phenomenological approach are the concepts of unique personal perceptions, acceptance, and nondirective leadership strategies. The teacher who accepts the notion of unique personal perceptions must incorporate it in group work at two levels: demonstration and discussion. Demonstration involves showing by doing, the actual implementation of a concept. Discussion refers to talking about a concept.

At the demonstration level, the teacher makes it a point to avoid rejecting or correcting any opinion, attitude, or idea put forth by a group member. Alternate opinions may be offered, but the individual's point of view is always respected. For example, a leader would never say "No, you're wrong about that," but would say "I see what you mean, but have you considered this idea."

At the discussion level, the teacher introduces topics that illustrate the uniqueness of personal perceptions, such as the influence of cultural background on an individual's point of view, the need for tolerance of alternate points of view, and the attitudes and feelings evoked by difference or deviance.

The concept of acceptance has similar implications for developmental group work. At the demonstration level the teacher makes clear with supportive remarks and good humor that each individual is a valued member of the group. The teacher may find that the group sessions provide a particularly valuable opportunity to communicate acceptance to problem children, who may not receive much positive reinforcement in the regular classroom situation. At the discussion level, concepts that pertain to acceptance, such as the fact that people generally respond more favorably when they feel liked and accepted, may be presented to the group.

By far the most significant aspect of the phenomenological approach is the concept of nondirective leadership. The nondirective leader permits group members to participate in discussion at their own pace, in accordance with their own needs. The teacher demonstrating nondirective strategies should listen to the children, accept their remarks without criticism, help them discuss the problems and issues that they want to talk about, respond in supportive fashion, reflect on children's comments, clarify children's ideas and attitudes, and provide suggestions to open group discussions.

The nondirective leader should avoid making interpretations about the dynamics that underlie the children's behaviors, telling children what's wrong with them, telling children what to do, probing too far into children's affairs, discussing sensitive topics, and dominating the group.

The methods required to implement nondirective leadership: leading, listening, reflecting, structuring, and reassuring, have been discussed elsewhere in this chapter. As with most methodologies, these techniques are effective only when the individual using them is committed to achieving success. Such commitment must be sufficiently strong to see the novice practitioner through periods of awkwardness until she or he feels comfortable using nondirective techniques.

The teacher will find the contributions from the phenomenological approach particularly applicable in developmental groups designed to increase self-awareness, develop social values, promote communication skills, and increase group cohesiveness. Obviously, mature children and adolescents are able to glean the messages from nondirective discussion groups far more efficiently than younger children.

The major contributions from the behavioral approaches are the techniques that efficiently reduce maladaptive overt behaviors and the emphasis on a systematic plan for therapeutic intervention. As noted previously, the behavioral orientation involves far more directive leadership strategies than the phenomenological approach. It may be adapted to developmental-group work to accomplish varied goals. Unlike the nondirective techniques, behavioral methodology is not designed to increase self-awareness or to develop social values. The therapeutic interventions are direct attempts to effect overt behavioral changes. As such, the procedures are particularly applicable to the solution of specific behavioral problems. For example, the teacher might be concerned with Bart, a boy whose excessive fighting interferes with his school work and his interpersonal relationships. His acceptance as a valued member of a discussion group may be contingent on the removal of the fighting behavior. Thus, the teacher must direct the group's attention to the problem of Bart's excessive fighting. The group's goals are to establish when the behavior occurs, what events appear to induce it, what might be done about it, and what criteria might be used to determine whether or not the behavior has been eliminated.

In our example, the group and Bart may agree that he begins to fight whenever he feels offended by another child's remarks. They may suggest that whenever he feels like fighting he report his anger to the teacher, hit a punching bag, or confine his displays of anger to verbal remarks, depending on Bart's preferences. His success may be evaluated on a weekly basis. Avoidance of fighting results in a letter to his parents praising his newly found self-control.

The example illustrates the second attribute of the behavioristic model, the systematic nature of the proceedings. Bart's problem is reduced to a specific behavior occurring in response to a specific environmental cue The effectiveness of the strategy for altering the maladaptive behavior can be measured directly. Should one option prove to be ineffective another may be substituted.

Behavioral strategies may be integrated most effectively into group sessions after the group members have developed feelings of confidence and trust in the good intentions of each participant. The greatest efficiency is obtained if Bart regards his fighting as a problem and is willing to cooperate with the group in finding a solution. Thus, the attitudes of acceptance and understanding are not precluded by the use of behavioristic interventions.

Two major related concepts that emanate from the rational approach are the *emphasis on reality* and the *importance of reason.* The teacher who incorporates these premises into developmental-group work may emphasize, without criticizing, arguing, or rejecting a child's opinions, the realistic consequences of certain ideas or behaviors. For example, if Bart were to justify his fighting, the teacher might say, "I understand how you feel, but fighting usually leads to trouble, doesn't it?" Such appeals to reason are predicated on the notion that usually individuals want to believe and do what is in their best interest. In the group sessions the teacher has the opportunity to help the group clarify the ideas and ensuing behaviors that inevitably are harmful rather than helpful.

The teacher may use the techniques associated with the rational approach to increase self-awareness, develop social values, and solve specific behavioral problems. Children who find it difficult to assume responsibility for their behavior may be helped to recognize that characteristic. Such recognition provides the motivation for attitudinal and behavioral change.

Appeals to reason are most effective with children who have reached the age of rational or logical thinking. Younger children are affected more by external manipulation of the consequences of their behavior, that is, behavioristic intervention.

In conclusion, it appears that the three major perspectives of group therapy offer unique concepts that can be integrated into developmental group work in school settings. The phenomenological school offers the attitude of acceptance, which promotes the best therapeutic environment. The behavioral school emphasizes the importance of goal specificity and the direct association between discussion and actual behavior. The rational approach focuses on the importance of ideas in determining behavior. Each of these therapeutic strategies associated with specific approaches will be explored more fully in following chapters.

STUDY QUESTIONS

1. Compare and contrast developmental and remedial groups.
2. Discuss alternate points of view on group formation. Select an approach that you favor and tell why.
3. Discuss ten leadership techniques that may be employed to promote group growth.
4. Discuss leading, reflecting, and structuring techniques used in group sessions.
5. Discuss the guidelines for using group techniques in education.

REFERENCES

Adler, A. *The practice and theory of individual psychology.* New York: Harcourt, Brace & World, 1927.

Bach, G. R. *Intensive group psychotherapy.* New York: Ronald, 1954.

Bach, G. The marathon group: intensive practice of intimate interactions. *Psychological Reports,* 1966, *18,* 995–1002 .

Barak, A. and La Crosse, M. Multidimensional perception of counselor behavior. *Journal of Counseling Psychology,* 1975, *22,* 471–476.

Berne, E. *Transactional analysis.* New York: Grove, 1961.

Berzon, B., and Solomon, L. The self directed therapeutic group: three studies. *Journal of Counseling Psychology,* 1966, *13,* 491–497.

Bion, Wilfred. *Experience in groups.* New York: Basic Books, 1962.

Bixler, R. Limits are therapy. *Journal of Consulting Psychology,* 1949, *13,* 1–11.

Brammer, L., and Shostrom, E. *Therapeutic psychology.* Englewood Cliffs, N.J.: Prentice-Hall, 1977.

Carnes, E., and Robinson, F. The role of client talk in the counseling interview. *Educational and Psychological Measurement,* 1948, *8,* 635–644.

Coffey, H. Group psychotherapy. In I. Berg and L. Pennington (eds.). *An Introduction to clinical psychology.* New York: Ronald, 1948.

Cohen, R. Military group psychotherapy. *Mental Hygiene,* 1947, *31,* 94–103.

Combs, A. *Florida Studies in the helping professions.* Gainesville, Fla.: University of Florida Press, 1969.

Crider, B. The hostility pattern. *Journal of Clinical Psychology,* 1946, *2,* 267–273.

Curran, C. Structuring the counseling relationship: a case report. *Journal of Abnormal and Social Psychology*, 1944, 39, 189–216.

Dollard, J., and Miller, N. *Personality and psychotherapy*. New York: McGraw-Hill, 1950.

Ellis, A. Rational psychotherapy. *Journal of General Psychology*, 1958, 59, 35–49.

Ellis, A. Toward a more precise definition of emotional and intellectual insight. *Psychological Reports*, 1963, 13, 125–126.

Freud, S. *Group psychotherapy and the analysis of the ego*. New York: Liveright, 1921.

Freud, S. *A general introduction to psychoanalysis*. New York: Liveright, 1935.

Fromm, E. *Man for himself*. New York: Farrar & Rinehart, 1947.

Ginott, H. *Group psychotherapy with children*. New York: McGraw-Hill, 1961.

Glatzer, H. The relative effectiveness of clinically homogeneous and heterogeneous psychotherapy groups. *International Journal of Group Psychotherapy*, 1956, 6, 258.

Grossman, D. Ego-activating approaches to psychotherapy. *Psychoanalytic Review*, 1964, 51, 65–88.

Hobbs, N. Group-centered psychotherapy. In C. Rogers (ed.). *Client-centered therapy*. Boston: Houghton Mifflin, 1951.

Horney, K. *New ways in psychoanalysis*. New York: Norton, 1939.

Horney, K. *Neurosis and human growth*. New York: Norton, 1950.

Joel, W., and Shapiro, D. Some principles and procedures for group psychotherapy. *Journal of Psychology*, 1950, 29, 77–88.

Jung, C. *Modern man in search of a soul*. New York: Harcourt Brace, 1933.

Levitshy, A., and Perls, F. The rules and games of gestalt therapy. In H. Ruitenbeek (ed.). *Group therapy today*. New York:Atherton, 1969.

London, P. *The modes and morals of psychotherapy*. New York: Holt, Rinehart and Winston, 1964.

Lowen, A. Bio-energetic group therapy. In H. Ruitenbeek (ed.). *Group therapy today*. New York: Atherton, 1969.

Maslow, A. *Motivation and personality*. New York: Harper & Row, 1954.

May, R. *The art of counseling*. New York: Abingdon-Cokesbury, 1939.

Menninger, K. *The theory of psychoanalytic technique*. Menninger Clinical Monograph Series 12. New York: Basic Books, 1958.

Perls, F. *Gestalt therapy verbatim*. Lafayette, Cal.: Real People, 1969.

Perls, F.; Goodman, P.; and Hefferline, H. *Gestalt therapy—excitement and growth in human personality*. New York: Julian, 1951.

Phillips, E. *Psychotherapy: a modern theory and practice*. Englewood Cliffs, N.J.: Prentice-Hall, 1956.

Powdermaker, F., and Frank, J. *Group psychotherapy*. Cambridge, Mass.: Harvard University Press, 1953.

Rank, O. *Will therapy and truth and reality*. New York: Knopf, 1947.

Rogers, C. *Counseling and psychotherapy*. Boston: Houghton Mifflin, 1942.

Rogers, C. *Client-centered therapy*. Boston: Houghton Mifflin, 1951.

Satir, V. *Conjoint family therapy*. Palo Alto, Cal.: Science and Behavior Books, 1966.

Schutz, W. *Elements of encounter*. New York: Bantam, 1975.

Slavson, S. *The Practice of group psychotherapy.* New York: International, 1947.

Sullivan, H. *The interpersonal theory of psychiatry.* New York: Norton, 1953.

Winder, L. Group psychotherapy. In J. Moreno (ed.). *Group psychotherapy— a symposium.* New York: Beacon, 1945.

Wolpe, J. *Psychotherapy by reciprocal inhibition.* Stanford, Cal.: Stanford University Press, 1958.

Yalom, I.; Lieberman, M.; and Miles, M. A study of encounter group casualties. *Archives of General Psychiatry,* 1971, *25,* 16–30.

6
Behavioral Therapy

The term *behavioral therapy* appears to have been introduced in the 1950's, first by Lindsley (1954), then with more popular impact, by Lazarus (1958). In its most general sense it refers to the application of principles derived from the field of experimental psychology to the study of abnormal behavior. Its earliest roots were the investigations into classical and instrumental conditioning undertaken by the Russian psychologists, Pavlov (1927, 1928), Bekhterev (1932), Ivanov-Smolensky (1927, 1928) and by the Americans Thorndike (1898), Watson (1916), Skinner (1953), and others. Interestingly, although much of the early research into conditioning principles was conducted with animals (Pavlov's famous salivating dog experiment), many of the fathers of behavioral therapy including Pavlov (1932, 1934) and Watson (1920, the equally famous "little Albert" experiment) applied those principles directly to abnormal behavior in humans. Thus, behavorial therapy existed in practice long before it existed in name.

Later in the twentieth century, the growth of experimental psychology to encompass general theories of learning also was reflected in the further development of behavior therapy. The development of theoretical models of learning based on the principles of conditioning enabled investigators to formulate more comprehensive hypotheses for the study of abnormal behavior. The work of Hull (1943, 1952) appears of particular importance in this respect. Of equal significance is the work of Albert Bandura (1969) who in *Principles of Behavior Modification* incorporated theoretical data on symbolic and cognitive processes into a behavioral model.

Clearly, the 1950's marked the flowering of behavior therapy, as the application of behavior principles to clinical cases began in earnest. Theorists such as Dollard and Miller (1950) and Mowrer (1950) translated psychodynamic constructs into the terminology of learning theory. To a large degree, however, the way was lead by B. F. Skinner, who demonstrated the effectiveness of operant conditioning with psychotic patients at the Metropolitan State Hospital in Waltham, Mass. and published his important book *Science and Human Behavior* (1953).

In England, the work of H. J. Eysenck and M. B. Shapiro at the Psychology Department of the Institute of Psychiatry moved behavior therapy one step further. Eysenck (1949, 1950, 1964a) was among the first to critique cogently the medical approaches to the study of abnormal behavior. He perceived clinical personnel as behavioral researchers who must apply methods of scientific inquiry to the solution of behavioral disorders. Similarly, Shapiro (1951, 1961, 1966) developed clinical procedures for assessment and treatment of disturbed conditions that were based on hypothesis formation and testing, rather than upon the traditional administration of psychodynamic tests. This emphasis on the utilization of experimental strategies in applied settings constitutes the foundation of what Davison and Neale (1974) have labeled an experimental–clinical approach to the study of abnormal behavior.

In America, Joseph Wolpe, later joined by Arnold Lazarus, drew from Hull's conceptualizations to formulate clinical procedures based on the theory of reciprocal inhibition. Their work encompasses many specific techniques associated with behavioral therapy and will be discussed in great length later in this chapter.

As this brief history suggests, behavioral therapy did not emanate from one particular source. In fact, the multiplicity of behavioral foundations has generated a certain amount of dispute regarding the definition of the term. Some individuals view behavioral therapy as the application of learning theory in clinical situations. For example, Eysenck (1964b) defines behavioral therapy as "the attempt to alter human behavior and emotion in a beneficial manner according to the laws of modern learning theory." Other experts dispute this definition, finding it too limiting. Yates (1970, p. 18)[1] typifies this attitude with his definition: "Behavioral therapy is the attempt to utilize systematically that body of empirical and theoretical knowledge which has resulted from the application of the experimental method in psychology and its closely related disciplines (physiology and neurophysiology) in order to explain the genesis and maintenance of abnormal patterns of behavior; and to apply that knowledge to the treatment or prevention of those abnormalities by means of controlled experimental studies of the single case, both descriptive and remedial."

---

[1] Source: Yates, *Behavior therapy*. New York: Wiley and Sons, 1970. Reprinted by permission of the publisher.

Yates's position emphasizes three related points: (1) that behavioral therapy involves the formulation and testing of unique experimental hypotheses for each specific individual, (2) that these hypotheses should be based on far more than learning theory, and (3) that behavioral therapy does not refer to routine applications of techniques, such as Wolpe's reciprocal inhibition principle, which are formulated as general theory, then applied clinically without controlled experimental investigations of the single case. To those sharing this point of view, any technique such as role playing or therapeutic art may be integrated into the behavioral intervention, provided it is applied in accordance with the experimental method.

Wolpe (1976, p. 24) responds emphatically to the "generalist" position with this definition: "Behavioral therapy is the application of experimentally established principles of learning and of related phenomena to the purpose of overcoming habits that are unadaptive. Every maneuver involves the deliberate use of knowledge of the learning process to weaken and eliminate unadaptive habits, to establish adaptive ones or both." His attitude toward the rationale that any techniques not associated with experimental learning theory may constitute components of behavioral therapy is conveyed in this statement: "To stretch the definition this way is to produce the same kind of semantic absurdity as to stretch the definition of 'automobile' to include horse-drawn vehicles. Anybody can slice the psychotherapy cake in a new way, but if he wants to label his slice he should not use a name already in use for a different slice" (p. 25).

Obviously, the application of any technique that alters behavior *could* be referred to as behavioral therapy. However, in this chapter, the use of the term will be restricted to the principles derived from conditioning and learning theory. Even with this restriction, the reader will find the discussion of behavioral therapy to be far more complex than many of the therapies presented in other chapters of this book, for example, drama, art, music. Those chapters refer primarily to therapeutic techniques, whereas behavioral therapy constitutes a distinct approach, a methodology for studying and treating abnormal behavior. Consequently, this necessarily long chapter will encompass: first, discussion of applied behavioral procedures such as applied behavioral analysis (ABA) and behavior modification; second, presentation of specific techniques more generally associated with clinical-behavioral therapy as distinct from behavior modification; and third, discussion of behavioral therapeutic interventions for specific pathological conditions. This information will be more clearly understood if the reader is familiar with the rationale and major concepts associated with behavioral psychology. Those persons lacking such familiarity might wish to consult the Appendix for a brief discussion of behavioral principles.

APPLIED BEHAVIORAL ANALYSIS

For ease of understanding, the term *applied behavioral analysis* is used predominately in this section and encompasses many of the procedures associated with the more common term *behavior modification.* The techniques discussed pertain primarily to procedures that are generally applicable in educational settings to control maladaptive behaviors. The following section, clinical-behavioral therapy, will pertain to applied procedures more generally associated with interventions in clinical settings. This distinction is obviously arbitrary, as both educational and clinical applications involve common procedures, that is, the practical application of behavioral theory.

Applied behavioral analysis is defined by Sulzer-Azaroff and Mayer (1977, p. 6) as "A systematic, performance-based self-evaluative method of changing behavior." Essentially, the principles of conditioning and learning, particularly reinforcement, are applied to manipulate behavior, to establish new behavior, to maintain satisfactory behavior, to increase or reduce behavior, and to extend or restrict behavior to specific settings. The four main components of ABA involve (1) focusing attention on specific activities or behaviors, (2) direct observation and recording of these behaviors, (3) formulation of behavioral objectives and goals from observation, and (4) treatment or intervention based on experimental analysis and data collection.

Regarding the first point, focusing attention on specific behaviors, ABA requires that terms denoting internal feelings such as *anger* or *sadness* be operationalized as specific behaviors. Thus, rather than describe an individual as angry, the interventionist might specify behaviors such as fights with peers, has temper tantrums, throws stones at passing cars, or uses profanity. Any or all of these may denote anger. The implication of this strategy is that anger, a construct that includes a variety of behaviors, is neither directly observable nor directly measurable. Unless it is defined operationally, in terms of specific behaviors, it cannot be incorporated into therapeutic interventions dependent on objective verification of behavioral change. In other words, the fact that an individual is less angry is best demonstrated by the performance of fewer angry behaviors.[2]

The second point, the importance of direct observation and recording of behavior provides the backbone of ABA because it involves the techniques that are used to obtain objective data for development of goals

---

[2] Some current experts in ABA no longer hold to the traditional Skinnerian rationale that only observable and measurable behaviors are important and that behavior modification is restricted to the manipulation of those behaviors. Modification of internal cognitive processes is viewed as a promising strategy for ABA (Craighead, Kazden, and Mahoney, 1976).

and strategies for behavioral change. Craighead et al., (1976)[3] list four classes of behavioral data: magnitude, temporal, frequency, and categorical. *Magnitude data* pertain to the intensity of a response—as in the amount of pressure a child puts on a pencil when writing. *Temporal data* involve measurements of time—as in the time required to complete an arithmetic assignment. *Frequency data* pertain to discrete, countable responses—as in the number of times a child talks out in class. *Categorical data* include measurements that differentiate responses—as when a child selecting food for lunch chooses to eat candy rather than nutritious food. All of these data are gathered through a variety of sampling techniques.

Sampling

The sampling technique used to gather data depends on whether the behavior to be measured is transitory or permanent. Behaviors such as the number of homework assignments completed or the number of arithmetic problems finished are readily observable since they are recorded permanently. The homework or arithmetic papers are samples of behavior and may be evaluated to determine accuracy, items completed, and so forth.

The observation and measurement of transitory behaviors, however, is far more difficult. Behaviors such as fighting or swearing leave no permanent record of their occurrence that may be assessed at a later time. They must be measured when they occur and recorded for later analysis. This type of observation usually requires a live observer or some type of taped record. The observation may be done by *event, duration,* or *interval time sampling*.

Event sampling simply involves counting the number of times a specific behavior occurs in a specific interval of time. It is useful for measuring discrete responses, such as correct answers, hand raising, or pencil sharpening. For example, an event recording would reveal that in four hour-long intervals, George sharpened his pencil, two, four, three, and four times.

Duration sampling focuses on the length of time required to complete a task. A clock is used to measure how long it takes Jane to complete her mathematics assignment.

Interval time sampling is employed when behaviors are not clearly discrete and it is difficult to tell where they begin and end. For example, a hyperactive child may engage in an ongoing pattern of activity, making it difficult to count each specific behavior or to measure its duration. In

---

[3] Source: W. E. Craighead, A. E. Kazdin, and M. J. Mahoney, *Behavior Modification: Principles, Issues and Applications.* Copyright © 1976 by Houghton Mifflin Company. Used with permission.

such cases an interval time sampling system can be used. If it is necessary to know if a behavior occurred throughout an entire interval, a *whole interval system* is established. Thus, if little Joey cried for an entire 15-minute interval, the behavior would be recorded. If he stopped half way through the interval, it would not be recorded. If the behavior only need appear during the interval, it is a *partial interval sampling*. This technique is useful to chart fleeting behaviors such as swearing. *Momentary time sampling* is used to chart behaviors that must be occurring as the interval ends. If Joey cried for 14 of 15 minutes in the interval, stopping one minute before the end of the interval, the behavior would not be recorded. However, if he began crying just as the interval ended, it would be recorded. This strategy is useful for reoccurring and relatively persistent behaviors such as thumb sucking. Finally, a *coded interval* can be used to sample several behaviors simultaneously. Each important behavior is assigned a letter on a recording sheet. If the behavior occurs during the time interval, the observer puts a slash through the letter. Interval time sampling of any type is best used with frequent behavior. As a rule of thumb it should not be used if the behavior occurs on an average of less than once in 15 minutes (Arrington, 1943).

Obviously, time is an important component for effective sampling. If data are not gathered *continuously*, that is, recorded 24 hours a day over extended time periods, various formulas can be used to determine when to sample. These are generally referred to as *fixed* and *randomized* sampling. Fixed sampling is undertaken at a set time period every day. With randomized sampling, data are gathered at varied periods of time throughout the day. The latter approach usually yields more accurate and reliable information since it is likely to tap more representative behavior, thus reducing the possibility of sampling error.

The possibility of sampling error is further decreased if the investigator ensures that the recorded data have not been biased by the implementation of the observational system. This is done by awareness that an *adaptation period* is usually necessary before representative behavior can be recorded. For example, an acting-out, hard-to-manage child who finds himself or herself being observed, might suddenly become a model of decorum. In a short time, however, after accommodating to the observer's presence, the child once again demonstrates more characteristic behavior. Once the adaptation period has passed, the data gathered from consistent observation of typical or representative behavior are referred to as *baseline measurements*. These data serve as a standard for evaluating the effects of the treatment to follow.

Analyzing Sample Data   Once gathered, the data are generally portrayed in the form of a graph. The curves provide a visual representation of behavior that is readily interpretable. The vertical line or ordinate represents the behavior measurement, such as number or rate of responses, and the horizontal line or the abscissa reflects the units of time. A baseline measure for Joey's out-of-seat behavior following a period of adaptation, might look something Fig. 6.1.

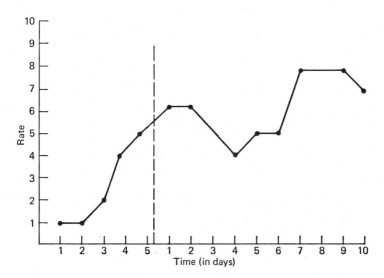

Fig. 6.1. *Joey's Out-of-Seat Behavior*

To aid the interventionist in analyzing the sample data, Goodwin (1969) has developed a format for sequence analysis. Called the "ABC" of behavior analysis it involves three categories: antecedent stimuli (A), problem behavior (B), and consequences of behavior (C). Antecedent stimuli are events that precede the response or problem behavior and include variables such as the child's activity, his or her location in the room, the activities of classmates and teacher, the time of day, and so forth. The problem behavior refers to the child's response—both the frequency and duration. The consequences include events such as the teacher's reaction and peer response, as well as other activities in the room. A sequence chart for Joey might look like this.

Antecedents	Behavior	Consequences
Activity: Reading lesson	Inappropriate laughter	Teacher: Criticizes child
Location: Front of room, reading circle	Ridiculing remarks to peers	Peers: Distracted, make negative remarks

Antecedents	Behavior	Consequences
Time: 10 to 11 A.M.	Frequency: 3 remarks 4 out- bursts of laughter	Activity: Work is interrupted
Peer Activity: Inde- pendent reading	Time: 1 hour	

With this type of chart all the environmental variables that pertain to the behavior are identified. The contingencies or relationship between the target behaviors and the antecedent stimuli and consequences are portrayed. Events not considered are those occurring inside the child, that is, what he or she thinks or feels about the situation. This type of cognitive information is not included in the ABC analysis because it is not considered pertinent for the implementation of treatment. The ABC approach reflects the principles of operant conditioning (see Appendix 1). The treatment depends on manipulation of reinforcement, that is, adjustment of external environmental events. Altering the consequences of Joey's behavior should reduce their occurrences, regardless of his thoughts or ideas about the situation. Presumably, once Joey is no longer engaging in maladaptive behavior and is receiving positive reinforcement from teacher and peers for more constructive activities, he will develop better feelings and thoughts about himself.

Setting Goals

As portrayed thus far, the name of the game in ABA is specificity—specificity not only in the procedures used to identify target behaviors, which require some type of modification or change, but also in the *formulation of goals and objectives* for behavioral modification, the third component of ABA. The key to effective behavioral intervention is that both the client and the interventionist have clear and precise knowledge about what must be accomplished.

By definition (Sulzer-Azoroff and Mayer, 1977), "A behavioral goal ought to be selected to provide both immediate and long term benefits to the client." Therefore, the goal of the behavioral intervention designed to help Joey would include increasing his popularity with his peers, increasing his academic skills, and increasing his enjoyment of the day-to-day events associated with attending school.

The clarity and usefulness of such goals are insured by refining them into behavioral objectives. A behavioral objective clarifies a goal by specifying the *desired response,* the *situation* in which it should occur, and the *criteria* for evaluating whether the objective has been met (Mager, 1962).

Sulzer-Azoroff and Mayer (1977) note that the response required may be delineated as to its characteristics including *topography*—where must the response be given (words must be written on the appropriate line of the paper with appropriate spacing between the letters), *intensity*—how strong must the response be (answer must be loud enough to be heard), *frequency*—how often must the response occur (hand must be raised before each remark), *duration*—how long must the response persist (30 minutes of seat work), and *accuracy*—what constitutes a correct response (100 percent correctly spelled words).

The second attribute of a behavioral objective, *specifying the situation* in which the response should occur, adds further precision to the planned intervention. The individual knows precisely when the adaptive response is to be demonstrated. Joey is attempting to complete more arithmetic problems, but is not expected to work on arithmetic during his reading lesson.

Specifying the criteria for determining whether or not the goal has been reached, the third characteristic of a behavioral objective, is probably the most critical, since it is most directly associated with the payoff—reinforcement. The criterion level for determining success must be realistic and feasible. It would be silly and harmful to plan an intervention that made reinforcement contingent on behavior the child could not possibly display. To ensure feasibility, the criterion level for success should be agreed to jointly by the child and the interventionist. It should reflect behavior the child believes she or he can demonstrate, as well as the interventionist's ideas regarding the child's capabilities. The guiding rule in establishing a criterion level is to set *minimal acceptable levels.* To be effective the objective must be attainable. The child needing to decrease out-of-seat behavior will probably fail if a criterion level of 100 percent is established for success. If the child fails, the behavior is not reinforced, and the desired behavior is less likely to be demonstrated again. He is more likely to be successful at an 80 percent level which, if it represents a substantial increase over his or her baseline rate of behavior, should be agreeable to the interventionist. As in-seat response becomes stronger, the criterion level can be elevated.

The best method of establishing a cooperative, mutually agreeable plan of behavioral objectives and goals is through behavioral *contracting.* A contract is a formal agreement between individuals that indicates their commitment to behavioral change. The contract specifies what adaptive behaviors will be demonstrated, how they will be monitored, what sanctions will accompany failure to display them, and what privileges will be earned. For example, Joey and his teacher might formally contract to diminish his out-of-seat behavior. A written agreement is drawn up

188 Part III Therapies

with terms calling for a progressive decrease in the maladaptive response over a 2-week period. The teacher agrees to monitor on an hourly basis. Tokens are to be awarded when the behavioral specifications are met and withheld when they are not met. If Joey proves unable to meet his commitment, the contract will be evaluated to determine its feasibility. Readjustment in the schedule of reinforcement might be necessary. In effect, the contract is renegotiated.

Treatment

The last step in ABA is *treatment based on experimental analysis and data collection.* This step is consistent with those that precede it, in that it is based on the application of scientific principles. The interventionist plans and implements treatment strategies in such a way that their effectiveness can be evaluated objectively. In other words, the treatment itself must be an experiment that demonstrates the intervention used was responsible for the behavioral change. Otherwise, even when behavior improves, the interventionist could not be certain why. Applied, experimental treatments of this type have been classified (Craighead et al., 1976) into two major categories: intrasubject and intersubject design.

In *intrasubject design,* an individual's or group's performance is measured under varied circumstances. No comparisons with other persons or groups are required. For example, John's rate of computing arithmetic problems may be assessed in the presence and absence of the reinforcer, praise. If he is more efficient when praised, it can be assumed that praise is an effective treatment. To ensure the validity of the conclusion, periods of praise and no praise should be alternated.

Intersubject design involves between-group comparisons. Two or more groups are exposed to different treatments and their performances are compared. For example, John and his classmates might be praised whenever they solve arithmetic problems, while another, control group receives no praise for that activity. The average performance of each group is compared. If John's group's average performance was significantly better than that of the control group, the praise treatment is verified.

Both intrasubject and intersubject designs have been used extensively in behavioral treatment. As the examples given above demonstrate, intrasubject designs permit the interventionist to draw conclusions about specific individuals, whereas intersubject or group research does not. In other words, when John's performance on arithmetic problems was analyzed under two conditions, praise and no praise, the conclusions drawn pertained specifically to John. However, when the performance of two groups was compared, the conclusions only pertained to the group's responses. No assumptions could be made about group member John's response to praise. Even if he appeared subjectively to perform well, there is no evidence that he would not have done as well or better if he had been in the no-praise group. Therefore, group or intersubject research is particularly valuable in demonstrating the general validity of an experimental assumption, that people do better work when they receive praise. In contrast, intrasubject research tests whether an assumption applies in each unique case, thus it minimizes the significance of individual differences in determining reinforcement or treatment strategies. When the treatment goal is the modification of an individual's specific problem behavior, intrasubject experimental design is extremely useful.

Intrasubject Designs   Four types of intrasubject research designs have been used in educational settings: *reversal* or *ABAB* design, *multiple-baseline* design, *changing-criterion* design, and *multielement* design. The reversal or ABAB design is based on the premise that behavior change is contingent on the absence or presence of the reinforcer. Therefore, the occurrence of the behavior is measured under reinforced and nonreinforced conditions (as in the intrasubject example testing John's response to praise). The initial data recorded, step A, was briefly discussed earlier in the chapter. Termed a *baseline,* it is evidence of the frequency or strength of the behavior without intervention. For example, John's usual performance on arithmetic problems can be measured as the number of problems completed correctly in one 30-minute period for 5 successive days. The amount of time required to establish a baseline varies with the behavior being assessed. However, care must be taken that the period of adaptation has passed, and the pattern of performance of the behavior should be relatively stable.

Step B is the treatment phase. The planned intervention is now implemented. John is praised for completing arithmetic problems in one 30-minute period for 5 successive days. No change in John's production suggests that the treatment is ineffective. John may not respond well to praise as a reinforcer, or other variables may be interfering with the effectiveness of the reinforcer in this instance. An increase in John's production does not signify that the praise was effective. John may do better simply because of novelty effect (a new experience), or Hawthorne effect (the tendency for individuals to perform better when they receive any type of special attention), or because of any number of other confounding variables.

At this point, step 3, a return to step A is implemented, and the program is reversed. The treatment is withdrawn and the conditions existing before treatment are reestablished. If John's performance again returns to his baseline rate, there is increased evidence that the treatment may be a causal factor in his improvement. Finally, the last step, B, is the reinstitution of the treatment. Once again John's performance should accelerate to previously obtained heights if the treatment is effective.

There are several variations of the reversal design. One involves no initial baseline measure and is used in instances where the individual has never demonstrated the target behavior. For example, an individual who cannot speak English has a zero baseline rate for uttering English sentences. The reversal design to be used is BAB. Another variation pertains to behaviors that cannot be reversed or returned to baseline conditions. If a child learned 100 new reading words under the experimental treatment condition of praise, the words will not be forgotten when praise is withdrawn. In these cases, the effectiveness of the reinforcer can be tested by withholding it from reading activities and applying it to a variety of other achievement activities such as spelling, arithmetic, and so forth. If the child's level of performance on the reading activities diminishes, while the degree of efficiency on other activities increases, it would appear that the praise is effective.

Although the reversal design is used often in educational research, it has certain limitations that frequently prevent the formation of definitive conclusions regarding treatment effectiveness. Kazdin (1975) has demonstrated that behavior usually does not return to baseline rate during the repetition of step A. The higher level of response without reinforcement may suggest that the treatment was not responsible for the change in behavior. However, it also may indicate that the treatment has resulted in other associations that tend to keep responses accelerated. For example, John may have received parental rewards for better arithmetic production during step 2. Although teacher praise initiated his new response, its withdrawal does not diminish the other reinforcers that may have developed.

Another persistent problem is the continued possibility of results caused by the Hawthorne effect. If the effects were due to being singled out for treatment, rather than caused by the reinforcer, the predicted decrease and elevation in performance during steps 3 and 4 would still be likely to occur. This problem is always true in single-case or N of 1 studies and is more serious where the efficacy of treatments other than praise or attention is being evaluated.

A final problem, most significant for an interventionist who would apply this design in schools or clinics, pertains to ethics. Once an individual shows improved behavior, it often is not ethical to deliberately reverse the treatment and bring about an increased incidence of problem behavior. Obviously, there is a firm line between applied research with human beings and experimental laboratory investigations with animals that cannot be crossed in the name of science. Therefore, in using this design the interventionist must maintain a clear vision of the general goal of behavioral therapy, to help the individual involved. If there is a question about the relative effectiveness of various reinforcers in increasing a child's adaptive behavior, it is perfectly reasonable to use the reversal steps in the design. In the long run, finding the best reinforcer will be in the child's best interest. Similarly, the reversal design may be used legitimately when the reversed step results in nothing more extreme than a brief period of decreased academic achievement. The child will quickly regain accelerated levels in step 4. The design is inappropriate when a child has improved control over debilitating behaviors such as fighting, stealing, setting fires, and so forth. Obviously, any technique that results even in a brief reoccurrence of those activities is not beneficial to the individual involved.

The *multiple-baseline design* demonstrates the causal relationship between treatment and behavior by introducing treatment at different points in time. (Baer, Wolf, and Risley, 1968). One type of strategy, termed *multiple-baseline across behavior*, involves two or more behaviors simultaneously. After baseline data have been gathered, treatment is provided for one behavior while the others remain untreated. When the treated behavior changes, the intervention is extended to the second problem behavior, and so on, until all problem behaviors are modified. If each behavior changes when the treatment is introduced, it is assumed that the treatment has caused the improvement. An example of this strategy might involve increasing John's achievement in reading and spelling as well as arithmetic. After his typical baseline performance is graphed in all three achievement areas, the treatment, teacher praise, is applied initially to increase performance on arithmetic tasks. If performance improves, the treatment is maintained for arithmetic and extended to reading activities. Once reading improves, the treatment is extended to spelling tasks. Since his performance in each of these areas improved only when John received the treatment, it can be concluded that praise was responsible for the changes in his behavior.

A slightly different version of this type of design is termed *multiple-baseline across individuals*. In this type of application, data are gathered on a single behavior for two or more persons. Treatment is applied to one person while the others continue at the baseline rate. If the first person's behavior changes, the treatment is extended to another person, and so on until all persons receive the treatment. For example, the teacher might decide to help Joey, Sally, and Sue improve their reading achievement. Reading is demonstrated by their ability to read short stories at 90 percent accuracy and answer correctly five comprehension questions. The treatment, reinforcement with tokens, is applied first to Joey. If his efficiency improves, the treatment is extended to Sally. If Sally also improves in reading, the treatment is extended to Sue.

A third version of this design is *multiple-baseline across situations*. This strategy involves one behavior, any number of individuals, and several situations. For example, the reading program for the three children above might be conducted twice daily. In one situation, the token reinforcement system is used with all three and their behavior is recorded. In the other situation, no reinforcement is provided. Presumably, the children will be more productive in the first situation. After a period of time, reinforcement is introduced in the second situation with a predictable acceleration in achievement.

Although multiple-baseline designs avoid the ethical problems associated with reversal designs, they too are not free from problems. There is some indication (Buell, Stoddard, Harris, and Baer, 1968) that reinforcement of one behavior indirectly affects the performance of other behaviors. For example, John may be reinforced only for achievement in mathematics, but his performance in other academic areas may also accelerate. Therefore, the evidence that the reinforcement caused his improved achievement is confounded.

Similarly, reinforcement provided for one individual may affect the behavior of others. When Joey earns tokens for his efforts, Sally and Sue may try harder, even though they are not being given direct reinforcement. The same problem applies to varied situations, as behavior reinforced in one place may be demonstrated in another situation.

Clearly, these problems are more important to the behavioral scientist seeking a precise method of validating the effectiveness of the treatment than they are to the practitioner, who is more concerned about improved behavior. The fact that the effects of direct reinforcement may spread to other persons' behaviors or situations is an important positive benefit of treatment. It suggests that the notion of reinforcement is far more complex than it may initially appear to be, and that individuals may begin patterns of self-reinforcements that are more powerful than the external variables controlled or manipulated by the interventionist. Possibly, the most significant aspect of direct overt reinforcement is to "turn the tide" toward a more generalized demonstration of adaptive behaviors.

The third intrasubject design, *changing-criterion* (Axelrod, Hall, Weis, and Rohrer, 1974), demonstrates the effectiveness of treatment by showing that it continues to change behavior when the criterion for reinforcement is altered. For instance, a single behavior, such as making negative remarks to others, may be selected for treatment. The initial criterion may be established at 50 percent of the average baseline utterances, which are ten per school day. Reinforcement, a token, is awarded every day the behavior is not demonstrated more than five times. As the behavior diminishes, the criterion for reinforcement is established at 20 percent of the baseline utterances. To earn the token, no more than two negative remarks per day may be uttered. Ultimately, the criterion may preclude any negative remarks. The fact that the child decreases his or her negative utterances to meet each new criterion level suggests that the treatment caused the behavioral change.

The changing-criterion design is extremely useful for gradually modifying behaviors. It reflects the behavioral emphasis on solving problems in small, sequenced steps, rather than attempting to effect all or nothing changes in behavior. Although it appears to validate the effects of treatment, like the other intrasubject designs the evidence is not definitive. It is possible that initial changes in behaviors evoke reinforcement from other sources that are responsible for the continued behavioral modification. For example, the child who reduces his or her negative utterances may receive positive reinforcement from other sources such as peer or parent approval. The token system may have relatively little to do with the eventual discontinuation of the behavior. These treatment validation problems are difficult to overcome in single-case studies.

The final intrasubject design to be discussed is called the *multielement design*. This approach uses the strategy of random application of alternate treatments in varied situations to establish causal relationships between treatment and behavior. For example, the teacher might wish to examine the effectiveness of four reinforcement strategies for altering John's inappropriate out-of-seat behavior. The teacher may devise treatment A—a token for 100 percent in-seat behavior every hour, treatment B—teacher praise for 100 percent in-seat behavior every hour, treatment C—a note home to parents informing them of John's progress if he avoids inappropriate out-of-seat behavior for 4 hours of the school day, and treatment D—no treatment or baseline conditions. The treatments are applied independently of John's behavior, on a random basis each day. John is informed each morning which treatment is in effect and his inappropriate out-of-seat behavior is tabulated under each treatment condition over an extensive period of time. A comparison of his performance under each treatment condition reveals the relative effectiveness of each approach.

The multielement design has been found effective for investigating complex behaviors, such as motivating a class of hard-core underachievers to attempt academic tasks. Among the intrasubject intervention designs, it provides the most valid data about the causal relationship between treatment and behavior. It also provides objective information regarding the relative strength of alternate interventions. The obvious disadvantage to this design is that it is elaborate and cumbersome. It also may be confusing to the individual involved and care must be taken to ensure that the objectives of the strategy are clearly understood.

For the most part, intrasubject designs are easily applied by teachers in classroom situations. In fact, many teachers have probably used strategies such as the multiple-baseline across individual design in an informal way. For instance, the teacher finds that awarding John the privilege of being teacher's helper reduces his disruptive behavior, and extends that reinforcer to another disruptive child. To apply such techniques more objectively requires only closer attention to data recording. The teacher no longer relies solely on impressions about treatment effectiveness, but bases conclusions on recorded events.

Intersubject Designs   The alternate approach to empirical investigation of treatment effectiveness, intersubject designs, is less likely to be used by teachers, as they do not provide data that are directly applicable to the solution of a specific individual's problems. However, the most basic design, *control-group design*, is not difficult to implement and should be used more consistently in classroom situations.

The control-group design compares the performance of at least two discrete groups of people. The treatment is administered to only one group (experimental group), while the other (control group) is maintained under normal or preexperimental conditions. The differences in the average performance of the experimental and control groups indicate the effectiveness of the treatment. To use this technique most effectively, children must be randomly assigned to each group. Random assignment assures that preestablished differences in variables other than the treatment will not affect the outcome of the experiment. For example, all kindergarten students in school X are randomly assigned to two classes. The techniques usually employed to assign children to kindergarten classes, such as their area of residence, are not employed to ensure that variables such as socioeconomic status do not influence the investigation. The experimental group is to receive concentrated instruction in oral language skills, while the control group receives the typical play-oriented kindergarten experience. At the end of the year, the respective oral language competence of the groups is measured and compared. If the treatment was effective the experimental group will exceed their non-treated peers in oral language skills.

The control group design has distinct advantages over the typical educational procedures used to measure children's gains in skill, the pretest–posttest approach. In school settings children are usually tested on a variable such as oral language ability, given a particular instructional intervention, and tested again at the end of the school year. Their gains in oral language skill are attributed to the instruction and it is concluded that the instructional approach is an effective method of teaching. Both the attribution and conclusion may be erroneous, however, as the gains may have been due to extraneous variables such as maturation or increased test-taking skill. Also, without establishing a control group as a basis of comparison, it is impossible to know whether or not the children would have made greater gains from an alternate instructional approach.

This simplistic discussion of control-group designs barely scratches the surface of the topic. Much more information could be provided about this design, as well as other intersubject designs, but it is beyond the scope of this book. The interested reader should consult Campbell and Stanley (1963). The intent of this discussion is to suggest that it is not beyond the teacher's capabilities to conduct simple group studies. For instance, a teacher who suspects that emotionally disturbed children behave better when they are given 15 minutes of strenuous physical exercise after every hour of academic instruction, can test that premise by randomly assigning the students to an experimental and control group, giving the experimental group physical exercise and the control group a passive activity and comparing their behavior on any number of criteria. This simple experiment should verify the teacher's impressions about how to best manage the students.

Before concluding this section on the general principles of ABA or behavior modification, one additional topic requires discussion. This topic pertains directly to the application of these behavior principles and techniques in the classroom.

Classroom Applications

The literature on behavior modification is replete with examples of successful classroom implementation of many of the procedures discussed in the previous section of the chapter. The bulk of this research appears to support certain conclusions regarding the classroom application of these techniques and also presents some helpful methodological procedures to facilitate intervention.

One set of four general stratagems of effective behavioral management in the classroom has been delineated by Blackham and Silberman (1975, p. 140).[4] They concern the optimal effects of combining certain behavior principles and are

1. *Extinction and positive reinforcement.* The teacher should alter undesirable behavior by simultaneously decreasing it and increasing a desirable behavior. If the teacher wants Mary to decrease the amount of time she spends daydreaming, she should provide a substitute behavior such as working on assignments that can be reinforced as the daydreaming is decreased. This principle is similar to what has been termed the "praise and ignore technique" (Drabman, 1976), which simply involves reinforcing socially appropriate behavior with praise and attention, while simultaneously ignoring inappropriate behavior. For example, if Patti's behavior is marked by her inability to play with others and observation proves that she receives most adult attention when she demonstrates behaviors incompatible with social play, for example, sitting alone, the

---

[4] Source: Blackham, G. and Silberman, A. *Modification of child and adolescent behavior.* 2nd ed., used with permission of the Wadsworth Pub. Co., Belmont, CA 94002.

treatment involves withholding adult attention when she is not interacting socially and reinforcing with praise and attention when she engages in social play. A multitude of studies exist that attest to the efficiency of the praise and ignore technique. Among the behaviors successfully modified are hyperactivity (Allen, Henke, Harris, Baer, and Reynolds, 1967), excessive fantasy play (Bijou and Baer, 1967), attending school (Copeland, Brown, and Hall, 1974), cooperation with peers (Hart, Reynolds, Baer, Browley, and Harris, 1968), crying (Harris, Wolf, and Baer, 1964), paying attention (Hawkins, McArthur, Rinaldi, Gray, and Schaffenaur, 1967) and the general behavior of an entire class (Becker, Madsen, Arnold, and Thomas, 1967). The pitfalls associated with this procedure are that some behaviors are too disruptive or dangerous to ignore, and that peer reinforcement often supercedes teacher responses and reinforces the behavior the teacher is trying to ignore (O'Leary, Becker, Evans, and Saudargas, 1969).

2. *Modeling and positive reinforcement.* The teacher may use this combination of techniques effectively to introduce a new behavior into the child's repertoire through modeling and to simultaneously increase the probability of its occurrence through positive reinforcement. If the teacher wants Suzy to zip up her jacket, she models the behavior and tells her to do as she does. When Suzy zips the jacket the teacher reinforces her with praise. The teacher will probably demonstrate the zipping skill in sequenced steps and will reinforce Suzy for each success in the sequence. In addition to direct teacher modeling of the desired behavior, the teacher can make use of peer models to set a good example (Bandura, 1965). In the case of relatively complex behaviors, such as employment interviewing, the teacher can make use of video-taped simulations to demonstrate the behaviors which must be imitated by the children (Bandura, 1965).

3. *Role shift and positive reinforcement.* In this instance an individual is reinforced for demonstrating behavior that is opposite to and incompatible with a problem behavior. For example, Tommy, a child who often makes unfriendly remarks to his classmates, is reinforced for smiling and making friendly remarks. The reinforced behaviors are not compatible with the problem behavior. Although the problem behavior is not deliberately extinguished, its incidence of occurrence decreases.

4. *Behavior contracts, positive reinforcement and withdrawal of reinforcement.* This procedure involves using behavior contracts to specify the consequences of both adaptive and maladaptive behavior. The association of these techniques permits the child to contrast the pleasurable results of adaptive behavior with the cost of maladaptive behavior. In effect, it supports the old truism that you don't miss what you don't have,

but you hate to lose what you have. Thus, if John contracts with his teacher to avoid fighting in school or on the playground, he earns an extra 10-minute free time period each day he is successful, and pays the price in loss of this free time on days when he is not successful. Although the withdrawal of positive reinforcement is not synonymous with punishment, children generally perceive it as punishing (Baer, 1962), and it depresses the incidence of maladaptive behaviors (Wolf, Risley, and Mees, 1964).

Figures 6.2, 6.3, and 6.4 show how contracts can be used in this fashion. Blackham and Silberman (1975) also have identified several ingredients that produce effective classroom management. They include specifying in positive terms the desired classroom behavior, individualizing learning tasks so that every child can succeed, modeling the behaviors that the students should emulate, using individual and group reinforcement systems, and determining when and how reinforcement will be

My Weekly Contract

During the week of _____,
I hereby agree to work on increasing
one of the following behaviors:

    O staying in my seat
    O completing class assignments
    O obeying class rules
    O getting along with others

    If I can exhibit appropriate behavior
in this category for ____ consecutive days,
I may choose as my reward one of the
following activities:

    O talking with a friend for 10 min.
    O playing the game of my choice for 10 min.
    O reading comic books and/or magazines for 10 min.
    O working out in the gym for 10 min.

We, the undersigned, agree to the above terms.

_____   _____
Student   Teacher

Fig. 6.2. Secondary-Level Contract

_____ and _____

agree to try to get along with each other.
For every recess without fighting, they will
each receive 5 points. Points may be traded in
for free time.

                    5 points = 5 minutes

_____
    Student's signature

_____   _____
    student's signature   teacher's signature

Fig. 6.3. _Intermediate-Level Contract_

administered. The first three points will be discussed in considerable detail in the succeeding chapter, Education Therapy. The latter points, particularly the information on the development of a reinforcement system, warrant further discussion here.

Most behaviorists recognize two general types of reinforcement systems, primary and secondary. Secondary reinforcement systems used in school settings may be broken down further into social, token, and contingency management systems.

Primary Reinforcers   Primary reinforcers such as food reduce drive state and are therefore highly reliable. Obviously, all persons get hungry and are susceptible to the reinforcement value of food. The limitation of using primary reinforcers is that individuals satiate quickly and the reinforcers lose their effectiveness. They also may be inconvenient to handle in class, and parents often object to the use of treat foods such as candy or cookies. Generally primary reinforcers have been used in the initial stages of a modification program to establish a stable adaptive response. At that point they usually are paired with social reinforcement to sustain the response. Also, primary reinforcers are useful with the severely handicapped including schizophrenics (Lovaas, Freitag, Kinder, Rubenstein, Schaeffer, and Simmons, 1966), retardates (Hundziak, Maurer, and Watson, 1965), and emotionally disturbed (O'Leary, O'Leary, and Becker, 1967), who may not be able to respond to alternate types of reinforcement. Even in these cases, however, some form of secondary reinforcement is paired with the primary reinforcement.

Social Reinforcement   Attention, social recognition, and praise are forms of social reinforcement. This type of reinforcement is most frequently used by teachers since it involves little effort and no cost. It is also less artificial in school settings than alternate types of reinforcement. Social recognition has been found to be successful when used with emotionally

Fig. 6.4. *Primary-Level Contract*

disturbed children (Zimmerman and Zimmerman, 1962), nursery-school students (Brown and Elliott, 1965), a nontalking boy (Brison, 1966), elementary school children (Barclay, 1967), high-school students (McAllister, Stachowiak, Baer, and Conderman, 1969), and a variety of others.

Similarly, praise and other verbal behaviors have been shown to be powerful enough to influence classes of verbal responses (Binder, McConnell, and Sjoholm, 1957; Vogel-Sprott, 1964), self-reference statements (Krasner, 1965), and information-seeking and decision-making responses (Krumboltz and Thoresen, 1964; Thorensen and Krumboltz, 1967). In other words, social reinforcement actually determines what an individual will say.

Of course, it must be recognized that social reinforcement is an equally effective reinforcer of maladaptive behavior (Hall, Lund, and Jackson, 1968). If Joan goes into a tantrum in class and the teacher responds with attention, even critical or negative attention, Joan is reinforced for her tantrum and will exhibit the behavior again. Therefore, teachers must carefully analyze their reactions to children's maladaptive behaviors to ensure that they are not inadvertently reinforcing them.

The disadvantages of social reinforcement are that some children do not respond positively to praise. In fact, it may decrease the probability of a behavior occurring, and in that case is not a positive reinforcer. In addition, the effectiveness of social reinforcement is related to the status of the agent supplying it. Praise from a highly valued individual may determine behavior more readily than similar remarks from a low-status person. This is particularly true among adolescents who value peer approval far more than adult approval and behave accordingly.

Token Reinforcement   This type of reinforcement uses a system that has the advantage of combining the principles of immediate and delayed gratification. Desired responses are reinforced immediately with tokens that may be exchanged at a later time for backup reinforcing items or events. For example, a child may earn one token every hour he or she works without calling out. After accruing 20 tokens, the child may exchange them for candy, the privilege of running the film projector, toys, extra recess, or a free time period.

When a system of token reinforcement is applied to a group, the effect is to establish an economy similar to that based on money. In effect, children earn tokens as a salary that they use to purchase items that give them pleasure. Because tokens are associated with a variety of backup reinforcers, they have very powerful reinforcement value.

Flexibility and administrative convenience are added advantages of token economies. The system is flexible in that it permits the behavior modifier to make simple adjustment in the rate or duration of responses necessary to earn the token reinforcer. Also, the price of backup reinforcers may be raised so that the child must work harder for the privilege or item. Administratively, the behavior modifier need not be concerned with problems such as satiation that accompany the direct use of primary reinforcers, nor with practical difficulties of having to select a reinforcer appropriate for a particular child.

The immediate administration of the token after the target behavior increases the probability of its reoccurrence. The later exchange of the token for a backup reinforcer teaches saving and planning and enhances self-control.

Generally, this system is particularly useful in school settings because it often works with children who do not respond to social reinforcement. Although token systems are easy to employ, Blackham and Silberman (1975, p. 145)[5] have summarized suggestions of requirements for successful programs from Phillips, Phillips, Fixsen, and Wolf (1973), O'Leary and Drabman (1971), and Vernon (1972).

1. The target behaviors that will earn tokens must be clearly specified and written on a chart or blackboard. If both individual and group token systems are used, the individual target behaviors should be posted on the student's desk. The rules governing individual and group contingencies should be reviewed frequently with the students.
2. The student must be able to perform the target behaviors for which tokens will be given.
3. The backup reinforcers for which tokens are exchanged must be appealing to the students and should not be available outside the token system.
4. The number of tokens earned must be consistent with the difficulty or effort required to perform the behavior. For example, if a student has great difficulty controlling his aggression, reinforcement for nonaggressive behavior must be sufficient to provide a potent incentive for proper behavior.
5. If possible, the teacher should keep a record of tokens earned by each child (and the group, when a group system is used). Student incentive is often enhanced when the number of tokens earned are recorded on a chart displayed for the entire class to see.
6. If the response cost (token fines) is also used, the exact conditions under which tokens will be earned or lost should be clearly designated to the student(s). When tokens are given or taken away, the teacher should relate the action to the student behavior involved (The teacher's statement should be to the point, and arguments regarding token loss should be avoided at all costs.)

---

[5] Blackham, G. and Silberman, A. *Modification of child and adolescent behavior.* 2nd ed., used with permission of the Wadsworth Pub. Co., Belmont, CA 94002.

7. Usually, token exchange for the backup reinforcer should occur at the end of the school day. If the material reinforcer (toy or game) is given to a student during the school day he is likely to play with it and distract other students from appropriate task behavior. When a student has earned enough tokens to exchange them for a tangible reinforcer, simply indicate to the child that his name tag will be placed on it so he can secure it at the end of the day.
8. Extend token reinforcement so that the target behavior will be encouraged in a wide range of situations (classroom, physical education class, playground). Desirable behavior is not likely to generalize to nonreinforced settings.
9. Devise the token system so that a student competes with himself rather than other students, i.e., on the basis of desirable improvements in his own performance and behavior.
10. Always combine praise with tokens so that social reinforcement ultimately can be used to maintain desirable academic and social behavior.
11. A well-devised token system should gradually withdraw material reinforcers and rely on reinforcing activities and events. Ultimately, social reinforcement and reinforcing events should maintain the desired behavior.
12. The token system should be simple, functional, and not distract from learning. Tangible tokens (chips, stamps) can be traded or stolen and disrupt the reinforcement system. In school situations, checkmark tokens are easiest to use. Each student is issued a card with his name on it. As he earns points or checkmarks, they are recorded on the card and initialed by the teacher. If the card is taken by another student, he cannot use it to obtain backup reinforcers.

Two additional points may be added to these statements. First, the student and teacher should prepare a formal contract specifying the relationship between the desired behavior and the token reinforcement. The arrangement must be negotiated. Second, the teacher can prepare a list of back up reinforcers that can be acquired with varied numbers of tokens. The object is to maintain a variety of reinforcers and to permit the student to save tokens for long-range reinforcement.

The token economy system appears to be gaining in popularity. It has been used in one form or another with retarded children (Birnbrauer, Wolf, Kidder, and Tague, 1965; Zimmerman, Zimmerman, and Russell, 1969), the autistic (Martin, England, Kaprowy, Kilgour, and Pilek, 1968; Craighead and Meyers, 1973), hyperactive children (Quay, Sprague, Werry, and McQueen, 1967), schizophrenic children (Drabman, 1973), emotionally disturbed children (O'Leary and Becker, 1967) and delinquents (Meichenbaum, Bowers, and Ross, 1968). It may be used with groups as well as individuals. A token economy called "The Good Behavior Game" (Barrish, Saunders, and Wolf, 1969) was used to decrease the out-of-seat and talking-out behavior of an entire class. The procedure involves dividing the class in half and having the two teams compete for tokens. Research suggests that group procedures, although less time consuming, are as effective as individual programs (Hermon and Tramontana, 1971; Drabman, Spitalnik, and Spitalnik, 1974).

Contingency Management   This is reinforcement technique based on the Premack principle (1959) that a low-probability behavior can be increased in frequency when its execution is followed by a high probability behavior. More simply, Homme (1969) calls this principle "Grandma's Law: first eat your vegetables, then you may have your dessert." With contingency management, a child is reinforced for completing a low-probability task, such as an arithmetic assignment, with a high-probability task, such as reading a mystery story.

There are two methods of implementing contingency management. One method simply permits the student free time to pursue a reinforcing activity after he or she completes an assigned task. The time allowed for completion of the assignment is not specified, but is always followed by a set period of free time.

A second, more precise method establishes specific time periods for each assignment. If the assignment is completed before the time elapses, the reinforcement is free time for the remainder of the time period. For example, the school day may be divided into 60-minute periods. An arithmetic assignment is estimated to take 45 minutes. Children who complete the task in 45 minutes, have 15 minutes of time to engage in a pleasurable activity. Children who fail to complete the assignment gain no free time reinforcement.

The key to using a contingency management system effectively is to ensure that the time periods allotted are fair to all students. Some individuals might be expected to complete twenty arithmetic problems in 45 minutes, whereas others might be capable of doing fifty problems. If assignments were not individualized, the contingency system would penalize the slower, less-capable students, who are in the greatest need of effective reinforcement.

The system is also more effective if the teacher provides a separate reinforcing events (RE) area in the room that contains a variety of appealing games, toys, books, and gadgets. The stock of this area should be changed periodically to prevent boredom. A good practice is to have the children suggest the items for the RE area. They also may contribute items.

In addition to the management tasks connected with this system, which obviously require effort and planning, the teacher should recognize that implementation requires a spacious room. Also, RE activities may distract other students, therefore, the program must be carefully introduced to the children and they must understand the limits to RE activities.

The contingency management system, while not used as extensively as alternative reinforcement systems, has been applied successfully with retarded children (Daley, 1969), as well as normals (Homme, 1966). It appears more effective when integrated with a token economy (Nolen, Kunzelmann, and Haring, 1967; Wasik, 1970).

Punishment   The topic of reinforcement, consequences that increase behavior, cannot be terminated without brief reference to punishment,[6] consequences that decrease behavior. Generally, in school settings three types of punishment are used: response cost, time out, and verbal reprimands.

Response cost is the loss of a previously acquired reinforcer contingent on inappropriate behavior. It is usually employed as a component of token economies: the child must give back a previously earned token. Iwata and Bailey (1974) have demonstrated that response cost is as efficient as positive reinforcement in reducing rule violations and off-task behavior. Apparently, children dislike losing tokens that they have earned just as adults dislike paying a traffic ticket.

Time out is a procedure that calls for placing a disruptive child in social isolation for a given period of time. Technically, the child is prevented from experiencing positive reinforcement during that period. Return to the classroom or to the group is determined by passage of time (usually about 10 minutes) and appropriate behavior during the last minutes of the time period. Studies (Whelan and Haring, 1966; Walker, Mattson, and Buckley, 1968) have demonstrated the usefulness of the time-out procedure in conjunction with positive reinforcement. Drabman and Spitalnik (1973) used time-out procedures exclusively to reduce the incidence of out-of-seat behavior and aggression among children residing in a psychiatric hospital.

The time-out procedure, as all behavioral procedures, is effective when it is contingent on a specific, clearly defined behavior. In establishing this response (punishment association), the teacher must ensure that the child's behavioral contract is not unrealistic, that is, that the child is not programmed to fail and that time out is not used too frequently. The association of time out with a positive reinforcement schedule is most desirable.

Verbal reprimands are an interesting class of punishment because they are the teacher's most often used method of behavior control. There is increasing evidence that although reprimands affect behavior, they do

---

[6] See Azrin and Holz (1966) for interesting and detailed information pertaining to the effects of punishment.

not decrease incidence as expected, but rather act as positive reinforcement and increase the incidence of occurrence (Thomas, Becker, and Armstrong, 1968). A typical example is reported by Madsen, Becker, Thomas, Koser, and Plager (1970), who tested the effectiveness of the teacher utterance "sit down" in reducing children's out-of-seat behavior. Using a modified reversal design, they established a baseline of typical teacher "sit down" comments, had the teachers triple the frequency of those comments, returned to a baseline level, returned to the elevated frequency, and finally had the teachers praise behaviors incompatible with out-of-seat behavior. They found a 37 percent increase in out-of-seat behavior during the high-frequency periods. The last stage, praising incompatible behaviors, resulted in a 33 percent decrease in those behaviors. The results show the ineffectiveness of verbal reprimands in reducing out-of-seat behavior. Apparently, however, the manner of delivery is a factor, as quiet reprimands have been shown to be more effective than loud reprimands (O'Leary and Becker, 1968; O'Leary, Kaufman, Kass, and Drabman, 1970).

Reinforcing Agents   The final section of the use of reinforcement systems pertains to the reinforcing agents. There is some evidence that peers can administer token economies (Johnson and Bailey, 1974; Drabman, 1973). The effectiveness of peer-delivered social reinforcement is less clear, as it appears influenced by the social relationships among the children. When peers are friends, social reinforcement is less effective (Hartup, 1964; Tiktin and Hartup, 1965). Parents have also been trained as reinforcing agents (Bijou, 1965; Russo, 1964; O'Leary, O'Leary, and Becker, 1967). The importance of such parent involvement appears to be achieving greater recognition among educators.

Finally, investigations have demonstrated that normal children can control their own token economies with no extensive training (Lovitt and Curtiss, 1969; Glynn, 1970; Glynn and Thomas, 1974). There is also evidence that a self-reinforcement program can be used by disruptive children if they are taught to rate their behavior as the teacher rates it (Drabman, Spitalnik, and O'Leary, 1973).

CLINICAL APPLICATIONS OF BEHAVIORAL PRINCIPLES: CLINICAL–BEHAVIORAL THERAPY

Thus far we have explored the general application of behavior principles through applied behavior analysis and behavior modification. The emphasis has been on depicting strategies typically used by teachers in a classroom. These strategies and others based on behavioral theory also are applied in clinical settings, that is, those that might be termed psychotherapeutic if it were not for the behavior therapists' insistence on distinguishing between traditional psychotherapies such as Freudian analysis, and behavioral therapy.

The separation of behavior modification from what is referred to in this section as clinical–behavioral therapy is arbitrary. It will become apparent in the discussion of clinical treatments that many of the simpler strategies could be implemented by teachers in classrooms. Essentially, the separation of these sections reflects the fact that behavioral interventions have been developed and applied in two settings, schools and clinics, by individuals with different professional backgrounds, educators and educational psychologists, and clinical psychologists and psychiatrists.

Reciprocal Inhibition   Possibly the most distinctive therapeutic technique applied in clinical–behavioral therapy is the reciprocal inhibition approach popularized by a psychiatrist, Joseph Wolpe, in his book *Psychotherapy by Reciprocal Inhibition* (1958). Wolpe's methods are based on an extension of the phenomenon of reciprocal inhibition in muscles (Sherrington, 1906), whereby the reflex excitation of a group of muscles automatically causes the inhibition of an antagonistic group of muscles and vice versa. For example, in a knee jerk reflex the excitation of the muscles that straighten the knee is accompanied by inhibition of the hamstrings that bend the knee. Wolpe (1976, p. 17) applies this principle to psychological behavior, theorizing that "an anxiety response habit can be weakened by evoking a response incompatible with anxiety in the presence of the anxiety-evoking stimulus." In other words, it is more difficult for an individual to experience anxiety in a situation that usually evokes that response, if an alternate response is evoked. The alternate response inhibits the anxiety response.

Wolpe identified three main categories of incompatible responses that inhibit anxiety. They are *assertive, sexual,* and *relaxation* responses. Assertive responses are defined as "Any overt expression of spontaneous and appropriate feelings other than anxiety." They are used primarily to overcome anxiety that is evoked in interpersonal situations and that inhibits verbal responses to others. The individual is taught to verbalize feelings such as anger and affection which are customarily inhibited. The verbal responses weaken the anxiety response habit.

Sexual responses are used when anxiety pertains to sexual situations. Sexual excitation is controlled by the parasympathetic nervous system and anxiety by the sympathetic nervous system. The arousal of one response inhibits the other.

Deep muscle relaxation is by far the most generally applied anxiety inhibitor. Originally, Jacobson (1938) recognized its effectiveness as an opposition response to anxiety and developed strategies of progressive relaxation in disturbing situations. Wolpe (1961, 1973) has developed and popularized a clinical technique to be used in conjunction with deep muscle relaxation called *systematic desensitization*.

Systematic desensitization is a procedure that involves developing a ranked list or hierarchy of unadaptive fears, ordered according to how much fear they evoke, and systematically deconditioning each sequenced fear response proceeding from low fear to high fear. For example, a hierarchy of fear of rats might at the lowest or least fear-evoking step, involve a picture of a rat, progress through sequenced steps that are progressively anxiety inducing such as viewing a live rat, and culminate with the most fear-evoking step, holding a rat. Although the rat fear example involved real life or *in vivo* experiences, that is, the person handled a real rat, systematic desensitization of complex fears may be conducted by having the client imagine situations that typically arouse anxiety. Thus, a claustrophobic person whose hierarchy pertains to fear of closed spaces, need only imagine himself or herself in a series of anxiety-evoking situations, such as being trapped in an elevator, to be desensitized. He or she need not actually live or directly experience the anxiety-evoking events.

Wolpe notes (1976) that most disturbed people require desensitization on more than one fear hierarchy. In fact, the identification and construction of the hierarchies is a critical step in effective treatment. Hierarchies are constructed from four main sources of information; the patient's clinical history, for example, the onset and vicissitudes of the maladaptive reaction; the patient's case history, for example, family background, childhood experiences; responses and reactions to probing questions; and responses to questionnaires such as the Willoughby Neuroticism Schedule and the Fear Survey Schedule (Wolpe and Lang, 1969). The hierarchies are not restricted to the patient's obvious or stated fears but may be developed for less apparent problems gleaned from the questionnaires or interviewing techniques. They may be thematic in nature, as is the fear of rats hierarchy that sequences steps involving reactions to the basic theme "rats," or they may be of temporal-spatial design (Yates, 1970). The steps of temporal-spatial hierarchies move the individual through varied time and space settings. For example, fear of leaving home may be desensitized by a hierarchy including sequences such as walking toward the door, opening the door, stepping outside for 5 seconds while holding the door knob, walking down the outside steps, walking to the edge of the curb, and so on. Often, temporal-spatial and thematic designs are combined.

When relaxation is used as the anxiety-inhibiting response in conjunction with systematic desensitization, the patient is trained in relaxation techniques as the hierarchies are being formed. When the individual is able to relax deeply, the weakest, least fear-evoking scene from the hierarchy is presented. The patient must imagine the scene briefly, then concentrate again on relaxation. The alternate pairing of imaginary experience and relaxation are continued until the initial scene no longer evokes anxiety. At that point, the next step on the hierarchy is introduced and the procedures are repeated. Theoretically, as each item is desensitized the item above it in the hierarchy becomes less threatening and also can be desensitized through the inhibiting effects of relaxation. Therefore, each scene of the hierarchy can be presented without causing the patient discomfort. When the final scene, which before treatment was the most anxiety-evoking event in the hierarchy, is presented, it too can be inhibited through relaxation procedures. The success of the procedure depends on beginning with an imagined scene that stimulates a weak anxiety response, that is, one that can be inhibited by relaxation. Relaxation and other anxiety-inhibiting responses will not immediately inhibit strong anxiety responses. Thus, if the individual experiences discomfort when confronted with a scene, the item must either be reduced into smaller steps on the hierarchy, or must be presented in a different way to build up desensitization.

Wolpe (1976) reports that the deconditioning of anxiety in imaginary situations is associated with an abatement of anxiety in corresponding real-life situations. Others, principally Yates (1970) question this assumption, pointing out that there are few investigations of the extent to which imagined desensitization transfers to real-life stimuli (as when the claustrophobic person actually gets trapped in an elevator). Also, there are few investigations of the relative effectiveness of imaginary desensitization as compared to real-life or *in vivo* desensitization. Apparently, however, there is a great deal of research that attests to the effectiveness of systematic desensitization *in vivo* (Freeman and Kendrick, 1960; Meyers, 1957; Bentler, 1962; Goldstein, 1969; Hamilton and Schroeder, 1973; Sherman, 1972) as well as in imagination (Borkovec, 1970, 1972; Lang, 1969; Paul, 1969; Rachman, 1967). The choice of imaginary versus *in vivo* procedures may simply be one of convenience.

More interesting criticisms of systematic desensitization pertain to each component of Wolpe's method: the importance of relaxation, the importance of constructing sequenced hierarchies, and the necessity of systematic progression through the hierarchies (Yates, 1975).[7] Yates reviewed research pertaining to relaxation and concluded that systematic desensitization is effective whether or not relaxation training is part of the program. In response, Wolpe (1973) notes that muscle relaxation is but one technique to inhibit anxiety. He points out that the emotion generated by the traditional patient-therapist relationship tends to inhibit anxiety when it is a weak response, and he attributed the beneficial effects of 40 percent of psychotherapy (nonbehavioral) to this fact. He believes that the efficiency of a specific system must be tested by recoveries above

---

[7] Source: Yates, A. *Theory and Practice in Behavior Therapy.* New York: Wiley and Sons, 1975. Reprinted by permission of the publisher.

that 40 percent baseline level and that systematic desensitization combined with relaxation is effective for these more-resistant patients.

The importance of specific, individualized hierarchy construction is questioned by Cotler (1970), Donner and Guerney (1969), McGlynn (1971), and Nawas, Fishman, and Pucel (1970) who found standard or group hierarchies as effective as individualized hierarchies, even when the standard items were in random order. More importantly, desensitization has been found to work when the sequence of low-anxiety to high-anxiety items is ignored, as when only high-anxiety items are presented (Cohen, 1969; Suinn, Edie, and Spinelli, 1970; Edelman, 1971) or when high-anxiety items are presented first (Krapfl and Nawas, 1970). These results suggest that it may not be necessary to proceed through step-by-step desensitization and that high-anxiety responses may be diminished when low-anxiety responses are ignored. The conclusion is supported by research that denotes the effectiveness of massed desensitization procedures, that is, moving quickly through the hierarchy, as opposed to the slow, cautious progress that characterizes standard desensitization procedures (Robinson and Suinn, 1969; Hall and Hinckle, 1972). It also gains support from the evidence that *flooding* or *implosive therapy*, in which the person is exposed quickly to the most frightening event for long periods of time, is effective (Stampfl and Levis, 1968).

Regarding this point, Wolpe (1973, pp. 193–200) has reported on the method of *flooding*, also referred to as *paradoxical intention* (Frankl, 1960) and *implosive therapy*. He regards flooding procedures as useful for treatment of compulsive neuroses based on fear of contamination (Rachman, Hodgson, and Marks 1971; Wolpe and Ascher, 1975), but as generally less effective than systematic desensitization and more prone to relapse (Willis and Edwards, 1969; DeMoor, 1970; Mealiea and Nawas, 1971).

Clearly, even the critiques of systematic desensitization do not dispute its effectiveness—anxiety is lessened when individuals are trained in controlled, safe circumstances, to relax in the presence of anxiety-inducing scenes or events. The debatable point appears to be the validity of Wolpe's firmly held conviction that the technique works because of reciprocal inhibition—that, in fact, "virtually all therapeutic changes (no matter how brought about) and perhaps all learning involve reciprocal inhibition" (p. 3, 1976). Others disagree and offer alternate explanations involving the concepts of counterconditioning, extinction, and habituation, Although these arguments are interesting, they are of limited importance to the practitioner, and the temptation to pursue them further will be resisted. The interested reader should consult Yates (1975) for a review of all positions, as well as an argument that deplores the development of any set of clinical procedures (particularly systematic desensitization) from an unverified theory.

Multimodal Therapy   This approach to clinical treatment is proposed by Lazarus in *Behavior Therapy and Beyond* (1971). Essentially, it is an eclectic, atheoretical set of therapeutic techniques, which, in Lazarus's words: "urges therapists to experiment with empirically useful methods instead of using their theories as a priori predictors of what will and will not succeed in therapy." In other words, the multimodal procedure is based on the position that behavioral therapy is not a methodology emanating from learning theory, as Wolpe maintains with his treatment built on the theory of reciprocal inhibition. Instead, it is the application of the scientific method in clinical situations to predict outcomes and assess their occurrence.

A multimodal approach is an attack on an emotional problem through as many avenues as possible. Lazarus advances the pragmatic rationale that "the more a person learns in therapy, the less likely he is to relapse afterwards." (p. 405, 1973) For example, a drug addict treated solely by aversion therapy would be more likely to relapse than an addict treated by aversion therapy, relaxation therapy, family therapy, and vocational guidance. Lazarus has developed seven categories that warrant investigation in each therapeutic situation: B—Behavior, A—Affect, S—Sensation, I—Imagery, C—Cognition, I—Interpersonal Relations, and D—Drugs (the acronym, BASIC ID). An example of problems and treatments in each category might be as shown in the accompanying table.

Category	Problem	Treatment
Behavior	Frequent crying	Positive self-talk assignments
Affect	Frequent anxiety	Relaxation training
Sensation	Stomach spasms	Abdominal breathing
Imagery	Father threatening punishment	Empty-chair technique
Cognition	Irrational self-talk	Corrective self-talk
Interpersonal Relations	Childlike dependence	Self-sufficiency assignments
Drugs	No problems	Not used

As might be expected, Wolpe takes a dim view of an eclectic approach, reporting that "there is no evidence that the specific interventions of other systems (not emanating from learning theory) add anything to therapeutic success. In fact, it may be disadvantageous; Lazarus (1971) had a 36% relapse rate at follow up, in contrast to the 3% or less that is characteristic of pure behavioral therapy" (p. 24, 1976).

Group Desensitization   This group adaptation of systematic desensitization was introduced by Lazarus (1961). It involves using a standard fear hierarchy with a group of disturbed persons and progressing to each step dependent on each group member's anxiety reaction. The group remains at a lower anxiety scene until all members are able to progress to the next step. Paul and Shannon (1966) found group desensitization as effective as the individualized technique.

Enriched Systematic Desensitization   This technique involves using alternate anxiety-inhibiting responses in addition to relaxation with the systematic desensitization. One such enriched technique is *emotive imagery* (Lazarus and Abramovitz, 1962). Emotive images are imagined events that arouse feelings of self-importance, joy, pride, and so forth. As the individual imagines himself or herself in circumstances that generate good feeling, a minimal anxiety-arousing stimulus from the hierarchy is introduced.

Another enrichment technique involves the introduction of *cognitive restructuring*. The patient is encouraged to think benign, helpful thoughts or to engage in positive self-talk that counters the fearful thoughts engendered by the anxiety-evoking stimulus.

Automated Systematic Desensitization   Migler and Wolpe (1967) have investigated the use of tape recordings to enable the patient to practice relaxation and desensitization to hierarchical scenes at home.

Aversion Therapy   According to Wolpe (1976), this approach is useful to inhibit unadaptive emotional responses other than anxiety, particularly those that are pleasurable, such as sexual deviance, alcoholism, and drug addiction. An aversion response such as electric shock is paired with the unadaptive pleasurable response and inhibits its occurrence. Thus, a sexual deviant would be encouraged to imagine himself or herself engaging in deviant sexual activities and would be shocked as this behavior began. The response to the shock would interfere with the excitation response to the sexual imagery.

An instrumental form of aversive therapy involves the application of an unpleasant stimulus that is terminated when the patient ceases the maladaptive behavior. For example, an individual may be shocked each time he or she smokes a cigarette, but the shock is terminated as soon as the cigarette is discarded.

A less drastic aversive technique involves *aversive imagery*. The patient is encouraged to imagine unpleasant scenes in response to the pleasure-evoking stimulus. For example, an alcoholic may imagine the unpleasant effects of a hangover in response to a bottle of alcohol.

In attempting to spread a word of caution about the use of aversive techniques, Wolpe points out that many maladaptive habits like excessive drinking and drug addiction usually are secondary to neurotic anxiety, and he notes that "aversion therapy should never be used before every attempt has been made to decondition the anxiety. If the basic anxiety is removed, the behaviors that stem from it will usually disappear, and there will be no need for aversive therapy" (1973, pp. 216, 238).

Massed Practice Techniques   This procedure is based on the theory of reactive inhibition (Hull, 1943), which states that the repetition of a response generates fatigue that acts to inhibit the occurrence of that response. Thus, unadaptive motor habits such as tics and stuttering may be eliminated by having the patient deliberately repeat the behavior.

Operant Techniques   This category refers to the use of the reinforcement procedures discussed throughout this chapter. Clinical applications vary with the case and the behavior problem. As these procedures are clearly most useful in educational settings, instances of their use to modify particular types of problem behavior will be discussed in detail. In addition to operant techniques, other behavioral procedures such as massed practice or systematic desensitization will be included to a lesser extent, so that their usefulness in real-life situations might be appreciated. This discussion of therapeutic interventions for specific pathological conditions is the third and final section of this chapter. Much of the material discussed follows Yates (1970, 1975), who should be consulted by the reader seeking more extensive information.

BEHAVIORAL THERAPEUTIC INTERVENTIONS

Temper Tantrums   Most operant procedures to control this unadaptive behavior involve withholding social reinforcement by ignoring the behavior (Williams, 1959) or combine ignoring the negative behavior with increased social reinforcement when it ceases (Patterson and Brodsky, 1966). Punishment through isolation is also useful, as Jensen and Womack (1967) report success with the time-out technique. The child was removed to an isolated room until the temper tantrum ceased.

Excessive Crying   Operant procedures are useful when crying appears related to and maintained by attention. As with temper tantrums, ignoring or withholding attention when crying occurs is paired with positive reinforcement for noncrying behavior in situations that normally produce crying, such as falls or tussles (Hart et al., 1964). In more severe cases of continuous crying, Blake and Moss (1967) have used the time-out technique effectively.

Head Bumping   Reported treatments for this behavior vary and obviously relate to the possibility of injury. In a case where the behavior is done in such a way that the child prevents injury, such as head bumping on clasped hands, Mogel and Schiff (1967) attempted to use massed practice. The child was instructed to demonstrate the behavior repeatedly. They report that when the child, a ten-year-old girl, understood what she would be required to do, she became embarrassed and stopped permanently. They attributed her change in behavior to the negative attention and to the girl's cognitive operations.

In other instances where head bumping is associated with severe disturbance and appears harmful to the child, the problem is more complex. Lovass, Freitag, Gold, and Kassarla (1964) reinforced schizophrenic children to display incompatible motor responses such as moving to music and bar pressing. They found that ignoring head banging did not reduce its incidence and that following it with positive verbalizations increased its incidence. Tate and Baroff (1966) also found that ignoring head banging increased the incidence of occurrence. Negative consequences, such as withdrawing bodily contact, reduced incidence, whereas mild electric shock eliminated it.

Thumbsucking This behavior has been reduced by the withdrawal of positive reinforcement whenever it occurs (Baer, 1962).

Isolate Behavior Allen et al. (1964) demonstrated that a socially isolated four-year-old girl altered her behaviors when she received reduced teacher attention for solitary activity or excessive association with adults and increased teacher attention for peer play. Eventually, teacher attention for peer interactions was faded as peer attention became a reinforcing stimulus. Clement and Milne (1967) found that socially withdrawn, maladjusted boys, aged 8 and 9, responded best to a token reward system for social play, proximity to others, and verbal statements to others. Verbal reinforcement also increased the incidence of these behaviors but not as effectively as tokens.

Elective Mutism This problem pertains to children who evidence normal speech with some individuals and total silence with others. The condition usually appears between the ages of 3 and 5. It often is associated with social timidity, poor social relationships, reluctance to attend school, fear of strangers (Salfield, 1950), or may be simply an attention-getting device (Reed, 1963).

Brison (1966) eliminated mutism by placing the child in a new class that had been instructed to ignore the mutism and all nonverbal behavior that might achieve the results normally achieved by talking. The child began talking in a whisper, was socially reinforced, and shortly began talking normally. Newcomer (1965) attained similar results by instructing the teacher of a mute kindergarten student to withhold all pleasurable items and activities, such as milk and cookies, games, and so on, unless the child asked for them. Also, the teacher was neither to express concern over the mutism nor to cajole the child to speak, but was to remain warm and positive about other aspects of the child's behavior such as his drawings, his appearance, and so forth. Within weeks, the child began talking normally.

Reid et al. (1967) used systematic desensitization procedures to overcome a child's fear of speaking in front of strangers. The child's mother fed him small portions of food as he asked for them. Reid entered the room and gradually approached the child. Eventually Reid substituted for the mother, feeding the child while maintaining the verbal behaviors. Other experimenters joined the group and all talked with the child. In this case, Reid judged the mutism to be representative of the child's general fear of strangers, whereas in the other cases cited, the mutism was deemed to be a negative or attention-getting behavior. Kauffman (1977) reports many other successful behavioral interventions combining desensitization and reinforcement for gradual approximations toward speaking freely.

Regressed Crawling or Talking   Occasionally children begin demonstrating behaviors developmentally characteristic of younger children. Regressed talking or "baby talk" is not uncommon and is reduced quickly when immature speech is ignored and chronologically appropriate speech is given social reinforcement (Newcomer, 1965).

Less frequently, children regress to younger locomotion patterns. Harris et al. (1964) used similar strategies with a kindergarten child who spent practically all her time crawling in class. They withheld all social reinforcement when she crawled and gave immediate reinforcement with praise and attention when she walked. Within two weeks she stopped crawling.

Restlessness and Excessive Mobility   Operant procedures have been applied successfully to reduce hyperactive behavior. Pihl (1967) used a system of token reinforcement to increase in-seat behavior of a neurologically impaired boy from 7–15 minutes at baseline to 42–45 minutes after eight sessions. He also extended the treatment to the child's home where he was reinforced for remaining seated for meals and other events.

Allen et al. (1967) reduced the hyperactive behavior of a kindergarten child by providing social reinforcement if he persisted in a single activity for more than a minute. Patterson (1965), Patterson et al. (1965), and Doubros and Daniels (1966) have had similar successes.

Aggressive Behavior   As both verbal and physical aggression are particularly troublesome in classroom situations, a study by Brown and Elliott (1965) is particularly revealing. Using a reversal design, basal rates of verbal and physical aggression were recorded for twenty-seven 3- and 4-year old children. Treatment required that the teachers ignore aggressive behavior and reward quiet, cooperative behavior. Both types of aggressive behaviors were substantially reduced. When the intervention was reversed and the teachers returned to their normal manner of dealing with aggressive behavior (verbal reprimand), physical aggression returned to baseline level, while verbal aggression increased but was still below baseline level. Reestablishment of the selected reinforcement treatment caused physical aggression to decrease as it had previously, and verbal aggression to decrease still further.

In a similar experiment, Scott et al. (1967) found that the incidence of physical aggression increased with attention from teachers and peers.

Mutism or Unintelligible Speech Absent or distorted speech is often symptomatic of severe disturbance or psychosis. Frequently, the development of speech or language skill is a critical component in determining the prognosis for future recovery. If these children cannot understand or communicate with others they remain locked in a world dominated by their own distorted thoughts. Consequently, many investigators have undertaken speech and language training with psychotic children through the application of operant principles. To do so they usually proceed systematically to train in sequence certain prespeech behavior, including attention to the vocal stimuli and reinforcers and eye contact with the teacher, before proceeding to train approximations of sound (Blake and Moss, 1967), words and sentences (Hewitt, 1965; Lovass et al., 1966), and spontaneous speech (Lovass, 1966; Jensen and Womach, 1967). Each sequenced step is accomplished by the immediate administration of positive reinforcement, usually food, for eliciting the desired response. In the early stages of training, positive reinforcement often must be paired with aversive techniques to eliminate competing behaviors such as crying or stereotyped motor responses. For example, Lovass (1966) used punishment, a slap, and the word "No" to reduce competing responses, that prevented the child from attending to the learning task.

In addition to the direct training of language and speech skills, investigators have undertaken to train generalization imitation. This type of program involves reinforcing imitative responses such as imitation of the word "car," with the expectation that the ability to imitate will be learned. If that occurs, verbal utterances and other behavior will be imitated without direct and specific training. Lovass et al. (1967) in a series of studies, demonstrated that psychotic children do develop generalized imitative ability.

Stuttering Although the remediation of stuttering is not generally a teacher's concern, it is of great interest because of the prevalence of the problem. A variety of operant techniques have been used with consistent success to eliminate stuttering. In some instances, an aversive consequence, such as time out, has been employed on each occasion that the subject stutters (Haroldson, Martin, Starr, 1968). In an interesting example, Martin, Kuhl, and Haroldson (1972) used a puppet to converse with two four-year-old stutterers. The negative consequence, time out, was a ten-second removal of the puppet for each stutter. Perkins (1973) also incorporated time out into treatment, combining it with delayed auditory feedback. Delayed feedback forces the stutterers to slow down speech, and the slower rate usually eliminates the stutter. Gradually the delay is diminished until the subject reaches no delay without stuttering. At this point time out is introduced. When the subject stutters twice in a five-minute period, she or he must sit in darkness for thirty seconds.

Delinquent Behaviors   Individuals who demonstrate a cluster of socially maladaptive behaviors such as stealing, lying, fighting, and other activities that defy authority and break social rules and laws, often are referred to as delinquents or criminals (depending on their age). Generally, these individuals have proved very resistant to therapeutic intervention, as apparently the positive social reinforcement provided by peer groups for deviant behaviors outweighs the effects of alternate reinforcement strategies (Buehler, Patterson, and Furniss, 1966). However, some behavioral techniques have been applied with relative success. Burchard and Tyler (1965) used a combination of isolation and tokens in the usual fashion to significantly decrease the number and frequency of deviant behavior in a thirteen-year-old child. Burchard (1967) found that with older male delinquents, token reinforcement was more effective in controlling behavior than were time-out punishment techniques. However, Tyler and Brown (1967) showed that, when punishment is used, time out (isolation) is far more effective in controlling behavior than verbal reprimand, which is not effective at all. Clements and McKee (1968) used the Premack principle with prison inmates. They used preferred recreational activities as reinforcers for increased work output. They negotiated contracts with each individual specifying the particular work tasks and reinforcers involved. Eventually, the inmates developed their own contracts and work production did not decrease.[8]

Conclusions regarding the effectiveness of operant techniques with delinquents are tentative, probably because research design has focused too extensively on group investigations. The term *delinquent* does not denote a homogeneous group. Children so labeled have some common characteristics, but also are dissimilar in many ways (Quay and Quay, 1965). Although teachers are confronted with many children demonstrat-

---

[8] Recently, behavioral therapy in prisons has come under attack for being similar to the dehumanizing procedures used in *A Clockwork Orange* (Burgess, 1963). The problem stemmed from inappropriate application of aversive therapy to unwilling prisoners, obviously not the types of procedures used by Clements and McKee.

ing delinquent behavior, it is important to remember that each individual may be responsive to alternate types and schedules of reinforcement. For example, some children might respond to time-out procedures and some might not. Only the experimental application of the treatment will determine its effectiveness.

Depressed Behaviors   Generally, behavioral psychologists believe that depression occurs when an individual sets unrealistic standards and engages in little self-reinforcement because of presumed or real failure to obtain goals. Also, sudden loss of external reinforcement may trigger self-derogation. Patterns of depressed behavior include self-derogatory remarks, inactivity, disinterest in the environment, low productivity, limited social interactions, excessive crying, and suicidal thoughts or attempts. Young children experience depressions, and it is becoming increasingly prevalent among adolescents.

Since depression is characterized by negative self-perceptions, much of the behavioral intervention has focused on increasing the incidence of positive self-statements. Therapeutic strategies often are modifications of the Premack principle, termed *covenant control therapy* (Homme, 1965). The idea is to pair positive self-statements, a low probability of occurrence behavior, with a high probability of occurrence behavior. Mahoney (1971) made cigarette smoking contingent on positive self-verbalization and self-thought and found that after 6 weeks, the individual generated positive self-talk without use of cigarettes as a reinforcer. Todd (1972) helped a depressed patient write out positive self-thoughts on index cards, made cigarette smoking contingent on reciting one of the cards, and also brought about increased incidence of positive self-verbalizations. Hannum, Thoresen, and Hubbard (1974) attempted to increase self-esteem while simultaneously decreasing negative self-talk through "thought-stopping," a technique that required the patient to interrupt his own self-derogative thoughts (Wolpe and Lazarus, 1966).

Jackson (1972) varied the approach somewhat and directed treatment toward the depressed persons overstringent standards for self-reinforcement. In sequenced fashion, the individual was helped to set goals that were realistic, then was instructed to self-reinforce with tokens when the goals were accomplished. The program initially was focused on one class of behavior, but later generalized to other behavior classes.

Wilcoxon, Schrader, and Nelson (1976) suggested a comprehensive intervention that involved an analysis of depressive verbalizations, performance deficits, self-reinforcement patterns, and external events. Such an analysis should lead to a therapeutic strategy that integrates components such as development of realistic standards, reinforced positive self-talk, and reorganization of the environment to establish opportunities for contingent reinforcement for events such as academic tasks, social interactions, and so on.

Enuresis and Encopresis   Enuresis is generally defined as the involuntary passing of urine after an arbitrary age limit of 3 years. The problem is most persistent at night, but may occur during the day as well. Unless the child is autistic or mentally deficient, daytime enuresis usually is modifiable with simple operant techniques (Yates, 1975). These may involve positive reinforcement for appropriate bathroom use, time-out and/or clean-up activities when wetting occurs. Although severely disturbed children require more elaborate strategies and persistent training, they too respond to a combination of positive reinforcement for eliminating appropriately and aversive consequences for incontinent behavior. These procedures usually involve electrical apparatus such as "wet-alarm pants" and "toilet-signal" apparatus and are fully explained in Foxx and Azrin (1973).

Producing nocturnal continence appears more difficult. Once again elaborate signalling equipment is used in strategies based on classical conditioning (Mowrer and Mowrer, 1938) and instrumental conditioning (Lovibond, 1964). A relatively simple method using social reinforcement involves training the child with praise to delay urination beyond the point of expressed need (Kimmel and Kimmel, 1970). Yates (1976) provides a detailed discussion of all these techniques.

Encopresis is defined as "disturbance in regulation of bowel evacuation" (Warson et al., 1954). Types of encopresis involve children who have never established control, those who had control but lost it, and those who play with or smear feces. Apparently, this condition occurs far less frequently than does enuresis; however, teachers of disturbed children still are confronted with it. Operant techniques that have been used successfully with encopretic children include rewards for appropriate expulsion (Neale, 1963; Gelber and Meyer, 1965; Keehn, 1965). In Neale's study, the subjects were initially placed on the toilet by an aide who also administered the rewards. Three of four children involved quickly accomplished self-control, attending to the task themselves on instruction from the teacher and returning to the room for reward. Other successes are reported by Edelman (1971a), who combined punishment (confinement to room for 30 minutes), and reward (not washing dishes), to overcome encopresis in a twelve-year-old girl, and Conger (1970), who convinced a mother to withhold attention from a nine-year-old boy.

Hysterical Conditions   These conditions, often referred to as *conversion hysteria,* involve loss of function that has no physiological or organic basis, such as hysterical blindness, deafness, anaesthesias, and paralysis. In hysterical cases such as functional blindness and deafness, it may be most important to determine whether the patient actually suffers from a conversion hysteria before attempting to plan an appropriate treatment. In that vein, Zimmerman and Grosz (1966), demonstrated that a functionally blind person tested in situations where visual acuity can increase the accuracy of performance, will respond below levels of accuracy based on chance. In other words, they perform worse than an organically blind person who would respond accurately on a chance basis.

Similarly, in studies of functional deafness, Malmo, Davis, and Barza (1952) demonstrated that affected individuals can be classically conditioned to respond to an auditory stimulus such as a buzzer but that the response is involuntary (muscle reactions), rather than voluntary. It seems that the functionally deaf individual consciously avoids hearing the stimulus but is unable to control involuntary muscle reactions.

Generally, functional blindness and deafness are not easy to treat with operant techniques since it is difficult to elicit the desired behavior (seeing and hearing) to reinforce it. Meichenbaum (1966) successfully used relaxation training with a functionally blind individual who was unable to open his eyes. Breathing exercises were combined with suggestion that his eyes would open with exhalation. Simultaneously, he was given assertiveness training to deal with difficulty in interpersonal relationships that contributed to his hysterical reaction.

Functional motor disabilities can involve elaborate cases of paralysis of arms or legs, unusual speech tonality termed *aphonia,* and the relatively common "writer's cramp." Meichenbaum (1966) successfully treated a hysterical patient who was unable to walk with physical therapy and a rewalking training program in which praise and ridicule were used as reinforcing and aversive stimuli.

Writer's cramp, that is, spasms of the muscles in the hand or forearm, has been treated by shock (Sylvester and Liversedge, 1960). However, Beech (1960) points out that in cases where the condition is associated with high anxiety, aversive stimuli such as shock could prove harmful by increasing anxiety. He suggests massed practice and systematic desensitization as more appropriate treatments.

Aphonia (loss of voice) has been treated successfully with systematic desensitization focused on the anxiety that appeared to cause the condition (Gray, England, and Mohoney, 1965). Another successful method used by Bangs and Freidinger (1949) involves training with positive reinforcement a sequence of speech skills from most basic breathing exercises through progressive steps such as uttering the easiest speech sounds, combining consonants with vowels, and uttering words.

The studies mentioned are but a few of many interesting treatments of hysterical conditions. The interested reader should consult reviews of studies of the applications of behavioral therapy to conditions such as anorexia nervosa (refusal to eat) (Kaufman, 1968), bronchial asthma (Freeman et al., 1964) and somnambulism (Arkin, 1966).

Obsessions and Compulsions Obsessions, persistent, intrusive thoughts such as preoccupation with death, and compulsions, repetitive acts or rituals, such as excessive hand washing or cleaning, have been successfully treated by a variety of behavioral interventions. Walton and Mather (1964) used systematic desensitization and assertiveness training with patients suffering from a recent onset of obsessive thinking. Their successful strategy involved reducing the anxiety that mediated the behavior. For patients with long-standing conditions, they demonstrated that treatment designed to decondition the anxiety did not remove the obsession or compulsion. The individuals became less anxious but continued to think obsessively or behave compulsively. Those behaviors had to be attacked directly in the therapy.

Taylor (1963) demonstrates a treatment focusing directly on a compulsive behavior. He was successful in curing a woman whose compulsion involved plucking her eyebrows. She was instructed to inhibit her hand from the first movement to her eyebrow and to say "No." Later, she was instructed to put her hand on her eyebrow until she felt the impulse to pluck, then to remove her hand. The treatment was successful in 10 days.

Weiner (1967) used successive approximations to reduce and finally eliminate a series of compulsive rituals in a fifteen-year-old boy. Each of the boy's rituals, such as spending 15 minutes to wash his face to ensure that germs were killed, or relocking his drawer three times to ensure that he would not be sent to Vietnam, were reduced to 5 minutes for washing and 1 relocking of the drawer. Also, they were associated with positive rather than fearful thoughts, washing made him handsome and drawer-locking kept out burglars. The rituals were progressively altered in this manner and eventually disappeared completely.

Meyer (1966) used the flooding technique to inhibit compulsive behaviors. He simply prevented the patients from performing their rituals when they felt impelled to do so, and instead had them perform acts incompatible with their ritualistic behaviors. For example, a compulsive hand washer was made to handle objects without washing them or her hands. Meyer demonstrated that obsessive or compulsive behavior can be eliminated when the unrealistic fear that disastrous consequences will follow when ritualistic activities are not performed is proved false. Similar results were obtained by Roper et al. (1975).

Obsessive-compulsive disorders are not uncommon in children. Although compulsive behaviors or rituals are relatively easy to identify, obsessive thoughts that are equally debilitating may be uncovered only by careful observation. Children experiencing such thoughts are often too frightened to discuss them. The obsessed child requires reassurance that she or he is not "crazy" and that the condition can be treated.

Phobia Phobias, exaggerated, unrealistic fears, are relatively common-place experiences for many normal individuals throughout their lifetimes. In cases where they either become so intense as to be more than an inconvenience, or persist in duration, behavior therapy has proved effective in eliminating them. Historically, behavioral treatments of fear responses began with Jones's (1924) classic efforts to decondition fear of animals in children by pairing the introduction of the feared object with an alternate stimulus, food (the principle of reciprocal inhibition used later by Wolpe). Currently, Wolpe's systematic desensitization techniques are, without a doubt, the preferred methods of treating phobic conditions. Those techniques have been discussed in detail previously, and a review of their effective use with phobias ranging from a fear of earthworms (Murphy, 1964), to inability to leave the house (Kraft, 1967), is provided in Yates (1970). It is sufficient to report here that these clinical cases of phobia have been successfully treated with imagined and *in vivo* techniques and that both methods appear equally effective. Applications with children included subjects as young as one year of age (fear of bathwater, Bentler, 1962) and as old as 17 (traffic phobia, Kushner, 1965), suggesting that desensitization may be a valuable tool for school-based intervention programs with phobic children.

In discussing childhood fears, it is worthwhile to devote specific attention to school phobias, since fear of attending school is apparently a common occurrence. In many instances, school phobia is associated with a cluster of neurotic responses including anxiety over separation from the mother and somatic complaints. Behavioral treatments have involved soliciting parental assistance in forcing school attendance, providing positive social reinforcement when the child enters school, and ignoring somatic complaints (Leventhal et al., 1971). Systematic desensitization techniques (*in vivo*) have been applied by leading a child, step by step, through the behaviors of entering school (Garvey and Hegrenes, 1966). Occasionally, parents and teachers have been used to provide positive reinforcement for *all independent* behavior during periods of systematic desensitization (Patterson, 1965). Generally, behavior therapy has been very effective in combatting school phobia (Kauffman, 1977).

This discussion of interventions used with specific problem behaviors has been designed to demonstrate the effectiveness of behavioral strategies for modifying many of the atypical behaviors encountered by teachers of emotionally disturbed children. This information has not been presented to suggest that the classroom teacher necessarily undertake all such treatment strategies in classroom situations, or that she or he is responsible for the treatment of complex conditions such as conversion hysteria, depression, or stuttering. The intent is to inform and thus to reduce teacher anxiety, confusion, and/or frustration when she or he encounters disturbed children manifesting such behavior.

On the other hand, teachers often must be prepared to cope personally with behaviors such as head banging, enuresis, phobic reactions, elective mutism, and so on. The evidence that operant principles may be applied to reduce the occurrence of these behaviors as readily as they are used in more typical classroom management efforts, for example, to reduce common disruptive behavior and to increase academic achievement, should increase the teacher's ability to provide a therapeutic environment for emotionally disturbed children.

STUDY QUESTIONS

1. List and discuss the four main components of applied behavioral analysis. Then develop a plan to use ABA with a student, friend, or relative.
2. Discuss the four intrasubject research designs. Select one and plan your own experiment.
3. Discuss the types of reinforcement systems and the type of punishment that can be used in school situations with disturbed children.
4. Plan a token economy.
5. Compare and contrast systematic desensitization and operant interventions.
6. Discuss the advantages and disadvantages of a behavioral approach to helping emotionally disturbed children. Integrate information from the behavioral section in Chapter 2.

REFERENCES

Allen, K.; Hart, B.; Buell, J.; Harris, F.; and Wolf, M. Effects of social reinforcement in isolate behavior of a nursery school child. *Child Development,* 1964, 35, 511–518.

Allen, K.; Henke, L.; Harris, F.; Baer, D.; and Reynolds, N. The control of hyperactivity by social reinforcement of attending behavior in a preschool child. *Journal of Educational Psychology,* 1969, 58, 231–237.

Arkin, A. Sleep-talking: a review. *Journal of Nervous and Mental Disorders,* 1966, 143, 101–122.

Arrington, R. Time-sampling in studies of social behavior: a critical review of techniques and results with research suggestions. *Psychological Bulletin,* 1943, 40, 81–124.

Axelrod, S.; Hall, R.; Weis, L.; and Rohrer, S. Use of self-imposed contingencies to reduce the frequencies of smoking behavior. In M. Mahoney and C. Thorensen, (eds.). *Self-control: power to the person.* Belmont, Cal.: Brooks/Cole, 1974, pp. 77–85.

Azrin, N., and Holz, W. Punishment. In W. Honig (ed.). *Operant behavior: areas of research and application.* New York: Appleton-Century-Crofts, 1966, pp. 380–447.

Baer, D. Laboratory control of thumbsucking by withdrawal and representation of reinforcement. *Journal of Experimental Analysis of Behavior,* 1962, *5,* 525–528.

Baer, D.; Wolf, M.; and Risley, T. Some current dimensions of applied behavior analysis. *Journal of Applied Behavior Analysis,* 1968, *1,* 91–97.

Bandura, A. Influence of models' reinforcement contingencies on the acquisition of imitative responses. *Journal of Personality and Social Psychology,* 1965, *1,* 589–595.

Bandura, A. *Principles of behavior modification.* New York: Holt, Rinehart and Winston, 1969.

Bandura, A. Psychotherapy based upon modeling principles. In A. Bergin and S. Garfield (eds.). *Handbook of psychotherapy and behavior change: an empirical analysis.* New York: Wiley, 1971, pp. 653–708.

Bandura, A., and Walters, R. *Social learning and personality development.* New York: Holt, Rinehart and Winston, 1963.

Bangs, J., and Freidinger, A. Diagnosis and treatment of a case of hysterical aphonia in a thirteen-year old girl. *Journal of Speech and Hearing Disorders,* 1949, *14,* 312–317.

Barclay, R. Effecting behavior change in the elementary classroom: an exploratory study. *Journal of Counseling Psychology,* 1967, *14,* 240–247.

Barrish, H.; Saunders, M.; and Wolf, M. Good behavior game: effects of individual contingencies for group consequences on disruptive behavior in a classroom. *Journal of Applied Behavior Analysis,* 1969, *2,* 199–124.

Becker, W.; Madsen, C.; Arnold, C.; and Thomas, D. The contingent use of teacher attention and praise in reducing classroom behavior problems. *Journal of Special Education,* 1967, *1,* 287–307.

Beech, H. The symptomatic treatment of writer's cramp. In H. Eysenck (ed.). *Behavior therapy and the neuroses.* Oxford: Pergamon, 1960, pp. 349–372.

Bekhterev, V. *General principles of human reflexology.* New York: International, 1932.

Bentler, P. An infant's phobia treated with reciprocal inhibition theory. *Journal of Child Psychology and Psychiatry,* 1962, *3,* 185–189.

Bijou, S. Experimental studies of child behavior, normal and deviant. In L. Krasner and L. Ullmann (eds.). *Research in behavior modification.* New York: Holt, Rinehart and Winston, 1965, 56–81.

Bijou, S., and Baer, D. *Child development: readings in experimental analysis.* Vol. 3. New York: Appleton-Century-Crofts, 1967.

Binder, A.; McConnell, D.; and Sjoholm, N. Verbal conditioning as a function of experimenter characteristics. *Journal of Abnormal and Social Psychology,* 1957, *55,* 309–314.

Birnbrauer, J.; Wolf, M.; Kidder, J.; and Tague, C. Classroom behavior of retarded pupils with token reinforcement. *Journal of Experimental Child Psychology,* 1965, *2,* 219–235.

Blackham, G., and Silberman, A. *Modification of child and adolescent behavior.* Belmont, Cal.: Wadsworth, 1975.

Blake, P., and Moss, T. The development of socialization skills in an electively mute child. *Behavior Research and Therapy,* 1967, *5,* 349–356.

Borkovec, T. The comparative effectiveness of systematic desensitization and implosive therapy and the effect of expectancy manipulation on the elimination of fear. Unpublished doctoral dissertation, University of Illinois, 1970.

Borkovec, T. Effects of expectancy on the outcome of systematic desensitization and implosive treatments for analogue anxiety. *Behavior Therapy*, 1972, 3, 29–40.

Brison, D. A nontalking child in kindergarten: an application of behavior therapy. *Journal of School Psychology*, 1966, 4, 65–69.

Brown, P., and Elliott, R. The control of aggression in a nursery school class. *Journal of Experimental Child Psychology*, 1965, 2, 103–107.

Buehler, R.; Patterson, G.; and Furniss, J. The reinforcement of behavior in institutional settings. *Behavior Research and Therapy*, 1966, 4, 157–167.

Buell, J.; Stoddard, P.; Harris, F.; and Baer, D. Collateral social development accompanying reinforcement of outdoor play in a preschool child. *Journal of Applied Behavior Analysis*, 1968, 1, 167–173.

Burchard, J. Systematic socialization: a programmed environment in the habilitation of antisocial retardates. *Psychological Record*, 1967, 17, 461–476.

Burchard, J., and Tyler, V. The modification of delinquent behavior through operant conditioning. *Behavior Research and Therapy*, 1965, 2, 245–250.

Burgess, A. *A clockwork orange*. New York: Norton, 1963.

Campbell, D., and Stanley, J. Experimental and quasi-experimental designs for research and teaching. In N. Gage (Ed.). *Handbook of research on teaching*. Chicago: Rand McNally, 1963, pp. 171–246.

Clement, P., and Milne, D. Group play therapy and tangible reinforcers used to modify the behavior of 8-year old boys. *Behavior Research and Therapy*, 1967, 5, 301–312.

Clements, C., and McKee, J. Programmed instruction for institutionalized offenders: contingency management and performance contracts. *Psychological Reports*, 1968, 22, 957–964.

Cohen, R. The effects of group interaction and progressive hierarchy presentation on desensitization of test anxiety. *Behavior Research and Therapy*, 1969, 7, 15–26.

Conger, J. The treatment of encopresis by the management of social consequences. *Behavior Therapy*, 1970, 1, 386–390.

Copeland, R.; Brown, R.; and Hall, R. The effects of principal-implemented techniques on the behavior of pupils. *Journal of Applied Behavior Analysis*, 1974, 7, 77–86.

Cotler, S. Sex differences and generalization of anxiety reduction with automatic desensitization and minimal therapist interaction. *Behavior Research and Therapy*, 1970, 8, 273–285.

Craighead, W.; Kazdin, A.; and Mahoney, M. *Behavior modification*. Boston: Houghton Mifflin, 1976.

Craighead, W., and Meyers, A. Behavioral modification with the autistic child in the classroom setting. Paper presented at the meetings of the Association for Advancement of Behavior Therapy, Miami, December, 1973.

Daley, M. The reinforcement menu: finding effective reinforcers. In J. Krumboltz and C. Thorensen (eds.). *Behavioral counseling, case studies and techniques*. New York: Holt, Rinehart and Winston, 1969, pp. 42–45.

Davison, R., and Neale, J. *Abnormal psychology: an experimental clinical approach*. New York: Wiley, 1974.

DeMoor, W. Systematic desensitization versus prolonged high intensity stimulation (flooding). *Journal of Behavior Therapy and Experimental Psychiatry*, 1970, 1, 45–52.

Dollard, J., and Miller, N. *Personality and psychotherapy*. New York: McGraw-Hill, 1950.

Donner, L., and Guerney, B. Automated group desensitization for test anxiety. *Behavior Research and Therapy*, 1969, *7*, 1–13.

Doubros, S., and Daniels, G. An experimental approach to the reduction of overactive behavior. *Behavior Research and Therapy*, 1966, *4*, 251–258.

Drabman, R. Child versus teacher administered token programs in a psychiatric hospital school. *Journal of Abnormal Child Psychology*, 1973, *1*, 66–87.

Drabman, R. Behavior modification in the classroom. In W. Craighead, A. Kazdin, and M. Mahoney (eds.). *Behavior modification*. Boston: Houghton Mifflin, 1976, pp. 227–242.

Drabman, R., and Spitalnik, R. Social isolation as a punishment procedure: a controlled study. *Journal of Experimental Child Psychology*, 1973, *16*, 236–249.

Drabman, R.; Spitalnik, R.; and O'Leary, K. Teaching self-control to disruptive children. *Journal of Abnormal Psychology*, 1973, *82*, 10–16.

Drabman, R.; Spitalnik, R.; and Spitalnik, K. Sociometric and disruptive behavior as a function of four types of token economies. *Journal of Applied Behavior Analysis*, 1974, *1*, 93–101.

Edelman, R. Operant conditioning treatment of encopresis. *Journal of Behavior Therapy and Experimental Psychiatry*, 1971a, *2*, 71–73.

Edelman, R. Desensitization and physiological arousal. *Journal of Personality and Social Psychology*, 1971b, *17*, 259–266.

Eysenck, H. Training in clinical psychology: an English point of view. *American Psychologist*, 1949, *4*, 173–176.

Eysenck, H. Function and training of the clinical psychologist. *Journal of Mental Science*, 1950, *96*, 710–725.

Eysenck, H. The effects of psychotherapy. *International Journal of Psychiatry*, 1964a, *1*, 99–144.

Eysenck, H. *Experiments in behavior therapy*. New York: Pergamon Press, 1964b.

Foxx, R., and Azrin, N. Toilet training the retarded: a rapid program for day and night time independent toileting. Champaign, Ill.: Research Press, 1973.

Frankl, V. Paradoxical intention: a logotherapeutic technique. *American Journal of Psychotherapy*, 1960, *14*, 520.

Freeman, E.; Feingold, B.; Schlesinger, K.; and Gorman, E. Psychological variables in allergic disorders: a review. *Psychosomatic Medicine*, 1964, *26*, 543–575.

Freeman, H., and Kendrick, D. A case of catophobia. *British Medical Journal*, 1960, *2*, 497–502.

Garvey, W., and Hegrenes, J. Desensitization techniques in the treatment of school phobia. *American Journal of Orthopsychiatry*, 1966, *36*, 147–152.

Gelber, H., and Meyer, V. Behavior therapy and encopresis: the complexities involved in treatment. *Behavior Research and Therapy*, 1965, *2*, 227–231.

Glynn, E. Classroom applications of self-determined reinforcement. *Journal of Applied Behavior Analysis*, 1970, *3*, 123–132.

Glynn, E., and Thomas, J. Effects of cueing on self-control of classroom behavior. *Journal of Applied Behavior Analysis*, 1974, *7*, 299–306.

Goldstein, A. Separate effects of extinction, counter-conditioning and progressive approach in overcoming fear. *Behavior Research and Therapy*, 1969, *7*, 47–56.

Goodwin, D. Consulting with the classroom teacher. In J. Krumboltz and C. Thorensen (eds.). *Behavioral counseling cases and techniques*. New York: Holt, Rinehart and Winston, 1969.

Gray, B.; England, G.; and Mohoney, J. Treatment of benign vocal nodules by reciprocal inhibition. *Behavior Research and Therapy*, 1965, *3*, 187–193.

Hall, R., and Hinkle, J. Vicarious desensitization of test anxiety. *Behavior Research and Therapy*, 1972, *10*, 407–410.

Hall, R.; Lund, D.; and Jackson, D. Effects of teacher attention on study behavior. *Journal of Applied Behavior Analysis*, 1968, *1*, 1–12.

Hamilton, M., and Schroeder, H. A comparison of systematic desensitization and reinforced practice procedures in fear reduction. *Behavior Research and Therapy*, 1973, *11*, 649–652.

Hannum, J.; Thoresen, C.; and Hubbard, D. A behavior study of self-esteem with elementary teachers. In M. Mahoney and C. Thorensen (eds.), *Self-control: power to the person*. Belmont, Cal.: Brooks/Cole, 1974, pp. 144–145.

Haroldson, S.; Martin, R.; and Starr, C. Time-out as a punishment for stuttering. *Journal of Speech and Hearing Research*, 1968, *11*, 550–566.

Harris, F.; Johnstone, M.; Kelley, C.; and Wolf, M. Effects of positive social reinforcement on regressed crawling of a nursery school child. *Journal of Educational Psychology*, 1964, *55*, 35–41.

Harris, F.; Wolf, M.; and Baer, D. Effects of social reinforcement of child behavior. *Young Children*, 1964, *20*, 8–17.

Hart, B.; Allen, K.; Buell, J.; Harris, F.; and Wolf, M. Effects of social reinforcement on operant crying. *Journal of Experimental Child Psychology*, 1964, *1*, 145–153.

Hart, B.; Reynolds, N.; Baer, D.; Brawley, E.; and Harris, F. Effect of contingent and non-contingent social reinforcement on the cooperative play of a preschool child. *Journal of Applied Behavior Analysis*, 1968, *1*, 73–76.

Hartup, W. Friendship status and the effectiveness of peers as reinforcing agents. *Journal of Experimental Child Psychology*, 1964, *1*, 154–162.

Hawkins, R.; McArthur, M.; Rinaldi, P.; Gray, D.; and Schaftenaur, L. Results of operant conditioning techniques in modifying the behavior of emotionally disturbed children. Paper presented at the 45th Annual International Council for Exceptional Children Convention, St. Louis, 1967.

Herman, S., and Tramontana, J. Instructions and group versus individual reinforcement in modifying disruptive group behavior. *Journal of Applied Behavior Analysis*, 1971, *4*, 113–119.

Hewett, F. Teaching speech to an autistic child through operant conditioning. *American Journal of Orthopsychiatry*, 1965, *35*, 927–936.

Homme, L. Perspectives in psychology, XXIV: control of coverants, the operants of the mind. *Psychological Record*, 1965, *15*, 501–511.

Homme, L. Human motivation and environment. In N. Haring and R. Whelan (eds.). *The learning environment: relationship to behavior modification and implications for special education*. Kansas Studies in Education, Vol. 16. Lawrence, Kans.: University of Kansas Publications, 1966, 30–39.

Homme, L. *How to use contingency contracting in the classroom*. New York: Research Press, 1969.

Hull, C. *Principles of behavior*. New York: Appleton-Century-Crofts, 1943.

Hull, C. *A behavior system*. New Haven: Yale University Press, 1952.

Hundziak, M.; Maurer, R.; and Watson, L. Operant conditioning in toilet training of severely mentally retarded boys. *American Journal of Mental Deficiency*, 1965, *70*, 120–124.

Ivanov-Smolensky, A. Neurotic behavior and the teaching of conditioned reflexes. *American Journal of Psychiatry*, 1927, *84*, 483–488.

Ivanov-Smolensky, A. The pathology of conditioned reflexes and the so-called psychogenic depression. *Journal of Nervous and Mental Disease,* 1928, *67,* 346–350.

Iwata, B., and Bailey, J. Reward versus cost token systems: an analysis of the effects on students and teacher. *Journal of Applied Behavior Analysis,* 1974, *7,* 567–576.

Jackson, B. Treatment of depression by self-reinforcement. *Behavior Therapy,* 1972, *3,* 298–307.

Jacobson, E. *Progressive relaxation.* Chicago: University of Chicago Press, 1938.

Jensen, G., and Womack, M. Operant conditioning techniques applied in the treatment of an autistic child. *American Journal of Orthopsychiatry,* 1967, *37,* 30–34.

Johnson, M., and Bailey, J. Cross-age tutoring: fifth graders as arithmetic tutors for kindergarten children. *Journal of Applied Behavior Analysis,* 1974, *7,* 223–232.

Jones, M. A laboratory study of fear: the case of Peter. *Journal of Genetic Psychology,* 1924, *31,* 308–315.

Kauffman, J. *Characteristics of children's behavior disorders.* Columbus, Ohio: Merrill, 1977.

Kaufman, M. (ed.). *Evolution of psychosomatic concepts: anorexia nervosa: a paradigm.* London: Hogarth, 1965.

Kazdin, A. *Behavior modification in applied settings.* Homewood, Ill.: Dorsey, 1975.

Keehn, J. Brief case-report: reinforcement therapy of incontinence. *Behavior Research and Therapy,* 1965, *2,* 239.

Kimmel, H. D. Instrumental conditioning of autonomically mediated behavior. *Psychological Bulletin,* 1967, *67,* 337–345.

Kimmel, H. D. Instrumental conditioning of autonomically mediated responses in human beings. *American Psychologist,* 1974, *29,* 325–335.

Kimmel, H., and Kimmel, E. An instrumental conditioning method for the treatment of enuresis. *Journal of Behavior Therapy and Experimental Psychiatry,* 1970, *1,* 121–123.

Kraft, T. Treatment of the housebound syndrome, *British Journal of Psychiatry,* 1967, *15,* 446–453.

Krapfl, J., and Nawas, M. Client-therapist relationship factor in systematic desensitization. *Journal of Consulting and Clinical Psychology,* 1969, *33,* 435–439.

Krasner, L. Verbal conditioning and psychotherapy. In L. Krasner and L. Ullmann (eds.). *Research in behavior modification.* New York: Holt, Rinehart and Winston, 1965, 211–228.

Krumboltz, J., and Thorensen, C. The effect of behavioral counseling in group and individual settings on information-seeking behavior. *Journal of Counseling Psychology,* 1964, *11,* 324–333.

Kushner, M. Desensitization of a post-traumatic phobia. In L. Ullmann and L. Krasner (eds.). *Case studies in behavior modification.* New York: Holt, 1965, pp. 193–196.

Lang, P. The mechanics of desensitization and the laboratory study of human fear. In C. M. Franks (ed.). *Behavior therapy: appraisal and status.* New York: McGraw-Hill, 1969, pp. 160–191.

Lazarus, A. Group therapy of phobic disorders by systematic desensitization. *Journal of Abnormal and Social Psychology,* 1961, *66,* 504–510.

Lazarus, A. *Behavior therapy and beyond.* New York: McGraw-Hill, 1971.

228   Part III   Therapies

Lazarus, A. Multimodal behavior therapy: treating the "basic id." *Journal of Nervous and Mental Diseases,* 1973, *156,* 404–411.

Lazarus, A., and Abramovitz, A. The use of "emotive imagery" in the treatment of children's phobias. *Journal of Mental Science,* 1962, *4,* 209–212.

Leventhal, T.; Weinberger, G.; Stander, R.; and Sterns, R. Therapeutic strategies with school phobics. *American Journal of Orthopsychiatry,* 1967, *37,* 64–70.

Lindsley, O. Studies in behavioral therapy: status report III. Waltham, Mass.: Metropolitan State Hospital, 1954.

Lovass, O. A program for the establishment of speech in psychotic children. In. J. Wing (ed.). *Early childhood autism.* London: Pergamon, 1966, pp. 115–144.

Lovass, O.; Berberich, J.; Perloff, B.; and Schaeffer, B. Acquisition of imitative speech by schizophrenic children, *Science,* 1966, 151, 705–707.

Lovass, O.; Freitag, G.; Gold, V.; and Kassarla, I. Experimental studies in childhood schizophrenia: analysis of self-destructive behavior. *Journal of Experimental Child Psychology,* 1965, *2,* 67–84.

Lovass, O.; Freitag, G.; Kinder, M.; Rubenstein, B.; Schaeffer, B.; and Simmons, J. Establishment of social reinforcers in two schizophrenic children on the basis of food. *Journal of Experimental Child Psychology,* 1966, *4,* 109–125.

Lovass, O.; Freitag, L.; Nelson, K.; and Whalen, C. The establishment of imitation and its use for the development of complex behavior in schizophrenic children. *Behavior Research Therapy,* 1967, *5,* 171–181.

Lovibond, S. *Conditioning and enuresis.* Oxford: Pergamon, 1964.

Lovitt, T., and Curtiss, K. Academic response rate as a function of teacher and self-imposed contingencies. *Journal of Applied Behavior Analysis,* 1969, *2,* 49–53.

Madsen, C.; Becker, W.; Thomas, D.; Koser, L.; and Plager, E. An analysis of the reinforcing function of "sit down" commands. In R. K. Parker (ed.). *Readings in educational psychology.* Boston: Allyn and Bacon, 1970, pp. 265–278.

Mager, R. *Preparing instructional objectives.* Palo Alto: Fearon, 1962.

Mahoney, M. The self-management of covert behavior: a case study. *Behavior Therapy,* 1971, *2,* 575–578.

Malmo, R., Davis, J., and Barza, S. Total hysterical deafness: an experimental case study. *Journal of Personality,* 1952, 188–204.

Martin, R.; Kuhl, P.; and Haroldson, S. An experimental treatment with two preschool stuttering children. *Journal of Speech and Hearing Research,* 1972, *15,* 743–752.

Martin, G.; England, G.; Kaprowy, E.; Kilgour, K.; and Pilek, V. Operant conditioning of kindergarten-class behavior in autistic children. *Behaviour Research and Therapy,* 1968, *6,* 281–294.

McAllister, L.; Stachowiak, J.; Baer, D.; and Conderman, L. The application of operant conditioning techniques in a secondary school classroom. *Journal of Applied Behavior Analysis,* 1969, *2,* 277–285.

McGlynn, F. Individual versus standardized hierarchies in the systematic desensitization of snake-avoidance. *Behavior Research and Therapy,* 1971, *9,* 1–5.

Mealiea, W., and Nawas, M. The comparative effectiveness of systematic desensitization and implosive therapy in the treatment of snake phobia. *Journal of Behavioral Therapy and Experimental Psychiatry,* 1971, *2,* 85–94.

Meichenbaum, D. Sequential strategies in two cases of hysteria. *Behavior Research and Therapy.* 1966, *4,* 89–94.

Meichenbaum, D.; Bowers, K.; and Ross, R. Modification of classroom behavior or institutionalized female adolescent offenders. *Behavior Research and Therapy,* 1968, *6,* 343–353.

Meyer, V. The treatment of two phobic patients on the basis of learning principles. *Journal of Abnormal and Social Psychology,* 1957, *55,* 261–266.

Meyer, V. Modification of expectations in cases with obsessional rituals. *Behavior Research and Therapy,* 1966, *4,* 273–280.

Migler, B., and Wolpe, J. Automated self-desensitization: a case report. *Behavior Research and Therapy,* 1967, *5,* 133–135.

Mogel, S., and Schiff, W. "Extinction" of a head bumping symptom of eight years duration in two minutes: a case report. *Behavior Research and Therapy,* 1967, *5,* 661–668.

Mowrer, O. *Learning theory and personality dynamics.* New York: Ronald, 1950.

Mowrer, O., and Mowrer, W. Enuresis: a method for its study and treatment. *American Journal of Orthopsychiatry,* 1938, *8,* 436–447.

Murphy, I. Extinction of an incapacitating fear of earthworms. *Journal of Clinical Psychology,* 1964, *20,* 396–398.

Nawas, M.; Fishman, S.; and Pucel, J. A standardized desensitization program applicable to group and individual treatments. *Behavior Research and Therapy,* 1970, *8,* 49–56.

Neale, D. Behavior therapy and encopresis in children. *Behavior Research and Therapy,* 1963, *1,* 139–149.

Newcomer, P. Establishing speech in a negativistic, non-talking kindergarten student. Unpublished case report, Beaver College, Glenside, Pa., 1965.

Newcomer, P. Eliminating "baby talk" through control of teacher attention. Unpublished case report, Beaver College, Glenside, Pa., 1966.

Nolen, P.; Kunzelmann, H.; and Haring, N. Behavior modification in a junior high learning disabilities classroom. *Exceptional Children,* 1967, *34,* 163–168.

O'Leary, K., and Becker, W. Behavior modification of an adjustment class: a token reinforcement program. *Exceptional Children,* 1967, *33,* 637–642.

O'Leary, K., and Becker, W. The effects of intensity of a teacher's reprimands on children's behavior. *Journal of School Psychology,* 1968, *7,* 8–11.

O'Leary, K.; Becker, W.; Evans, M.; and Sandargas, R. A token reinforcement program in a public school: a replication and systematic analysis. *Journal of Applied Behavior Analysis,* 1969, *2,* 3–13.

O'Leary, K., and Drabman, R. Token reinforcement programs in the classroom: a review. *Psychological Bulletin,* 1971, *75,* 379–398.

O'Leary, K.; Kaufman, K.; Kass, R.; and Drabman, R. The effects of loud and soft reprimands on the behavior of disruptive students. *Exceptional Children,* 1970, *37,* 145–155.

O'Leary, K.; O'Leary, S.; and Becker, W. Modification of a deviant sibling interaction pattern in the home. *Exceptional Children,* 1967, *33,* 637–642.

Patterson, G. A learning theory approach to the treatment of the school phobic child. In L. Ullmann and L. Krasner (eds.). *Case studies in behavior modification.* New York: Holt, 1965, pp. 279–285.

Patterson, G. An application of conditioning techniques to the control of a hyperactvie child. In L. Ullmann and L. Krasner (eds.). *Case studies in behavior modification.* New York: Holt, 1965, pp. 370–375.

Patterson, G., and Brodsky, G. A behavior modification programme of a child with multiple behavior problems. *Journal of Child Psychology and Psychiatry*, 1966, 7, 277–295.

Patterson, G.; Jones, R.; Whitter, J.; and Wright, A. A behavior modification technique for the hyperactive child. *Behavior Research and Therapy*, 1965, 2, 217–226.

Paul, G. Outcome of systematic desensitization I: background procedures and uncontrolled reports of individual treatment. In C. M. Franks (ed.). *Behavior therapy: appraisal and status*. New York: McGraw-Hill, 1969, pp. 63–104.

Paul, G., and Shannon, D. Treatment of anxiety through systematic desensitization in therapy groups. *Journal of Abnormal Psychology*, 1966, 71, 124–135.

Pavlov, I. *Conditioned reflexes*, trans. by G. Anrep. London: Oxford University Press, 1927.

Pavlov, I. *Lectures on conditioned reflexes*, trans. by W. Gantt. New York: International, 1928.

Pavlov, I. Neurosis in man and animals. *Journal of the American Medical Association*, 1932, 99, 1012–1013.

Pavlov, I. An attempt at a physiological interpretation of obsessional neurosis and paranoia. *Journal of Mental Sciences*, 1934, 80, 187–197.

Perkins, W. Replacement of stuttering with normal speech: clinical procedures. *Journal of Speech and Hearing Disorders*, 1973, 38, 295–303.

Phillips, E.; Phillips, E.; Fixsen, D.; and Wolf, N. Behavior-shaping for delinquents. *Psychology Today*, 1973, 7, 74–108.

Pihl, R. Conditioning procedures with hyperactive children. *Neurology*, 1967, 17, 421–423.

Premack, D. Toward empirical behavior laws: I. Positive reinforcement. *Psychological Review*, 1959, 66, 219–233.

Premack, D. Reinforcement theory. In D. Levin (ed.). *Nebraska symposium on motivation*. Lincoln, Neb.: University of Nebraska, 1965, pp. 123–180.

Quay, H., and Quay, L. Behavior problems in early adolescence. *Child Development*, 1965, 36, 215–220.

Quay, H.; Sprague, R.; Werry, J.; and McQueen, M. Conditioning visual orientation of conduct problem children in the classroom. *Journal of Experimental Child Psychology*, 1967, 5, 512–517.

Rachman, S. Systematic desensitization. *Psychological Bulletin*, 1967, 67, 93–103.

Rachman, S.; Hodgson, R.; and Marks, I. The treatment of chronic obsessive compulsive neurosis. *Behavior Research and Therapy*, 1971, 9, 237–248.

Reed, G. Elective mutism in children: a reappraisal. *Journal of Child Psychology and Psychiatry*, 1963, 4, 99–107.

Reid, J.; Hawkins, L.; Keutzer, C.; McNeal, S.; Phelps, R.; Reid, K.; and Mees, H. A marathon behavior modification of a selectively mute child. *Journal of Child Psychology and Psychiatry*, 1967, 8, 27–30.

Robinson, C., and Suinn, R. Group desensitization of a phobia in massed sessions. *Behavior Research and Therapy*, 1969, 7, 319–321.

Roper, G.; Rachman, S.; and Marks, I. Passive and participant modeling in exposure treatment of obsessive-compulsive neurotics. *Behavior Research and Therapy*, 1975, 13, 271–279.

Russo, S. Adaptations in behavioral therapy with children. *Behavior Research and Therapy*, 1964, 2, 43–47.

Salfield, D. Observations on elective mutism in children. *Journal of Mental Science*, 1950, 96, 1024–1032.

Scott, P.; Burton, R.; and Yarrow, M. Social reinforcement under natural conditions. *Child Development*, 1967, 38, 53–63.

Shapiro, M. B. A method of measuring psychological changes specific to the individual psychiatric patient. *British Journal of Medical Psychology*, 1961, 34, 255–262.

Shapiro, M. B. An experimental approach to diagnostic psychological testing. *Journal of Mental Science*, 1951, 97, 748–764.

Shapiro, M. B. The single case in clinical-psychological research. *Journal of General Psychology*, 1966, 74, 3–23.

Sherman, A. Real-life exposure as a primary therapeutic factor in the desensitization treatment of fear. *Journal of Abnormal Psychology*, 1972, 79, 19–28.

Skinner, B. F. *Science and human behavior*. New York: Macmillan, 1953.

Stampfl, T., and Levis, D. Implosive therapy, a behavioral therapy. *Behavior Research and Therapy*, 1968, 6, 31–36.

Suinn, R.; Edie, C.; and Spinelli, P. Accelerated massed desensitization: innovation in short-term treatment. *Behavior Therapy*, 1970, 1, 303–311.

Sulzer-Azaroff, B., and Mayer, G. *Applying behavior-analysis procedures with children and youth*. New York: Holt, Rinehart and Winston, 1977.

Sylvester, J., and Liversedge, L. Conditioning and the occupational cramps. In H. Eysenck (ed.). *Behavior therapy and the neuroses*, Oxford: Pergamon, 1960, pp. 334–348.

Tate, B., and Baroff, G. Aversive control of self-injurious behavior in a psychotic boy. *Behavior Research and Therapy*, 1966, 4, 281–287.

Taylor, J. A behavioral interpretation of obsessive-compulsive neurosis. *Behavior Research and Therapy*, 1963, 1, 237–244.

Thomas, D.; Becker, W.; and Armstrong, M. Production and elimination of disruptive classroom behavior by systematically varying teacher's behavior. *Journal of Applied Behavior Analysis*, 1968, 1, 35–45.

Thoresen, C., and Krumboltz, J. Relationship of counselor reinforcement of selected responses to external behavior. *Journal of Counseling Psychology*, 1967, 14, 140–144.

Thorndike, E. Animal intelligence: an experimental study of the associative processes in animals. *Psychological Review Monograph Supplement*, 1898.

Titkin, S., and Hartup, W. Sociometric status and the reinforcing effectiveness of children's peers. *Journal of Experimental Child Psychology*, 1965, 18, 50–64.

Todd, F. Coverant control of self-evaluation responses in the treatment of depression: a new use for an old principle. *Behavior Therapy*, 1972, 3, 91–94.

Tyler, V., and Brown, G. The use of swift, brief isolation as a group control device for institutionalized delinquents. *Behavior Research and Therapy*, 1967, 5, 1–9.

Vogel-Spott, M. Response generalization under verbal conditioning in alcoholics, delinquents and students. *Behavior Research and Therapy*, 1964, 2, 135–141.

Vernon, W. *Motivating children: behavior modification in the classroom*. New York: Holt, Rinehart and Winston, 1965.

Walker, H.; Mattson, R.; and Buckley, N. Special class placement as a treatment alternative for deviant behavior in children. In F. Benson (ed.). *Modifying deviant social behaviors in various classroom settings*. Eugene, Oregon: University of Oregon, 1968.

Walton, D., and Mather, M. The application of learning principles to the treatment of obsessive-compulsive states in the acute and chronic phases of illness. In H. Eysenck (ed.). *Experiments in Behavior Therapy*. London: Pergamon, pp. 117–151.

Warson, S.; Caldwell, M.; Warriner, A.; Kirk, A.; and Jensen, R. The dynamics of encopresis. *American Journal Orthopsychiatry*, 1954, *24*, 402–415.

Wasik, B. The application of Premack's generalization on reinforcement to the management of classroom behavior. *Journal of Experimental Child Psychology*, 1970, *10*, 33–43.

Watson, J. Behaviorism and the concept of mental disease. *Journal of Philosophical, Psychological Scientific Methods*, 1916, *13*, 587–597.

Watson, J., and Rayner, R. Conditioned emotional reactions. *Journal of Experimental Psychology*, 1920, *3*, 1–14.

Weiner, I. Behavior therapy in obsessive-compulsive neurosis: treatment of an adolescent boy. *Psychotherapy*, 1967, *4*, 27–29.

Whelan, R. and Haring, N. Modification and maintenance of behavior through systematic application of consequences. *Exceptional Children*, 1966, *32*, 281–289.

Wilcoxon, L.; Schrader, S.; and Nelson, R. Behavioral formulations of depression. In W. Craighead, A. Kazdin, and M. Mahoney (eds.). *Behavior Modification*. Boston: Houghton Mifflin, 1976.

Williams, C. The elimination of tantrum behavior by extinction procedures: case report. *Journal of Abnormal and Social Psychology*, 1959, *59*, 269.

Willis, R., and Edwards, J. A study of the comparative effectiveness of systematic desensitization and implosive therapy. *Behavior Research and Therapy*, 1969, *7*, 387–395.

Wolf, M.; Risley, T.; and Mees, H. Application of operant conditioning procedures to the behavior problems of an autistic child. *Behavior Research and Therapy*, 1964, *1*, 305–312.

Wolpe, J. *Psychotherapy by reciprocal inhibition*. Stanford: Stanford University Press, 1958.

Wolpe, J. The systematic desensitization treatment of neuroses. *Journal of Nervous and Mental Disorders*, 1961, *132*, 189–203.

Wolpe, J. *The practice of behavior therapy*. New York: Pergamon, 1973.

Wolpe, J. *Theme and variations: a behavior therapy casebook*. New York: Pergamon, 1976.

Wolpe, J., and Ascher, L. Outflanking "resistance" in a severe obsessional neurosis. In H. Eysenck (ed.). *Case studies in behavior therapy*, London: Routledge and Kegan Paul, 1975.

Wolpe, J., and Lang, P. *Fear survey schedule*. San Diego: Educational and Industrial Testing Service, 1969.

Wolpe, J., and Lazarus, A. *Behavior therapy techniques*. New York: Pergamon, 1966.

Yates, A. J. *Behavior therapy*, New York: Wiley, 1970.

Yates, A. J. *Theory and practice in behavior therapy*. New York: Wiley, 1975.

Zimmerman, J., and Grosz, H. "Visual" performance of a functionally blind person. *Behavior Research and Therapy*, 1966, *4*, 119–134.

Zimmerman, E., and Zimmerman, J. The alteration of behavior in a special classroom situation. *Journal of Experimental Analysis of Behavior*, 1962, *5*, 59–60.

Zimmerman, E.; Zimmerman, J.; and Russell, C. Differential effects of token reinforcement on instruction-following behavior in retarded students instructed as a group. *Journal of Applied Behavior Analysis*, 1969, *2*, 101–112.

7
Educational Therapy*

The term *educational therapy* has no specific historical precedent. It is used in this text to mean the therapeutic value of typical school-related activities. These activities include individualized instructional techniques in academic skill or content areas such as reading, arithmetic, and written expression that correct or remediate learning deficits in all children; instructional arrangements or organizational procedures that facilitate learning for disturbed children; and general classroom management strategies that effectively reduce maladaptive, disruptive, or unproductive activities in disturbed children. The basic assumption underlying educational therapy is that affective and cognitive functions are intertwined and that effective teaching that promotes improvement in academic skills indirectly leads to improvement in nonacademic behaviors. In this context, teacher is synonymous with therapist, and therapy is an ongoing process throughout the school day.

INDIVIDUALIZED INSTRUCTION AS A THERAPEUTIC TECHNIQUE

One of the primary characteristics of emotionally disturbed children is academic failure (Hewett, 1969; Haring and Phillips, 1962; Bower, 1961). Some children are so disturbed due to a variety of developmental, biophysical, and/or acquired problems that they simply cannot absorb subject matter in a typical school environment. However, many other children show increasing symptoms of emotional disturbance as they progress through their school careers *because* they cannot achieve successfully in school. Essentially, these children might remain well adjusted,

---

* This chapter was co-authored by Patricia Magee and Phyllis L. Newcomer.

were it not for the frustration experienced in school. In light of this fact, it has become apparent that individualized instruction is an important treatment for improving children's self-concepts and for promoting their general emotional well being. Individualized instruction can be explored most efficiently by examining first, established instructional models and, second, general teaching procedures.

Models of Individualized Instruction

Models for individualizing instruction have been gaining steadily in popularity in the past 10 to 15 years as educators have become increasingly concerned with the issue of accountability for student learning. As the responsibility for a student's success in school shifted from the student and his or her parents, to those who plan and implement the educational program, it became increasingly clear that teachers required effective strategies and methodologies for making their instruction meaningful to each child. In addition, the schools required a new operational systems model that would help them become more child-centered in their approach to education.

As part of this educational revolution many programs and plans were designed to alter both school and teacher operations. Three of the most popular, Individually Guided Education (IGE)—a model for school operations, Precision Teaching, and Prescriptive Teaching—models for teacher efficiency, will be discussed here. These particular models have been selected for discussion from among many similar models because they are among the most innovative examples of behaviorally based instructional systems.

These three models differ in that IGE was designed as a comprehensive approach to total school reorganization, obviously applicable in regular education. Both Prescriptive Teaching and Precision Teaching originally were developed as specific methodologies for use with underachieving students, primarily in special-education settings. Their application was later expanded to include regular-education students.

Individually Guided Education   Individually Guided Education (Klausmeier, Morrow, and Walter, 1968) is essentially a school-management system built around the concept of individualized instruction. It embodies the notion that each child is an individual and should progress at her or his own rate of skill development in academic subjects. In an IGE school, several classes are grouped together into a unit. Units can be composed of classes at the same grade level, or of classes spanning several grades. In each unit, the children are given placement tests to determine their level of functioning in the various academic subjects. Students are grouped for instruction within the unit on the basis of these test results. For example, Leslie is a third-grade student in a school using the IGE model. She is in a unit composed of one first grade, two second grades, and two third grades. Her test results place her at the fifth-grade level in reading and language arts, the second-grade level in math, and indicate that she still needs many readiness activities to develop the fine-motor coordination necessary for handwriting. In a traditional self-contained third grade, Leslie would receive lessons in reading and language arts that were too easy for her and lessons in math that were too difficult. If the majority of Leslie's classmates did not need instruction in handwriting, probably none would be given, and she would continue to write illegibly. However in her IGE school, Leslie would be grouped for instruction with students who shared similar competencies and deficits. She would receive reading and language arts instruction at a fifth-grade level, math instruction at a second-grade level, and be placed in a readiness group for handwriting.

Children in an IGE program are instructed by their teachers, classroom aides, volunteer parent aides and peers. Teachers are responsible for teaching new concepts and skills. They also plan the lessons taught by the classroom aides and parent volunteers. Classroom aides and parent volunteers work with groups on lessons designed to review and reinforce concepts and skills taught by the teacher. From time to time, parent volunteers may tutor individual students in specific skills. Peer tutoring primarily involves drill activities. Classmates drill each other on rote tasks such as multiplication tables, sight words, and spelling patterns.

Learning centers are used extensively in an IGE school. A learning center is an area or place in the room devoted to a specific academic activity, such as math, social studies, or reading, or to a nonacademic activity such as art. Often more than one learning center is established in a classroom. The students are expected to work without teacher direction at each center and to move from center to center as they complete their assigned tasks. They may work alone or in small groups. To facilitate independent work the teacher ensures that the necessary directions and materials for task completion are available at each learning center.

Tests are given to all students at regular intervals to monitor their progress. Both the commercial tests that accompany the basal reading series, mathematics programs, and so on, and teacher-made tests are used. The children's scores are used to reform their instructional groups. Some children advance to new instructional levels, whereas others must be reexposed to content they did not master. Records and charts are kept for each child in each academic subject. They are used to plan the children's future programs and to communicate information about their progress to their parents.

The IGE model is designed to encourage problem solving and decision making by the school's teachers. A teacher from each unit is elected unit leader and is responsible for conducting regularly scheduled unit

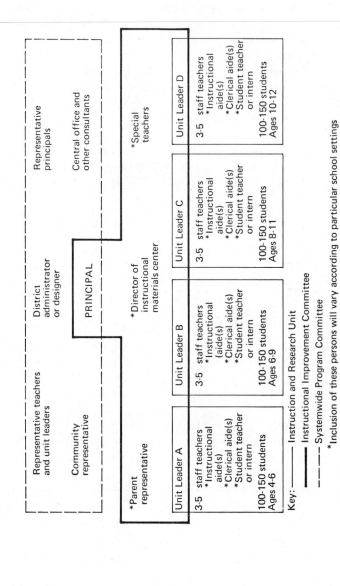

Fig. 7.1 Multiunit organization of an IGE school of 400–600 students. Source: Klausmier, H.; Morrow, R.; and Walter, J. *Individually guided education in the multiunit school.* Reprinted by permission of the Wisconsin R & D Center for Cognitive Learning, Madison, Wisc. 53706.

meetings to facilitate cooperative planning among the unit teachers. She or he also is responsible for supervising and coordinating the unit activities.

The principal format for decision making is the instructional improvement committee (IIC). The IIC consists of the unit leaders, the school principal, and, in some instances, additional persons such as a parent, the school guidance counselor, and special teachers. The IIC meets on a regular basis to discuss and resolve problems pertaining to school instructional policy. Figure 7.1 illustrates the multiunit organization of an IGE school. The actual functioning of the model depends on the extent to which teachers have the specific competencies to individualize instruction. These competencies will be discussed later in this chapter.

Precision Teaching The Precision Teaching model (Lindsley, 1971; Kunzelmann, et al., 1970) was devised as a system for monitoring each student's daily academic progress. This model employs the measurement and data collection procedures of behavior modification: (1) target a response, (2) collect and chart baseline data, (3) devise and implement a change strategy, and (4) continue to chart the resulting response. According to Lindsley (1971), precision teaching differs from behavior modification in that the focus of the change strategy (step 3) is curricular, that is, it involves the academic skills and concepts the child is trying to master. Precision teaching tries to help the child "do more successful classroom work by making curricular changes . . . rather than trying to jack up a dull curriculum with rewards for doing tasks" (Lindsley, 1971, p. 115). The use of precision teaching involves the daily measurement of performance rate (frequency divided by time) on various academic tasks. When a student is not making progress, curricular changes are made. These changes might involve lowering the difficulty level of a task, changing the instructional material the student is using, or changing the teaching strategy being used by the teacher. These curricular changes are made in lieu of giving the student tangible incentives such as candy, tokens, and prizes for completing inappropriate curriculum tasks.

A principal tool used in precision teaching is the standard behavior chart. The precision teaching behavior chart has a special six-cycle semilogarithmic design (see Fig. 7.2) that allows the recording of behavioral data on a frequency-per-minute basis ranging from 0 to 1,000 times per minute. The upper limit for behaviors—1,000 times per minute—represents the time in a day when a person typically is awake and functioning. A behavior that occurred once a day would occur at a rate of 0.001 times per minute (1−frequency divided by 1,000−minutes), and would be recorded near the bottom of the chart. A student who correctly worked twenty math problems in 10 minutes would have a math performance rate of 2 (20−frequency divided by 10−time). A student who correctly

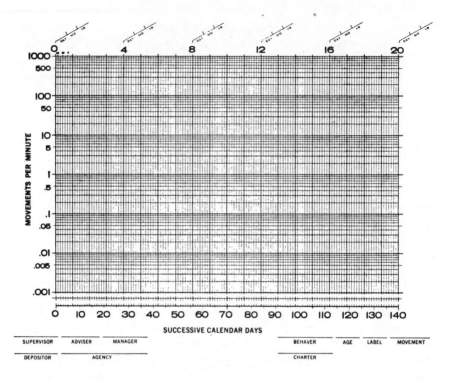

Fig. 7.2 This is a reproduction of a sheet of six-cycle semi-logarithmic chart paper produced by Behavior Research Co., Box 3351, Kansas City, Kansas 66103. Reprinted by permission of the publisher.

read 100 words in 2 minutes would have a reading rate of 50. These behaviors would be recorded in the appropriate place on the chart. The use of the frequency-in-minutes figure permits great flexibility in charting a wide variety of behaviors. In turn, the chart enables teachers to know exactly how their students are progressing in each academic subject.

Lindsley states that precision teaching is not a new methodology. It is a structure imposed on tried-and-true teaching procedures that provides more precise information about a child's rate of progress and indicates how instruction can best be individualized.

Prescriptive Teaching   Prescriptive Teaching is "an organization of definable and observable components of the process of instruction to achieve a predetermined or prescribed objective" (Peter, 1972, p. 3). The Prescriptive Teaching model of individualized instruction is similar to Precision Teaching, although it is not as rigorous in its methodology. However, it too stresses the systematic application of behavioral learning principles to children's educational experiences.

The conceptual model of Precision Teaching is composed of three elements: (1) elicitors or events occurring before a behavior, (2) the

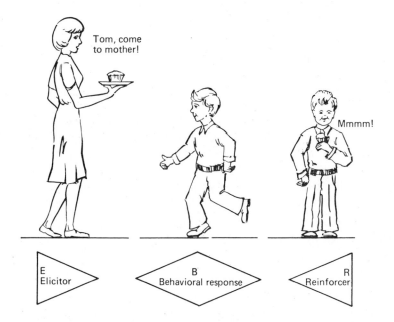

Fig. 7.3 Elements of the conceptual model. The conceptual model is composed of these three elements: elicitor (E), behavior (B), and reinforcer (R). Source: Peter L. Individual instruction. New York: McGraw-Hill, 1972. Reprinted by permission of Wadsworth Publishing Co.

behavioral response itself, and (3) reinforcers or events occurring after a behavioral response that serve to maintain, strengthen, or weaken the response (see Fig. 7.3). For example, a mother calls her child, the child comes to her, and she gives him a cupcake. The elicitor is the mother calling to the child, the behavioral response is the child coming to the mother, and the reinforcer is the cupcake. The reinforcer probably will strengthen the response since it is something the child likes (a positive reinforcer). Had the reinforcer been something the child dislikes such as a spanking (negative reinforcer), the behavior response probably would have been weakened, and in the future the child would avoid coming when his mother called.

This conceptual model is used in four stages that comprise the Prescriptive Teaching process. The first stage involves *describing the students entering behavior,* that is, the student's present level of academic functioning. This description is obtained by observing the student in the classroom and by working individually with the student. Direct observation of classroom behavior reveals the maladaptive behaviors that interfere with achievement, as well as their elicitors and reinforcers. Specific academic strengths and weaknesses are assessed through diagnostic teaching on an individual basis. In diagnostic teaching, academic tasks of varying degrees of difficulty are presented to the child under varied conditions of reinforcement (praise, tokens, food). The child's performance should indicate where he or she functions best academically and which reinforcers are most motivating.

The second stage of Prescriptive Teaching involves *delineating the goals* or final outcomes of a student's program. These goals are called *terminal objectives* and are written according to the elicitor-behavior-reinforcement model of Prescriptive Teaching. For example, Steve, a fifth-grade student, was having difficulty with social studies. When given an independent assignment to do (seatwork), he would gaze around the room, tap his feet on the floor, drum his fingers on the desk, and wiggle around in his seat. Rarely did Steve finish an assignment. A terminal objective for Steve might be:

> Given the fifth-grade social studies book, Steve will read the assignment and correctly answer on paper the questions at the end of the chapter while receiving only regular teacher attention.

This terminal objective would fit in to the model in this manner:

Elicitor	Behavior	Reinforcer
Fifth grade social studies book.	Read the assignment and correctly answer on paper the questions at the end of the chapter.	Regular teacher attention.

The third phase involves *writing enroute objectives*. Enroute objectives are a series of steps or skills that the student must learn or accomplish to move from his or her entering behaviors to the terminal objectives. Usually, the teaching procedures and curricular materials are specified in the enroute objectives. Enroute objectives are also written according to the elicitor-behavior-reinforcement model. Enroute objectives for Steve might include the following:

Elicitor	Behavior	Reinforcement
1. Fifth-grade social studies book	Read one paragraph and answer correctly on paper two questions about the paragraph.	Five minutes free time to listen to the radio.
2. Fifth-grade social studies book	Read three paragraphs and answer correctly on paper three questions about the paragraphs.	Four minutes free time to listen to the radio and teacher praise.
3. Fifth-grade social studies book	Read one page and answer correctly on paper five questions about the content.	Good progress note to take home and teacher praise.

This list of enroute objectives should continue until the desired terminal objective is reached. In behavioral terms, Peter is employing the concept of successive approximation (see Chapter 6), to move a student from his or her entering behaviors to the terminal objectives.

The fourth stage of Prescriptive Teaching is the *evaluation*. This step can be accomplished subjectively by simply observing the student in the classroom to see if the terminal objective has been attained. Evaluation also can be conducted objectively by observing the student in the classroom and collecting data regarding the frequency of the terminal behavior.

General Procedures for Individualizing Instruction

The teacher who plans to use any of the specific programs described above, or who simply wants to individualize instruction for her students, must have certain competencies. First, the teacher must be able to use and interpret various formal and informal tests and assessment techniques. Second, he or she must be able to translate the information gained from the assessment into goals and instructional objectives. Third, the teacher must be able to deliver instruction to the students. Fourth, he or she must be able to monitor and evaluate the student's progress.

Assessment A student should be tested in all curricular areas to determine specifically the concepts and skills already known and those that need to be learned. Assessment can be conducted both formally and informally. Formal assessment involves administering standardized tests such as those listed in Table 7.1. Standardized tests "yield information of a quantitative nature and tend to compare a specific child's performance with national or regional normative data" (Hammill, 1971, p. 343). Raw scores, usually the total number of correct responses, can be converted to

Table 7.1 *Standardized Tests Useful for Formal Assessment*

Test	Academic Area
Peabody Individual Achievement Test (Dunn and Markwardt, 1970).	Math, Reading Recognition, Reading Comprehension, Spelling, General Information
Psycho-Educational Test Battery (Woodcock and Johnson, 1978)	Cognitive Skills, Academic Skills, and Interest Inventory.
Test of Reading Comprehension (Hammill, Weiderholt, and Brown, 1978).	Reading
Woodcock Reading Mastery Test (Woodcock, 1974)	Reading
Durrell Analysis of Reading Difficulty (Durrell, 1955)	Reading
Peabody Picture Vocabulary Test (Dunn, 1959)	Spoken Language

Table 7.1 *Continued*

Test	Academic Area
Test of Language Development (TOLD) (Newcomer and Hammill, 1977)	Spoken Language
Northwestern Syntax Screening Test (Lee, 1969)	Spoken Language
Test for Auditory Comprehension of Language (Carrow, 1975)	Spoken Language
Key-Math Diagnostic Test (Connolloy, Nachtman and Pritchett, 1973)	Math
Stanford Diagnostic Arithmetic Test (Beatty, Madden, and Gardner, 1966)	Math
Test of Written Spelling (Larsen and Hammill, 1977)	Spelling
Picture Story Language Test (Myklebust, 1956)	Written Language
Test of Written Language (Hammill and Larsen, 1978)	Written Language

age equivalents, grade equivalents, stanines, or percentiles to make such normative comparisons. Generally, teachers use standardized tests to determine how a student's level of achievement compares to others at the same grade or age level. Although they are helpful tools for this purpose, standardized tests have distinct limitations. According to Wallace and Larsen (1978, pp. 22–23)

> The teacher is provided with little data that can be used in actually teaching the child. The more exact information upon which daily instruction is usually formulated is omitted in the results obtained from most formal assessment instruments. Grade level scores do not describe the specific behaviors that encompass the scores . . . this is one of the most serious shortcomings of formal tests.

In other words, standardized tests are good starting points in assessment; however, they must be followed by more specific assessment that yields information needed to plan instruction. This step in information gathering is accomplished best through informal assessment. Informal assessment is used to: "detect areas of [academic] strength and weakness; to verify, probe or discard the conclusions and recommendations based on the formal evaluation; to deduce the child's particular instructional or behavioral needs; and to formulate a remedial program for (the student)" (Hammill and Bartel, 1975, p. 7). There are several kinds of informal assessment instruments. One type is termed *criterion-referenced tests*. Criterion-referenced tests are designed to evaluate a child's specific level of mastery on educational tasks without making reference to the performance of other children. An absolute or specific criterion is set for the individual's achievement, for example, reaching a level of 90 percent accuracy on a spelling test. The object of the test is to discover what a particular student knows or does not know. Criterion-referenced tests have been developed by commercial publishers to accompany particular basal reading, math, and spelling textbook series. These commercial criterion-referenced tests are often referred to as monitoring systems. They may include pretests, which are given before an instructional period, progress tests, given to measure daily achievement, and posttests, given after the instructional period. Most monitoring systems usually include some method of record keeping.

Criterion-referenced tests also can be constructed by teachers. For example, the weekly spelling test may include words that the teacher selected randomly from the child's reading series. Gronlund (1973) has proposed six simple guidelines to aid teachers in the use of behavioral procedures for test construction. They are:

1. Clearly define and delineate the domain of learning tasks
2. Express instructional objectives in behavioral terms
3. Clearly specify a standard of performance
4. Adequately sample student performance within each performance area
5. Select test items based on how well they reflect the behavior specified in the instructional objective
6. Devise a scoring and reporting system that adequately describes student performance on clearly defined learning tasks

The first guideline refers to the scope of the subject matter to be included on the test. For example, if the subject matter is arithmetic, the teacher must decide if the scope should include only computation or should involve arithmetic vocabulary and problem-solving skills. If the scope is restricted to computation, the teacher must decide what specific computational skills should be included.

The second guideline will be discussed in detail in an upcoming section of this chapter. Most simply, it consists of forming instructional objectives that are observable and measurable. For example, a statement such as "the student will be able to recognize and name the numerals 1, 2, and 3, when shown them on flash cards, states precisely what the student must do after being instructed, whereas, the statement "the student will learn the numerals 1, 2, and 3," does not.

Stating objectives behaviorally leads directly to the third guideline. A standard of performance pertains to components such as level of accuracy and rate of response. For example, the statement "the student will be able to recognize and name the numerals 1, 2, and 3 without error, within five seconds after viewing each flash card," includes standards.

Guideline four pertains to including enough items in each skill area on the test. For example, an arithmetic test of the four basic computational skills must have a representative number of addition, subtraction, multiplication, and division problems included. Too few items in one area would preclude the formation of accurate conclusions about the child's skills in that area.

Guideline five, also about the selection of test items, suggests that each item used must pertain to the instructional objectives. If an instructional objective pertained to recognition and naming of numerals, it would be poor testing strategy to ask the child to write a numeral on the test.

The final guideline indicates that the teacher should convert test results to charts, graphs, or records that permit him or her to monitor the child's progress in academic areas.

Skills checklists are another tool for informally evaluating a student's academic abilities. They are simply lists of skills that a student should be able to demonstrate if he or she has mastered certain material and is ready to progress to a higher level of instruction. They differ from criterion-referenced tests in that the skills represented on checklists are not defined behaviorally, nor do they involve a specific standard of performance. An example of a commercial skills checklist is the *Barbe Reading Skills Checklist* (Barbe, 1975) presented in Figure 7.4. Teachers

Fig. 7.4 Barbe Reading Skills Check List (Advanced Level). Source: Reprinted with permission of the owner of the copyright. Individual copies may be obtained from Dr. Walter Barbe, The Ohio State University, Columbus, Ohio 43210.

| (Last Name) | (First Name) | (Name of School) |

| (Age) | (Grade Placement) | (Name of Teacher) |

PART ONE

I. Vocabulary:
   A. Word Recognition in Content:
      English _____
      Mathematics _____
      Social Studies _____
      Science _____
   B. Identifies Compound Words
   C. Root Words
      1. Recognizes and understands concept of root words
      2. Knows meaning of common roots
   D. Prefixes
      1. Recognizes and knows concept of prefixes   _____

   2. Knows meaning of common prefixes: _____

anti-	against	antibiotic
co-	together with	cooperate
de-	down, from, away	deploy
dis-	apart from, reversing	dismantle
en-	in	encourage
ex-	out of, beyond	extrovert
pre-	before	preview
pro-	for, forward	propeller
un-	not	unkind

E. Suffixes
   1. Recognizes and knows concept of suffixes   _____
   2. Knows meaning of common suffixes: _____

ary	place where	primary
ist	one who acts	scientist
ive	relating to	constructive
less	without	fearless
ly	similar in manner	definitely
ment	state, quality, act	contentment
ness	state of being	happiness
ous	abounding in	righteous
hood	condition of	statehood

F. Knows meaning of terms in vocabulary of language:
   1. simile __ metaphor __
   2. synonyms __ antonyms __ homonyms __
   3. onomatopoeia __

II. Word Attack Skills:

A. Knows consonant sounds
   1. Initial single consonants of one sound
   2. Sounds of c and g   _____
   3. Blends __ digraph __ diphthong __
   4. Medial sounds
   5. Final sounds   _____

B. Hears and can make vowel sounds   _____
   1. Long vowels __ short vowels __
   2. Can apply vowel rules   _____

C. Knows elements of syllabication
   1. Knows rules   _____
   2. Can apply rules   _____

D. Uses accent properly
   1. Knows and applies rules   _____
   2. Can shift accent and change use of word   _____

III. Comprehension:

A. Understands structure of story or paragraph:
   main idea   _____
   topic sentence   _____
   sequence of ideas   _____
   subordinate ideas   _____

B. Can repeat general idea of material read   _____

C. Can remember specific important facts   _____

Fig. 7.4 Continued

    D. Can relate material read to known information or experience   _____

    E. Can follow printed directions   _____

    F. Can interpret hidden meaning   _____

IV. Silent and Oral Reading:

    A. Reads silently without lip movements   _____

    B. Reads silently at twice oral rate   _____

    C. Adjusts silent rate to material

        1. Reads popular fiction at 200+ words per minute   _____

        2. Uses skimming techniques when applicable   _____

    D. Eye-voice span 3 to 5 words (in oral reading)   _____

    E. Reads aloud with comprehension   _____

can construct their own skills checklists by listing the tasks that a student must master and providing a place to record whether mastery has been accomplished. An example of a teacher-made skills checklist is presented in Figure 7.5.

Fig. 7.5 Prereading and primary reading skill checklist

	Has Mastered	Needs Review	Has Not Mastered
1. Can follow oral directions:			
a. One specific direction			
b. Two specific directions			
c. Three specific directions			
d. Four or more specific directions			
2. Can listen to an oral story			
a. Can answer questions concerning the story			
b. Can retell the story in his/her own words			
c. Can retell the story's events in correct order			
3. Recognizes the differences between letters and words			
4. Relates his/her experiences verbally			
5. Can relate his/her experience in complete sentences			
6. Can say the alphabet in order			
7. Can say the alphabet while pointing to each letter			
8. Can write the alphabet in order			
9. Can supply rhyming words for simple poems			

	Has Mastered	Needs Review	Has Not Mastered
10. Can recognize words that begin with the same sound			
11. Can recognize words that end alike			
12. Knows the sounds of the consonants			
13. Knows the sounds of the short vowels			
14. Can name the beginning, medial and final sound of a word			
15. Can recognize a c-v-c word after the teacher says each sound			
16. Can blend c-v-c words			
17. Can substitute beginning and ending sounds in word families			
18. Recognizes the sight words a, is, the, I, and, come,			

Skills checklists are useful for verifying information obtained from standardized tests. For example, a student, Donnie, scored below grade level on the *money* subtest of the KEY-MATH Diagnostic Test (Connolloy et al., 1973) by missing the four items involving coin identification and making change. Since these four items only tap certain aspects of money knowledge, the teacher may not be sure of the extent of Donnie's problem. The teacher can gather more information by constructing a skills checklist that samples all of the skills involved in identifying coins and making change, such as the one presented in Fig. 7.6. Not only has the teacher verified Donnie's deficiency in identifying coins and making change, but specific information for writing instructional objectives has also been gathered.

A final type of informal assessment consists of *daily anecdotal records* written by the teacher regarding the child's progress. Anecdotal records are simply written statements about the child's performance in the various academic areas. This relatively informal procedure can be useful if it is done systematically. The accumulated information is helpful in determining whether to reteach a skill, devise a different teaching strategy, or proceed to the next skill. Some useful sources of information regarding the construction of informal assessment instruments are:

Reading: *Informal Reading Inventories* (Johnson and Kress, 1965)

Spelling: "Developmental Spelling Inventories." In *Handbook in Diagnostic Teaching* (Mann and Suiter, 1974)

Math: "Guidelines for Preparing a Teacher-made Diagnostic Test." In *A Guide to the Diagnostic Teaching of Arithmetic* (Reisman, 1978).

Written   "Written Expression and Spelling by G. P. Cartwright.
Expression: In *Teacher Diagnosis of Educational Difficulties* (Smith,
             1959).

Other helpful sources of information concerning both formal and informal
assessment are: *Educational Assessment of Learning Problems: Testing
for Teaching* (Wallace and Larsen, 1978); *Corrective and Remedial
Teaching* (Otto, McMenemy, and Smith, 1973); *Assessment in Special
and Remedial Education* (Salvia and Ysseldyke, 1978).

Fig. 7.6 Skills checklist—money

1. Knows names of: penny   _____

                      dime   _____

                      nickel   _____

                      quarter   _____

                      half-dollar _____

2. Knows the equivalent in cents for:

                      penny   _____

                      dime   _____

                      nickel   _____

                      quarter   _____

                      half-dollar _____

3. Can add change involving:

                      pennies   _____

                      nickels   _____

                      dimes   _____

                      quarters   _____

                      half-dollars _____

4. Uses the signs ¢ and $ properly _____

5. Can make change for amounts under $.50 _____

6. Can make change for amounts under $1.00 _____

7. Can solve computational problems involving a decimal point _____

8. Can solve verbal problems involving addition and subtraction of monetary
   amounts under $1.00 _____

Annual Goals and Instructional Objectives   The next area of competence involves translating the information gained from the educational assessment into annual goals and short-term instructional objectives. Annual goals are written statements covering what the student is expected to gain from his or her educational program. They generally reflect the progress a student is expected to make in each academic area over the course of a year. Suggestions or prototypes of annual goals can be found in teacher's manuals of published curriculum materials. For example, an annual goal for a fourth-grade student in most mathematics programs is to learn division of whole numbers. To develop annual goals for each learner, the teacher must consider typical developmental and curricular expectations based on chronological age, consult the child's assessment data, examine his or her past learning history, and draw on her or his own experience working with children. The teacher's goals for each child must be a realistic reflection of that child's capabilities.

Short-term objectives are based on annual goals. They represent the learning tasks a student must master to reach the annual goal. The number of short-term objectives written for each annual goal will vary depending on the degree of specificity of the objective and the needs of the student. To develop short-term objectives, teachers should draw from published lists of objectives and scope-and-sequence charts that are provided with most commercial curriculum materials. Additionally, teachers can construct their own sequences of short-term objectives, often referred to as *skill hierarchies*. To do so, they must perform a *task analysis* of each annual goal. Task analysis is simply the process whereby the annual goal is reduced to its smallest component parts, the short-term objectives. For example, an annual arithmetic goal for a student might be to learn to add and subtract three-digit numbers when regrouping is involved. This annual goal could be task analyzed into the following components or subskills:

1. Can construct and count sets of varying number
2. Understands number/numeral relationships
3. Can add one-digit numerals
4. Can subtract one-digit numerals
5. Can add two-digit numerals
6. Can subtract two-digit numerals
7. Can add two-digit numerals that require regrouping
8. Can subtract two-digit numerals that require regrouping
9. Can add and subtract two-digit numerals with zeros that require regrouping
10. Can add three-digit numerals
11. Can subtract three-digit numerals
12. Can add three three-digit numerals that require regrouping

13. Can subtract three-digit numerals that require regrouping
14. Can add and subtract three-digit numerals with zeros that require regrouping

Depending on the characteristics and needs of the student, the annual goal could be task analyzed with regard to the psychomotor skills needed, such as holding a pencil, writing numerals, working from right to left, or it could be task analyzed in terms of the social–emotional behaviors needed, such is staying in his or her seat, attending to the task, or task completion. Once an annual goal has been task analyzed, the teacher consults the assessment data to determine which of the subskills has already been mastered by the student. Short-term objectives are then written for those skills the student needs to learn to reach the annual goal.

As stated earlier, the degree of specificity in writing short-term objectives can vary. The most widely used method of devising instructional objectives has been developed by Mager (1962). He refers to his objectives as behavioral objectives. The process involves:

1. Stating the behavior to be learned in very specific terms (*What*)
2. Stating the *conditions* under which the behavior is to occur (*How* and *When*)
3. Stating the *criteria* for acceptable performance (*How much*)

A behavioral objective for step 11 of the above task analysis might be formulated in the following manner:

> During a math practice session, when given a pencil and a piece of paper with ten subtraction problems requiring no regrouping, the student will write all the answers correctly.

In the above statement, all of the components of a behavioral objective are present.

Behavior: Write the answers to ten subtraction problems that have three-digit numbers and do not require regrouping.
Conditions: During a math practice session, with pencil and paper.
Criteria: All must be done correctly (100 percent accuracy).

Delivering Instruction   The next area of competence for individualizing instruction involves the actual delivery of instruction—teaching. This area incorporates four components: (1) instructional arrangements, (2) classroom management strategies, (3) the selection of instructional materials, and (4) the adaptation of instructional materials. Topics 1 and 2 will be discussed later in this chapter. We will elaborate on the latter two components here.

When selecting materials for teaching, three factors should be considered: the needs of the student, the needs of the teacher, and the dictates of the curriculum (Wilson, 1978). When examining student needs, the teacher must consider the children's levels of academic skill development as well as their social and emotional needs. He or she should select materials that not only teach necessary academic skills but also motivate and arouse the student's interest. Moreover, it is important to investigate which instructional materials have been previously successful with the student and which materials have been associated with anxiety, frustration, and failure. In a therapeutic educational program, it is not wise to reintroduce materials associated with past failure.

The needs of the teacher are a most important element in the process of selecting materials, for teachers are the main facilitators of instruction (Starkel, 1978). Their theoretical biases, teaching styles, and levels of teaching competence must influence materials selection. First of all, teachers will not deliver effective instruction if their materials reflect a theory they do not espouse. For example, a teacher who dislikes the phonetic approach to teaching reading would not use a phonetically based reading series effectively. Similarly, a teacher will not use materials that require a teaching methodology that is incompatible with his or her particular teaching style. For example, a teacher who prefers an experimental approach to teaching science would not be happy with a science series that emphasized lectures on concepts. Finally, it is doubtful that a material with content beyond the teacher's scope of understanding can be employed successfully in delivering instruction. If the teacher doesn't understand algebra, he or she cannot effectively use the materials that teach that subject.

The third factor, dictates of the curriculum, are the limits imposed on the selection of materials by the general school curriculum. Many times students must master certain skills or certain content areas before they can move to the next grade level. This is especially true at the middle-school and high-school levels where certain courses are required for graduation. In cases such as these, instructional materials pertaining to particular subject areas must be identified and purchased.

Another component of teaching involves the adaptation of instrucional materials to meet individual needs of students. Often, a student will not experience success with a particular instructional material. In these instances, the teacher must alter or modify the material so that it is more appropriate for the student. Wilson (1976) presents a range of options for adapting and developing materials in terms of a four-level hierarchy that includes: first, altering regular materials; second, selecting another material; third, combining several diverse materials; and fourth, developing new materials.

The first step can be done in a variety of ways.

1. Limit the length of assignments. The number of pages that a student must read or the number of math problems he or she must work can be reduced.

2. Color-code directions. Directions can be highlighted with a magic marker so students can find them easily on the page.
3. Use outlines and study guides. This is especially important at the secondary level with such subjects as history, health, or literature.
4. Rewrite explanations and directions on a lower readability and syntactic level.
5. Use tapes and slides to accompany written material. This helps accent important facts and key concepts.
6. Place written material on cassette tapes. Students can hear the reading matter as they follow along in their texts.
7. Break skills into smaller steps. Many times a workbook or textbook will teach a new skill in only one or two pages. Supplementary lessons can be built into the workbook or text to teach the skill in smaller steps and provide for more reinforcement and/or drill.

If none of these modifications is successful, the teacher can move to the second level of the hierarchy and select another material. The task is to find a material that encompasses the same content or skills as the regular material that is written at a lower reading level, uses a simpler format, is easier to understand, and is interesting to the student.

If no solutions to the curricular problem are found at levels one or two, the teacher must drop to level three of the hierarchy. This level involves developing a program or teaching sequence by combining several diverse materials. To do this effectively, the teacher must select materials that cover the required content area, for example, regrouping in addition, the life-cycle of the toad, the history of the Equal Rights Amendment, and that are at the same instructional level with regard to format, readability, and interest. An example of a level three adaptation, a unit in map skills, is presented in Figure 7.7. In this lesson, the teacher incorporated four separate books and one kit of four filmstrips. The teacher notes the pages from each source used, and the concepts combined in the lesson.

When all else fails, teachers can move to the fourth and lowest rung of the hierarchy—developing new materials. Starkel (1978) warns that this task is very time consuming and may prove surprisingly expensive if the teacher considers the cost of his or her time. Also, teacher-made materials often are poorly designed, unattractive, and unappealing to the children. Generally, teacher-made materials are best when limited to instructional games and flash cards intended for drill and reinforcement.

INSTRUCTIONAL ARRANGEMENTS

This section will deal with several formats for classroom organization for emotionally disturbed children including the structured classroom (Haring and Phillips, 1962), the engineered classroom (Hewett, 1969),

Fig. 7.7 Outline for a unit in map skills. Source: Ruth Berkowitz. Used with permission.

Material	Page	Concept
Map Skills Book 1 (MSB1)	(3,4)	Introduction to maps
Filmstrip (What is a Map?)		Comparing maps and globes
MSB1	(5)	"
How Maps & Globes Help Us (HM&GHU)	(6,7)	"
Readiness for Map Skills 2 (RFMS2)	(3,4,28)	"
MSB1	(7)	Determining positions
HM&GHU	(10,11)	"
RFMS2	(10,11,12,13,14,15, 16,20,22,23-30)	"
MSB1	(8,9)	Determining size
RFMS2	(12-16,19,20,22, 29,30)	"
Basic Skills in Getting Around (BSIGA)	(15,16)	"
MSB1	(10,11)	Using map symbols
RFMS2	(5,6)	"
Filmstrip (Lakes, Rivers and Their Symbols)		"
RFMS2	(7,8)	"
Filmstrip (Towns, Cities and Their Symbols)		"
RFMS2	(9,10)	"
Filmstrip (Landforms and Their Symbols)		"
MSB1	(12-17)	Using map keys
MSB1	(18-23)	Determining direction
BSIGA	(8,9)	"

and the open classroom (Knoblock, 1975). In conjunction with this discussion of organizational models, the general role of the teacher of emotionally disturbed children will be presented. Finally, the use of resource personnel including pro essionals, such as principals, psychologists, psychiatrists, and resource teachers; children, in such activities as peer tutoring, cross-age tutoring, and self-management; and parents for parent tutoring, will be explored.

Classroom Organization

The models for classroom organization to be presented in this chapter largely reflect the philosophical orientations of those who developed them. Haring and Phillips primarily espouse a behavioristic perspective. Thus the structured classroom organization they present in *Educating Emotionally Disturbed Children* (1962) places emphasis on using the child's natural learning process as a means of remediating emotional disabilities. They believe that the child who learns to accept behavioral limits and who is successful in academic learning begins to feel better about himself or herself.

Hewett's engineered classroom model is an integration of behavioristic and developmental principles. In his classic book *The Emotionally Disturbed Child in the Classroom* (1969), Hewett applies the behavioristic principles of reinforcement to help the disturbed child progress through a highly structured sequence of hierarchical developmental skill areas.

Knoblock (1975) espouses a humanistic orientation. Therefore, the open classroom concept reflects the psychoeducational philosophy that teaching strategies must primarily emphasize children's feelings and attitudes, and to a lesser extent, their cognitive skills.

The Structured Classroom Model   This type of classroom organization for emotionally disturbed children was developed, in part, as a reaction to psychoanalytically oriented classrooms. The guiding principle of the psychoanalytic approach is permissiveness. Disturbed children are seen as being too ill either to cope with the stresses of academic achievement or to observe social rules. They are encouraged to display bizarre, acting-out behaviors to release the repressed emotions causing their disturbance. Teachers are expected to be accepting, loving, and to impose few behavioral limits. Academic instruction is a secondary goal, emotional development is of primary importance.

In contrast, the structured classroom reflects the premise that emotionally disturbed children require firm limits on their behaviors, and that academic achievement is extremely important. Haring and Phillips state "children suffer from emotional disturbance because they lack order or structure or definiteness in their daily living at home and at school, and that within the confines of the school program it would be desirable and constructive to rectify past excesses in habits, attitudes, and achievement" (p. 10). Similarly, in presenting a synopsis of their general attitudes toward children they note: "discipline, or structure, is not a negative condition—not merely a matter of restraint. Proper self-discipline promotes achievement, and achievement develops self-discipline" (p. 181). Also, "Avoid leaving too many decisions up to the child that have to do with his daily routine. Some teachers follow the dictum

'If you learn, fine; if you do not learn, that is up to you.' This attitude of purporting to leave a mature choice up to the immature student without teaching him the consequences of his action in more concrete terms is unrealistic; it is bound to cause the student trouble and to adversely affect society in many ways" (p. 181).

The establishment of structure in the classroom depends on the following variables: individualized instruction, seating limits, play and recreational limits, conduct limits, movement privileges, and parent discussion groups. *Individualized instruction* has been discussed extensively in the first section of this chapter. Briefly, it involves gearing instructional activities to the child's level of competence, presenting academic tasks in brief, sequenced steps, and using consistent follow-up of academic progress. *Seating limits* involve the use of small study booths equipped with movable chairs and fixed desks. Children who become distracted while sitting in their regular seats can retreat to the more subdued environment of the study booth. *Play limits* are rules that ensure that children complete their work assignments before they engage in play or recreation activities. In the structured classroom, play serves as a reinforcer for work. Academic tasks are assigned in the morning, and the afternoons are devoted to fun activities if the child's work is completed. *Conduct limits* involve three rules for coping with a disorderly or upset child: provide the child with time to calm down, administer one warning of consequences if he or she does not comply, and isolate the disruptive child. *Movement privileges* involve rules for controlling movement activities such as trips to the rest room and errands. Some movement activities are used as rewards, for example, passing out paper, emptying wastebaskets. *Parent discussion groups* are held approximately once a month to coordinate parent-school efforts in handling problems, help parents improve control techniques, and to gather more information about children's home life.

Obviously, the teacher's role is of critical importance in the structured classroom. Haring and Phillips make four assumptions about the attitudes teachers must possess. They believe "That the teacher's essential motivation, beyond earning a living, is the utilization of the natural learning process of children to the fullest possible extent; that the teacher believe that all children have potential for learning useful, constructive skills which can be utilized now and in the future for the benefit of society; that the teacher employ throughout his teaching experiences, efficient and complete methods of child study; and that the teacher respond warmly, sensitively and empathetically to all of the children" (p. 42).

Having presented these general characteristics, they proceed to delineate the specific teacher behaviors that are effective with emotionally disturbed children. These are:

1. *Teach academic subject matter as soon as possible.* Such emphasis is consistent with the reality of an educational environment.

2. *Use concrete assignments.* Emotionally disturbed children benefit from well defined, specific tasks in which completion can be easily recognized.

3. *Be aware of each child's developmental level.* Material must be appropriate for each child to experience success.

4. *Give immediate feedback.* Score tasks on the spot and allow the child to see and correct errors and earn reinforcement.

5. *Sequence achievement tasks.* Show the child his or her progress through each step of a task.

6. *Allow increased freedom of choice as the child progresses.* Initially much structure is required. The child must be presented with specific tasks and must be made aware of the contingencies of task completion. Once the child learns that he or she can succeed and can control himself or herself, then he or she can be permitted to make more and more decisions for himself or herself.

7. *Be consistent.* The child must know precisely what to expect. Consistency promotes stability.

8. *Modify achievement tasks.* Give highly specific instructions, use short assignments, monitor work closely, and make adjustments if the work is too easy or too difficult.

9. *Enforce work requirements.* Initially children will try to avoid working. Make sure that the task is appropriate and, if so, enforce the consequences of not working.

10. *Prepare consequences that avoid punishment.* Intersperse enjoyable activities throughout the school day. Failure to work leads to forfeit of an enjoyable activity.

11. *Limit verbalizations.* Don't talk excessively and train children not to listen. Demonstrate materials or activities instead of talking about them. Enforce consequences of behavior but don't harangue or engage in verbal threats. Don't argue or debate issues.

12. *Don't overlook significant misbehavior.* Children require firm, clear enforcement of behavioral limits. Inconsistency results in an increase in compulsive, acting-out behavior.

13. *Have missed work made up.* Insist that children complete all assignments, even when they are absent from school. Otherwise children often attempt to stay home to avoid difficult tasks.

14. *Make return to the regular classroom the goal.* Plan to integrate the child as he or she begins to improve. Early exposures to regular class

should be on a gradual, part-time basis. The regular educator should be selected carefully, prepared in advance of receiving the child, and given back up support when necessary.

15. *Conduct follow-up.* Once the child is integrated into regular education, follow his or her progress. Help if problems begin to develop.

Haring and Philips compared the effectiveness of the structured approach with a permissive approach and an approach that used typical classroom procedures. They demonstrated that emotionally disturbed children placed in their structured program showed an increase in both academic achievement and behavior adjustment. They concluded that the structured classroom, "one in which clear direction, firm expectations and consistent follow-through are paramount, is presumably a healthy state of affairs for normal children, as well as necessary for optimal growth of emotionally disturbed children" (p. 80).

The Engineered Classroom Model   Hewett's model is based on the underlying premise that "all children [emotionally disturbed] are ready to learn something and despite their deviant behavior, the major educational goal is to get them ready for school while they are actually in school" (p. 7). To accomplish this task, Hewett has integrated strategies for interpersonal behavior, sensory and perceptual-motor behavior, and behavior modification into a total developmental approach. His basic conceptualization is a developmental hierarchy that encompasses the essential skills that all children require to be successful in school. This "Developmental Sequence of Educational Goals" is illustrated in Figure 7.8. This sequence occurs as normal development in most children, but not in emotionally disturbed children. The teacher of the emotionally disturbed must assess children's competence at each developmental level and must help them acquire the skills they lack. The methodology used to do so is derived from behavior modification.

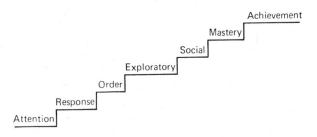

Fig. 7.8 A developmental sequence of educational goals. Source: Frank M. Hewett, *The emotionally disturbed child in the classroom.* Boston, MA; Allyn and Bacon, 1968. Reprinted with permission of the publisher.

The initial educational level, *attention,* is basic to all other learning. A child must use his or her sense organs to attend to stimulation. The next step, *response,* is the child's reaction to the stimuli. *Order* introduces the organizational factors that help determine that learning will occur. The *exploratory* stage is most critical in promoting learning about the environment. Beyond these four stages, which focus primarily on the child's development as a learner, is the *social* stage. This level involves the element of social approval as a critical factor in learning. *Mastery* involves conquering the basic intellectual and adaptive skills that permit independent functioning. Fundamental mastery skills include language and concept formation, as well as academic competence. Finally the *achievement* level involves self-motivation in learning, the desire to learn because of a desire for knowledge.

In addition to the developmental sequence of educational goals, Hewett presents a learning triangle to illustrate the three ingredients that must be provided in an instructional program to ensure that the child learns. Fig. 7.9 depicts the equal ingredients: the task, the reward, and the structure.

The task is "any activity, lesson or assignment given to the child which is directed toward assisting him in achieving one or more goals on the developmental sequence" (p. 61). Each goal must be reduced to a sequence of tasks that the child can learn to perform successfully. For example, to help a child obtain the goal of order on the developmental

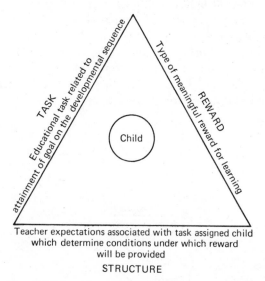

Fig. 7.9 The learning triangle (child). Source: Frank M. Hewett, *The emotionally disturbed child in the classroom.* Boston, MA: Allyn and Bacon, 1968. Reprinted with permission of the publisher.

sequence, the teacher should emphasize discrete tasks such as seat sitting, turn waiting, and so on, rather than the global concept of good citizenship. Hewett cautions that a "thimbleful" accomplishment related to the goal is far more obtainable than the "bucket" approach of a major change in behavior.

Reward is a positive consequence that maintains or increases the strength or frequency of a desired behavior. Hewett recognizes that emotionally disturbed children require rewards to learn and that those available must range from tangible items to intrinsic satisfaction.

Structure "refers to the limits or 'strings' the teacher or the school attaches to particular tasks assigned the child which determine whether or not he will be rewarded. In essence, it is the degree of teacher control present in the learning situation" (p. 67). For example, to earn a reward for arriving at school on time, the child must arrive at 9:00 A.M. sharp, not 9:05. The structure pertains to the specific time lines established.

To aid in evaluating a child's functional level in each developmental area, Hewett has designed a hierarchical checklist that is depicted in Table 7.2. The basic problem at each level, as well as the task, reward,

Table 7.2 *Student Assessment According to a Developmental Sequence of Educational Goals*

TASK

Attention

1. Child does not pay attention to learning tasks.

☐	☐	☐
(ALWAYS)	(SOMETIMES)	(RARELY)
Child never pays attention to learning tasks	Child often does not pay attention to learning tasks	Child occasionally does not pay attention to learning tasks

2. Child prefers fantasy to reality.

☐	☐	☐
(SEVERE)	(MODERATE)	(MILD)
Child out of contact with reality	Child often daydreams	Child occasionally daydreams

3. Child engages in repetitive behavior which interferes with learning.

☐	☐	☐
(SEVERE)	(MODERATE)	(MILD)
Child preoccupied with constant self-stimulation	Child preoccupied with rituals or other compulsive behavior	Child preoccupied with neatness, cleanliness, or correctness

Table 7.2 *Continued*

---

4. Child's beliefs and interests are inappropriate.

☐
(SEVERE)
Child has
extremely
bizarre beliefs
and interests

☐
(MODERATE)
Child has distorted be-
liefs about his environ-
ment

☐
(MILD)
Child's beliefs and
interests immature for
sex and age

5. Child does not pay attention to teacher.

☐
(ALWAYS)
Child never
pays attention
to teacher

☐
(SOMETIMES)
Child often does not
pay attention to teacher

☐
(RARELY)
Child occasionally does
not pay attention to
teacher

6. Child does not profit from instruction.

☐
(ALWAYS)
Child never
retains and
uses instruc-
tion he has
been given

☐
(SOMETIMES)
Child often does not
retain and use instruc-
tion he has been given

☐
(RARELY)
Child occasionally does
not retain and use in-
struction he has been
given

Response

7. Child does not respond to learning tasks.

☐
(ALWAYS)
Child will
never under-
take a learn-
ing task

☐
(SOMETIMES)
Child often will not
undertake a learning
task

☐
(RARELY)
Child will occasionally
not undertake a learn-
ing task

8. Child maintains a constricted level of performance.

☐
(ALWAYS)
Child always
controlled and
rigid with
learning tasks

☐
(SOMETIMES)
Child often controlled
and rigid with learning
tasks

☐
(RARELY)
Child occasionally con-
trolled and rigid with
learning tasks

9. Child exhibits a narrow range of learning interests.

☐
(ALWAYS)
Child will
never try a
new or differ-
ent learning
task

☐
(SOMETIMES)
Child often will not try
a new or different
learning task

☐
(RARELY)
Child occasionally will
not try a new or differ-
ent learning task

10. Child withdraws from teacher and peers.

□
(ALWAYS)
Child always
avoids contact
with teacher
and peers

□
(SOMETIMES)
Child often avoids con-
tact with teacher and
peers

□
(RARELY)
Child occasionally
avoids contact with
teacher and peers

11. Child cannot function in a regular classroom.

□
(SEVERE)
Child does
not respond to
tasks in in-
dividual tutor-
ing

□
(MODERATE)
Child does not respond
to tasks in a special
class or program

□
(MILD)
Child does not respond
to tasks in a regular
classroom except for
brief periods of time

Order

12. Child does not follow directions.

□
(ALWAYS)
Child never
follows direc-
tions when
doing learning
tasks

□
(SOMETIMES)
Child often does not
follow directions when
doing learning tasks

□
(RARELY)
Child occasionally does
not follow directions
when doing learning
tasks

13. Child is uncontrolled in learning.

□
(ALWAYS)
Child always
approaches
learning tasks
in an impul-
sive, uncritical
manner

□
(SOMETIMES)
Child often approaches
learning tasks in an
impulsive, uncritical
manner

□
(RARELY)
Child occasionally ap-
proaches learning tasks
in an impulsive, un-
critical manner

14. Child is disruptive in group.

□
(ALWAYS)
Child always
is disruptive
in group

□
(SOMETIMES)
Child often is disrup-
tive in group

□
(RARELY)
Child occasionally is
disruptive in group

15. Child does not finish learning tasks.

□
(ALWAYS)
Child never
finishes learn-
ing tasks

□
(SOMETIMES)
Child often does not
finish learning tasks

□
(RARELY)
Child occasionally does
not finish learning tasks

Table 7.2 *Continued*

Exploratory

16. Child does not adequately explore his environment.

☐ (ALWAYS)	☐ (SOMETIMES)	☐ (RARELY)
Child's exploration of his environment extremely limited	Child's exploration of his environment moderately limited	Child's exploration of his environment limited to a few specific areas

17. Child overly dependent on others for choice of interests and activities.

☐ (ALWAYS)	☐ (SOMETIMES)	☐ (RARELY)
Child completely dependent on others for choice of interests and activities	Child excessively dependent on others for choice of interests and activities	Child usually dependent on others for choice of interests and activities

18. Child cannot do learning tasks because of motor, physical, sensory, perceptual, or intellectual deficits.

☐ (SEVERE)	☐ (MODERATE)	☐ (MILD)
Child severely impaired by motor, physical, sensory, perceptual, or intellectual deficits	Child moderately impaired by motor, physical, sensory, perceptual, or intellectual deficits	Child mildly impaired by motor, physical, sensory, perceptual, or intellectual deficits

Social

19. Child does not gain approval from others.

☐ (SEVERE)	☐ (MODERATE)	☐ (MILD)
Child never gains approval from others	Child often does not gain approval from others	Child occasionally does not gain approval from others

20. Child overly dependent on attention or praise from others.

☐ (SEVERE)	☐ (MODERATE)	☐ (MILD)
Child will only work with constant supervision and attention from teacher	Child will only work for brief periods of time without attention and praise from others	Child often seeks attention and praise from others while doing learning tasks

Mastery

21. Child's functioning level in self-care and intellectual skills below capacity.

(self-care)

▽ (SEVERE)
Extreme discrepancy between child's capacity and functioning level in self-care

▽ (MODERATE)
Considerable discrepancy between child's capacity and functioning level in self-care

▽ (MILD)
Slight discrepancy between child's capacity and functioning level in self-care

(intellectual skill)

◿ (SEVERE)
Extreme discrepancy between child's capacity and functioning level in intellectual and academic skills

◿ (MODERATE)
Considerable discrepancy between child's capacity and functioning level in intellectual and academic skills

◿ (MILD)
Slight discrepancy between child's capacity and functioning level in intellectual and academic skills

REWARD

a. Child not rewarded by tangible rewards (e.g., food, money) in learning.

☐ (ALWAYS)
Child's responses never controlled by tangible rewards

☐ (SOMETIMES)
Child's responses often not controlled by tangible rewards

☐ (RARELY)
Child's responses occasionally not controlled by tangible rewards

b. Child not rewarded by social attention in learning task.

☐ (ALWAYS)
Child's responses never controlled by social attention

☐ (SOMETIMES)
Child's responses often not controlled by social attention

☐ (RARELY)
Child's responses occasionally not controlled by social attention

Table 7.2 *Continued*

c. Child is not rewarded by finishing learning tasks.

□ (ALWAYS)	□ (SOMETIMES)	□ (RARELY)
Child's performance never controlled by task completion	Child's performance often not controlled by task completion	Child's performance occasionally not controlled by task completion

d. Child not rewarded by multisensory experiences in learning.

□ (ALWAYS)	□ (SOMETIMES)	□ (RARELY)
Child's responses never controlled by multisensory rewards	Child's responses often not controlled by multisensory rewards	Child's responses occasionally not controlled by multisensory rewards

e. Child not rewarded by gaining approval and avoiding disapproval for learning tasks.

□ (ALWAYS)	□ (SOMETIMES)	□ (RARELY)
Child's responses never controlled by social approval and disapproval	Child's responses often not controlled by social approval and disapproval	Child's responses occasionally not controlled by social approval and disapproval

f. Child not rewarded by doing learning tasks correctly.

□ (ALWAYS)	□ (SOMETIMES)	□ (RARELY)
Child's responses never controlled by knowledge of results	Child's responses often not controlled by knowledge of results	Child's responses occasionally not controlled by knowledge of results

g. Child not rewarded by acquiring knowledge and skill.

□ (ALWAYS)	□ (SOMETIMES)	□ (RARELY)
Child's performance never controlled by acquisition of knowledge and skill.	Child's performance often not controlled by acquisition of knowledge and skill	Child's performance occasionally not controlled by acquisition of knowledge and skill

Source: Frank M. Hewett, *The emotionally disturbed child in the classroom.* Boston, MA: Allyn and Bacon, 1968. Reprinted with permission.

and structure components are presented in Table 7.3. Specific teacher behaviors that are needed at each level are

Attention
1. Remove distracting stimuli
2. Present small, discrete units of work
3. Heighten the vividness of important stimuli
4. Use concrete tasks

Response
1. Reduce criterion for success
2. Guarantee success

Order
1. Maintain fixed environmental expectations
2. Define starting point and series of steps leading to a conclusion which may be evaluated
3. Require "student" behavior, i.e., behavior which meets basic levels of acceptability in school

Exploratory
1. Provide a wide range of multisensory experiences
2. Place emphasis on reality
3. Make outcomes of behavior predictable

Social
1. Emphasize communication with teachers and peers
2. Emphasize appropriate social behavior
3. Introduce social situations which temper individual gratification such as "waiting turn," deferring to others, etc.

Mastery
1. Promote self care skills which enable independent functioning in the environment
2. Promote cognitive development in areas of speech, concept formation, and problem solving
3. Work for expected levels of academic achievement

Achievement
1. Present an enriched curriculum
2. Allow freedom in selection of learning tasks
3. Stimulate critical thinking ability, increase power and speed reading

Hewett goes on to present many suggested activities to teach skills related to each of the developmental areas. He also has redesigned the classroom to provide the needed space for his instructional model. His plan is represented in Fig. 7.10. Clearly, Hewett is an advocate of a well-organized, well-planned instructional program for emotionally disturbed children. The methodology that makes the engineered classroom function is the behavioral principles explained in Chapter 6. The classroom is "structured" in the same manner as Haring and Phillips classroom. The following type of classroom environment, the open classroom, offers an alternate approach.

Table 7.3 *Summary of the Developmental Sequence of Educational Goals*

Level	Attention	Response	Order	Exploratory	Social	Mastery	Achievement
Child's Problem	Inattention due to withdrawal or resistance	Lack of involvement and unwillingness to respond in learning	Inability to follow directions	Incomplete or inaccurate knowledge of environment	Failure to value social approval or disapproval	Deficits in basic adaptive and school skills not in keeping with IQ	Lack of self motivation for learning
Educational Task	Get child to pay attention to teacher and task	Get child to respond to tasks he likes and which offer promise of success	Get child to complete tasks with specific starting points and steps leading to a conclusion	Increase child's efficiency as an explorer and get him involved in multisensory exploration of his environment	Get child to work for teacher and peer group approval and to avoid their disapproval	Remediation of basic skill deficiencies	Development of interest in acquiring knowledge
Learner Reward	Provided by tangible rewards (e.g., food, money, tokens)	Provided by gaining social attention	Provided through task completion	Provided by sensory stimulation	Provided by social approval	Provided through task accuracy	Provided through intellectual task success
Teacher Structure	Minimal	Still limited	Emphasized	Emphasized	Based on standards of social appropriateness	Based on curriculum assignments	Minimal

Source: Frank Hewett, Educational engineering with emotionally disturbed children, *Exceptional Children*, 1967, 33, pp. 459–467. Copyright © 1967, Council for Exceptional Children. Reprinted by permission.

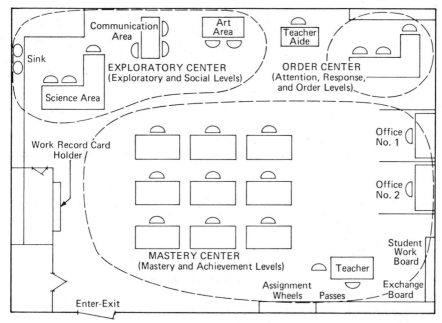

Fig. 7.10 Floor plan of an engineered classroom. Source: Frank Hewett, Educational engineering with emotionally disturbed children, *Exceptional Children*, 1967, 33, pp. 459–467. Copyright © 1967, Council for Exceptional Children. Reprinted by permission.

The Open-Classroom Model

In introducing the open-classroom model, Dupont (1975) traces its philosophical roots to the following humanistic principles:

1. The child is valued and his or her rights as a person are respected.
2. The children are seen as part of a democratic learning community and they have responsibility for what they do and what happens.
3. Each child is guaranteed an equal opportunity and his or her point of view, skills and goals are accepted and respected (p. 449).

He also points out that humanistic open education assumes the following psychological principles about how children learn:

1. Each child has a unique learning style and his own strategy and timetable for learning.
2. Children learn best when provided with a rich complex environment they are encouraged to explore.
3. Children learn best when their interaction with their environment and other persons is self-directed (p. 449).

These principles are similar to those espoused by Carl Rogers (1969) and Abraham Maslow (1968) in their applications of humanistic theory to education. Peter Knoblock applies these principles and what he terms a *psychoeducational perspective,* in his alternative school for excluded children and youth in Syracuse, New York. In providing guidelines for the application of the open-classroom model, Knoblock (1975, pp. 453–454) targets first the child behaviors encouraged in these settings, and second the teacher behaviors that are required.

Child Behaviors

A premium would be placed on the learning becoming self directed. Depending on the psychosocial development of the child and his interests, the environment of the classroom should allow him as much self choice about what he should learn and how he should learn it.

Children are encouraged to specify their learning needs and interests and seek ways to meet these needs.

Children engage in exploratory activity in an attempt to find the relationship between themselves and the materials in their environment.

Children spend time with other children assisting them in learning activities and engaging in a variety of play activities.

Children offer feedback to teachers, parents, and others concerning the viability of the learning environment.

Children evaluate their own progress and contribute to the charting and analysis of their activities.

Children play a vital role in working out their problems, disagreements and conflicts with other children and adults.

Teacher Behaviors

Adults function as partners and facilitators of children's learning. There is a tendency to respond to individual children and small groups.

Adults function as organizers of the learning resources (materials, adults, and other children), making such resources known and available to the children.

Frequently, the adults will design learning activities and encourage children to participate in them. There are a variety of teacher behaviors having to do with the initiation of activities. In one classroom I observed that a teacher had certain time periods for designated activities—free choice, reading, math, vocabulary development, or playground. Within several of these activities the teacher encouraged children to pursue the activity or task (finding words that begin with /th/, /cr/, etc.) in their own way.

Teachers tend to ask many questions of the children and encourage them to solve problems rather than ask for or accept answers from adults.

Teachers often view themselves as resources and catalysts for learning for the children and other adults. This implies that teachers need to be explicit about their skills and interests so that their skills can be used most efficiently.

Teachers expend considerable energy assisting the children in committing their time and in setting reasonable and realistic goals for themselves.

Regarding materials, Knoblock suggests open-ended, activity-based approaches that utilize the specific interests of each child as the basis for the instructional component of school. For example, if a child is interested in dinosaurs, the teacher can develop stories for reading activities, spelling tasks, writing lessons, mathematical problems, and so on, all of which pertain to dinosaurs in some way. Since, for the most part, children determine what they wish to do, it is helpful to have a wide variety of materials available. It is also important to avoid evaluation of a child's performance on a particular task.

Knoblock has identified five problem areas or concerns for troubled children and has provided the response that is appropriate in open education. These are presented in Table 7.4. The actual teaching procedures suggested to deal with these five concerns also are presented:

Table 7.4 *Concerns of Troubled Children and the Response of Open Education*

Concerns of Troubled Children	*Response of Open Education*
Conflict with authority.	Nonauthoritarian adults and environments in which less is decided for the child and more is done with him.
Tendency to move away from people and concerns; an unwillingness and inability to capitalize on their resources.	Emphasis placed on providing support to the child for becoming more active in self defining; provision of an environment that holds appeal to the child.
Concern with establishing relationships with adults who are trustworthy.	Adults who firmly believe in the growth potential of children and communicate this in words and practices.
Feelings of loss of control over their own feelings and their learning environments.	Mutuality between all participants in the learning environment thus enhancing active participation; response to the feelings and emotions of children.
Deep feelings of inadequacy leading to negative self concepts.	Provisions for a variety of activities and behaviors which supply the child with many ways to self evaluate.

Source: From *Educating Emotionally Disturbed Children: Readings*, 2nd Edition, edited by Henry Dupont. Copyright © 1969, 1975 by Holt, Rinehart and Winston, Inc. Reprinted by permission of Holt, Rinehart and Winston.

Conflict with authority—the teacher avoids win-lose situations, for example, "do this now." Instead, each child is given choices about activities and is guided by the teacher in pursuing his or her own choice.

Moving away from others—the teacher stimulates involvement with the environment and other people by providing a variety of learning materials and the opportunities to manipulate them.

Establishing adult relationships—the teacher trusts the child's intrinsic interests and builds learning experiences around those interests. External evaluation, grading or comparisons with others, is avoided. Also, group discussions and classroom meetings are held daily and provide an opportunity for the teacher to communicate unconditional positive acceptance of the child and his or her behavior.

Feelings of loss of control—the teacher helps the child engage in activities that reflect his or her strengths. The child is permitted to pursue more threatening activities at his or her own pace, in a nonevaluative atmosphere. Teachers and aides help when the child falters. Slowly the child gains confidence in his or her ability to control his or her life.

Feelings of inadequacy—the teacher provides diversification in the environment, thus, the child need not view himself or herself as "bad" because he or she cannot handle certain types of activities. For example, if the child defines himself or herself as "No good in math," the discovery that there are math tasks that he or she can handle should alter that opinion.

Perhaps in keeping with the humanistic philosophy that underlies this model, there is little structure presented that pertains to its implementation. Educational programs are reflections of the unique talents and interests of the teachers and students involved. No two classes would be organized in precisely the same way.

Interestingly, Knoblock's personal preference for an open-classroom model is not shared by others who profess a psychoeducational orientation. The approach adopted by Carl Fenichel (1965) at the League School for Seriously Disturbed Children in Brooklyn, New York, is, in fact, more reminiscent of the structured or engineered models discussed previously. He makes the following points regarding effective classroom functioning.

First, *the teacher must recognize the divergence among the children to be served.* Even children labeled schizophrenic differ greatly. Their behavior ranges from extreme passivity and lethargy to excessive impulsiveness and hyperactivity. Some appear regressed or defective mentally, whereas others are relatively intact intellectually. Often the same child demonstrates characteristics of schizophrenia, autism, retardation, and neurological damage.

Second, *the teacher must provide a structured, well-organized environment for the children.* An atmosphere of permissive acceptance that encourages children to act out their psychic conflicts such as that recommended by psychoanalytically oriented persons like Bettelheim (1950), produces chaos. Most disturbed children fear losing control over their behavior and desire protection from their impulses. They need behavioral limits incorporated into a well-organized educational program. The only exceptions to this rule are the overly inhibited, obsessive-compulsive children who must be helped to function in unstructured situations.

Third, *the teacher must focus immediately on overcoming learning deficits.* The psychoanalytic notion that instruction, even at a preacademic level, should be postponed until the child develops sufficient ego strength has little validity. Ego strength cannot develop unless the learning and behavioral deficits that contribute to it are remediated. Pathological behavior such as disorientation and withdrawal is associated primarily with learning and language disorders, not psychic conflicts.

Fourth, *the teacher should assume that the removal of one pathological behavior will facilitate the removal of others as the child's anxiety is reduced and his or her self-esteem increases.* This premise is contrary to the psychoanalytic idea that altering one behavior ignores the root of the problem and leads to symptom substitution.

Fifth, *instruction usually must begin on an individual, tutorial basis.* Children often need training in sitting, attending, listening, responding to directions, and so forth, before they can be integrated into a group. The individualized program should reveal the child's learning potential, that is, whether he or she can progress beyond simple concrete responses.

Sixth, *teacher verbalizations must be terse, simple, and direct.* Combined problems of attention and comprehension make it obligatory to limit remarks to those that are essential.

Seventh, *the group setting has important implications for growth.* These children must have the opportunity to learn social skills and this type of learning can take place only in a group. For example, they must learn to share, to wait their turn, to have respect for other persons and their property, to assert themselves.

Eighth, *the curriculum must be reality oriented.* Achievement in accordance with potential is emphasized. Routine, stable daily living skills also are stressed. When possible, educational techniques and materials used in normal school settings are employed.

Fenichel's observations are shared by the authors of this chapter who have derived the following set of "be's" for teachers of emotionally disturbed children.

1. Be well prepared for instructional activities. Emotionally disturbed children are quick to exploit situations where they have time to

be idle. They rarely use such time constructively. They must be guided from activity to activity in a well-organized, efficient manner. Such organization is highly dependent on the extent to which instructional programs are individualized for each child, as well as the use of a consistent reinforcement schedule. Remember that low frustration tolerance breeds disruption if work assignments are too long or difficult, or if task completion does not result in a predictable consequence.

2. Be calm when confronted with disruptive behavior. Recognize the behavior for what it is, the attempt of a maladjusted child to gain control over his or her environment. Try not to personalize the incident by assuming that the child's behavior is directed specifically at you. Don't permit yourself the luxury of outraged indignation and the companion feelings of betrayal and anger. Deal with the child's behavior as a problem that must be solved as rationally as possible.

3. Be prepared for maladaptive behaviors. Observe the children in your class. Make notes about the types of maladaptive or unproductive behaviors they are likely to engage in. Make tentative plans about your reactions. All people deal more efficiently with problems when they are prepared for them. When you are caught by surprise and must react on the spot, try to take a few moments to consider the situation, don't "gut react."

4. Be fair—establish clear, realistic rules, then enforce them. Don't weaken in your resolve because you either like or dislike a particular student. When you meet a "tough nut" who resists your attempts to help and flatly rejects you, make sure you are as fair with him or her as you are with the child who immediately responds to your efforts. Also, don't punish yourself by setting such idealistic or perfectionistic standards for behavior that you are acting as an enforcer or policeman constantly. Finally, don't get trapped into setting rules that you can't enforce. A teacher who tells a child: "You must eat your snack," or "You must finish your spelling assignment," is inviting defiance. The child cannot be forced to comply. An effective, enforceable rule involves the contingency of behavior, the event that the teacher can control, for example, "If you don't eat your snack, you will not receive one tomorrow," or "If you don't finish your assignment, you will not go outside to recess." Watch out for overkill, remember the dilemma of the mother who told her child: "If you don't stop that, I'll break your neck."

5. Be human—don't try to pretend that you are perfection personfied. When you make errors, admit it to yourself and to the children. Apologize if you have behaved inappropriately.

6. Be courteous—treat the children with the same respect you show adults. Don't respond to rudeness on their part with rude behavior.

Remember that they, not you, are emotionally disturbed. They will not learn civil behavior unless they are treated civilly.

7. Be a leader. Much has been written in recent years about the importance of establishing a school environment that facilitates independent thinking and self-rule. Such goals are important for all children, including the emotionally disturbed. However, these aspirations do not imply that the teacher should renounce his or her position as the leader in the classroom setting. The teacher is responsible for the educational welfare of each student. Thus, he or she must make behavioral rules, promote social values, supervision, make instructional decisions; in short, actively direct the children.

Use of Resource Personnel

The smart teacher of emotionally disturbed children takes all the help he or she can get. In fact, if it isn't offered, he or she seeks it out or arranges it, using the resources of other professionals, the children, and their parents to improve the instructional program.

Professional Resources Among the professionals who can be of help to the teacher are the school principal, resource or consulting teachers, the school psychologist, guidance counselors, and the school-affiliated psychiatrist.

School principals are educational policy makers, thus their support of special-education programs for emotionally disturbed children is important. Unfortunately, their interest and attention are focused on many diverse elements in the school, and often the needs of "problem" children are low-priority items. It behooves a teacher of emotionally disturbed children to make sure that his or her program is not ignored or simply tolerated as a "necessary evil." In effect, he or she must conduct a propagandizing campaign for administrative support. One strategy in such a campaign is frequent but brief teacher-initiated meetings that involve discussions of constructive, positive topics such as children's progress, or that draw the principal into the instructional program, such as seeking her or his opinion about an instructional decision, discussing plans for class activities, and warning of potential trouble such as parental discontent. Another strategy is to interest the principal in visiting the class to observe the children. In the usual course of events, these visits are limited to times when a problem occurs rather than times when normal instruction is occurring. If the principal is familiar with the classroom operation, she or he can be of greater assistance as a "troubleshooter." The third strategy is to involve the principal in classroom functions. She or he might conduct classroom discussions or serve as a crisis-intervention specialist (see Chapter 9). Obviously, the extent to which these goals can be realized will depend on the attitudes of the individual involved. At the very least, however, the teacher should try to build a positive rather than a negative relationship.

Another invaluable asset is the services of a variety of resource teachers who might be associated with the school. Most elementary schools and some secondary schools have resource programs designed to provide corrective and remedial academic instruction to children who experience achievement problems. Resource teachers are available to work with slow or nonlearning children or to act as consultants to other teachers in the school. Although these programs usually are supplemental to regular education services, that is, they provide support for mainstreamed children, they can and should be used by special educators who teach emotionally disturbed children. Some children, despite efforts to individualize instruction in the self-contained special classroom, require additional tutorial or small-group instruction. Often the additional attention the child receives from a "special" teacher adds the necessary impetus for breakthroughs in academic achievement areas. Obviously such desirable outcomes can occur only when teachers cooperate closely and when instructional programs are planned carefully.

The resource room can also serve as an initial step in a program culminating in the reintegration of the emotionally disturbed child in the regular classroom. In this circumstance, the child must be taught the types of coping skills that will help him or her function in the more normal and more stressful regular class environment. For example, in the resource room he or she may be required to self-start independent assignments and to work to completion without teacher attention. Also, he or she may need practice in controlling behavior while moving from one room to another. The resource teacher, who usually is a special educator, should be a helpful assistant in teaching such coping skills.

Another use of resource personnel is as a crisis or helping teacher (Morse, 1975). This role is based on the idea that crises are valuable periods for helping children, that intervention provided at the time of a crisis can be extremely effective. Theoretically, during a crisis an individual is more susceptible to suggestions from others than at other times. He or she is less defensive and the realistic aspects of the problem are more likely to penetrate the individual's consciousness. Thus, the crisis teacher must be available to deal with the disturbed child immediately, not as is usually true in schools, when the time happens to be available or when the child has "cooled down." Often the classroom teacher of emotionally disturbed children has too many responsibilities to take advantage of an opening in a particular child's defenses. The availability of a back-up resource teacher is a valuable addition to the program.

The teacher's interaction with other specialists, including the guidance counselor, school psychologist, and psychiatrist, can be particularly useful in situations where each professional uses the expertise associated with his or her particular discipline. The teacher should find that the information available in psychological and psychiatric reports increases her or his knowledge about the children and their problems, and provides alternate opinions for problem solutions. Confusion and inefficiency can result from an interdisciplinary approach to problem solving only when the teacher attempts to surrender the responsibility of classroom management to noneducators. These instances usually culminate in the preparation of an elaborate plan of teaching strategies and behavioral management techniques by individuals who have never attempted to teach or manage groups of normal, not to mention disturbed, children. This point is not meant to imply that consultant services by noneducators are not useful. Good advice and assistance in problem solving is a valuable resource. Usually, the more familiar ancillary personnel are with the reality of the classroom situation, the more useful is their advice.

Another variable concerning the effective use of nonteaching school personnel is their specific competence and interests. Some guidance personnel and school psychologists function excellently in a crisis-intervention capacity (Chapter 9). They also may be willing and able to conduct individual therapy sessions with certain children who need more attention than the teacher can provide. Generally, the professionals who offer the greatest assistance in dealing with the problem of emotional disturbance are those housed in the school as opposed to those who visit periodically.

Child Resources   The idea of using peer or cross-age tutoring to help emotionally disturbed children is totally consistent with the notion of using in-house resources. Peer tutoring involves having members of a class instruct other members. In cross-age tutoring, older children help younger students. The keys to success of both types of programs are *training* and *program structure*. Children interested in helping other children do so best when they are trained in advance to understand the benefits of positive reinforcement, and to understand the content to be taught. Unless they are cautioned that tutorial programs are based on offerings of encouragement and support, child tutors easily lapse into a critical, demanding attitude with their charges. They are particularly prone to adopt this type of role, or to lapse into silly, time-wasting behavior, when they are confused about the content to be presented. The teacher must ensure that the tutor has thoroughly mastered the concepts that he or she will be teaching. Mastery involves the ability to present the concept to others in a clear, concise fashion.

In addition to training in advance of the program, the program itself must be well structured. Structure implies that the teacher has identified the goals of the program and has explained them to the tutors. Also, specific behaviors appropriate for the tutor and his or her charge are clarified. Both children know what is expected of them. The teacher monitors the session to identify problems and acts to reduce them before the tutorial session has deteriorated into a sham or a source of conflict.

The final and possibly the most significant child resource involves the training of self-management techniques. Lovitt (1973) has led the way in the systematic training of self-management techniques with emotionally disturbed children. Using behavior modification principles, he has demonstrated that children can be taught to correct, count, chart, and evaluate their own performance on academic tasks. He also has demonstrated that children trained in self-management skills become more highly motivated to achieve. The student involved in Lovitt's program was led, step by step, through eight phases of self-management activity: (1) scheduling morning and afternoon assignments, (2) scheduling the entire day, (3) correcting his or her work, (4) evaluating daily academic response rate, (5) examining his or her overall record of academic performance, (6) charting achievement data in reading and in math, (7) charting achievement rates in six academic subjects, and (8) setting his or her own contingencies in three of six academic areas. Apparently it is not beyond the competence of some emotionally disturbed children to accept responsibility for their academic production if they are carefully shown how to do so.

Parent Resources   Parent involvement in programs for emotionally disturbed children, after having been regarded with a certain amount of suspicion for many years, is finally gaining rightful recognition as an important ingredient. It has always been obvious that optimal benefits for children occur when school authorities and parents cooperate. The less-obvious information pertained primarily to how to arrange such cooperation, or, more precisely, how to help parents help their children. Currently, a great deal of information on this topic is available. New books in special education deal specifically with parenting (Cooper and Edge, 1978; Kroth and Simpson, 1977).

Commercial programs like *Parent Effectiveness Training* (Gordon, 1975) and *Systematic Training for Effective Parenting* (Dinkmeyer and McKay, 1976) also are available. These useful sources will not be discussed in detail in this text. It is sufficient to suggest that the wise teacher might wish to consult them or other similar sources for information, since she or he stands to benefit from the arrangement of some type of constructive activities for the parents of her or his students. At the very least, the teacher might plan any or all of the following: parent discussion groups, parent tutoring, and group training in effective parenting.

Parent discussion groups are relatively informal groups held by the teacher and principal and attended by other interested professionals such as the school psychologist or guidance counselor. These sessions should meet for approximately one hour once a month, and should deal primarily with problem-solving strategies. Problems at school and at home should be discussed. Parents and educators should develop consistent methods of handling shared problems.

Parent tutorial services pertain to the in-school involvement of parents as tutors. For any child but their own, parents can be a helpful resource if the tutorial program is carefully planned. Typically, parents are far more tolerant and effective in tutorial roles when they do not work with their own children. Similarly, the children are more responsive when a comparative stranger offers them help. Using parents as tutors has the combined advantages of permitting them to make a direct contribution to their child's school program and allowing them to learn and practice specific instructional techniques that later might be used at home. As in all other tutorial programs, effectiveness depends on systematic planning and structure. Parent volunteers must be aware of the goals of the program and must have observed and practiced sequenced instructional techniques, combined with positive reinforcement methods. Demonstrations by the teacher may help parent volunteers understand and model the roles they are expected to play.

Group training in effective parenting sessions, conducted by the school psychologist, guidance counselor, or other individual proficient in these techniques, involves training parents in all aspects of the parent-child relationship. For example, the goals of STEP, the Dinkmeyer and McKay (1976, p. 14) program, are:

> To help parents understand a practical theory of human behavior and its implications for parent-child relationships.
>
> To help parents learn new procedures for establishing democratic relationships with their children.
>
> To help parents improve communication between themselves and their children so all concerned feel they are being heard.
>
> To help parents develop skills of listening, resolving conflicts, and exploring alternatives with their children.
>
> To help parents learn how to use encouragement and logical consequences to modify their children's self-defeating motives and behaviors.
>
> To help parents learn how to conduct family meetings.
>
> To help parents become aware of their own self-defeating patterns and faulty convictions which keep them from being effective parents who enjoy their children.

Presumably, such training will indirectly benefit the teacher whose job should become far simpler when critical home problems are alleviated or minimized.

CLASSROOM MANAGEMENT STRATEGIES

In effect, the two preceding sections of this chapter pertain directly to this topic. Individualized academic instructional techniques obviously aid the teacher in controlling classroom behavior. A child who does not experience the frustrations of failure is far less likely to demonstrate maladaptive behaviors than one who has no hope of experiencing academic success. Also, instructional arrangements incorporating effective classroom organization and using resource services are likely to result in improved classroom management. This section of the chapter differs from the others in that it pertains specifically to strategies that the teacher will need to handle on-the-spot problems. In addition, it presents curricular resources that are useful in teaching self-control and other affective information.

Curricular Material

Throughout this book, references have been made to the importance of incorporating affective curricular material into the general instructional program. The basis for these references is that children, both normal and disturbed, need to learn about feelings and emotions. Topics for such instruction may be developed informally from the events that occur in the school. For example, children may be encouraged to discuss the emotional outbursts of a classmate; conjecturing about the individual's feelings, their own feelings, the events that provoked the occurrence, and so forth. They might offer alternate strategies to use in such instances, and possibly role play similar events. Other informal instructional topics might be gleaned from local or national news events. For example, the feelings associated with war, losing in a sporting event, a neighborhood robbery, school vandalism, and so forth, provide interesting material for discussion. Such material has the advantage of being highly relevant to the children. Therefore, they are likely to attend to it.

Formally developed, commercial affective curricula also are available to the teacher. Cheney and Morse (1976) discuss the key components of several programs. These include an approach developed by Weinstein and Fantini (1970), which concentrates on three classes of children's concerns: self image, disconnectedness, and control over one's life. The techniques presented to illustrate these concerns include:

1. Creating situations to arouse pupil emotion, such as deliberately denying privileges to blue-eyed children.
2. Assessing students' opinions about their lives through verbal games such as The Faraway Island, where children identify and describe six people to accompany them to a deserted island, Ten Years From Now, where children project about their lives in ten years time, Time

Capsule, where children select significant items from their lives to preserve for posterity.
3. Increasing self-esteem with games such as Complain, Gripe, and Moan, where children get coupons that allow them to buy the right to complain about aspects of their lives, Spies from Xenon, where children from outer space must report on events that make earthlings unhappy, afraid, and so on, and Mirror, where children look at themselves in a mirror and say something nice.

Similarly, Raths, Harmin, and Simon (1966) have developed a curriculum that deals with value formulation and clarification. Their techniques include:

1. Value clarification responses—children are helped to clarify their feelings or attitudes through questions such as "How did you feel when that happened?" or, "Did you have to make that choice?"
2. Role playing—children act out scenes depicting their values.
3. Value sheets—children are asked provocative, value-related questions.
4. Contrived incident—the teacher plans situations to shock students into recognizing their attitudes about certain issues.
5. Open-ended questions—children respond to questions such as "How did you feel?"
6. Public interviews—the teacher conducts interviews with students about an emotional issue.
7. Action projects—children plan projects involving the values they have discussed.

Other affective curricula are *Dimensions of Personality* (Limbacker, 1969), *Guidance* (Bruck, 1970), *Developing Understanding of Self and Others (DUSO)* (Dinkmeyer, 1973), *Human Development Program* (Palomares and Ball, 1974), *The Coping With Series* (Wrenn and Schwarzroch, 1973), *Target Behavior* (Kroth, 1973), *First Things* (Grannis and Schone, 1970), *The Child's Series on Psychologically Relevant Themes* (Fasler, 1971), and *Teaching Self-Control in the Elementary School: A Curriculum for Preventing Learning and Emotional Problems* (Fagen, Long, and Stevens, 1975), *Toward Affective Development (TAD)* (Dupont et al., 1974), *My Friends and Me* (Davis, 1977).

Limbacker's curriculum focuses on self awareness ("Getting to Know Myself"), feelings ("My Feelings Are Real"), and other people ("How Different Are We?"). The "Guidance" series is similar in format.

DUSO consists of two programs, one for kindergarten-aged children and one for primary-aged children. The program used in kindergarten involves eight units of study: Understanding and Accepting Self; Understanding Feelings; Understanding Others; Understanding Independence; Understanding Goals and Purposeful Behavior; Understanding Mastery,

Competence and Resourcefulness; Understanding Emotional Maturity; and Understanding Choices and Consequences. The other program also includes eight units: Towards Self-Identity, Towards Friendship, Towards Responsible Interdependence, Towards Self-Reliance, Towards Resourcefulness and Purposefulness, Towards Competence, Towards Emotional Stability, and Towards Responsible Choice Making.

The Human Development Program, an extremely comprehensive program, is designed for children from preschool to sixth grade. Its lessons are similar to others that have been discussed. They are designed to increase self-control and responsibility, and to improve self-concept and interpersonnel relationships.

The Coping With Series involves twenty-three books that deal with contemporary social and personal problems such as: *Parents Can Be a Problem* and *Facts and Fantasies about Drugs.* Each book is designed to serve as a focal point for group discussions. The program is useful for children at the junior high and high school level.

Target Behavior, as its name suggests, reflects a behavioristic orientation. It involves the use of a Q-sort technique to identify behaviors that need to be modified. *First Things,* a program for primary-level students, is designed to promote group interaction and discussion of feelings through videotapes and role playing. The general themes explored are "Who do you think you are?", "Guess who's in a group!", "What happens between people?", "You got mad, are you glad?", and "What do you expect of others?"

The *Child's Series on Psychologically Relevant Themes* is for both preschool and primary-level students. This program reflects a psychoanalytic format through a series of six videotapes. In "Man of the House" a boy assumes daddy's role, then must surrender it when daddy returns home; in "All Alone with Daddy" a girl relates closely with daddy and resents mommy; in "Grandpa Died Today" a child reacts to his or her grandparent's death; in "Don't Worry Dear" a girl's behavior regresses because of stress; in "Boy with a Problem" repression of a problem leads to many hypochondriacal symptoms; and in "One Little Girl" a girl compensates for her weaknesses.

The curriculum designed by Fagen, Long, and Stevens teaches self-control: "the capacity to flexibly and realistically direct and regulate personal action (behavior) in a given situation" (1976, p. 272). It consists of eight skill clusters: *selection*—ability to take in information, *storage*—ability to retain information, *sequencing and ordering*—ability to organize actions, *anticipatory consequences*—ability to relate actions to outcomes, *appreciated feelings*—ability to identify and use affective experiences, *managing frustration*—ability to cope with stress-producing events, *inhibition and delay*—ability to delay action, and *relaxation*—ability to calm down.

The information is a condensed illustrative unit for the *managing frustration* area (adapted from Fagen, Long, and Stevens, 1976, p. 273).

Unit 1—Accepting Feelings of Frustration

Goals   To help children accept feelings of frustration as unavoidable occurrences.

Tasks   Sharing Group Frustration—the teacher and group plan a satisfying activity. The teacher frustrates the group by interfering with the completion of the activity. Discussion then centers on the feelings evoked by frustration, e.g., anger, sadness, etc.

TAD is designed to be used with students in grades 3 through 6. TAD has 180 lessons organized into 5 units: *Reaching In, Reaching Out, Your Feelings and Mine, Working Together, Me: Today and Tomorrow,* and *Feeling, Thinking and Doing.* TAD focuses on the child's real-life experiences. TAD's objectives include helping the children understand feelings in relationship to themselves, their interpersonal relationships, and their adult careers. TAD also helps children develop a way of solving their problems and making choices.

My Friends and Me is designed especially for the preschool child. It's purposes involve helping each child develop (1) a confident and realistic personal identity, and (2) essential social skills and understandings. This program is organized into eight units. Four of these units involve personal identity. They are: *Social Identity, Emotional Identity, Physical Identity,* and *Intellectual and Creative Identity.* The other four units involve social skills and social understanding. These units include: *Cooperation, Consideration for Others, Ownership and Sharing,* and *Dependence and Help.* These programs are but a few of the many that are available to the teacher.

Guideline for On-the-Spot Management Decisions

The teacher's ability to control emotionally disturbed children depends greatly on her or his competencies, specifically the ability to understand each individual and the ability to react efficiently to classroom dynamics. Long, Alpher, Butt, and Cully (1976) note that these competencies are reflected in three types of classroom activities: *decoding, labeling,* and *redirecting* behavior.

Decoding behavior pertains to understanding both verbal and nonverbal communication. A disturbed child's verbal communication often is used to disguise true feelings. For example, a child tearfully reacting to the loss of a privilege might say: "I didn't want to do that anyway." His or her entire demeanor belies such a statement—obviously the child very much wanted the lost privilege. The teacher must attend more to how a child speaks, than to what is said.

Nonverbal communication can be observed in body language, eye movements, breathing patterns, posture, muscle rigidity, and so on. All these indicators convey messages about the child's true feelings. The observant teacher can tell when a child is ready to "blow up" or is feeling particularly depressed by reading his or her nonverbal messages.

Labeling involves the ability to make an accurate interpretation of the child's feelings and to state it clearly. For example, the teacher might say to the child referred to above, "I know you're upset over losing your privilege."

Redirecting behavior involves the techniques of ventilation, skill development, and verbal insight. Ventilation typifies the old maxim "Sticks and stones will break my bones but words will never hurt me." Emotionally disturbed children often must be encouraged to talk about their angry feelings instead of engaging in aggressive or destructive physical activity.

Skill development involves helping the child express feelings in socially acceptable ways, through art, music, dramatic play, sports, and so on. Verbal insight involves the use of interviewing techniques such as life-space interviewing to ascertain how the child feels and to help him or her learn coping behaviors.

Long and Newman (1976) provide additional suggestions to aid teachers in managing disturbed children. These teacher reactions include *permitting, tolerating, interfering,* and *preventive planning.* Permitting behaviors simply involve informing children of the times and places where they will be allowed to engage in behaviors that are usually taboo in school. For instance, the teacher might want the children to scream, run, and otherwise expend a great deal of energy on the playground. The teacher should inform the children that they have this privilege and that they will not be penalized for such behavior. By directly informing them of permitted behaviors, the teacher avoids confusion and prevents them from developing the notion that they are "getting away with something."

Tolerating behavior involves ignoring acts that are not sanctioned. In most cases this involves activities that are typical of a developmental stage. For instance, five-year-old children usually are impulsive, pre-adolescent girls are often giddy, and adolescents often are suspicious of adults. The teacher is more likely to maintain equilibrium if these behaviors are ignored.

The most important reaction category, interfering with behavior, pertains to those acts that the teacher cannot permit to continue. Redl and Wineman (1951) suggest that teachers should interfere under the following circumstances.

1. Reality dangers—when injury to the child or others might be involved
2. Psychological protection—when a child is being abused by name calling or ridicule
3. Protection against overexcitement—when the children appear to be getting carried away
4. Protection of property—when the children attempt to destroy school property or the property of others
5. Protection of an ongoing process—when one child threatens to disrupt an activity everyone else is enjoying
6. Protection against negative contagion—when a child begins a behavior that could ignite the class
7. Highlighting a value area or school policy—when the teacher wants to make a point about a general rule, for example, how borrowing another child's pen without permission can cause a misunderstanding, or how throwing a ball against the school wall is against the rules because a window might be broken
8. Avoiding conflict with the outside world—when the children are confronted with behavioral expectations outside the classroom, such as the class trip
9. Protecting the teacher's inner comfort—when the teacher simply is unwilling to accept certain behavior, such as threats of personal harm

Long and Newman (1971) present twelve influencing techniques that may be used to stop or interfere with surface behaviors. They are planned ignoring, signal interference, proximity control, interest boosting, tension decontamination through humor, hurdle help, restructuring the classroom program, support from routine, direct appeal, removal of seductive objects, antiseptic bouncing, and physical restraint.

Planned ignoring is the traditional behavioral technique of extinguishing a behavior by withholding reinforcement. The teacher simply does not react to the child's activity, assuming that it will not spread to others and will soon cease. An example is the behavior of a first-grade student who habitually straggled behind his classmates when they left the room for lunch or recess. The behavior stopped as soon as the teacher began ignoring it.

Signal interference refers to the teacher's nonverbal behaviors such as looks, nods, or gestures that ask the child to stop his or her activities. *Proximity control* simply involves moving close to the child who is beginning to act up. In some instances this technique involves touching the child to help him or her gain self-control. *Interest boosting* has two components. The simpler one refers to spurring a child on in his or her work with interested questions or comments. The more elaborate component involves using a child's specific interests to build a course of study.

Tension decontamination through humor is self-explanatory. *Hurdle help* and *restructuring the classroom program* are similar techniques pertaining to helping children who are stymied by assignments. The former involves increasing individual attention to help the child by the rough spot, whereas the latter pertains to abandoning planned lessons and teaching about situations that arise spontaneously.

Support from routine draws on the premise that children feel more secure when they know what to expect. The teacher may reduce a child's anxiety by clearly delineating projected classroom activities. *Direct appeal to values* can be a personal plea from the teacher to the student, "Do this for me," an appeal to consequences, "If you continue this behavior, you will not go to recess," an appeal to group opinion, "You will hurt the class's chances in the school contest," and an appeal to teacher authority, "I like you so much that I can't let you do this."

Removing seductive objects simply is taking away toys and other attractive nuisances that are likely to be used during class. *Antiseptic bouncing* involves giving a child beginning to have problems the opportunity to leave class temporarily. For example, a child, angry at classmates, might be asked to run an errand and thereby have time to cool off.

Physical restraint is necessary occasionally when a child loses control and threatens to injure himself or herself, or others. The most efficient method is to cross the child's arms around his or her side while standing behind. Hold on despite protestations of physical pain as the child is not being hurt. Typically, children out of control who must be held engage in four phases of response. First they fight being held and demonstrate frustration by swearing, biting, or kicking. Second, they realize they cannot break away and begin to cry. Third, they ask to be released. If their language is more coherent and logical the teacher might release the hold. Finally, they attempt to save face by pulling away or making a negative remark. At this time they have regained control.

It should be stressed that these twelve techniques interfere with or help control surface behaviors. They are effective only when used by an individual who consistently seeks understanding of the children's problems. Understanding the children permits the teacher to display the fourth reaction for good classroom management—preventive planning.

Preventive planning involves projecting where problems develop and taking steps to prevent them. For example, if Billy fights every time he goes to recess with older children, the problem may be prevented by scheduling Billy's recess with younger children.

SUMMARY

This chapter included a discussion of a range of teaching strategies and activities that may be used in the classroom or school, either to treat emotionally disturbed children, or to help normal children retain their emotional equilibrium. It has reviewed several approaches to individualization of instruction, three types of classroom organization models, and a variety of classroom-management strategies.

The material incorporated in the chapter has been drawn from various theoretical perspectives. The techniques for individualizing instruction were clearly behavioral in orientation; the classroom organization models reflected behavioral, modified behavioral, and humanistic orientations; and the management strategies were drawn primarily from the writing of ecological or sociological theorists. The use of approaches emanating from alternate perspectives was designed to provide the teacher with a relatively complete overview of available techniques and strategies and to enable him or her to use those that best meet his or her unique needs.

STUDY QUESTIONS

1. Discuss six guidelines for teachers to follow when constructing tests.
2. Discuss the differences between norm-referenced and criterion-referenced tests.
3. Discuss three factors to be considered when selecting instructional materials.
4. Describe Hewett's engineered classroom.
5. Discuss several ways in which parents can be involved in programs for the emotionally disturbed.
6. Select several of the techniques presented in this chapter and explain how they can be applied in a teaching situation.

REFERENCES

Barbe, W. *Barbe reading skills checklist and activities.* Honesdale, Pa., 1975. Center for Applied Research and Education, 1975.

Beatty, L.; Madden, R.; and Gardner, E. *Stanford diagnostic arithmetic test.* New York: Harcourt Brace Jovanovich, 1966.

Bethelheim, B. *Love is not enough.* Glencoe, Ill.: The Free Press, 1950.

Bower, E. *The education of emotionally handicapped children.* Sacramento, Cal.: California State Department of Education, 1961.

Brown, V. L.; Hammill, D. D.; and Weiderholt, J. L. *The test of reading comprehension: a method for assessing the understanding of written language.* Austin, Texas: Pro-ED, 1978.

Bruck, C. *Guidance series for the elementary school.* New York: Bruce, 1970.

Carrow, E. *Test for auditory comprehension of language.* Austin, Texas: Learning Concepts, 1973.

Cartwright, R. Written expression and spelling. In R. Smith (ed.). *Teacher diagnosis of educational difficulties.* Columbus, Ohio: Merrill, 1969.

Cheney, C., and Morse, W. Psychodynamic intervention. In N. Long, W. Morse, and R. Newman (eds.). *Conflict in the classroom,* 3rd ed. Belmont, Cal.: Wadsworth, 1976.

Cohen, C., and Abrams, R. *Spellmaster.* Exeter, N.H.: Learnco, 1974.

Connolloy, A.; Nachtman, W.; and Pritchett, E. *Key-math diagnostic test.* Circle Pines, Minn.: American Guidance Service, Inc., 1973.

Cooper, J., and Edge, D. *Parenting: strategies and educational methods.* Columbus, Ohio: Merrill, 1978.

Davis, L. *My friends and me.* Circle Pines, Minn.: American Guidance Service, Inc., 1977.

Dinkmeyer, D. *Developing understanding of self and others.* Circle Pines, Minn.: American Guidance Service, Inc., 1973.

Dinkmeyer, D., and McKay, G. *Systematic training for effective parenting.* Circle Pines, Minn.: American Guidance Service, Inc., 1976.

Dunn, L. *Peabody picture vocabulary test.* Circle Pines, Minn.: American Guidance Service, Inc., 1959.

Dunn, L., and Markwardt, F. *Peabody individual achievement test.* Circle Pines, Minn.: American Guidance Service, Inc., 1970.

Dupont, H. (ed.) *Educating emotionally disturbed children.* New York: Holt, Rinehart and Winston, 1975.

Dupont, H.; Gardner, O.; and Brody, D. *Toward affective development.* Circle Pines, Minn.: American Guidance Service, Inc., 1974.

Durrell, D. *Durrell analysis of reading difficulty.* New York: Harcourt Brace Jovanovich, 1976.

Fagen, S.; Long, N.; and Stevens, P. A psychoeducational curriculum for the prevention of behavioral and learning problems: Teaching self-control. In N. Long; W. Morse; and R. Newman (eds.) *Conflict in the classroom.* 3rd ed. Belmont, Cal.: Wadsworth, 1976.

Fasler, J. *The child's series on psychologically relevant themes.* Westport, Conn.: Videorecord Corp. of America, 1971.

Fenichel, C. Psycho-educational approaches for seriously disturbed children in the classroom. In P. Knoblock (ed.). *Intervening approaches in educating emotionally disturbed children.* Syracuse, N.Y.: Syracuse University, 1965.

Gordon, T. *Parent effectiveness training.* New York: Wyden, 1975.

Grannis, J., and Schone, V. *First things.* Pleasantville, N.Y.: Guidance Associates, 1970.

Gray, W., and Robinson, H. *Gray oral reading test.* Indianapolis: Bobbs-Merrill, 1967.

Gronlund, N. *Measurement and evaluation in teaching.* New York: Macmillan, 1976.

Hammill, D. Evaluating children for instructional purposes. *Academic Therapy,* 1971, 6, 341–353.

Hammill, D., and Bartel, N. *Teaching children with learning and behavior problems.* Boston: Allyn and Bacon, 1975.

Hammill, D., and Larsen, S. *The test of written language.* Austin, Texas: Pro-Ed, 1978.

Haring, N. and Phillips, E. *Educating emotionally disturbed children.* New York: McGraw-Hill, 1962.

Hewett, F. *The emotionally disturbed child in the classroom.* Boston: Allyn and Bacon, 1969.

Johnson, M., and Kress, R. *Informal reading inventories.* Newark, Del.: International Reading Association, 1969.

Klausmier, H.; Morrow, R.; and Walter J. *Individually guided education in the multiunit school.* Madison, Wis.: Wisconsin Research and Development Center for Cognitive Learning, 1968.

Knoblock, P. Open education for emotionally disturbed children. In H. Dupont (ed.). *Educating emotionally disturbed children.* New York: Holt, Rinehart and Winston, 1975.

Kroth, R. *Target behavior.* Olathe, Kans.: Select-Ed., 1973.

Kroth, R., and Simpson, R. *Parent conferences as a teaching startegy.* Denver, Colo.: Love, 1977.

Kunzelmann, H.; Cohen, M.; Hulten, W.; Martin, G.; and Mingo, A. *Precision teaching.* Seattle, Wash.: Special Child Publications, 1970.

Larsen, S., and Hammill, D. *Test of written spelling.* San Rafael, Cal.: Academic Therapy Pub., 1976.

Lee, L. *Northwestern syntax screening test.* Evanston, Ill.: Northwestern University Press, 1969.

Limbacker, W. *Dimensions of personality: here I am.* Dayton, Ohio: Pflaum, 1969.

Lindsley, O. Precision teaching in perspective. *Teaching Exceptional Children,* 1971, *3,* 114–119.

Long, N.; Alpher, R.; Butt, F.; and Cutty, M. Helping children cope with feelings. In N. Long, W. Morse, and R. Newman (eds.). *Conflict in the classroom.* 3rd ed. Belmont, Cal.: Wadsworth, 1976.

Long, N., and Newman, R. The teacher and his mental health. In N. Long, W. Morse, and R. Newman (eds.). *Conflict in the classroom.* 2nd ed. Belmont, Cal.: Wadsworth, 1971.

Long, N., and Newman, R. Managing surface behavior of children in school. In N. Long, W. Morse, and R. Newman (eds.). *Conflict in the classroom.* 3rd ed. Belmont, Cal.: Wadsworth, 1976.

Lovitt, T. Self-management projects with children with behavioral disabilities. *Journal of Learning Disabilities,* 1973, *6,* 15–28.

Mager, R. *Preparing instructional objectives.* Palo Alto, Cal.: Fearon, 1962.

Mann, P., and Suiter, P. Developmental spelling inventories. In *Handbook in diagnostic teaching.* Boston: Allyn and Bacon, 1974.

Maslow, A. Some educational implications of the humanistic psychologies. *Harvard Educational Review,* 1968, *38,* 385–696.

Morse, W. Crisis intervention in school mental health and special classes for the disturbed. In N. Long, W. Morse, and R. Newman (eds.). *Conflict in the classroom.* 3rd ed. Belmont, Cal.: Wadsworth, 1976.

Myklebust, H. *Picture story language test.* New York. Grune and Stratton, 1965.

Newcomer, P. and Hammill, D. *Test of language development.* Philadelphia: Empirical Enterprises, 1977.

Otto, W., McMenemy, R., and Smith, R. *Corrective and remedial teaching.* 2nd ed. Boston: Houghton Mifflin, 1973.

Palomares, V., and Ball, G. *Human development program.* LaMesa, Cal.: Human Development Training Institute, 1974.

Peter, L. *Individual instruction.* New York: McGraw-Hill, 1972.

Raths, L.; Harmin, M.; and Simon, S. *Values and teaching.* Columbus, Ohio: Merrill, 1966.

Redl, F., and Wineman, D. *Children who hate: the disorganization and breakdown of behavior controls.* Glencoe, Ill.: The Free Press, 1951.

Reisman, F. *A guide to the diagnostic teaching of arithmetic.* Columbus, Ohio: Merrill, 1972.

Roger, C. *Freedom to learn.* Columbus, Ohio: Merrill, 1969.

Salvia, J., and Ysseldyke, J. *Assessment in special and remedial education.* Boston: Houghton Mifflin, 1977.

Starkel, J. Selection and adaptation of materials for learning disabled adolescents. Unpublished manuscript, University of Kansas, 1978.

Wallace, J., and Larsen, S. *Educational assessment of learning problems: Testing for teaching.* Boston: Allyn and Bacon, 1978.

Weinstein, G., and Fantini, M. *Toward humanistic education: a curriculum of affect.* New York: Praeger, 1970.

Wilson, J. *Adapting instructional materials.* Unpublished manuscript, University of Kansas, 1976.

Wilson, J. Selecting educational materials and resources. In D. Hammill and N. Bartel (eds.). *Teaching children with learning and behavior problems.* 2nd ed. Boston: Allyn and Bacon, 1978.

Woodcock, R. *Woodcock reading mastery tests.* Circle Pines, Minn.: American Guidance Service, 1974.

Wrenn, C., and Schwarzroch, S. *The coping with series.* Circle Pines, Minn.: American Guidance Service, 1973.

8
Rational–Cognitive
Therapy

Rational–cognitive therapy, in the most general sense, refers to therapeutic approaches that depend on changing an individual's internal cognitive operations, that is, thoughts, ideas, beliefs, perceptions, or attitudes. It focuses on such mental functions as problem-solving strategies, attribution of causes to events, and self-verbalizations; in short, any of the internal cognitive strategies that determine an individual's external behaviors. Although all therapeutic approaches are designed to alter an individual's thoughts and ideas, rational–cognitive therapies are distinguished by the *directness* of concentration on these events. In other words, whereas other approaches through indirect techniques such as reflection of thoughts and exploration of feeling, eventually may help the individual develop new ideas, rational–cognitive therapies feature direct communication about harmful, illogical thoughts. The underlying assumptions are that *maladaptive or disturbing feelings are triggered by harmful, unrealistic, and illogical thoughts.* Thus, a person feels unhappy because he or she literally is telling himself or herself things that evoke unhappiness. Second, it assumes that *deliberate, conscious efforts to alter destructive, illogical thoughts will diminish disturbed emotion.* The person who substitutes helpful thoughts for those that cause unhappy feelings will no longer feel disturbed.

The simplicity and concreteness of these basic assumptions make the rational–cognitive approach to therapy very attractive to educators. As is true of the behavioral approach, emotionally disturbed states are stripped of mystique. They are represented as conditions primarily caused by inappropriate learning and alterable through new learning. Rational–cognitive therapy is distinct from the applied behavioral approach because, whereas behavioral therapy focuses primarily on the external events that influence behavior, for example, the reinforcement principles, rational–cognitive therapy is concerned with internal symbolic functions such as reasoning processes. Although this distinction is minimized in the work of certain behavioral theorists, most prominently Albert Bandura (1969), who extended the behavioral model beyond overt stimuli and responses to encompass the symbolic functioning of the mind, the primary difference between these two approaches remains the degree of emphasis placed on cognitive functioning. The principles and methods to be presented in this chapter will be those developed not from a particular theoretical orientation, but from the clinical experience of two prominent cognitively oriented therapists, Albert Ellis and William Glasser. Although these individuals are by no means the only ones espousing a rational orientation, their ideas and methods are particularly useful in school settings. Each of their approaches, Ellis's *rational-emotive therapy* and Glasser's *reality therapy* will be discussed in detail. Those discussions will include the educational application of their techniques.

ELLIS'S RATIONAL-EMOTIVE THERAPY

Albert Ellis, formerly a psychoanalytical therapist, is a prolific author (1957, 1958, 1960, 1962, 1970, 1972a, 1972b, 1973, 1974) who presents the essence of his theory and applied procedures in his book *Reason and Emotion in Psychotherapy* (1962). His basic tenets have been mentioned in Chapter 5, Group Therapy. An amplification of those tenets will illustrate the manner in which they are applied in clinical situations.

Rational-emotive therapy is based on the assumption that "man is a uniquely rational, as well as a uniquely irrational animal; that his emotional or psychological disturbances are largely a result of his thinking illogically or irrationally; and that he can rid himself of most of his emotional or mental unhappiness, ineffectuality and disturbance if he learns to maximize his rational and minimize his irrational thinking" (1962, p. 36).

Implicit in this assumption is the notion that *thinking and emotion are not two different processes, but are essentially the same thing.* More accurately, thinking and feeling are so closely related that they cannot realistically be considered independently. Ellis explains that emotion is caused by several noncognitive events such as sensorimotor stimulation (the sight of a large animal causes fear), and biophysical stimulation through the autonomic nervous system and hypothalamus (electric shock causes fear). However, the most important cause is the thinking process (anticipation of meeting a large animal or of being shocked causes fear). Thinking also involves the recirculation of previous emotional experiences that regenerate feeling (thoughts about an angry encounter experienced last week evoke fresh anger). Thus, much of what is termed *emotion* is in fact "emotional thought," that is, strongly evaluative or biased thought (attitudes) triggered when the individual perceives events as good or bad, pleasant or unpleasant, beneficial or harmful, and responds accordingly.

Similarly, emotions can be controlled by a variety of means including biochemicals (tranquilizing or sedative drugs), using the sensori-motor system (exercises or controlled breathing), using existing emotional feeling (changing out of love for someone) and, most critically, using cerebral processes (thinking, or telling the self to calm down). Rational-emotive therapy does not negate the importance of sensorimotor or biophysical techniques, as is reflected by the inclusion of the word *emotive* in the title. However, the obvious emphasis is on the rational techniques used to alter feeling. Since emotions are principally a certain type of evaluative or judgmental thought, they are most efficiently altered through thought manipulation.

In applying this fact to the problem of emotional disturbance, Ellis defines emotionally maladjusted individuals as intelligent, potentially logical persons who demonstrate illogical behavior. In other words, these are persons who, through their negative, self-defeating thoughts, cause themselves extensive unhappiness, despite the fact that they are capable of thinking and behaving in a more healthy, adaptive manner. Therefore, treatment always includes delineating the person's past and present illogical thinking and self-defeating remarks by: "1) bringing them force-fully to his attention or consciousness, 2) showing him how they cause and maintain his disturbance, 3) identifying the illogical links in his internalized sentences, and 4) teaching him how to rethink and re-verbalize these internalized thoughts" (1962, p. 59).

Illogical Ideas Underlying Disturbance

The crux of Ellis's (1962) position are the illogical thoughts or ideas that appear to be prevalent forces in causing and maintaining emotional disturbance. Each will be presented and discussed in detail.

1. *"The idea that it is a dire necessity for an adult human being to be loved or approved of by virtually every significant other person in his community"* (p. 61). Ellis regards it as irrational to believe that one must be admired and accepted by most other people. He argues that such expectations are perfectionistic and ultimately unattainable since it is not possible for all persons to be approving. In fact, some people will invariably be disapproving for reasons of their own. Thus, an overwhelm-ing desire to be loved and approved of can never be satisfied. Even when offered love and admiration, the individual remains fearful that he or she will be rejected eventually. This approval seeking drains energy that should be expended elsewhere, and frequently earns disdain from others.

An overwhelming need for affection and acceptance actually interferes with the individual's ability to love.

For all of these reasons, Ellis argues that a healthy individual should try to extirpate overwhelming love needs. The need for approval should be directed toward significant relationships such as those needed to maintain a job or keep a viable marriage. The fact that other persons may dislike or disapprove of one would be regarded in perspective, as inconvenient or annoying rather than as horrible or catastrophic, and as far less important than one's own opinion of one's actions.

2. *"The idea that one should be thoroughly competent, adequate, and achieving in all possible respects if one is to consider oneself worthwhile."* (p. 63) The irrationality of this idea is illustrated by the fact that no person could ever be perfectly competent in all avenues of life. Expecting success of oneself in every endeavor promotes fear of failure, reduces enjoyment of activities, and eventually generates feelings of anxiety and worthlessness. The acceptance of a philosophy of achievement limits effectiveness in pursuing the genuine discovery of self-rewarding activities. A more healthy attitude is that one should try to *do* rather than always try to *do well*. The goal should be enjoyment and intrinsic satisfaction, not achievement for its own sake. Errors should be used to promote improvement, rather than viewed as indicators of incompetence.

3. *"The idea that certain people are bad, wicked or villainous and that they should be severely blamed and punished for their villainy"* (p. 65). This concept is irrational because it ignores the fact that most people who behave badly do so because they are stupid, ignorant, or emotionally disturbed rather than because they are evil. The concept of evil implies free will, that people consciously choose to behave wrongly. It is more likely true that their behavior is determined by their previous learning. All individuals are fallible and can be expected to make mistakes. Those who perform "bad" acts usually are not helped to understand the nature of their behavior or to avoid repetition by being blamed for their errors or by being punished severely. In dealing with them, the goal is to help them learn from their mistakes. That goal is not facilitated by the notion that they are evil or worthless.

A rational approach is to avoid becoming overly upset about other people. It is helpful to attempt to understand the reason for the behavior, to avoid criticism or blame, and to offer assistance when possible.

4. *"The idea that it is awful and catastrophic when things are not the way one would very much like them to be"* (p. 69). Ellis points out that there is no reason for people to expect that they will always get what they want or that they will avoid frustration. Overreaction to frus-

trating events is absurd since it inevitably must cause unhappiness and worsen a bad situation. He recommends that individuals try to change undesirable events and when they cannot effect change, adjust to reality as calmly as possible. A moralistic, indignant reaction to frustration often causes hostility and aggression, whereas acceptance of reality diminishes unhappiness.

Ellis notes that rational human beings try to differentiate between external frustrating events and events perceived as irritating because of internal upset. They also recognize the human tendency to catastrophize about frustrating situations as in "This situation is terrible," and are able to alter that type of response with a reaction such as "This situation is bad but it is not going to ruin me."

5. *"The idea that human unhappiness is externally caused and that people have little or no ability to control their sorrows and disturbance"* (p. 72). This irrational notion pertains to the human tendency to view external people and events as responsible for personal unhappiness. Ellis notes that other people or events actually do relatively little harm to an individual. The harm or unhappiness is due to the self-verbalizations, or destructive thoughts and attitudes that individuals indulge in when they encounter problems with others.

Also, people appear to believe that they cannot control their emotions. Therefore, when they feel unhappy, they can do nothing to alter those feelings. Ellis believes that, although it is difficult for individuals to control their emotions, they can do so if they work at it calmly. Becoming overly upset is definitely avoidable if an individual will acknowledge that he or she is causing the negative emotions and that he or she need not react in an upset fashion. The individual can avoid turmoil, if he or she will think about the negative emotions, and associate his or her feelings with illogical verbalizations and attempt to replace the illogical verbalizations with logical, realistic self-talk.

6. *"The idea that if something is or may be dangerous or fearsome one should be terribly concerned about it and should keep dwelling on the possibility of its occurring"* (p. 75). The irrationality of this idea pertains to the fact that anxiety about a possible occurrence often limits rather than enhances the individual's ability to react effectively. Also, most fears are not realistic, they are exaggerated by worry. Finally, some fears that are realistic are unavoidable (fear of death). Worry doesn't alter the situation.

A more effective means of dealing with fear or danger is to logically examine it. Such examinations will illustrate that most worries are not caused by external dangers, but by negative, anxiety-evoking self-talk. Self-statements indicating that irrational worry does not prevent dangerous events from occurring reduce such irrational thoughts. Also individuals can reduce fear by doing that which is fear-evoking and discovering that there is nothing harmful in these situations. The key to conquering fear is to face it.

7. *"The idea that it is easier to avoid than to face certain life difficulties and self-responsibilities"* (p. 78). This idea is irrational because withdrawal from difficult situations, although it provides temporary relief, never engenders an ultimate feeling of satisfaction. Troublesome situations that are avoided only reappear again. Also, effort devoted to avoidance behavior may deplete the individual's energy.

A second point pertains to the dubious assumption that individuals who are passive and irresponsible are happy. Seemingly, happiness is related to involvement in goal-oriented activities. Prolonged vacations become boring and unsatisfying. Dealing with challenges and problems is exciting and interesting.

Ellis recommends that individuals should do the things that are necessary in life, regardless of personal preferences. Such behavior requires discipline that is obtainable by logically deducing that such activities are necessary and therefore must be done. Self-disciplined behaviors are aided by planned work schedules, reasonable subgoals, and rewards for accomplishments.

8. *"The idea that one should be dependent on others and needs someone stronger than oneself on whom to rely."* (p. 80) This irrational idea pertains to an individual's tendency to maximize dependency on others by permitting them to make important decisions. Such dependency is inversely related to individualism. The dependent individual sacrifices his or her unique desires to the will of another. Also, dependency reduces self-confidence and increases anxiety. The individual never learns that he or she can cope because he or she is able to avoid challenges.

The better-adjusted individual accepts the fact that in many respects a person is always alone in the world and is basically responsible for his or her own decisions. Each person must pursue his or her own desires, not to the detriment of others, but for personal welfare.

9. *"The idea that one's past history is an all-important determiner of one's present behavior and that because something once strongly affected one's life, it should indefinitely have a similar effect"* (p. 82). The irrational aspect of this belief is that it is based on a logical error of overgeneralization, the assumption that because a thing is true in some circumstances, it is equally true in all circumstances. The fact that a certain behavior produced a certain outcome at one period of life doesn't mean it will continue to do so. A child may use a temper tantrum to get what is wanted, but such behavior is unlikely to work for an adult. Individuals who cling to past solutions are unlikely to develop new solutions to problems.

According to Ellis, it is more beneficial for individuals to accept the fact that they are influenced by past experience, but that it is present behaviors that will influence the future. Thus, what is done now is of critical importance. Also, individuals need not continue to engage in activities simply because they have always done so. Pernicious influences from the past can be countered by verbal and active behavior that forces change. For example, an individual who fears social encounters, and has always avoided them, can systematically engage in such activities and learn that he or she *is capable* of enjoying them.

10. *"The idea that one should become quite upset over other people's problems and disturbances"* (p. 85). Ellis points out that other people's problems usually have little impact on one's own life. Therefore, there is no reason to become overly upset, angry, or even involved when individuals engage in behavior that we disapprove of. For instance, when someone is impolite, this behavior is annoying but not worthy of outraged indignation.

Becoming upset with other people's behavior rarely changes it. Individuals may change themselves but they rarely are changed from without. Often intense anger over another's behavior is a means of avoiding dealing with one's own problems.

Ellis recommends that individuals ask themselves if the behavior of others is really worth such annoyance. Usually, we do not care enough about others to help them change and those we do care about are helped, not by outraged behavior, but by calm objective discussions of their problems.

11. *"The idea that there is invariably a right, precise, and perfect solution to human problems and that it is catastrophic if this perfect solution is not found"* (p. 86). Clearly there is no perfection or absolute truth in the world, therefore it is irrational to believe that one cannot be happy in an imperfect world. Expectations to the contrary raise false expectations and create unnecessary anxiety. The fact is that imagined disasters do not materialize when persons do not arrive at "correct" solutions to their problems. Even less than optimal decisions are not catastrophic.

Ellis recommends that individuals faced with significant problems should devise several possible solutions and choose the one that is most practical. The decision should be accepted, not as a perfect solution, but as a realistic compromise. In the event that the decision is not beneficial, the individual should accept the fact that errors are bound to occur and can lead to better decisions in the future.

Role of the Therapist

Having isolated the types of illogical beliefs that cause neurotic or disturbed behavior, Ellis presents the role of the therapist. Succinctly, the therapist must help the disturbed individual recognize illogical thinking. The first step in this process may be identifying how he or she originally developed neurotic attitudes. The following and more critical therapeutic steps, however, involve showing the person how he or she is maintaining illogical thinking, and helping the client recognize what must be done to replace irrational ideas with more logical attitudes toward life. According to Ellis, the therapist is a "frank counterpropagandist" who directly contradicts and denies the illogical, self-defeating statements of the disturbed person. The therapist "encourages, persuades, cajoles, and occasionally even insists" that the disturbed person act in some manner that will counteract illogical thoughts. The ultimate goal is to convince the individual to internalize a logical, rational philosophy about life, that is, to abandon any or all of the eleven irrational ideas that destroy confidence and create countless problems. By assumption, the disturbed person has made himself or herself disturbed and can "cure" himself or herself. Although the therapeutic relationship is enhanced by establishing a warm, supportive relationship with the troubled individual, this trusting bond will not be sufficient to help resolve problems and improve behavior. To accomplish these events, the therapist has an obligation to consistently reiterate the illogical ideas at the root of the problem. The patient must not be permitted to evade or elude the essence of the problems by dwelling on superficial aspects or by hiding behind the rationalizations that are part of irrational defenses against reality. For example, an adolescent who maintains that he fails in school because *his* teacher dislikes him, must be convinced that *his* negative self-talk pertaining to feelings of inadequacy and fear of failure contribute more to the problem than does the teacher's attitude. He also must learn to dismiss the irrational notion that because he dislikes a task, he need not deal with it. He must accept responsibility for his life situation. Unless he resolves these basic problems, even a superficial modification of current school performance would have no lasting effect on behavior.

Although Ellis recommends that the therapist attempt to form a supportive, trusting relationship with the client, he does not accept the premise of the nondirective school formulated by Carl Rogers (1957), that the therapeutic relationship can only be successful if the therapist has unconditional positive regard for the patient. Nor does he believe that the therapist must communicate empathetic understanding of the patient's experience. On the contrary, Ellis believes that the therapist should not literally feel the patient's disturbance, and more emphatically, should not believe the patient's irrationalities.

In place of an emphasis on total acceptance of the patient, Ellis has devised a series of important considerations that constitute the basis of effective therapy. The first consideration is that *therapy should not involve the assignment of blame*. It is important that the therapist help the patient recognize that problems do not mean that he or she is an evil, worthless person. The therapist must insist that blame is destructive rather than helpful—patients should not blame themselves, others, or fate for their problems. Ellis recommends that patients be encouraged to think about themselves in unmoralistic words such as *wrong doing* and *irresponsible* rather than as *bad* or *evil*. Stress must be placed on the "intrinsic value" of all human beings in accordance with Hartman's notion (1959) that human beings have worth simply because they exist, despite the fact that they encounter problems.

The second consideration is that the disturbed patients *must act to help themselves feel better*. They must work hard to restructure their thinking and to face the reality of their faulty logic. Therapy involves changing through doing and therefore is difficult and threatening. Although the therapist cannot single-handedly solve the patient's problems, he or she must provide the emotional support and direct suggestion that will enable the patient to solve his or her own problems.

The third consideration regarding therapy is the key to helping the patient clarify his reasoning. It is a process termed *the A B C of emotional disturbance*. In this process, hypothesis A reflects a fact about the patient's life, such as "My father dislikes me," and hypothesis C is the presumable logical corollary of A, "My father's dislike has caused me to be a sick person." Rational-emotive therapy points out that the essential step in producing C—one often omitted from the patient's logic, is hypothesis B. This hypothesis is the patient's self-talk, such as "I tell myself that my father should love me and feel outraged about his attitude." Hypothesis B always causes C, although usually the disturbed patient attributes the cause to A.

The fourth condition associated with rational-emotive therapy pertains to the emphasis on the *present as the cause of difficulties*. Disturbed persons rarely recognize the underlying ideologies they hold that lead to neurotic behavior. However, these ideas *are not* deeply hidden in the dark recesses of the mind (as psychoanalytically oriented therapists maintain). They are readily discernible and may be quickly introduced into consciousness. Such illogical thoughts may have been formulated in the past as a reaction to unhappy environmental situations. The important aspect of each thought, however, is its current existence. Thus, in therapeutic situations, patients are not encouraged to dwell on early history or past personal trauma. They must find and counteract hypothesis B—their ongoing self-verbalizations.

The fifth consideration is that rational-emotive therapy regards the *didactic method as a powerful means of producing change in others*. Propagandistic techniques, that is, the persuasive presentation of ideas, changes people's attitudes and behavior. For example, an individual can be convinced to buy certain automobiles or can develop new ideas about breakfast food when presented certain types of information. That being the case, there is no reason to believe that once a person adopts a premise about his or her personality or emotionality, that he or she cannot be led to abandon it in favor of a more logical premise. Therefore, rational-emotive therapy involves *teaching* an individual to see and alter illogical or erroneous premises. However, the therapist must realize that these illogical ideas are tenaciously held by the patient. They have been learned by exposure to powerful propagandizing teachers—often including the patient and patient's parents. To be displaced, they must be attacked vigorously, by an insistent, persistent therapist who refuses to permit the patient to comfortably cling to self-defeating rationalizations and who consistently redirects attention to step B in the "A,B,C," of emotional disturbance. This emphatic teaching behavior may be taken to the point of indicating that the patient's utterances about his or her problems are nonsense. Such a direct frontal attack on illogical premises often is met with resistance, as patients cling to familiar attitudes and ideas rather than risk adapting new ones. The therapist should regard such behavior as typical and should not stop teaching because an individual resists learning. In fact, the therapist must work harder to present the information that represents essential new learning.

The sixth consideration is the importance of *homework assignments* to effective therapy. The rational-emotive therapist does not rely solely on talking about problems. The disturbed individual is assigned tasks to be performed in the real world that will help break down irrational ideas. For example, a boy who is afraid of social encounters may be assigned the task of going to his high school dance. He may be required simply to attend, not to dance. This first step in a sequence of such activities eventually helps the patient overcome his fears and learn that social events hold no dire consequences.

The seventh consideration is that *rational-emotive therapy must be unpampering*. The chore of gaining emotional health falls squarely on the shoulders of the patient. The disturbed individual must recognize that his or her improvement will be a direct consequence of his or her effort. The therapist must not humor or indulge the patient who fails to work. He or she must directly inform the patient that the patient's rationalizations are foolish and that a failure to carry out homework assignments wastes time. To be sure, such direct confrontation will make the individual feel uncomfortable. These uncomfortable feelings and the anxiety associated with them influence the patient to try harder. Similarly, when disturbed individuals deny their feelings of anger, tension, guilt, and so on, the therapist must persistently confront them with evidence of their own behavior that makes it obvious that they do in fact hold these feelings. When they insist that they are not using negative self-talk to perpetuate their disturbance, the therapist must contend that they must be engaging in such self-verbalizations or they would cease to feel upset. The therapist never permits the patient to avoid responsibility for behavior.

The eighth consideration involves the *language of rational-emotive therapy*. The therapist is responsible for helping the patient modify his or her language to make it more representative of reality. Thus, when an individual suffers rejection, he is taught to say "I don't like being rejected," rather than the irrational sentence: "It is terrible or catastrophic to be rejected." The latter sentence simply is not true and leads to feelings of depression and despair that can be avoided by keeping such an event in perspective.

Rebuttals to Criticisms

Having forcefully stated how therapy should be conducted, Ellis is equally forceful in answering criticisms of his approach. One of the most prevalent attacks on rational-emotive therapy is that it is *too intellectualized and ververbal*. In response, Ellis notes that rational-emotive therapy does not ignore a person's current feelings. The emotionally disturbed person is asked to discuss feelings about events, not to talk about conceptions of his or her condition. When negative, self-harming feelings are recognized, the patient is led to identify his or her cognitive sources.

A more important rebuttal is that rational-emotive therapy does not differentiate between emotions and ideas. Sustained or prolonged emotions are self-evaluative thoughts. Therefore, to isolate and correct such thoughts is to directly alter emotion.

A second criticism is that the use of *realism is limited in human affairs, that is, realism is not the only authority in determining opinions or behaviors*. Ellis agrees, but finds the statement irrelevant. He maintains that regardless of the subjective, unrealistic forces that influence behavior, clear, logical thought can aid people in overcoming their disturbances. Actually, rational-emotive therapy is based on the idea that attitudes are not necessarily developed from realistic, external events but spring from internal interpretations of external forces. The treatment seeks to alter those internal, subjective interpretations, not simply to manipulate the environment.

A third attack is that *rational-emotive therapy is superficial* and that *it depends solely on suggestion and "positive thinking."* As a surface treatment only, it cannot be used to uncover the patient's deep unconscious thoughts, therefore it results in symptom removal rather than in a real cure. In response, Ellis argues that rational-emotive therapy is designed to alter an individual's basic philosophy of life and that such goals are not superficial. Suggestion is used extensively in treatment, but the suggestions pertain to underlying irrational thoughts, not the superficial problems that may be espoused by the patient. Therefore, suggestion directly promotes healing activities, activities that help the patient overcome fears.

Also, the unconscious emotions that underlie disturbed states are identified and introduced to conscious awareness in rational-emotive therapy through examination of an individual's self-talk. This process is decidedly different from those associated with "positive-thinking" techniques (Peale, 1952). Positive thinking simply involves the parroting of positive statements, such as "I am a loved person." It does not assist an individual in understanding and analyzing thoughts as a prelude to replacing them with more constructive or realistic ideas, as rational-emotive therapy does. Rational-emotive therapy does not gloss over problems but tries to solve them.

A fourth attack charges that rational-emotive therapy is *too directive and authoritarian*. Ellis responds that all psychotherapy involves authoritarian attempts to control behavior. Rational-emotive therapy simply takes a more open, direct path to helping the individual alter the attitudes and behaviors that make him or her troubled. The more efficiently the therapist can accomplish this task, the more effective the therapy. It must be expected that the therapist will impose values on the patient and that presumably the disturbed patient needs to acquire new values, since he or she is not doing well with those previously acquired.

Finally, rational-emotive therapy is attacked as being *ineffective with extremely disturbed or mentally limited patients*. Ellis argues that it is more effective with such individuals than are other approaches by virtue of the fact that the techniques are directive and systematic. Thus, patients who are too sick to function efficiently such as schizophrenics, or who are too limited intellectually to gain insights through their own cognitive processes, are able to recognize certain problems and to make adjustments in their behavior. Obviously, the goals of therapy vary with the patient and those set for severely disturbed or mentally limited persons must be more modest than those evolved for mildly maladjusted, intelligent persons. However, if used correctly, rational-emotive therapy is effective with all types of people.

Educational Adaptations

Ellis makes perfectly clear that the use of rational-emotive therapeutic techniques is not restricted to psychotherapists. He has authored many books for public consumption, such as *How to Live with a Neurotic* (1957) and *A New Guide to Rational Living* (1975). He maintains that individuals who read about rational-emotive techniques may apply them to improve their own lives and to help others lead more productive lives. It is interesting to note that although Ellis reports the success of his techniques with children and adolescents, and obviously would regard teachers as capable of applying his ideas, he has not written specifically of the adaptation of his principles in school situations. Therefore, this section on educational adaptations is a logical extension of Ellis's ideas. They are guidelines that should aid the teacher in using rational-emotive therapy in the school.

1. *Rational-emotive techniques should be most effective when used with children whose stage of development permits them to reason logically.* Although there are no substantiating empirical data available, Piaget's stage of formal operations, at age 11 or 12, appears to be a sensible lower limit for this type of therapy. At this age the children should be capable of identifying harmful self-verbalizations and of eventually recognizing the influence they have on behavior. Before reaching that age, it is likely that the children will be unable to see how their attitudes and expectations influence their perceptions. Such children are likely to be more readily influenced by the simple manipulation of external consequences. However, it is not necessary to automatically exclude a child from this type of treatment on the basis of age alone. Obviously, intelligence is an important factor, and, in fact, Ellis (1962) reports that he used rational-emotive therapy successfully with a bright eight year old. The best way to determine the effectiveness of this approach with any child is to try to use it.

2. *Rational-emotive techniques may be used with children whose emotional disorders range from mild to severe.* The key to successful treatment is to establish realistic goals. If a child is so severely disturbed that he or she avoids all contact with other children, the establishment of one social relationship may be a goal of therapy. However, a realistic goal for a mildly disturbed child who has minor problems with peer relationships may involve not only identifying and altering the self-talk that causes the current difficulty, but the development of a more constructive total philosophy of life.

3. *Rational-emotive techniques may be used with so-called normal children as part of a daily program in affective education.* All children would benefit from learning how to control their self-derogatory thoughts that are only too prevalent in most competitive classroom situations. They should also learn to be more tolerant and understanding of the problems shown by their more maladjusted peers. Finally, they can be helped to cope more effectively with the inevitable stressful situations that they will encounter in the process of living.

4. *Rational-emotive techniques are useful with the parents of disturbed children.* Often such persons have problems of their own that limit their effectiveness at child rearing. More importantly, they generally react

to their children's problems with feelings of resentment, anger, and embarrassment—all of which counteract effective therapeutic techniques. The use of rational-emotive techniques might alter destructive parental attitudes and help them become positive forces in their children's therapeutic programs.

5. *Rational-emotive therapy may be used with individuals or with groups.* The teacher may wish to work with certain disturbed children independently. However, for most individuals group proceedings have decided advantages. Ellis (1975) has found that group members learn the therapeutic techniques very quickly and literally replace the therapist in offering pragmatic, logical suggestions to each other. Often, suggestions that might be voiced originally by the therapist are given added credibility when reinforced by group members. Also, certain self-defeating behaviors that might be overlooked by the therapist are readily recognized by group members.

6. *Rational-emotive techniques that deal with thoughts rather than mysterious, unconscious psychic processes are not likely to elicit defensiveness and resistance on the part of parents and school administrators.* In effect, altering thought is the business of educators, therefore, rational-emotive techniques appear to belong in school.

The actual application of rational-emotive therapy involves the following procedures and techniques.

The teacher must create, through frankness and objectivity, an atmosphere among the children that invites open discussion of feelings. This is best done by modeling the behavior, that is, by openly discussing her or his own feelings. For example, the teacher may cite an instance when she or he became very angry because of rude treatment, inefficient service, mechanical failure, or any of a variety of such events that occur in daily living. She or he can point out that the initial feelings of anger were spontaneous but that prolonged anger over the incident could only have been due to self-statements such as "People have no right to be rude," or "I should never be kept waiting," or "That clerk always has been a mean, stupid person." The teacher must emphasize that everyone engages in this type of self-talk to a certain extent, and that these utterances maintain upset feelings, prolonging them long after the precipitating event has occurred. She also must show that it is not shameful or degrading to admit to feeling angry or upset.

Through examples such as that presented above, *the teacher teaches the children the relationship between self-verbalizations and emotion.* This is a lesson that must be thoroughly taught, since it is not always an easy matter for individuals to identify the subvocal verbalizations that accompany their emotions. At this step the teacher must provide practice sessions to ensure that the children understand this relationship. They must discuss events that generally arouse strong emotion, then attempt to isolate the self-statements that might be part of such emotion. For example, a child who is upset and angry because he or she was disciplined by his or her mother, should be helped to identify the self-talk that perpetuates upset feelings. Typical thoughts might be "My mother doesn't love me," or "She always picks on me." The training should extend to actual instances where a child becomes emotionally upset. The teacher should attempt to help the youngster isolate self-talk by asking questions such as "What are you telling yourself?", or "What are you thinking?" Some children may be able to identify their negative self-talk when they are experiencing strong emotion. Others, however, may be able to track down their destructive self-talk only after a cooling-off period.

Once the children appear to understand the relationship between self-talk and emotion, *the teacher should introduce each of Ellis's eleven irrational ideas.* The children should be informed that these illogical notions underlie most disturbed emotions and account for many of the problems that people experience in their daily living. The teacher should present as many examples as possible to illustrate the effects of the irrational convictions.

At this point, *the teacher is ready to establish weekly sessions designed to assist children in counteracting any of the eleven irrational ideas that may be causing disturbed behavior.* She or he may use a variety of formats. For instance, the teacher may decide to work once per week with the entire class, and on a daily basis with several children whose problems are more demanding. As a rule of thumb, children with more complex problems should be worked with individually before they are integrated into a group situation.

When using rational-emotive techniques with groups, the teacher must establish firm procedural ground rules. The basic by-law of this approach is *frankness without blaming.* All participants must understand that their role in the group is to help each other participant identify any irrational beliefs that may cause maladaptive or unconstructive behavior. Although such a role obviously demands that each group member learn to speak frankly and openly, it does not imply that members speak in a manner that is hostile, negative, or demeaning. In fact, it is critically important that the teacher emphasize the difference between honest criticism and insults. Mastery of this distinction is based on the extent to which the children understand that people who have emotional or social problems are not bad or evil individuals destined to be in perpetual trouble, but instead are confused, unsatisfied persons capable of changing their behavior. Remarks in group sessions should be aimed at identifying irrational self-talk, "John thinks nobody likes him," rather than at describing general personality traits, "John is a dope."

The key technique in conducting the therapy sessions is *the A,B,C paradigm of disturbance* that was discussed previously. The teacher, as the group leader, must take every opportunity to illustrate the relationship between B, the individual's irrational self-talk, and C, the disturbed behavior, and must consistently point out the inaccuracy of the individual's perceptions of a relationship between A—external events, and C. Thus, when a child says "My classmates don't like me" (A), therefore, "I don't like school" (C), the teacher must help him or her identify step B—the irrational ideas that he or she holds that one *must* be liked by others, that others are responsible for or cause one's behavior, and that the situation is intolerable and unchangeable—as the real reasons why he or she either cannot face attending school or feels uncomfortable when attending.

Throughout the therapy sessions, *the teacher must recognize that rational-emotive therapy is an active-directive approach*. Group sessions are not designed simply to talk about problems, but to work out solutions. As leader, the teacher must be prepared to offer concrete suggestions to the children in the form of homework assignments. First, the concept of *homework* must be explained so that the children understand their responsibility for improving their situations. Then, appropriate assignments must be developed for each individual. Shy individuals must practice meeting and speaking to others in small sequenced steps until the uncomfortable feelings associated with social interaction have diminished. Phobic children must engage in activities that will systematically desensitize them (see Chapter 6). Children in conflict with their parents must make a certain number of positive, helpful statements to them every evening. Children who fight frequently must practice alternate responses such as yelling or hitting a punching bag. Children who are overly dependent on adults must complete certain simple tasks without adult support or advice. Children who are irresponsible must take charge of certain activities. Overly competitive children must be responsible for helping other children improve in certain skills. Children who are disliked because they make unfriendly, hostile, or supercilious remarks to others must practice making positive, supportive remarks.

Every child must report to the group, which then evaluates the sincerity of the effort to complete the homework. Excuses or rationalizations are not accepted. Group members who have been unsuccessful are encouraged to try again. Possibly, homework assignments are modified. No child is permitted to remain a passive bystander.

Once the group becomes familiar with the therapeutic techniques and accustomed to easy verbalization, the teacher may find, particularly with older children and adolescents, that many of the *leadership activities are assumed by group members*. This turn of events is very desirable, since adolescents in particular are far more prone to listen to their peers than to adults. Ellis and his associates encourage client autonomy and self-reliance and recommend the use of educational aids to increase client independence. One educational aid is the Disputing Irrational Beliefs (DIBS) instruction sheet (Ellis and Harper, 1975, p. 216). The DIBS sheet is simply a format that requires an individual to write down answers to questions about his or her irrational beliefs. The first question is "What irrational belief do I want to dispute and surrender?" The person formulates an answer such as "I must receive love from someone for whom I really care." The following questions pertain to the falseness or truthfulness of this belief. As the individual thinks about the belief in order to answer, she or he becomes better able to recognize and combat the force of the irrational idea.

Another therapeutic aid that should make the teacher's job simpler is a "Homework Report Sheet" that each group member completes on a daily basis and discusses during group sessions. Depending on the age of the children, this sheet may list the child's daily assignment, the steps taken to implement the assignment, and the apparent outcome, or may involve an A-B-C-D format developed by Maultsby (1971). The A section consists of perceived external facts (Billy fought again at recess). The B section is the self-talk pertaining to A (Billy is a rotten person) and C is a description of the emotions caused by A (anger). The final step D is the rational alternative self-talk section where the individual analyzes A objectively and generates realistic sentences that challenge B (Billy is still too explosive to go to recess with the class. I must discuss possible alternatives with him and try not to let his problem upset me). Maultsby (1971) has demonstrated the effectiveness of the homework technique using the A-B-C-D format with a wide variety of neurotic and psychotic people.

Ellis also recommends the use of bibliotherapy, having children read about rational-emotive therapy,[1] videotapes of group activities, and games illustrating rational versus irrational thinking. He stresses that rational-emotive therapy is essentially an educational technique and that ultimately the terms *emotional education* or *tolerance training* may replace the term *psychotherapy* to describe it.

The teacher who implements rational-emotive techniques in the school must be prepared for an initial period of confusion as the children become accustomed to speaking about their emotions. He or she should not be discouraged if early sessions are fraught with awkward silences or nervous laughs. A good procedure is to begin with short group sessions— 20 to 30 minutes—and to lengthen the time period to 45 to 60 minutes as the children become more comfortable. The teacher also should not

---

[1] Inexpensive books and articles may be obtained from: Associated Rational Thinkers, University of Kentucky, Lexington, Ky. 40506.

feel upset when, despite the correct application of the therapeutic techniques, some children do not respond positively. Therapeutic techniques are never effective with all persons and it would be illogical to expect rational-emotive therapy to be the perfect answer to the problem of emotional disturbance. Obviously, some children may simply be so resistant to attempts to help them that they effectively stymie the teacher's efforts. Others may be too immature to understand the ideas that underlie the approach. Still others may be overwhelmed by other influences in the environment, such as parental attitudes. The teacher encountering a child who cannot benefit from rational-emotive group work, can always use the techniques on an individual basis. If the child progresses he or she can be reintegrated into the group. If individual sessions are not successful, the teacher may de-emphasize efforts to alter self-verbalizations and focus extensively on reinforcement for improved behaviors. It is worth noting that certain behavioral therapists (Wolpe, 1976) believe that it is the active homework assignments, reinforced by group or therapist approval or disapproval, that make rational-emotive therapy successful, not the emphasis on rethinking or the adaptation of more rational ideas. Others such as Maultsby have incorporated the emphasis on self-talk into behavioral therapy (rational behavioral therapy).

Illustrative Cases

As noted, Ellis has not worked in school settings; however, some of the techniques discussed in the previous section are demonstrated in three of his clinical case reports. One case reported by Ellis (1963, p. 224) pertains to a young girl who, at age 25, had never dated. She was attractive, well-educated, and eventually wanted to marry and have a family. When invited for dates she either made an excuse or, after accepting, found reasons to break the dates at the last minute. In the A,B,C terminology, she believed that C—her phobia of men was caused by A—an unpleasant rejection by a boy she once wished to date. When asked about her self-talk to uncover B, she denied that it occurred. After persistent questioning, she finally revealed her debilitating thoughts—that she would not be found a suitable candidate for marriage and that such an event would be catastrophic because women who remain unmarried are incompetent and worthless.

Therapy attacked the girl's irrational notions that marriage is the only good state of female existence and that a female who fails to marry is inept and worthless. After three months of therapy, during which the therapist challenged these premises directly, the girl began to have dates, and shortly got engaged to marry. She also returned to college to finish her education (she had dropped out because of her poor social life). Her improvement appeared directly related to her acceptance of the idea that there are options or alternatives in life—if one channel closes another may open.

Another type of treatment described by Ellis (1963, p. 290) involved a twenty-five-year-old male psychopath. This person was the son of a well-to-do family and since age 14 had committed a variety of antisocial offenses including lying, stealing, sexual irresponsibility, and physical assaults on others. He had been arrested five times, convicted once, and had served a year in a reformatory. He came to therapy to substantiate a plea of emotional disturbance and avoid a jail sentence for his latest offense—robbing vending machines. He evidenced no guilt about his crimes nor any real desire to change.

Therapy focused on the manner in which the patient's irrational beliefs inevitably led him to grief. Like a spoiled child, he thought he could have what he wanted whenever he wanted it, despite the attitudes of others. Therapy also pointed out that although it was sane to want things, it was insane to demand them, since demanding something turned it into a necessity and produced either stupid, antisocial behavior to obtain it, or anger and frustration over failing to get it. Finally, the patient was shown that to maintain his current life-style required "tough skin," since he felt no guilt over his exploitation of innocent people, and that his "tough skin" could only be maintained by feelings of hatred toward others which, in the long run, were self-destructive.

Finally, after a year of discussion of this type during which the patient gave lip-service to these ideas but actually did not change his behaviors, the patient admitted that he was afraid he couldn't change— he felt unable to control his antisocial behavior and feared failure if he tried to live honestly. Therapy then attacked these fearful ideas, for example, the self-talk "I can't stop myself from doing these things." The patient also revealed severe feelings of inadequacy in self-talk such as "I am utterly worthless unless I exploit others," which also was attacked in therapy.

After months of talking about these ideas, the patient, then on probation, entered college to study accounting and decided to "do things the hard way and not to worry about failure." He eventually graduated and has been relatively problem free ever since.

A third case involved a young male (1963, p. 182) who committed violent crimes against women. Discussion revealed that he felt hostile to everyone, particularly toward his mother. He held the irrational idea that other persons should love him despite his behavior and that his mother was responsible for his current behavior because she was not loving toward him.

Therapy centered on the premise that, although it would have been nice if his mother had loved him as she did his siblings, it was not mandatory that she do so, nor was it mandatory for any other person to give him things because he thought he deserved them. He was taught to examine his own self-talk—the things he said to himself that made him angry, such as "My mother shouldn't behave this way." The counter-suggestion was the alternate self-talk "Why shouldn't she be the way she always has been." On accepting these options, his hostility abated and he stopped all violent behavior.

The examples presented involved relatively seriously disturbed individuals, and although these people were not children, the success of the rational-emotive techniques in these cases suggests that they would be equally effective if used with children suffering from similar or less-serious types of disorders. These cases illustrate several features of rational-emotive therapy that apply to school settings. First, the teacher *must expect* the children initially to be unable to identify their negative self-talk. Probably the more seriously disturbed children will be most emphatic in their denials that they say or think certain things when they behave badly or become upset.

Second, the teacher must persist in communicating his or her own perceptions of the child's debilitating self-talk. As was apparent in the first clinical case, the fact that certain behaviors occur means that the child *must* be engaging in precipitating self-talk despite denials.

Third, the teacher must be patient and realize that cognitive change takes time. Each of the cases presented showed that clients may profess to understand and accept a point long before they actually do so. The fact that a child may not be successful in changing behavior after initial exposure to therapy doesn't mean that he or she will not do so eventually.

Fourth, the teacher should always look at overt behavior to evaluate the success or failure of the therapeutic intervention. What an individual says can be deceptive and misleading; what he or she does is a far more reliable index of where he or she is psychologically.

GLASSER'S REALITY THERAPY

The theory and methodology that constitute *reality therapy* have been presented in two books: *Reality Therapy* (1965) and *Schools Without Failure* (1969). Like Ellis, William Glasser was trained in traditional psychoanalytic philosophy and procedures but found them inadequate and evolved his own unique approach to psychotherapy and the problem of emotional disturbance. Glasser's approach, unlike that of Ellis, is not highly theoretical. The tenets of reality therapy are few and simple, as Glasser emphatically avoids the "whys" of emotional disturbance. His position is more akin to that of the most externally oriented behaviorists, since he focuses attention exclusively on what can be altered—overt behavior. However, unlike most behaviorists, he espouses a rationale for behavior change that involves the development of feelings of *responsibility* and *commitment*—a focus that indirectly illustrates the general cognitive–rational aspects of his approach. Other indications of the similarity between reality and rational-emotive therapy can be discerned in Glasser's representation of the differences between his approach (reality therapy) and conventional therapy (strict or loose psychoanalytic procedures). Many of these differences also exist between rational-emotive therapy and conventional therapy. They are as follows:

1. Conventional approaches hold that an individual is a passive victim of mental or emotional disease and is not responsible for behavior whereas reality therapy holds that a person becomes disturbed because he or she behaves inappropriately, that he or she can and must change that behavior, and that the designation of mental illness is misleading and meaningless.

2. Conventional therapy believes that probing in the patient's past to unearth the roots of the problem will lead to insight and changes in attitude and behavior, whereas reality therapy emphasizes only the present and the future because past events cannot be altered and need not influence current behavior.

3. Conventional therapy depends on transference, that is, the patient's transferring to the therapist the attitudes and feelings that he holds toward other persons, whereas reality therapy simply advocates that the therapist become truly involved with the patient.

4. Conventional therapy emphasizes the importance of unconscious mental processes that are discovered through indirect methods such as dream analysis, free association, and so on. (Glasser's term is educated psychiatric guessing), whereas reality therapy is not concerned with unconscious forces, but focuses on overt behavior.

5. Conventional therapy avoids the issue of the rightness or wrongness of behavior, whereas reality therapy emphasizes that deviant behavior is wrong and that the patient is responsible for it.

6. Conventional therapy is not concerned with teaching people to behave better, assuming that they will discover better behavior once they understand their problem, whereas reality therapy focuses directly on teaching people about better behavior.

As these tenets indicate, reality therapy depends on the patient's cognitive efforts to consciously monitor his or her activities and to cast away the rationalizations that sustain disturbance. To that significant extent, Glasser's approach is similar to Ellis's procedures and deserves to be called a cognitive–rational approach.

The underlying tenets of reality therapy can be summed up in what Mowrer, in the foreword of *Reality Therapy*, has termed the "psychiatric version of the three R's, namely: *reality, responsibility* and *right-and wrong*." Glasser holds that emotional disturbance evolves when an individual is unable to fulfill two basic needs—"the need to be loved and to love and the need to feel that we are worthwhile to ourselves and to others" (1965 p. 9). This failure is caused when an individual does not behave in a manner that is realistic, responsible and right. In other words, people encounter emotional difficulty when their behavior falls below acceptable social standards, when they consistently engage in immature, self-serving behaviors without regard for the rights of others and without appreciation of the consequences of their behavior.

The right-wrong aspects of reality therapy hold for all traditional classifications of disturbed conditions—neurosis, psychosis, psychopathic, and delinquent behavior. All disturbed persons suffer conduct disorders in that they behave badly and, as part of their disturbed condition, engage in rationalizations, justifications, and other exploitative activities that enable them to maintain their wrong patterns of behavior. Their maladaptive behavior problems are related to the most important of Glasser's basic tenets, responsibility.

Responsibility is "the ability to fulfil one's needs, and to do so in a way that does not deprive others of the ability to fulfil their needs" (1965 p. 13). Glasser believes that all disturbed persons are irresponsible. More importantly, he notes that they are "ill" because they are irresponsible, rather than the traditionally accepted converse position, that they are irresponsible because they are ill. Because they are irresponsible, they cannot earn the respect or admiration of others and cannot maintain a sense of their own self-worth. Thus, in time, because their basic needs for love and respect remain unfulfilled, they must suffer emotionally.

Glasser believes that acquiring responsibility is a complicated, life-long problem. Individuals must learn how to fulfill their need for responsibility. They do so best as children of loving parents who teach them with appropriate use of affection and discipline. Parents who love their children and wish the best for them must discipline them. Discipline differs from punishment in that it is simply the enforced consequences of the child's behavior; a child who does not complete his or her homework, doesn't go outside to play baseball. Unlike punishment, discipline need not cause pain and always is limited to a specific behavior. It teaches the child that he or she must behave according to society's standards, that he or she must meet obligations and not infringe on the rights of others.

The third "r" concept, realism, is related to those concepts discussed previously. Glasser notes that disturbed persons have common characteristics; they all deny the reality of the world around them. In other words, the symptoms of their disturbance: breaking laws, being disagreeable with others, justifying their behavior, all reflect the disturbed individual's inability to recognize and accept the manner in which society functions. They deny that certain behaviors evoke certain consequences, whether they like it or not. Thus, they cannot be excused when they ignore reality and blame their problems on other people or on external events. They must be brought to recognize the long-term impact or consequences of their actions—to become responsible.

Educational Applications

Reality therapy is an attempt to teach responsible, socially adaptive, realistic behavior. The therapist does so by *involvement* with the patient. In effect, the therapist must demonstrate that he or she cares enough about the person to confront him or her when the patient is irresponsible and to work to strengthen the patient's ability to make rational decisions. When reality therapy techniques are applied to children the methodology is relatively simple. The teacher–therapist attempts to have the child make a value judgment about his or her behavior and to suggest a more realistic beneficial alternative. Once the child makes a value judgment and a commitment to change, no excuse is accepted for not following through. This *discipline,* having the child face the consequences of behavior, is critical to the success of the program. To involve the child in working toward improved behavior, the teacher responds to misbehavior with two key questions: "What are you doing?", followed by "Is your behavior helpful to you or others?" Note that the teacher–therapist never asks "Why are you doing that?" This question is irrelevant—the person's motivation for the behavior (even if known) is unimportant. In fact, answers to "why" questions usually are justifications for behavior and should be avoided.

If the child responds honestly to the first two questions, the teacher–therapist asks "What could you do differently?" Thus, the child is put in a decision-making role regarding his or her behavior and is helped to learn responsibility.

If the child cannot make an accurate value judgment about the behavior, that is, if he or she believes the behavior is acceptable— the child cannot be changed and the teacher–therapist *should not* tell the child what is being done wrong. He or she simply must suffer the social consequences of misbehavior. Importantly, no attempt should be made to adjust those consequences. However, the child should be asked repeatedly for a value judgment until he or she can recognize the advantages of an honest appraisal of his or her activity.

If the child cannot select a better course of behavior, the teacher should offer alternatives. However, the child should select the actual course to be pursued. For example, a child who fights constantly at recess may not be able to formulate a plan to help him or her control this behavior. The teacher may suggest options such as going to recess with another class, remaining inside to assist the office staff with errands, or joining in recess activities but leaving the playground when angry feelings begin to develop. The child must select a preferred course of action and, in so doing, accept responsibility for avoiding fights.

If the child, after making a commitment for improvement, fails to keep the commitment, he or she must accept realistic consequences. The child who agrees to participate in recess activities until feeling angry, but who once again fights on the playground, has failed to keep the commitment. He or she may offer excuses, for example, he or she was attacked by someone, someone hit him or her with a ball, or he or she forgot not to fight. Though all these explanations may be true, none are acceptable. The ensuing discipline—restriction from recess activities for a day—must be enforced or the child will never develop the internalized controls to accept responsibility for personal behavior.

These simple procedures are predicated on the establishment of a warm, supportive relationship between the child and the teacher–therapist. It is essential that the child recognize that discipline does not convey dislike, and that, in fact, the teacher–therapist enforces discipline because she or he cares enough about the child to want him or her to change. Thus, the teacher–therapist must forego the luxury of feeling anger or outraged indignation when a child fails to keep a commitment. The child is involved in a painful process of new learning that cannot succeed if he or she isn't secure about the teacher–therapist's positive regard.

In *Schools Without Failure,* Glasser presents a plan for redirecting the focus of modern education. He believes that many emotional problems are instigated and nurtured by modern instructional procedures, which he sees as de-emphasizing thinking and problem solving in favor of rote memory activities. He offers a model of group meetings designed to teach children concepts like decision making, social responsibility, and cooperation. In short, concepts that currently are de-emphasized in competitive, achievement-oriented classrooms. His model involves three types of classroom meetings: the social-problem-solving meeting (most important for the purpose of this book), the open-ended meeting, and the educational-diagnostic meeting.

The social-problem-solving meeting deals with the individual and group problems of the class and school. They are designed to teach children to assume some degree of control over their own destiny. Issues such as class attendance, grades, and individual behavior problems may all be introduced. The discussion *should* be directed toward problem solving, and *should not* affix blame, provide an outlet for griping, or culminate in punishment. Specific problem behavior by a given child is a legitimate topic but should be discussed during one meeting only. It should not remain a topic of discussion over additional meetings unless the problem child has done something positive that deserves recognition. Meetings should not seek to find perfect answers to problems, but should clarify that many problems have no correct solution and must be met with the alternatives that are most helpful. The benefits to the children lie in thinking and discussing problems and in recognizing the fact that there is more than one way of dealing with them.

Open-ended meetings are not directed at problem solving but are for the discussion of any thought-provoking question related to the children's lives. In these situations, the teacher is not looking for factual answers but is trying to stimulate thought.

Educational-diagnostic meetings are related directly to content being studied by the class. They provide a means other than objective testing to ascertain whether or not the children are mastering the information being taught. They too provide an atmosphere for free discussion and relieve the children of the burden of being wrong. They should never be used to grade children but simply to learn how much they really understand.

To conduct these meetings, Glasser recommends that the teacher and students be seated in a tight circle. The teacher should sit in a different place each day and should arrange the children to reduce the possibility of problems arising. The meetings should be short, 10 to 30 minutes for primary children, 30 to 45 minutes for older children, and should be held regularly; once a day for elementary students and two to three times a week for secondary students. Topics for discussion may be introduced by the teacher or by the children. Initially the teacher may need to take much of the responsibility for topic selection as the children will be reticent until they become familiar with the operation. In addition the teacher should be prepared for initial difficulty in eliciting open discussion by the children. They are not accustomed to having an open format for their opinions in school and it takes them some time to learn to contribute. Open-ended questions such as "Suppose I were to select two children to accompany me to the zoo? Who should I select?", serve to stimulate discussion. Another method is to use argumentative questions such as "Are poor people lazy?", "Are people on welfare lazy?", or "What would you do if you had a million dollars?"

Practical issues such as when to talk can be solved by having the children raise their hands. This method also prevents certain children from dominating the sessions. Also, reluctant speakers who fail to volunteer might be brought into the discussion by a remark such as "You are listening carefully, would you like to comment?" It is important that the teacher always be supportive of the children's efforts and that no attempt be made to criticize them. Children whose remarks are overly personal or boring to the group may be stopped with a polite "Thank you for your comments, let's hear from someone else now."

Glasser's techniques are not complex. They are direct and designed for educational application. Like Ellis, he views therapy as the business of teachers. In fact, he believes that teachers have an advantage in working with disturbed children—they see them on a daily basis and can establish a trusting relationship very quickly. The group situations obviously are to be applied with all students to promote more constructive problem-solving efforts. However, the key to changing maladaptive behavior is the application of the principles of *right-wrong, responsibility,* and *reality* through questioning and discipline.

COMPARISON OF APPROACHES

To briefly contrast these two approaches, Ellis's ideas are much more thoroughly evolved and reflect much greater concern with altering the underlying causes (negative self-talk) of behavior. Ellis believes that changing self-talk causes changes in behavior.

Glasser attends basically to the consequences of behavior and takes the behavioristic position that changes in behavior bring about changes in feeling. It appears that, although Glasser reports effectiveness with adolescents (1975), his approach might have the greatest effectiveness with young children who can not understand the logic associated with Ellis's self-talk hypothesis. It also might be particularly effective when the therapist has great control over the consequences of irresponsibility. For example, Glasser's discipline would be effective at an institution for delinquents, where uncooperative individuals can be restricted, but would be far less effective in a situation where the therapist had no such controls.

In contrast, Ellis's techniques might be more applicable with older children in instances where behavior change depended on internal events rather than control of external contingencies. In any event, both Glasser's and Ellis's approaches are useful in educational settings. Obviously, the clever teacher can draw upon Glasser's structure for group meetings and use either rational–cognitive approach. The basic tenets of both approaches: (1) of demonstrating how the person's maladaptive behaviors harm him or her, and (2) of insisting that the individual is responsible for his or her behavior, and (3) of insisting that the individual can change behavior if an honest commitment to do so is made, are totally in keeping with basic educational philosophy of growth through learning.

STUDY QUESTIONS

1. Discuss the basic tenets of rational–cognitive therapy.
2. Compare and contrast the tenets underlying rational–cognitive therapy with those underlying behavioral therapy.
3. Describe how thoughts can cause emotional disturbance.
4. According to Glasser, how are three basic tenets: reality, responsibility, and right-and-wrong, related to emotional disturbance?

5. Discuss the similarities and differences between Ellis's and Glasser's theories.

6. Describe how the rational–cognitive approach can be integrated into a comprehensive school-based program for emotionally disturbed children.

REFERENCES

Ellis, A. *How to live with a neurotic.* New York: Crown, 1957.

Ellis, A. *Sex without guilt.* New York: Lyle Stuart, 1958.

Ellis, A. *The art and science of love.* New York: Lyle Stuart, 1960.

Ellis, A. *Reason and emotion in psychotherapy.* New York: Lyle Stuart, 1962.

Ellis, A. Rational-emotive therapy. In L. Hersher (ed.). *Four psychotherapies.* New York: Appleton-Century-Crofts, 1970.

Ellis, A. *Growth through reason.* Palo Alto, Cal.: Science and Behavior Books, 1971.

Ellis, A. *How to master your fear of flying.* New York: Curtis, 1972.

Ellis, A. Psychotherapy and the value of a human being. In J. W. Davis (ed.). *Value and valuation: essays in honor of Robert S. Hartman,* Knoxville: University of Tennessee Press, 1972.

Ellis, A. *Humanistic psychotherapy. The rational-emotive approach.* New York: Julian, 1973.

Ellis, A., and Harper, R. *A new guide to rational living.* Hollywood, Cal.: Melvin Powers, 1975.

Glasser, W. *Reality therapy.* New York: Harper & Row, 1965.

Glasser, W. *Schools without failure.* New York: Harper & Row, 1969.

Hartman, R. *The measurement of value.* Crotonville, N.Y.: General Electric Co., 1959.

Maultsby, M. Systematic written homework in psychotherapy. *Psychotherapy: Theory, Research and Practice.* 1971, 8(3), 195–198.

Peale, N. *The power of positive thinking.* Englewood Cliffs, N.J.: Prentice-Hall, 1952.

Wolpe, J. *Theme and variations: a behavior therapy casebook.* New York: Pergamon, 1976.

9
Milieu Therapy[*]

Milieu therapy is a generic concept implying the creation of a social organization for the express purpose of providing a treatment program for groups of people. The concept has grown out of a belief that social-psychological forces play an important and active part in both the causes of disturbed behavior and in its eventual treatment. The structure needed to organize a treatment program and to provide the social relationships necessary is called the *therapeutic milieu* or the *therapeutic community*.

Several aspects of milieu therapy will be covered in this chapter: the development of the concept, components of the therapeutic milieu, the life-space interview, crisis intervention, ecological models (specifically Project Re-ED), therapeutic camping, and a general discussion applying the theories to the school setting.

THE DEVELOPMENT OF THE CONCEPT OF THE THERAPEUTIC MILIEU

In the eighteenth and early nineteenth centuries, a humanistic, social philosophy surrounded the care of the mentally ill in Europe. Essentially, the philosophy held that mentally ill people were susceptible to and unable to cope with ordinary environmental stresses that did not disturb well-adjusted people. Thus, disturbed people could be helped by being taught to cope with stress-inducing environmental influences. This attitude of social responsibility faded with the advent of the medical model in the late nineteenth century when the two-person treatment, psychotherapy emerged.

---

* This chapter was co-authored by Judith Levitan and Phyllis L. Newcomer.

The philosophy was reborn in England in 1946, when Dr. Thomas F. Main, an army psychiatrist, coined the term *therapeutic community* when writing about residential centers created to handle the enormous numbers of emotionally disturbed military personnel that emerged from World War II (Rossi and Filstead, 1973). In the therapeutic community, therapy was an ongoing social process throughout the day, not an isolated verbal exchange between patient and psychiatrist. The staff and patients interacted freely in all aspects of normal living, and the responsibility for improved behavior and better adjustment were equally shared by all. For some reason, possibly because there was a great shortage of psychiatrists, or because there was a true belief that social factors and group treatment could facilitate a return to normal life, these wards were created throughout England, Scotland, and France, both in hospitals and as self-contained treatment centers. These centers not only provided psychiatric treatment, but also attempted to resettle patients in the communities where they had previously failed to adjust. The techniques used to change social attitudes within the hospital community aided in changing general social attitudes in the community at large.

The concept of the therapeutic community continued to develop and grow under the leadership of Dr. Maxwell Jones, who wrote extensively on the subject and who headed two residential programs in England. Not only were his patients involved in an in-hospital community with a definite group culture, but they were expected to participate in a vocational program usually outside of the hospital. Jones felt that although the work goal was difficult for the patient, it was a realistic part of therapy and added to the success of the program (Jones, 1953).

Jones also believed it was important to involve the family in the treatment process. Patients were encouraged to return home for periodic visits and were helped to deal with the problems they experienced. Family members were counseled as a prelude to the patient's eventual release. Thus, Jones created a bridge between the therapeutic hospital community and the patient's natural family setting. The hospital community in which the patient temporarily lived and the social and vocational milieu to which he or she must return, were all components of treatment.

Interestingly, Main and Jones, both psychiatrists, differed in their feelings about the role that classical psychotherapy should play in the therapeutic community. Main found the two therapies entirely compatible. In fact, one of his reasons for establishing therapeutic communities for former military personnel was the lack of psychiatrists available after the war (Main, 1946). Jones, on the other hand, believed that traditional psychotherapy had limited value, particularly in the hospital setting. Although the psychiatrist played an active role in Jones's model, it consisted primarily of casual contacts with a patient or with groups of patients in the therapeutic community rather than of the traditional individual hour-long session held once or twice a week (Jones, 1953). The doctor's supportive role was linked to his or her social role in the community. Although Jones was not against psychiatric intervention, he felt that social and environmental dimensions played a much more important role in the rehabilitation of socially disturbed adults (Jones, 1968).

In America, the concept of the therapeutic community received only nominal attention until the late 1950's and early 1960's. Prior to that time, only Bettelheim and Silvester (1948) made any substantial reference to the notion of a therapeutic milieu. They discussed establishing a therapeutic milieu in the Orthogenic School at the University of Chicago to avoid the syndrome, "psychological institutionalism," found among many children in typical hospital-like settings. According to Bettelheim, psychological institutionalism is the impoverishment of personality that results from the lack of a warm, trusting personal interaction between patient and therapist. Therefore, in Bettelheim's model of milieu therapy, unlike later models, the most important aspect of the therapeutic community was the establishment of a relationship between the patient and the counselor. It was less important that the severely disturbed children establish themselves as members of a social community than that they form a one-to-one relationship with an understanding and flexible adult.

Further development of the therapeutic milieu concept in the European tradition occurred with the work of Fritz Redl. In 1959 he published an article entitled, "The Concept of the 'Therapeutic Milieu,'" which presented twelve variables that should be included in an artificially created milieu for disturbed children in a residential setting. These variables will be discussed later in this chapter.

Long before this article appeared, Redl was exploring the rationale of clinically exploiting the life events of children in a residential setting. In 1946, Redl began Pioneer House, a group home for a small number of severely disturbed children. In what he called "a hygienically prepared climate," Redl structured the entire environment of the home, to program for ego support and to use the group atmosphere as a diagnostic and therapeutic tool. Redl had three major goals for Pioneer House: to know what these children were really like, to know what needed to be done to change their surface behavior so that therapy could begin, and to design a long-range therapy for their treatment (1951).

Redl takes note of Bettelheim's term "milieu therapy," in his early book on Pioneer House, *Children Who Hate*. Whereas Bettelheim thought of the milieu only as exposure to a total environment designed specifically for treatment, Redl felt that the prepared milieu could include part of the child's natural environment such as a therapy group once a week or a specifically designed summer camp. Its application in the school setting becomes a real possibility under these circumstances. Redl felt, however, that for the severely disturbed child the residential treatment design is the most supportive and effective way to provide treatment.

Redl does not eliminate psychotherapy as a treatment resource in the social milieu. However, he points out that most of the emotionally disturbed children in residential treatment centers are poor candidates for classical psychiatric treatment. Not only are they often nonverbal, but the enormous experiential gap between their natural life-style and the atmosphere of the psychiatrist's office creates total lack of relevance for the child (Redl, 1951). Their acting-out behaviors are often so destructive that the psychiatrist cannot function in his or her traditional role. Therefore, the prepared environment of the therapeutic community where treatment can be ongoing, twenty-four hours a day, in the child's own life setting, is, according to Redl, a much more valid model.

THE THERAPEUTIC MILIEU: WHAT IT INCLUDES

The therapeutic milieu is usually thought of as a residential treatment program where staff has total control over the patient's environment. Redl, however, points out that understanding what constitutes a residential treatment milieu for severely disturbed children can aid in the designing of school and community programs for less disturbed children and also can help in establishing preventive programs for all children (Redl, 1966). There are many therapeutic milieu models in existence today, particularly in drug- and alcohol-treatment centers and in psychiatric hospitals. However, this chapter will concentrate on Redl's model, since it deals exclusively with children and it lends itself to wide application outside of the hospital or residential setting.

Redl includes twelve variables in the therapeutic milieu: the social structure; the value system; routines, rituals, and behavioral regulations; the impact of the group process; the trait clusters; the staff, their attitudes and feelings; behavior received; activity structure and nature of constituent performances; space, equipment, time, and props; the seepage from the world outside; the system of umpiring services and traffic regulations between environment and child; and the thermostat for the regulation of clinical resilience (Redl, 1959a).[1]

The Social Structure   The typical hospital setting is oriented toward a fixed-status hierarchy, beginning with the doctor at the top, progressing downward with the nurse and culminating with the patient. Each member has a prescribed role, and the patient relates in a fixed, dependent

---

[1] Source: Redl, F. The Concept of a Therapeutic Milieu. *American Journal of Orthopsychiatry,* 1959. Reprinted with permission from the author and the *American Journal of Orthopsychiatry:* copyright 1959 by the American Orthopsychiatric Association, Inc.

manner. Redl suggests that a better structure resembles that of an American summer camp where many adults, the counselors, cooks, office staff, teachers, and so on, touch the children's lives. This type of environment forces the child to learn about people's professional and social roles and to determine which individual can help him or her with problems, who has the authority to make decisions, and so on.

The social structure is organized to take advantage of the natural relationships among the patients and among the patients and the staff. The idea is to maintain a social structure that resembles the child's real world, not to create an artificial environment. Thus, the children must interact with a variety of other individuals and not passively allow things to be done *to* them by adults in command. They must become active agents of their own treatment.

In these treatment centers, the usual hospital class system is overcome by establishing patient governments and community meetings where the patients have a great deal to say about how the community is to be run (Rossi and Filstead, 1973).

The Value System   Children are acutely aware of the real values of the adults who deal with them. When an adult's comments do not represent his or her real values, the child becomes aware of it. On the other hand, if an adult is truly concerned with a child's well being, it can be made known to the child even though the adult seems to be acting contrary to the child's wishes. For example, the adult who stops a child from banging his or her head against the wall makes it clear that his or her interest is in the welfare of the child and not the preservation of the wall.

Routines, Rituals, and Behavioral Regulations   Redl states that all individuals have rituals or repetitive behaviors in their life space. Many individual rituals may need to be discouraged. However, others can be used therapeutically and can promote a sense of security and adaptation to the milieu. Redl cites an example of a routine developed in one setting that involved rubbing the children's backs before they went to bed at night. Not only did this routine relax the children, but it presented a time for quiet talk that often led to important revelations between adult and child. Routines will exist in any therapeutic milieu, but there is no formula describing how many or how few should be included.

The Impact of the Group Process   Redl lists several components of the group process: "over-all group atmosphere, scapegoating, mascot cultivation, subclique formation, group-psychological role suction, exposure to group-psychological intoxication, dependency on contagion clusters, leadership tensions and so forth" (1959a, p. 723). These aspects of group interaction often are difficult to identify, but they are as much a part of the child's surroundings as the food he or she eats. Many of these components will be explained later in this chapter.

The Trait Clusters Although the therapeutic milieu is built around a group concept, there is no question that each individual reacts to other individual personalities as well as to the group. Redl claims that an individual's personality traits "swing . . . around his body like a wet bathing towel, and they are going to hit whoever gets in its path" (1959a, p. 729). To create a useful milieu, personality traits must be considered as psychological entities. It is very possible that one child's particular personality can raise havoc with another's. It would be foolish to place two children whose personalities obviously clash, together as roomates. The therapeutic community affords each member the possibility of forming relationships with those he or she is most attracted to and of learning to avoid conflict with those whose personalities clash with his or her own.

The Staff, Their Attitudes and Feelings The attitudes and feelings of the staff are perhaps the most important component of the milieu. When Redl speaks of staff, he means everyone who comes in contact with the child: psychiatrists, psychologists, teachers, aides, medical personnel, dieticians, cooks, and so on. The staff must be able to give emotionally, to share feelings and opinions, and to communicate with understanding and without judgment.

Behavior Received Each child receives behaviors and feelings from other children, as well as from the staff. The underlying feelings are as important, if not more so, than what is actually physically done to or for the child. The staff has to try to help the patient sort out the behaviors received from others and to react to them in a beneficial way.

Activity Structure and Nature of Constituent Performances A large part of the impact of the milieu on a child are the things he or she is asked or allowed to do. Exposing an emotionally disturbed child to games or activities that have rules and regulations is of clinical significance. Certain kinds of constituent performances are required, and the way a child learns to meet expectations has a great impact on the milieu at large as well as on the child's own life space.

Space, Equipment, Time, and Props The distribution of time and the arrangement of space and equipment are important properties of the milieu. A staff member must be sure that sufficient time exists to accomplish his or her goals. If he or she has begun to discuss an important problem with a group of children and the bell rings for swimming, then the effort should not have been made. The children will not attend to him or her. It also is necessary to use good judgment when selecting a place for a discussion. If a child is given an intense life-space interview in a gym filled with tantalizing sports equipment, the effort is in vain. The child's attention will be focused on a basketball, hockey stick, or some other attractive distraction.

The Seepage from the World Outside   No matter how insulated a residential program may seem, it is not a vacuum. Outside influences enter through television, movies, and visitors, and through stories the children and staff tell each other. Other types of planned outside influences are introduced through trips and walks in the neighborhood. Both planned and unplanned outside influences constitute a real impact on the milieu and need to be accounted for in the planning of any therapeutic community.

The System of Umpiring Services and Traffic Regulations Between Environment and Child   This system takes two forms. The first involves protecting a child from a situation or from other children, particularly if he or she is new to the program. The second is to interpret experiences that a child may not understand. Although some "milieu impacts" hit children like the proverbial ton of bricks, and need no explanation to illustrate the lesson to be learned, others are more subtle. To have any influence on the child they need interpretation.

The Thermostat for the Regulation of Clinical Resilience   This variable refers to flexibility. The milieu must reflect the changing needs of the children who are part of it. Not only individual children, but entire groups change over a period of time. If the milieu is rigid and does not consider the needs of its members, it cannot have the kind of therapeutic influence it should.

These twelve variables describe Redl's basis for the therapeutic community in a residential setting. However, many features of the total therapeutic milieu are applicable to school settings. Rossi and Filstead (1973) relate these premises to school environments and define the therapeutic community as a "method of organizing the social structure of a treatment setting to cultivate and take advantage of natural social relationships." They point out that a teacher, whether in a mainstreamed or self-contained special-education class, can adapt these principles and use the class and school milieu in a therapeutic way.

Redl and Wattenberg (1959) suggest several ways that a teacher can focus on the individuals in his or her class as members of a group.

1. *Sociometric studies:* The use of a sociogram or friendship chart can be very revealing to a teacher who may not be aware of anything but the most obvious relationships in the class. Asking questions such as "Who would you like to sit next to you?", "Which children in the class would you like to have spend the weekend with you?", "Who would you least like to have sit with you at lunch?" can give the teacher insight into the entire social structure of the class. The construction of a sociogram (illustrated in Chapter 4) can make the teacher aware of the friendless children who would like to relate to other children. It also will reveal the patterns of negative and positive social relationships in the group.

2. *The group as an organism:* A class generally assumes its own distinctive personality after being together for a considerable amount of time, for example, some classes are competitive, others are cooperative. Although it may be difficult to predict what personality a group will assume, there are often indications that can be drawn from the group's previous behavior. Placing an emotionally disturbed child in a class that appears able to accommodate him or her may make a great deal of difference in the child's behavior.

3. *Cliques and subgroups:* The personality of a group is due in part to the cliques and subgroups that form within it. Cliques vary in their attitudes and behaviors. A troubled child must be placed in a receptive clique or subgroup. Practical events such as carefully selecting a child's class seat, lunch hour, or gym or reading group may enable a teacher to attach the child to a group whose influence will be beneficial or to remove him or her from one that is harmful.

4. *Role concepts and expectations:* Role expectations affect the tone of the whole group as well as individual members. For example, a particular clique may think of themselves as leaders and work hard to maintain the role. Individuals, too, fall into certain role classifications. Redl lists five that can be found in most classes: (1) *Leaders*—In some groups, the leader remains constant, whereas in others the role is assumed by many different people. Redl describes a leader as a superior group member, exceeding the other members in intelligence, scholarship, responsibility, social participation, and socioeconomic status. However, he also points out that not all groups will tolerate a "superior leader." In some cases, a group selects an individual who is deficient in the above characteristics and who exerts a negative influence on them. When this occurs, as it does often in school situations, the teacher has to analyze the sources of the leader's power. Is he or she using fear tactics or blackmail? It may then be necessary for the teacher to destroy the leader's influence by direct intervention or exposure. (2) *Advocates*—Some children, who may not themselves be leaders, may be thought of as such because they are facile and creative talkers. They become the negotiators or lawyers for the group. The adult, however, must realize that their influence over the group may not be very strong. (3) *Clowns*—These children are generally placed in this position by the group. Their sense of humor usually is leveled at themselves and self-display tactics frequently are used to draw attention away from the group. Often, but not always, the clown is very fat or very thin and many times feels inferior in some way. Occasionally, the class clown sets himself or herself up as a reliever of tension, which can be a positive factor for the group. The teacher needs to understand this child's motivation to help the child understand his or her own behavior. (4) *Fall guys*—In some cases, the child who

takes the blame for the group's mistakes is satisfied by this role because she or he may feel that it impresses the group. The teacher should recognize that in most cases this is a weak and often incompetent child who thinks of herself or himself as a dope and therefore feels she or he deserves everything she or he gets. The teacher must be careful not to place the blame where it is so easily laid, but to find the real source of the problem. (5) *Instigators*—These children often are responsible for class problems, but they are careful to remove themselves from direct involvement. The teacher must expose these tactics so that the group, and particularly the fall guy, can disengage from the instigator. It is also necessary for this kind of child to understand what he or she is doing and to know that suggestions of wrong doing are often more serious than the actual deeds.

5. *Group Atmosphere and Group Morale*   The atmosphere and morale of a group are extremely important when setting up a therapeutic milieu. There are various ways that a teacher can change or influence the social climate of a classroom. The first way is by lessening control of the classroom activities. A teacher-directed class provides few free choices to children and differs dramatically from an open, individually paced program with activities that require little teacher intervention. The second way is to lessen his or her role as the center of attention in the class. In a teacher-centered class, a child must wait until the teacher tells him or her whether he or she is right or wrong, acceptable or unacceptable. In a learner-centered class, where problem solving is a goal, the teacher reassures rather than directs. Relationships are as important as completing certain tasks. The third teacher influence over the social climate involves the group morale. The morale of the group is determined largely by the teacher's attitude toward the children. The teacher may be cynical or enthusiastic. She or he may regard it as a sin to be "different" or may encourage creativity. She or he may attend excessively to one child's poor behavior and thereby cause it to spread to other children.

Obviously, although the concept of the therapeutic milieu implies a total community in a residential treatment center, many of its concepts can be applied to group situations in other environments. Examining class groups and school atmospheres and employing tactics such as the life-space interview make it possible to create supportive and therapeutic environments in school settings.

Redl (1966, p. 68) suggests that it "might pay . . . to learn from the problems that emerge in the treatment of the sick what needs to be known in order to plan the life of the healthy."

THE LIFE-SPACE INTERVIEW

Perhaps the most important component of the therapeutic milieu as Fritz Redl conceived it is the life-space interview. Although occasionally the impact of the environment is enough therapy for a given child, more often it takes a trained adult to serve as mediator between the environment and the child. The child's experiences in the therapeutic milieu may go unnoticed if there is no interpretation of those events. Even in an ordinary school environment, an adult's well-thought-out reaction to an event can clarify it for a child and prevent misinterpretation.

In contrast to the interview techniques used in traditional psychotherapy that refer to events long since past, the life-space interview is based on immediate events in the child's life. A particular incident serves as the focus of the interview that is held immediately after, and in the same vicinity of, the incident. In most cases, the interview is held by a person who is part of the child's life-space and who has directly observed or even participated in the event leading up to the interview. Although Redl developed his method of interviewing in a residential setting, he makes it clear that the techniques are entirely applicable to both the school and the home setting (1966).

Redl (1959b) divides the goals of the life-space interview into two categories: clinical exploitation of life events and emotional first aid on the spot. The difference between the two goals depends upon the demands of the particular situation and the manner in which the interviewer wants to deal with the event.

Clinical Exploitation of Life Events

This category involves using a situation to focus the child's attention on reality and meet a long-term treatment goal. According to Redl, this strategy has various components. They can be used alone or in combination whenever an opportune life event presents itself.

1. *Reality rub-in:* Some children consistently distort the reality of an event to protect their egos. In this phase of the life-space interview, the adult on the spot must immediately focus the child's attention on the meaning of a sequence of events so that there can be no misinterpretation. The child must be helped to see the relationships between behavior and realistic consequences.

2. *Symptom estrangement:* Some children have learned to use the symptoms of their disturbance for their own benefit. In the past, much of the attention they have received has been in response to their pathological symptoms. In the life-space interview, these events are discussed to illustrate the fact that they pay few dividends to the child. For example, a child may be shown that his or her aggressive behaviors in-

variably land him or her in trouble. An alternate reaction to anger, such as telling a counselor about his or her feelings, might have a more beneficial pay off.

3. *Massaging numb value areas:* No matter how emotionally disturbed these children may be, Redl believes that there are still areas of value sensitivity that can be appealed to. Using various events from daily life, it is possible to use the interview technique to point out and appeal to certain codes of fairness or other values. Particularly in fight situations, any value sensitivity that the child has can be exploited through the interview technique. For example, a child might be reached because he or she really thinks it's wrong to hit smaller children.

4. *New tool salesmanship:* The life-space interview, drawing on life experiences, can immediately teach a child that there is more than one way to handle a given situation. Although classical therapy often emphasizes the fact that there are other defenses besides the ones a child has been using, the life-space interview moves to the practical demonstration of the inadequacy of the defenses a child has chosen.

5. *Manipulation of the boundaries of the self:* For the child usually exploited by stronger peers, some life incidents can be used to give a feeling of self-worth and to allow an expansion of feelings for himself or herself. For instance, a child's good performance on a test can serve as a praiseworthy incident. In the same vein, expanding the child's boundaries to include other caring people can encourage the development of a healthier attitude of self-worth and pride.

Each of the above forms of life-space interviewing makes it possible to move toward the goal of clinical exploitation of life events. In other words, the aim of this type of interview is to use momentary life experiences to accomplish long-range therapeutic goals, as opposed to the temporary relief that is sought in the following techniques.

Emotional First Aid on the Spot

This use of interviewing is designed to give immediate support to a child in a stressful situation without the added purpose of a long-term therapeutic goal. Although the children that Redl treated while developing the goals of the life-space interview were extremely disturbed, they were still growing youngsters. Often with these children, as with other less disturbed children, situations arose that needed to be dealt with on the spot and that offered no long-range gains. For example, a child being picked on by two larger children needs to be rescued from the situation and given support by an adult. The child is not capable of dealing with involved interviews. Probably the other two children can benefit from clinical exploration of the event. Redl enumerates five subcategories under the goal of emotional first aid on the spot.

1. *Drain off of frustration acidity:* In this case, the life-space interview becomes a hygienic device for the draining off of anger resulting from the frustration of being interrupted from some pleasurable activity. Especially in situations where something the child has planned on has gone wrong, the sympathy or genuine sharing of indignation with an adult helps to drain off hostility and avoid adding to an already well-stocked storehouse of hate.

2. *Support for the management of panic, fury, and guilt:* Because these children cannot handle highly charged emotional states, Redl suggests that it is important that an adult remain with a child while he or she goes through a tantrum so that immediate aid and therapeutic support can be given when the attack is over. It is necessary that the child know that he or she will be protected, not only from the attacks of other children, but also from his or her own highly charged emotions, and that he or she will be helped to put things back in focus and return to the day's events without suffering from guilt or hostility.

3. *Communication maintenance in moments of relationship decay:* The most feared reaction to an emotional experience in disturbed children is the autisticlike withdrawal and breaking off of all communication to which many are prone. At the point where a child is ready to withdraw from reality, the life-space interviewer must keep communication flowing on any subject, no matter how trival or how removed from the point it seems to be.

4. *Regulation of behavioral and social traffic:* In any community, therapeutic or not, certain rules and regulations are necessary for the well being of all. The children may know the rules of the community but the extent to which they have internalized them may depend on the severity of their disturbance. It is a function of the life-space interviewer to remind the children of the rules of the social structure in a benign and guiding way. Moralizing or preaching have no place in the therapeutic milieu.

5. *Umpire services—in decision crises as well as in loaded transactions:* Umpiring can take two different forms; first, helping the child decide between his or her worse or better self, and, second, physically mediating in fights, conflicts, and any tension-loaded situations in the child's life.

Both of these goals, clinical exploitation and emotional first aid, may be found in the same interview, and the interviewer may find that he or she switches from one to the other, depending on many factors. Regardless of the goal, Redl has devised various criteria for conducting the interview. In the first, *central theme relevance,* Redl cautions against moving in for a life-space interview too often or for too shallow a reason. A child's momentary misbehavior in the classroom does not warrant an interview. A child, either in a residential treatment center or a classroom situation, can become immune to adult intervention if it is overdone and the point of life-space interviewing can easily be lost.

The second criterion, *ego proximity and issue clarity,* involves making the choice between whether an issue is relevant for an interview and needs attention right away or whether it is too threatening and should be left alone. It also cautions against choosing issues cluttered with sub-issues that are so distracting that the child would have a great deal of trouble focusing on the central theme. For instance, if a child has been fighting over the last piece of cake at the dinner table and another child has gotten it, it would probably not be a good time for a life-space interview. The child's attention will be focused on the loss of the piece of cake and not aggressive behavior.

Third, the *role compatibility* of the interviewer and the child can affect the outcome of an interview. Because the child has expectations of the role a certain adult will play in his or her life, it is important that the adult interviewer not overstep the boundaries of that role. An interview held by a teacher would differ from that conducted by a parent or a camp counselor even though the incident precipitating the interview might be the same.

The fourth criterion, *mood manageability—the child's and our own,* speaks for itself. Even though the issue may be perfect for an interview, if the child (or the interviewer) is bored, tired, grouchy, or overexcited it would be better to wait for another occasion to arise.

Fifth, *issues around timing,* are what set the life-space interview apart from other interview techniques. The child does not have to remember what happened on Saturday to tell the therapist on Tuesday; he or she is able to discuss it on the spot. Even if emotional first aid has to be used to calm the child down so that in the future the impact of that event can be discussed with some insight, the initial interview takes place directly following the event. The interviewer needs also to be sensitive to whether the time is right to conduct an interview. If the bell for recess has just rung and the child's entire class has just run outside to play, any interview conducted will be a wasted effort.

The last criterion, *the impact of terrain and of props,* is important, but because of the immediacy of the life-space interview is usually beyond the interviewer's control. Although the site is germane to the success or failure of an interview, it is apt to be anywhere from underneath a desk to the child's bathtub. Redl (1959b, p. 17)[2] summarizes by saying:

> The choice of a given technique must be dependent on the specific goal we have in mind within a given phase of his therapeutic movement. There is no "odd" or "bad" technique in itself. The very procedure that "made" one situation all by itself may be the source of a mess-up in another or may have remained irrelevant in a third. This reminder, although disappointing, would not be too hard to take, for we have learned that lesson from the development of concepts of strategy and techniques for the psychiatric interview long ago. Rather than relearn it, we simply need to remember the difference between a pseudoscientific technical trick-bag, and a more complex, but infinitely more realistic concept of multiple-item conditioned choice of criteria for the selection of strategy as well as of techniques.

Although Redl does suggest that the life-space interview can be used in the school setting for both disturbed and healthy children (1969), he implies that it is most useful in a crisis situation as an intervention and learning tool.

William Morse (1969) calls for the use of the life-space interview by classroom teachers not only in crisis incidents, but in less emotionally charged situations with normal children experiencing some type of problems. Morse believes that many techniques commonly used by teachers have little effect on today's children, particularly those with adjustment problems. He suggests the theoretical framework of the life-space interview for working through problems that occur in any classroom.

According to Morse, teachers first must accept the concept of the school as a large part of the child's milieu. Second, teachers must be sensitive to the child's behavior as a reflection of his or her life-space and must learn to interpret it as a cue to how he needs to be handled. Third, teachers must be able to put themselves in the child's position and understand how the child expresses feelings through social behavior, language, gesture, and so on. With experience, a teacher, aide, or principal can learn to look beyond surface behavior to what motivates the child to manipulate his or her life-space.

To be effective, a teacher needs a theoretical framework for interviewing, and Redl's concept provides such a framework. However, along with the theory, the teacher needs guidelines or operational steps. Morse (1976b) provides a worksheet on life-space interviewing to help teachers

---

[2] Reprinted, with permission, from the author and from the *American Journal of Orthopsychiatry:* copyright 1959 by the American Orthopsychiatric Association, Inc.

implement the technique. Seven steps with goals and processes are presented, not necessarily as a set sequence, but as a guide.

1. *Instigating condition:* The interview begins with an incident that calls for intervention by the teacher. In a nonmoralistic, nonthreatening way, the teacher listens to the child's (or group's) perception of the event. The child's psychological perception of the event becomes much more important than the usual, "who did what first and why" stories that teachers often encourage. Generally, the teacher's ability to listen establishes a relationship with a child because it shows interest in his or her opinions. As Morse has said, "to listen is to accept: it requires empathic feeling" (1976b, p. 338).[3]

2. *Testing for depth and spread:* In this case, the teacher looks for problems related to the event chosen for interview. Was it an isolated incident? Does it represent a more extensive problem? Is it a symbol of something basic to the child's life? What is the real reason for the child's explosive reaction? Again, the teacher's ability to listen without assuming responsibility for providing a solution, can allow the child to expose important and meaningful material.

3. *Content clarification:* This part of the interview is unlike the traditional approach to discipline where morality and compliance is the goal. Neither is it like psychological counseling, where fantasy, dreams, and conflicts are taken into consideration. Instead, the emphasis is on a nonjudgmental discussion of the events. At this point the teacher may ask what the child thinks should be done about the situation. She or he may explore the child's values without imposing her or his own.

4. *Enhancing a feeling of acceptance:* Often at, or just before, this stage a possible solution to the problem has been reached. If the child is defensive and cannot propose a realistic solution, the teacher must respond to the feeling behind his or her defense and must not attack the defense itself. For example, in dealing with an aggressive child who insists on having no responsibility for a fight, the teacher must not attack the denial as untrue, but must deal with the underlying feelings—"you feel unable to admit that you began fighting."

5. *Avoiding early imposition of value judgments:* At this point the teacher should point out to the child that, although she or he accepts the child's perception of the event, others may perceive the event differently. The teacher should convey that she or he is not being judgmental, and should suggest coping skills that the child can use when similar situations arise.

---

[3] Morse, W. Worksheet on Life Space Interviewing for Teachers. In *Conflict in the Classroom*, 3rd ed. Belmont, CA.: Wadsworth, 1976. Reprinted with permission.

6. *Exploring the internal mechanics for "change" possibilities:* At this stage, the teacher and child explore ways to prevent or change what has been happening. This step is the time for realism and relevance. The teacher asks such questions as "What will happen if this incident is repeated?", "How can the teacher help?", "Who else can help?" The solutions explored by the child and teacher must fit realistically into the school milieu. The child must be encouraged to become more aware of the reality of his or her surroundings and the implication of his or her behavior on it.

7. *The two resolution phases:* In life-space interviewing there may be no resolution to the problem, although the children can gain support and may learn some coping behaviors. However, one of the goals of the interview should pertain to preventing a similar incident from recurring. Two processes may be used to obtain this goal. The first process involves presenting the adult point of view. This perspective of the situation reflects the reality of the child's milieu. For instance, the teacher might say "It is a school rule that fighting on the playground means no recess for two days." The presentation of the adult point of view should not appear to be a moralistic judgment of the child's behavior. It is simply a statement of fact—no more, no less.

The second resolution process includes strategic planning, working through to a solution. It is here that a realistic plan is worked out and all its implications are explained. The teacher may have to explain such things as what will happen if the behavior is repeated, if parents will be involved, if more intensive help is needed, and who is going to help the child carry out the plan. The child should be left with a feeling of support and solidarity from the milieu.

Brenner (1963) points out the difficulties of conducting life-space interviews in school settings. If there is no aide in the classroom, the best a teacher may be able to do is to take the troubled child into the hall for a few minutes to talk to him. Brenner suggests that schools should have a person to assist the teacher in crisis situations, to conduct life-space interviews if the teacher cannot get away from the class to do it himself or herself. In many cases, the natural person to handle crisis situations is the principal. If the principal and teacher are mutually supportive and if the principal does not think of herself or himself solely as a disciplinarian, she or he can effectively conduct a life-space interview. Brenner (1963) suggests ten points to make the interview useful to the child.[4]

---

[4] Abstracted with permission from the author and from the *American Journal of Orthopsychiatry:* copyright 1963 by the American Orthopsychiatric Association, Inc.

1. *Be polite:* Treat the child as you would the parent, listening to what he or she has to say and not answering your own questions to him or her.

2. *Don't tower over a little child:* Offer the child a chair and sit down on her or his level. Don't put a child in a situation where she or he feels trapped.

3. *When you are sure of your ground, it can be a good approach to confront a child with your knowledge of his or her misdeed:* This tack will not work with a child who thinks everyone is against him or her, but it can give most children a sense of security to know where they stand.

4. *Be sparing with your use of "why?":* It is better to suggest talking about what happened or, if that is not working, to suggest a solution rather than backing a child into a corner by asking why she or he thought of doing such a terrible thing.

5. *Get the conversation going about the actual situation:* Stay on the subject and listen to the child's description of the event.

6. *If you think a child is overwhelmed with guilt or shame, begin by minimizing the weightiness of the problem at hand:* Suggest that the child is not the only one who has been in this situation, that a solution is possible, and that you will work together to find it.

7. *Say what you know the child wants to say but can't put into words:* Such words as, "you were angry, weren't you?" or, "your feelings were hurt, weren't they?" are helpful because they are said without judgment, whereas, "you're sorry, aren't you?" might well be judgmental and is therefore less desirable.

8. *Be aware of the kinds of thinking demanded by the situation:* Beware of assuming that a young child's thinking resembles that of an adult. Don't put him or her in the position of having to work out a situation the way an adult might. He or she probably cannot do so.

9. *Help the child with plans for specific steps to improve the situation:* Some children become so frightened by what they think might happen at home that they cannot think rationally about a solution to the problem. Their anxiety must be reduced and they must feel assured that the teacher means to help before any solution can be found. In these cases, it often is best to assure the children that the problem will be handled at school.

10. *At some point in the interview, give the child an opportunity to ask you questions:* A lot of information can be gathered by listening to a child's questions. A frightened child may have blown an incident totally out of proportion and your answers may serve to put it in perspective.

These suggestions are given specifically for a principal or person who has not witnessed the actual situation, but who must conduct the interview. Of course, they can be used by the teacher or adult involved. It is most important that the teacher and principal work together to improve techniques such as the life-space interview that are helpful aids when working with disturbed children.

CRISIS INTERVENTION

Since many more regular classroom teachers will be faced with the problem of dealing with emotionally disturbed children because of the passage of P.L. 94–142, the crisis or helping teacher may become a necessary feature in many schools. A crisis teacher is not only trained in behavioral management, but is also a well-qualified remedial teacher who is available to offer immediate emotional and academic support to the child unable to cope with a particular situation.

The concept of crisis intervention was developed to meet the same needs that produced the life-space interview. However, rather than developing in a residential setting, crisis intervention developed in schools that maintained children in least-restrictive settings. Traditionally, within these schools a child in the throes of an emotional crisis was sent to the principal to be disciplined. As though by magic, these visits were expected to change the child into a "'good citizen" who would not misbehave again. These visits to the principal usually were removed from the situation where the emotional crisis occurred and sometimes took place hours or even days after the crisis.

Even when crises were dealt with more "therapeutically," the traditional approach was to focus on the immediate behavior during the upheaval and to delegate the real corrective therapy to an individual who would see the child at a later date. In crisis intervention, the helping teacher combines both steps: managing the surface behavior while dealing with the deeper significance of the incident.

Morse (1976) points out that even though a child may not be teachable in the immediate crisis situation, he needs to know on the spot how to cope with stressful situations. Inability to cope has produced the crisis in the first place. The use of crises as a resource for helping disturbed children was suggested by Caplan (1963). He noted that feelings such as guilt, shame, anger, fear, and anxiety throw the child into a state of confusion. By helping the child cope with these feelings, the crisis teacher can promote growth and change. Intervention is not only verbal; the environment also is manipulated to help provide change. The more traditional concept of cooling the child down before discussing the situation is reversed. The helping teacher may manipulate the environment by perpetuating the crisis, or even by creating a crisis to teach coping skills at the moment of greatest disequilibrium.

Morse (1976) states that the crisis or helping teacher (a more preferred term) works with children's emotional and academic problems. They often occur together, since severely disturbed children often are not able to cope with academic pressures any more effectively than they cope with social pressures. In fact, many crises are perpetuated by a child's frustration over academic failure. Morse advocates no single theoretical approach. The helping teacher must find the best possible technique to help a child cope with a particular problem. Thus, intervention can come in many forms: conducting a life-space interview, providing remedial instruction, or teaching simple study skills. It may involve the child's regular teacher, his or her friends and family, or it may involve only the child.

To provide the appropriate intervention at the appropriate time, the helping teacher must understand the child's milieu. He or she must know the curriculum in the child's regular classroom as well as life-space interviewing techniques. He or she must have a good relationship with classroom teachers, who have the most accurate ideas of the children's behavior patterns. She or he must not serve as a dumping ground or as a punitive agent for misbehaving children. Rather, the helping teacher should see only children who cannot cope with environmental events. Those children should be helped to return to their classrooms as soon as possible. In some cases that event will occur almost immediately, whereas in others it may take some time until the child feels able to cope with the precipitating problem.

The helping teacher must take on any role to help children cope with various problems: surrogate parent, therapist, and teacher. He or she must be a member of the school staff and not an itinerant teacher, in order to alter his or her role to meet the needs of the children. The helping teacher's primary obligation is to help find solutions to problems. He or she can function effectively only as part of a cooperative school milieu. The entire staff must be dedicated to assisting all children to function well in a regular class setting. Management procedures must be the result of total staff decisions. The helping teacher's specific contribution to the total effort is to help in problem solving and includes intervention at the moment of severe crisis.

Morse (1971) questions the effectiveness of the traditional school approach to crisis when the principal intervenes. He believes that unless a person is well versed in life-space interviewing techniques, the intervention is likely to be haphazard and will only curb the behavior, not change it. The helping teacher should have the skills to bring about behavioral change. The availability of this type of professional is critical because teachers of large classes that include emotionally disturbed children often need more than advice. They need the support and assistance of a person available at the moment of crisis to take advantage of the situation in the most effective way.

Little research has been done on the efficacy of the crisis intervention approach. The few studies available suggest that the technique helps children to increase self-esteem, motivation, and to establish social relationships (Morse, 1976).

ECOLOGICAL MODELS

The theory underlying the therapeutic community approach, that an emotionally disturbed child must be treated in his or her environment or milieu, essentially reflects an ecological or social-competence view of emotional disturbance. In general, the proponents of ecological theory reject both individual and group psychotherapy as viable methods of treatment. Hobbs, (1966), an ecological theorist, states that the early acceptance and commitment to psychotherapy stemmed from the belief that disturbed children had curable illnesses. Hobbs rejects the disability or medical view of emotional disturbance, arguing that disturbed children have learned bad habits from their interactions with the environment.

Rhodes (1967) also suggests that emotional disturbance is the result of a reciprocal relationship between the child and the environment. Both components, the environment and the child, contribute to the problem. Behavior that departs from that sanctioned by the culture disturbs conforming members of the society and generates certain reactions toward the nonconforming individual. In one society, deviant behavior may be defined as a crime, in another as a sin, and in a third as a sickness. Each society responds differently, depending on the accepted definition. For example, the sick person is cared for, the criminal punished, and so forth.

Clearly, from this perspective emotional disturbance must be regarded as culturally relative. For example, a child who moves from a tough innercity neighborhood where fighting is necessary for survival, to a suburban community where fighting is frowned on, obviously is not emotionally disturbed if he or she fights in school. He or she is reflecting unique cultural conditioning. Therefore, attempts to treat children's emotional problems must take into consideration not only the children, but the environmental forces surrounding them, including the other individuals disturbed by their behavior.

Hobbs states that the treatment of emotionally disturbed children must emphasize social realities as well as the individual's perception of events. The child is part of an ecological or social system that includes family, neighborhood, community, school, and often a social agency. Any goals for changing the child must involve strategies for adjusting the environment, the realities the child lives with. Rhodes and Paul (1978) point out that if the ecological view of emotional disturbance is valid, treatment of disturbed conditions is quite complex. It is relatively simple to change a child's view of his or her relationship to the environment, but it is much more difficult to change the environmental conditions that led to the problem in the first place. If the community can accept the fact that it contributed to the child's problem, it is feasible that changes can occur. The most important factor in effecting treatment is its focus. Instead of concentrating the total treatment effort toward changing the child, the emphasis must move toward the child's adaptation to his or her environment and vice versa. This focus has significant implications in school settings where the emphasis primarily has been on changing the child so that he or she fits into the system. The ecological position assumes that effecting behavioral change requires modification of the school setting as well as alteration of the child's reactions to the school.

PROJECT RE-ED

The best-known example of a therapeutic program based on ecological principles is project Re-ED, which stands for "a project for the Re-education of Emotionally Disturbed children." (Hobbs, 1969) Based partially on Hobbs's observation of both day schools and residential programs in Glasgow, Scotland, and in France, the concept for the project gradually emerged over a period of several years. The Re-ED model, as might be gathered from the name, views emotional disturbance as an educational problem rather than as an illness. Treatment involves relearning and a readjustment of the child's total social system, rather than psychoanalytic therapy.

Re-ED began in 1962–1963 with two schools, Cumberland House in Nashville, Tennessee and Wright School in Durham, North Carolina, funded through a grant from the National Institute of Mental Health. The children involved were between the ages of 6 and 12, had average or above-average intelligence, and displayed behavior problems that made it impossible to keep them in regular schools or community facilities. They resided at the Re-ED school during the five-day week and went home to their families on weekends. At the school the children were divided into groups comprised of eight to ten individuals. Each group was assigned to a team of teacher-counselors whom Hobbs (1974) describes as the heart of the Re-ED program.

Three teacher-counselors were assigned to each group of children: a day teacher-counselor, a night teacher-counselor, and a liaison teacher-counselor. These people, along with aides and special consultants, were totally responsible for the children in their group. The day teacher-counselor designed a program for each child based primarily on achieving competence in academic areas. The night teacher–counselor's role was to develop social and emotional competence. The liaison teacher-counselor was responsible for the children's ecological system or the children's relationship with individuals in their home, school, and community environment. All three members of the team worked to bring the children and their ecological systems into balance. Hobbs (1974, p. 156)[5] explains:

> Teacher-counselors work with increasingly well-defined and tested strategies. They are not concerned with psychodynamic formulation of a child's problem; rather they are concerned with the behaviors and expectations of those who define his life space here and now as well as in the future. . . . They work first to build trust, with the sure surmise that this is requisite to all further achievement. They are committed to the notion that life is to be lived *now*, not in the past nor in the distant future, but *now*—this ten minutes, this hour, this day—knowing that in the mastery of this hour, the child masters in principle the living of all hours . . . they modulate all events to the readiness for experience for each child, so that success, not failure, is the bright mark of most of every day for most of the children and for the teacher-counselors as well.

It is important to note that although the original concept of Re-ED was developed in residential settings, Hobbs made sure that those settings were part of the child's ecological system, not an escape from it. His goal was to make the system work without Re-ED. The philosophy underlying Re-ED was that the child remain in the program for as short a time as possible, only as long as it takes to readjust his or her ability to adapt to an environment that, it is hoped, has become better able to accept the child.

Although the techniques and practices for implementing Re-ED may change from program to program, or even group to group, certain basic educational assumptions are maintained. Hobbs (1966) lists twelve concepts that are at the core of the Re-ED process.

1. *Life is to be lived now.* The first assumption is that every moment is important to a child. Each hour is a special hour that needs to be filled with purposeful and consequential learning. Such learning is enhanced by the provision of opportunities for success that far surpass the possibilities of failure.

2. *Time is an ally.* This assumption reflects Hobbs's belief that treatment speeds up therapeutic processes that might occur naturally in many children and that a long stay in a treatment center may actually slow down that process. Thus, the average stay of a child in a residential Re-ED program is six months. From an ecological perspective, the child's family should be prepared to accept his or her return after a short period of time.

---

[5] Reprinted, with permission, from the Charles E. Merrill Pub. Co.

This efficient use of time varies from the approach associated with traditional psychotherapy, which takes much longer either to succeed or to
fail because the goal includes reorganizing the child's personality. The
goal of Re-ED is to teach the child to adapt and to react more constructively to his or her ecological system.

3. *Trust is essential.* In almost every case, the child who comes to
Re-ED has learned to distrust adults. To learn from adults, trust has to be
reestablished. The first step in the child's reeducation is to prove that
adults are not necessarily punishers, rejectors, or withdrawers of love.
Once the child learns that the adults who surround him or her can be
trusted, he or she is well on the way to learning how to use them to teach
him or her the things he or she needs and wants to know.

4. *Competence makes a difference.* Obviously, a child who can do
nothing well lacks not only self-confidence and self-respect, but the respect and confidence of others. Therefore, a goal of the Re-ED program
is to teach each child to be very good at something. Developing competence in school subjects is the greatest aid to increasing self-confidence.
Usually consistent failure in this area contributes greatly to the child's
disturbance in the first place. Therefore, Re-ED concentrates heavily on
improving academic achievement, since school is one of the most important components of a child's ecological system. In the classroom,
individualized instructional techniques are used. However, academics
are not limited to the formal classroom presentations but are taught in
conjunction with all aspects of living such as cooking, learning to row a
boat, or sitting around a campfire. Although competence in school subjects is a primary goal, a child may win respect because he or she is a
fine swimmer, artist, or table tennis player as well. It is important, however, that the teacher-counselors accept the children even when they are
not productive.

5. *Symptoms can and should be controlled.* Re-ED does not adhere
to the traditional psychoanalytical premise that surface behaviors interfering with the child's ability to form normal relationships should not be
treated because they will be replaced by other, more severe symptoms.
In Re-ED the symptoms that prevent the establishment of the normal
contacts that provide the child with support and affection from others are
the important ones to remove.

6. *Cognitive control can be taught.* The Re-ED approach attributes
little importance to the acquisition of insight as it is presented in traditional psychotherapy. However, the teacher-counselors and the children
talk extensively about the solution of personal problems. On-the-spot
interviewing is a technique used constantly, not only to increase the
child's ability to adapt to his or her surroundings, but to teach the child

how to recognize the signals that indicate the onset of behavioral problems. For instance, the child might clench his or her fists just before losing his or her temper and beginning to fight. Children are encouraged to learn to talk things over to gain more control over their lives both in the Re-ED setting and at home. Immediate experiences are used as a basis for interviewing, and the children are taught that it is never the wrong time to talk. A nightly council ring or powwow is held by each group to discuss the day's events; the successes or failures that were experienced and the means to function better tomorrow.

7. *Feelings should be nurtured.* Some emotionally disturbed children are overly inhibited and unable to express feelings openly. Therefore, in Re-ED they are encouraged to express feelings even toward animals when they cannot do so toward humans. Even negative feelings are not suppressed and the use of clay, drawing, painting, and puppetry are encouraged as media for the expression of emotion. The friendships developed among the children often turn into long-standing bonds that last even after they have returned to their own communities. Re-ED training helps them learn to control fear, to be alone, and to work out problems for themselves.

8. *The group is important to children.* Groups are kept together for almost all Re-ED activities and become an important source of support, motivation, and control. The nightly powwow allows children who may never have related to other children before, to influence and be influenced by others.

9. *Ceremony and ritual give order, stability, and confidence.* Most of the children at Re-ED have led disorganized and chaotic lives and many are from unstable families and environments. Including ritual as part of the program provides a kind of stability and security that is extremely therapeutic. For instance, the nightly powwow is looked forward to as a comforting event at the end of the day.

10. *The body is the armature of the self.* A great amount of physical activity through sports and games gives the children the opportunity to learn about themselves. It is hoped that understanding their physical selves will result in greater understanding of all aspects of their personalities.

11. *Communities are important.* Since the Re-ED child generally has been referred because of disturbed behavior in the home and the community, and since experiences probably have alienated that child from realizing that the community exists for the people in it, the school encourages trips to community agencies and institutions. An effort is made to show the child that community institutions exist for his or her benefit and should not be destroyed.

12. *A child should know joy.* Hobbs (1966, p. 1113) says "We try to develop skill in developing joy in children. We believe that it is immensely important, that it is immediately therapeutic if further justification is required, for a child to know some joy in each day and to look forward with eagerness to at least some joy-giving event that is planned for tomorrow."

These twelve assumptions provide the foundation for the residential Re-ED program that Hobbs (1974) defines as being for children whose behavior, emotional, and academic problems are so profound that they are at the point of no return. Re-ED is a last resort before institutionalizing the child. However, the principles of Re-ED and ecological intervention are extremely adaptable to the regular school setting. Self-contained classes, mainstreamed classes, and classes made up of so-called normal students can be planned to incorporate the principles of Re-ED.

One very important extension to regular school settings is the role of the liaison teacher-counselor. If Re-ED principles are to be effective, the ecological system of each disturbed child must be dealt with and the liaison teacher (or child advocate) serves as the link between the child, the school, the home, and the community. This teacher must try to restore the effective functioning of all components of the child's environment. To do so she or he must have the following skills: first, *understand the child*. Before designing a curriculum for a child, the teacher-counselor is obligated to gather all the information available about the individual. This information includes social history, parent questionnaires, behavioral checklists, medical and psychological assessment, and results of academic testing and evaluation. It also is important that an ecological assessment pertaining exclusively to the child's educational setting be conducted. Variables such as teacher expectations, peer acceptance, parental pressure, and many others affect a child's performance and behavior in the classroom (Wallace and Larsen, 1978). Evaluations focused only on the child provide very limited feedback.

Second, the teacher-counselor must *understand curricula*. The teacher-counselor must keep up with new information in the field of curriculum and materials. New techniques and materials should be studied with the needs of individual students in mind.

Third, the teacher must be able to *design and implement* curricula. Each child must be designed an individual curriculum that is defined by the following characteristics:

1. It must be *relevant* and have meaning to the daily life of the child. It must be functional, taking into account the competencies a child needs to function in his or her own world.

2. It must be *appropriate*, considering the individual's strengths and

weaknesses, conceptual level, physical development, age, interests, and so on. It must have both behavioral and academic objectives.

3. It must be *well organized.* Appropriate sequence and continuity must be present and the child's prior learning must form a base for new skills and concepts.

4. It should be *reinforcing.* If a child's learning experiences are too abstract, too far removed from real life, the child will tend to lose interest. Far more motivating are experiences that satisfy and reinforce the child's natural curiosity.

5. It should include *naturalized teaching.* Either planned or spontaneously, a teacher can use experiences outside the classroom for instruction. For example, a walk through a littered playground can lead to a discussion of ecology and a sudden thunderstorm can become a lesson on the weather.

6. It must include *actualized teaching.* A child needs to use the learned skills for practical reasons. Motivation, which often is a great problem, becomes less of a problem when the child feels that what is being learned has a real purpose.

7. It must include direct and immediate *feedback and evaluation.* For disturbed children, feedback must immediately follow behavior. If the child is ever to monitor his or her performance, he or she must be informed immediately about the level of performance. Immediate feedback is made easier by the use of programmed, individualized instructional materials, rather than by the usual method of collecting, correcting, and returning a child's paper two or three days later.

8. It must be *directed toward the total child.* The curriculum must be directed not only to the child's academic needs, but also to his or her social and emotional needs. Goals in behavioral areas need to go hand in hand with academic goals. The needs of the total child have to be met.

Fourth, the teacher must *coordinate the curricula.* Although a child may be taught by several teachers during the day, it is up to the teacher-counselor to coordinate the program so there will be a high degree of continuity. Experiences in one area should coordinate with those in another. The cooperation of the entire staff is necessary to the success of the program.

Fifth, the teacher must *communicate.* Communication on many levels is necessary for a coordinated program. Communication with teachers, with supervisory personnel, with parents, and with community members, as well as with the child, is essential.

Project Re-ED provides a viable model for the school setting. As Hobbs (1974, p. 164) says, "every one of the principles manifested in Re-ED schools is a principle that has been recognized at one time or another as simple, straightforward, effective pedagogy."

Weinstein (1976) has investigated the effectiveness of Re-ED schools. Parents, counselors, and referring schools were asked to evaluate a child's progress using various checklists and scales. Results from home and school follow-up showed improvement in both academic and behavioral performance generally being maintained a year after the chlid had left the program. Further research needs to be done on Re-ED programs in day-school settings.

THERAPEUTIC CAMPING

Therapeutic camping programs are very similar in theory and design to the Re-ED schools. Usually operated in the summer, they are approximately six to eight weeks long and are often funded by a university, residential treatment center, or psychiatric hospital. Their emphasis is on the establishment of a simple environment that can be manipulated by the child. Theoretically, in a simple environment, the child can learn cause-and-effect relationships, that is, that the child's behavior affects what happens to him or her. In adapting the ecological perspective of the Re-ED schools to camping situations, not only is attention focused on the child and his or her social system, but also it is extended to the broader natural environment. An example of the ecological camp can be seen in the Camp Woodland Springs program near Dallas, Texas (Loughmiller, 1972). This camping experience operates as a full-time program for emotionally disturbed boys aged 6 to 16 who have been referred by schools, social agencies, psychiatric clinics, private psychiatrists, and others.

In Camp Woodland Springs, boys deal with a primitive environment by providing and maintaining all the facilities of the camp including their living quarters. Theoretically, these constructive activities provide valuable learning experiences. Also, the children are not likely to destroy what they have built themselves. Although many of these children have never been able to establish a sense of security in their relationships with others, it is presumed the natural setting of camp will help develop secure feelings. The child discovers the ability to adapt to the realities of nature, and to survive in a supportive atmosphere.

Within the general structure of the camp, small groups of children are assigned to an adult counselor and they plan their own activities, something most of them have never done. Each evening the entire group meets at a powwow to look back on the day, to talk about the new skills or behaviors learned, and also to look forward to the next day's activities.

The powwow provides a time for the children to evaluate their experiences and to express themselves freely on any subject without being criticized by others. The focus of the discussion is on values, attitudes, and relationships, particularly those pertaining to the group.

The emphasis at Woodland Springs is on problem solving, group living, and the acquisition of skills and knowledge through goal-directed activities. No formal academics are taught, but the opportunities for informal, useful acquisition of academic skills are widespread. Loughmiller (1972, p. 5)[6] cites the need for success experiences when he notes that most of these disturbed children have experienced many more failures than successes.

> Society loses contact with these boys along the way. Communication breaks down. They choose sides. Their resentment, hostility, and hatred cause them to behave in ways that are unacceptable to society and at the same time make them less amenable to ordinary forms of help. . . . We see our job at camp as one of helping these boys correct the distortions in their point of view by providing them with corrective experiences tailored to individual capacity, and to assist them in the development of more appropriate patterns of behavior, growing out of a different set of values.

Many therapeutic camps exist that are strictly summer programs. They are based on a philosophy similar to Loughmiller's camp program. There is maximum interaction with a natural, primitive environment, and the formation of small groups under the leadership of a competent adult. Four basic commitments can be stated (Shaw, 1969):

1. The health and safety of all campers,
2. Adequate food and shelter.
3. The preservation of the ecological balance of the land.
4. The remediation of the specific deficits for which the child was referred.

Theoretically, the teacher or counselor at camp has an easier time helping the children develop conceptual understanding from concrete experiences than the classroom teacher. The use of nature makes lesson planning simpler and more flexible for any child at any stage of development. The counselor also benefits from the fact that the group of children at camp work together for their mutual basic needs, thus, a cohesiveness forms that is much stronger than that found in the school setting. The group becomes the major agent for change in the social environment.

It is important to note that the benefits of camping can accrue to normal children as well as to poorly adjusted children. However, the children involved in therapeutic programs are characterized by any

---

[6] Source: C. Loughmiller, *Wilderness Road*. Hogg Foundation for Mental Health, 1972. Reprinted with permission.

number of serious deficits in personality adjustment. For them, camp provides a flexibility in time, space, and resources that cannot be matched elsewhere.

APPLYING ECOLOGICAL AND MILIEU THEORIES
TO THE SCHOOL SETTING

Each section of this chapter contains suggestions for applying certain aspects of ecological and milieu theories to school settings. In addition to those suggestions, there are general applications and certain other principles that may be integrated into educational programs (Morse, 1974).

1. *Attention to the values, attitudes, and implicit-explicit aspects of the total life space.* In the classroom or school environment this principle means responding with total concern to a student, demonstrating values that take into consideration the child's ability to adapt to a situation. Rules should not be set up for the comfort and well being of the adults in the school, but should establish limits that provide a secure atmosphere. The environment must reflect the values implicit in the child's total life-space or the reconstruction of his or her personality is impossible. For emotionally disturbed children, building a rescue system that incorporates some form of crisis intervention and that provides a nonpunitive alternative when direct confrontation between teacher and student is not productive, is very important.

2. *The role of the teacher in this view is not only that of an academic learning engineer, it is that of a figure for identification.* This principle does not mean that the teacher should fancy himself or herself a member of the child's peer group or, on the other hand, should assume the role of authoritarian. Rather, it suggests that the teacher should demonstrate through daily living, the behavior that the child needs to model. The teacher's attitude in life-space interviewing procedures provides a model for the child.

3. *There are curricular opportunities to incorporate affective learning into the life stream of education.* There are some very well thought out affective materials on the market, but occasionally, particularly in special education classes, they are overused at the expense of the academic curriculum. Some value may be gained from planned affective lessons incorporating role playing and psychodrama (see Chapter 11). Teachers should be encouraged to incorporate the use of expressive media into their programs. Art, music, dance, drama, and play are natural ways for children to express their feelings and to learn to deal with them.

4. *Since the peer culture is the youngster's most potent teacher, any*

educational design that does not become involved in it leaves real influence to chance. The group is enormously important, particularly to older children and adolescents. The value of teaching children how to cope with their peer group and how to learn from each other cannot be over-emphasized. Under the leadership of a flexible and nonjudgmental teacher, the group can be an important therapeutic aid for many children.

5. *The availability of therapeutic resources.* There are many times when a teacher needs specific assistance in dealing with certain children, their families, and their environment. There have been several suggestions in this chapter for therapeutic intervention by experts other than the classroom teacher: crisis teachers, liaison teacher-counselors, and so on. There are other, more traditional psychological or psychiatric resources that may need to be made available to particular children. The point is that assistance needs to be planned so that it is not haphazard. The child's total milieu must be considered when the therapeutic program is planned and the needs of others in the environment must be considered as well.

The therapeutic milieu is not a new or complicated idea. However, its importance in helping the emotionally disturbed child cannot be minimized. William Rhodes (1970, p. 437) sums it up well.

> The view presented here suggests that intervention into the surroundings of the child should occur simultaneously with any intervention into the condition of the child, because the disturbing events are reciprocal products rather than isolated attributes of the child—live products of the encounter between a child and a participating community.

STUDY QUESTIONS

1. Compare and contrast milieu therapy with educational therapy.
2. Discuss the life-space interview. How can this concept be applied in school settings?
3. What is Project Re-ED?
4. Discuss the role of the crisis or helping teacher.
5. Trace the theoretical roots, in terms of the models presented in Chapter 2, that have contributed most to the development of milieu therapy.

REFERENCES

Bettelheim, B., and Sylvester, E. The therapeutic milieu. *American Journal of Orthopsychiatry,* 1948, *18,* 121–206.

Brenner, M. B. Life space interview in the school setting. *American Journal of Orthopsychiatry,* 1963, *33,* 717–719.

Caplan, G. *Prevention of mental disorders in children.* New York: Basic Books, 1961.

Caplan, G. Opportunities for school psychologists in the primary prevention. *Mental Hygiene,* 1963, *47,* 525–539.

Hobbs, N. Helping disturbed children: psychological and ecological strategies. *American Psychologist,* 1966, *21,* 1106–1115.

Hobbs, N. A brief history of project Re-ED. *Mind Over Matter,* 1969, *14,* 9–14.

Hobbs, N. Personal perspective. In J. M. Kauffman and C. D. Lewis (eds.), *Teaching children with behavior disorders.* Columbus, Ohio: Merrill, 1974.

Jones, M. *The therapeutic community: a new treatment method in psychiatry.* New York: Basic Books, 1953.

Jones, M. *Beyond the therapeutic community.* New Haven: Yale University Press, 1968.

Long, N. Personal perspective. In J. M. Kauffman and C. D. Lewis (eds.). *Teaching children with behavior disorders.* Columbus, Ohio: Merrill, 1974.

Loughmiller, C. *Wilderness road.* Austin, Texas: The Hogg Foundation for Mental Health, 1972.

Main, T. F. The hospital as a therapeutic institution. *Bulletin of the Menninger Clinic,* 1946, *10,* 66–70.

Morse, W. C. Training teachers in life space interviewing. In H. Dupont (ed.). *Educating emotionally disturbed children: readings.* New York: Holt, Rinehart and Winston, 1969.

Morse, W. C. Crisis intervention in school mental health and special classes for the disturbed. In N. J. Long, W. C. Morse, and R. G. Newman (eds.). *Conflict in the classroom: the education of children with problems.* Belmont, Cal.: Wadsworth, 1971.

Morse, W. C. Personal perspective. In J. M. Kauffman and C. D. Lewis (eds.). *Teaching children with behavior disorders.* Columbus, Ohio: Merrill, 1974.

Morse, W. C. The crisis or helping teacher. In N. J. Long, W. C. Morse, and R. G. Newman (eds.). *Conflict in the classroom: the education of emotionally disturbed children.* Belmont, Cal.: Wadsworth, 1976a.

Morse, W. C. Worksheet on life space interviewing for teachers. In N. J. Long, W. C. Morse, and R. G. Newman (eds.). *Conflict in the classroom: the education of emotionally disturbed children.* Belmont, Cal.: Wadsworth, 1976b.

Redl, F., and Wineman, D. *Children who hate.* New York: The Free Press, 1951.

Redl, F. The concept of a therapeutic milieu. *American Journal of Orthopsychiatry,* 1959a, *29,* 721–734.

Redl, F. The concept of the life space interview. *American Journal of Orthopsychiatry,* 1959b, *29,* 1–18.

Redl, F. *When we deal with children.* New York: The Free Press, 1966.

Redl, F. Why life space interview? In H. Dupont (ed.). *Educating emotionally disturbed children: readings.* New York: Holt, Rinehart and Winston, 1969.

Redl, F., and Wattenberg, W. W. *Mental hygiene in teaching.* New York: Harcourt, Brace and World, 1959.

Rhodes, W. C. The disturbing child: a problem of ecological management. *Exceptional Children,* 1967, *33,* 449–455.

Rhodes, W. C. A community participation analysis of emotional disturbance. In N. J. Long, W. C. Morse, and R. G. Newman, (eds.) *Conflict in the classroom: the education of emotionally disturbed children.* Belmont, Cal.: Wadsworth, 1976.

Rhodes, W. C., and Paul, J. L. *Emotionally disturbed and deviant children: new views and approaches.* Englewood Cliffs, N.J.: Prentice-Hall, 1978.

Rossi, J. J., and Filstead, W. J. *The therapeutic community.* New York: Behavioral Publications, 1973.

Shaw, K. L. Camping in re-ED. *Mind Over Matter,* 1969, *14,* 47–50.

Wallace, G., and Larsen, S. C. *Educational assessment of learning problems: testing for teaching.* Boston: Allyn and Bacon, 1978.

Weinstein, L. Project Re-ED schools for emotionally disturbed children: Effectiveness as viewed by referring agencies, parents, and teachers. In N. J. Long, W. C. Morse, and R. G. Newman (eds.). *Conflict in the classroom: The education of emotionally disturbed children.* Belmont, Cal.: Wadsworth, 1976.

10
Play Therapy

Play therapy is a method that permits children to air their feelings through the medium of play. It is presumed that children, particularly young children, are most natural and comfortable when at play. Thus, they express themselves as readily through play as adults do through speech.

The introduction of play as a therapeutic technique has been attributed to a psychoanalytically oriented therapist, Melanie Klein (Segal, 1972). However, play therapy has been adopted by individuals embracing a wide variety of theoretical perspectives, including psychoanalytic, phenomenological and behavioral; thus the leadership methods used may range from nondirective to highly directive. Regardless of the therapeutic orientation underlying play therapy, the term *play* is not used in the ordinary sense of recreation. Instead, it connotes a method by which a child is given the freedom to act out and say what he or she thinks and feels. The keystone of play therapy is *permissiveness*. In a permissive play situation, the child is accepted as a competent human being and is treated with the same respect that is usually afforded to adults. Anna Freud (1965, p. 110) conveys the importance of an accepting, permissive attitude when she cautions: "Don't be too cocky and imagine that children can't do everything that grown-up people do . . . . And don't ever say, 'You must do this, you must do that.' No one must do things, neither therefore must children do things."

Axline (1947b, p. 16) in her classic book *Play Therapy* also emphasizes the importance of a permissive environment in play therapy; she states: "The play-therapy room is a good growing ground. In the security of this room where the child is the most important person, where he is in command of the situation and of himself, where no one tells him what to do, no one criticizes what he does, no one nags, or suggests, or goads him on, or pries into his private world, he suddenly feels that here he can unfold his wings; he can look squarely at himself, for he is accepted completely . . . ."

The agreement between the psychoanalyst, Anna Freud, and the nondirective, phenomenologically oriented theorist, Virginia Axline regarding the importance of an accepting, permissive environment is shared by the majority of play therapists. However, such agreement does not extend to issues pertaining to the direct implementation of play therapy. Apparently, there have been few efforts to establish systematic play-therapy procedures. Consequently, the techniques employed largely reflect the attitudes and preferences of each practitioner. Many of the suggestions pertaining to the implementation of play therapy presented in this chapter have been drawn from the work of Axline (1947a and b, 1949) and Ginott (1961), since both authors present practical suggestions which are applicable to educational settings. The issues to be discussed are

1. The children who benefit from play therapy,
2. The composition of play-therapy groups,
3. The methods and techniques that the therapist uses during therapeutic sessions,
4. The physical plant and equipment required,
5. The application of play therapy in school settings,
6. The efficacy of using play therapy.

CHILDREN ELIGIBLE FOR PLAY THERAPY

Axline, possibly the most enthusiastic of the play therapists, advocates the use of play therapy with any type of problem child "including those with behavior problems, study problems, speech problems, and even somatic problems" (1947b, p. 59). By behavior problems she means children whose maladjustment ranges from highly inhibited, withdrawn behavior to overly aggressive, acting-out behavior. She maintains that speech problems such as stammering, stuttering, baby talk, repetitious language, garbled language, and even nontalking, are also rectified by play therapy. She reports several research studies (1947a, 1949) that she interprets as demonstrating that play therapy causes disturbed children to become better readers. In short, Axline seems to regard play therapy as the best cure for a variety of problems that may befall children. She touts its use for preventive purposes with children who are not seriously disturbed, as well as for remedial or curative purposes. Although her enthusiasm for this technique may be somewhat excessive, her interesting reports of case studies appear to demonstrate that play therapy may be used successfully with a wide variety of children. Of course, Axline usually reports cases of individual play therapy rather than group therapy.

When she uses groups they often consist of one disturbed child and that child's selection of nondisturbed friends and playmates. Axline advocates group therapy only when the child's problem centers on social relationships and regards individual therapy as more helpful for treating children with deep-seated emotional difficulty.

Ginott (1961) provides a great deal more specific information about the selection of children for play therapy because he regards group sessions as the preferred method of treatment. The success of group therapy for each individual depends largely on the formation of the group, thus it is important to ensure that the correct mix of children is brought together.

Ginott presents a series of subjective guidelines for the selection of children for group play therapy. His foremost criterion is Slavson's (1952) concept of "social hunger." Slavson believed that children develop social hunger when they have experienced parental care and love during infancy. Ginott defines social hunger as "a person's desire to gain acceptance by his peers, to act, dress, and talk as they do and to attain and maintain status in his group" (p. 17). In other words, social hunger is the necessary force that motivates children to change their behavior. Children lacking this force are unconcerned about group acceptance and unwilling to delay gratification of their own impulses. Therefore, they do not experience any strong desire to change their behavior. Children with social hunger who are good risks for group play therapy are classified as: (1) withdrawn, (2) immature, (3) phobic, (4) effeminate, (5) having pseudo assets, (6) having habit disorders, and (7) having conduct disorders.

According to Ginott, withdrawn children "are unable to express ordinary feelings of affection and aggression, have no friends or playmates, and avoid social give and take" (p. 19). They respond to group play therapy because the presence of other children makes it easier for them to join in play activities. They are not faced with the pressure of interacting singly with the therapist. A group that is active but mild is recommended for withdrawn children.

Immature children are those who generally might be described as spoiled, or overindulged. They lack the capacity to cooperate with their peers, are often selfish with material objects, and are overly solicitous of the spotlight of adult attention. In the group situation they learn socially acceptable behaviors in order to win peer approval.

Phobic children have a variety of inordinate fears. They may be upset by loud noises, darkness, animals, and so on. The feelings of panic that their fears induce cause them to avoid many activities. Consequently they often are restricted in their mobility. In group play therapy, such children must encounter their peers who invariably expose them to fear-inducing stimuli such as dirt, darkness, or noise. Thus, they must face their problems directly. Such direct encounters with their fears are more difficult to induce in individual therapy.

Effeminate boys are defined by Ginott as meek and submissive, lacking the characteristic aggressiveness expected of boys. They are usually reluctant to participate in boys' games and are regarded as sissies by the other children. An all-male group and masculine toys and activities are recommended as the optimal curative elements for treatment.

Children with pseudo assets are "too good." They are overly obedient and worry excessively about pleasing their parents. They lack normal assertiveness and the ability to gratify their own wishes. Association with the group teaches them that assertive behaviors will not evoke adult retaliation and that it is legitimate for them to express their own feelings.

Children with habit disorders demonstrate symptoms such as temper tantrums, eating problems, bed wetting, and so forth. Such problems often are superficial reactions to frustration. In the group situation, their maladaptive habits do not evoke responses that the children have learned to expect. The group members either ignore or censure children who engage in disruptive behaviors such as temper tantrums. Consequently, the offending behavior is eliminated in the group situation and replaced with more constructive reactions.

Children with conduct disorders are generally destructive and overly aggressive. Many such children are suspicious of adults and are therefore unwilling to relate to a therapist in an individual setting. They respond well in group settings because they feel insulated by the presence of the other children. They are more likely to develop self-control in group therapy.

Children Unsuitable for Play Therapy Groups

The children Ginott deems unsuitable for inclusion in groups are those who demonstrate: (1) intense sibling rivalries, (2) sociopathic behaviors, (3) accelerated or deviant sex drives, (4) tendencies to steal, (5) extreme hostility and aggression, and (6) gross stress reaction.

Children who are extremely hostile toward their siblings tend to displace their feelings onto the other children in the group. Since the atmosphere in the group is permissive, they may actually harm others. Such children respond more favorably to individual play sessions. Once they have gained control over their hostility they can be integrated into a play group.

Sociopathic children lack concern about others and interact with them for purposes of exploitation. They are incapable of introspection and are without feelings of guilt or responsibility for wrongdoing. They detest authority and refuse to abide by rules. In group situations they prey on others and disrupt their activities. They are unable to benefit from therapeutic techniques. Neither indirect reflection of their feelings nor direct interpretation of their behavior is effective. They are poor risks for individual therapy also, since they cannot relate to the therapist.

Children with accelerated or deviant sex drives are generally better assigned to individual therapy because they might frighten other children or involve them in their activities. Similarly, children who steal should be excluded from group situations because they might steal from the other children or teach them to steal. This general guideline does not extend to children who steal only at home. These children are often either bidding for affection or seeking revenge on parents. Such stealing usually does not transfer to the group situation.

Highly aggressive children whose behavior appears to stem from deep-rooted hostility cannot benefit from group sessions. They require forceful restraints on their behavior to prevent them from injuring others. Such restraint cannot be applied in the group session without destroying the permissive environment and proving detrimental to the other children.

Children who have suffered emotional trauma because of a catastrophe such as a death, accident, or fire, respond best to individual therapy. Usually their anxiety is generated by one particular event and can be resolved most efficiently if symbolic play is focused on a reenactment of this event. The presence of other children only interferes with the child's progress.

GROUP COMPOSITION

The discussion of group composition in Chapter 5, Group Therapy, illustrated the disagreement among professionals over the best strategies to employ. As was noted, some individuals recommend that groups consist of persons having important characteristics in common, for example, age, sex, problems, personality type, educational background, or socioeconomic status. Other experts believe that groups should include persons with diverse backgrounds, problems, or personality types to provide role models. Clearly, the dilemma about group composition applies to play therapy groups just as it does to verbal discussion groups. Ginott offers another series of guidelines to aid the practitioner in deciding which children to group together.

First, he maintains that groups should consist of children with *varying types of symptoms* so that each individual can identify with persons who are different from himself or herself. For instance, a passive, withdrawn child is aided by his or her observations of an active, acting-out child. A dependent, fearful individual gains courage from observing the behavior of stronger, more independent children.

A second guideline is an *absence of ridicule within the group*. The group should not be comprised so that one child is the butt of barbs from more assertive peers. For instance, a fat child who has been ridiculed for obesity should not be included in a group of dominant, thin children. A group with other obese members, or with mild, unassertive children, would be more beneficial.

Ginott's third guideline deals with *group tension level.* Effective therapy occurs when the interaction of the group members produces a moderate level of tension. Some groups fail to generate enough tension, whereas others generate too much. For example, a group composed solely of aggressive children would be fraught with encounters creating too much tension, when a group of withdrawn children would lack tension-generating encounters.

As a fourth guideline, Ginott recommends that the therapist *avoid grouping friends and siblings.* Ginott believes that therapy should promote new attitudes and relationships and that the intrusion of friends or siblings in the group blocks this type of new learning.

The fifth guideline concerns *eliminating wrong heroes.* Care must be taken to ensure that antisocial children do not dominate the group. The inclusion of delinquent children in a group of neurotic or immature youngsters who are not antisocial should be avoided.

Guideline six concerns *neutralizers.* A neutralizer is a child who is not greatly disturbed and who controls his or her overt behavior. The neutralizer is expected to influence less-controlled children by example and by comments that illustrate socially acceptable behaviors.

Guidelines seven and eight concern *group size and the age of group members.* Ginott recommends no more than five children per group and as few as three if the therapist lacks experience. Chronological age of the group members generally should not differ by more than twelve months. However, socially immature children or mentally retarded youngsters who are rejected by their chronological peers might fit comfortably into groups of younger children. As a general rule, preschool children are at the optimal age for play therapy techniques and the procedure loses effectiveness with children beyond the age of 8.

The ninth guideline concerns *opened an dclosed groups.* Open groups accept new members periodically and integrate them into the existing group. Closed groups exclude new members once the group is operating. Ginott notes that open groups are more practical and economical because children regularly drop from therapy and must be replaced. Obviously the new group member must be chosen as carefully to avoid upsetting the other children. Whenever possible it is beneficial to prepare the group for the departure of one member and the entrance of another child several weeks in advance.

Ginott's final guideline concerns *mixed-sex groups.* He accepts the Freudian notion of a period of latency in children's sexual development and recommends like-sex groups for children of school age who are in that period of sexual development. He notes the importance of reinforcing sexual identification and the pursuit of conventional masculine and feminine interests. Preschool children of both sexes may be grouped together, however, since they have not entered the latency period.

As stated previously, Ginott's criteria for group composition are highly subjective. By no means are they uniformly accepted. Lippman (1956) maintains that play-therapy groups should consist solely of withdrawn children and exclude all aggressive individuals. Lebo (1956) believes that play therapy is effective until children reach twelve years of age. Slavson (1955) recommends closed play-therapy groups to prevent disruption of treatment by new members. Axline (1947b) would not exclude friends and classmates from her groups nor would she segregate children on the basis of sex. Generally, Axline and others of a phenomenological persuasion (Buhler, 1962; Moustakas, 1966) are not inclined to judge in advance how children will interact in group sessions and are prone to permit each group to develop uniquely. In fact, it seems clear that for most practitioners decisions to include or exclude children from group therapy are difficult and must be based on extensive observation. For example, the conclusion as to whether a child's excessive aggressive behavior stems from deep-rooted hostility or from a relatively minor conduct disorder cannot be based solely on psychometric evaluation or even on examination of the child's past history. The bottom line in such a diagnosis is the child's response to the group situation and the extent to which his or her maladaptive behaviors are alleviated or heightened by the permissive group atmosphere.

In short, there are no hard-and-fast criteria for formulating play-therapy groups (Dorfman, 1951; Lippman, 1956). Newman (1971, p. 231) notes this fact and its unfortunate implications when she writes: "The screening methods presently in use are either overly pedantic or too loose to be effective. There are few experiences more immobilizing than that of the child who is placed in a group which repeatedly excludes him. Eventually he develops a pattern of self-exclusion, so that he holds himself apart whenever he meets new groups of people. There is a need for some good research into the requirements of grouping . . . ." Until such research appears however, the person interested in forming play-therapy groups must proceed with caution and, at the very least, attempt to integrate each child into the group after considering his or her impact on the other children.

THERAPEUTIC TECHNIQUES

As play therapy is not based primarily on verbal interchanges between therapist and child, it differs dramatically from most forms of psychotherapy. Many experts believe that the demands on the play therapist are at least equal to, if not exceeding, those made on the verbal psychotherapist. The play therapist must *first* understand normal play and recognize the unusual characteristics in the play of disturbed children, and *second*, play the therapeutic role by interpreting and responding to the psychological messages conducted in the play activities.

Play

The characteristics of children's normal play are determined by their stage of development. The norm varies with age. Three-year-old children typically engage in parallel play without social interaction. They may stare at one another and covet each other's toys, but they rarely cooperate in play activities. Even their speech is most accurately described as independent monologue rather than shared dialogue. Conversely, normal children aged 4 through 8 engage in few solitary play activities and do little passive watching of other children. Instead they initiate cooperative activities. They tend to share toys, show affection through hugs and pats, yield to each other's demands or suggestions, offer and ask for approval, help, or sympathy, and generally increase their dependence on each other while they decrease their dependence on adults. As children mature they tend to become more assertive and aggressive. Conflicts erupt suddenly but are usually of short duration. Rules become increasingly important in games or other group play activities.

At any age, normal children enjoy play. They experiment freely, show imagination, and create new learning experiences. As they mature they discuss their activities enthusiastically, accept restrictions without resentment, and use their toys carefully.

Disturbed patterns of play are readily apparent and usually characterized by too much or too little inhibition. Overly inhibited children are extremely wary of play situations. They tend to be passive observers rather than active participants. Toys are treated like rare jewels. The child is afraid to touch them and when he or she does use them is concerned excessively about breakage. Play activities lack spontaneity and bring little joy. Undue concern is expressed about getting dirty and cleaning up any mess.

In addition to their general passivity and timidity in play situations, overly inhibited children tend to rely greatly on adult support. They solicit suggestions for play activities from adults, seek permission for each act they plan to undertake and try to gain favor from adults by doing what they believe will please them. They are not assertive in group situations, nor do they show appropriate aggression when challenged. They rarely offer social reinforcement to others. In fact, they tend to depreciate the activities of their peers by ridiculing their efforts and products.

On the other hand, children with too few inhibitions see no need to restrict impulse-gratifying behaviors. Their notion of interacting with others is to exploit or dominate. As they are overly assertive and excessively aggressive, they become furious if others resist following their suggestions and respond either by disrupting group activities by taking toys, knocking down buildings, scribbling on drawings, or with physical and verbal abuse. Underinhibited children typically resent authority and resist behavioral limits. Their preferred toys are usually weapons and their symbolic play generally involves aggressive behavior. They often deliberately break toys.

Evidence of severe emotional pathology such as psychosis also is evidenced in play activity. Psychotic children engage in a variety of bizarre behaviors. They are often impervious to the existence of other children and unresponsive to all attempts at social interaction. Even their faces are devoid of expression as they sit passively in one position or engage in some type of self-stimulating behavior such as body rocking or hand waving. Toys are used inappropriately, often repetitiously, as when a block is banged repeatedly on the floor. Disruption of familiar routines and established patterns such as the rearrangement of furniture or toys is resisted with tantrums.

In short, children's play patterns often clearly reveal the state of their mental health. Of course, children with other types of handicapping conditions also display abnormal play patterns. For example, the play of mentally retarded children lacks creative imagination and appears immature. However, most children, even those with handicaps, find joy in their play activities that is not experienced by emotionally disturbed children.

The Therapeutic Role

As is true of all types of psychotherapy, there is no universally accepted best way to conduct play therapy. Preferred techniques often depend on the psychological orientation of the therapist. However, a series of nondirective techniques that have been found useful by a variety of play therapists (Axline, 1947; Hobbs, 1955; Moustakas, 1959) appear most applicable to educational settings.

Nondirective therapy is designed to minimize the therapist's control over the events in the therapy session. The child is viewed as a rational being, motivated toward self-actualization. To overcome problems and fulfill potential, the child must be permitted to engage in activities that reflect his or her needs or desires. Thus, the therapist's role is not to instruct, direct, counsel, censure, shape, praise, or reward, but is to respond to the child's direction by reflecting his or her feelings and by helping him or her become aware of the significance of his or her behaviors. Axline advises the non-directive therapist to:

1. Establish rapport—communicate an attitude of acceptance to the child,
2. Set and maintain a permissive atmosphere,
3. Recognize and reflect the child's feelings,
4. Permit the child, at his or her own pace, to reach solutions to problems,
5. Set behavioral limits that do not violate the permissive atmosphere.

The first step, that of establishing rapport with the child, underlies the entire therapeutic relationship. The therapist must begin this introductory stage by depicting himself or herself as a nonthreatening, nonpunitive person primarily concerned with the child's interests and desires. This attitude is conveyed to some extent by pleasant remarks and a smiling countenance, but it depends on other behaviors as well. Rapport depends on the therapist's ability to convince the child that he or she is as important as any adult, and to avoid falling into the superior adult–inferior child relationships that often are common elsewhere. Children, particularly those experiencing emotional problems, are very adept at testing the sincerity of an accepting attitude and often probe to unearth underlying authoritarian attitudes. For example, a child might not respond to the therapist's initial friendly overtures. He or she might refuse to talk to the therapist and cry for his or her mother. To establish proper rapport, the therapist must avoid forcing the child to comply with his or her suggestions. The therapist must not urge, tease, coerce, argue, or in any way attempt to convince the child to do what he or she wants. The therapist should *not* say: "There's nothing to cry about," "Don't cry honey, I won't hurt you," "Big boys don't cry," "Stop crying and I'll give you a surprise," "Are you a mommy's boy?", "Play with these toys, you'll like them." All of these responses, no matter how kindly meant, ignore the child's feelings about the events. Instead, the therapist must accept the child's attitude and respond only to the feelings being conveyed. She or he should say: "You are upset and would like your mother." This statement deals with the child's reality and informs the child that the therapeutic situation is special and is unlike most situations in which the child must interact with adults. In the therapeutic situation the child's feelings and desires will be given as much consideration as those of the adults present. In an instance such as the one just described, it might be necessary for the mother initially to accompany the child. When the child becomes absorbed in some of the play material and is less fearful, the mother can leave. It is far more important that the child's attitude toward the therapy be shaped properly than it is that the therapist's plan for a private opening session remain unaltered.

Acceptance of the child is a continuation of the attitude conveyed while establishing rapport. Acceptance is conveyed by avoiding either direct or implied criticism of the child. For example, if the child smears paint on his or her clothes, the therapist neither tells the child directly that it was wrong to do so nor implies criticism by telling him that a lovely shirt has been spoiled. Similarly, if a child spends all his or her time scribbling on paper with a black crayon, the therapist does not suggest that he or she draw pictures, use crayons of varied colors, or engage in more interesting activities. The child's behavior reflects what he or she feels like doing. When prepared to try an alternate activity, the child will.

It is important to note that acceptance does not imply approval of a child's activity. In fact, approval, even the mildest compliment, may have adverse effects. For example, the child who paints a pretty picture might, if complimented, spend an excessive amount of time painting pictures to win more of the therapist's approval. The goal of play therapy is not to have the child do as the therapist wishes. It is to have the child express what he or she thinks and feels.

The key to acceptance is that the child learn not to fear rejection regardless of his or her activities. He or she may utter statements such as: "I'd like to kill my brother," and receive only reflection of his or her feelings as in: "You feel like killing your brother," rather than a shocked reprimand for uttering such a socially unacceptable filial attitude. The child accustomed to being told what he or she should and should not say and how he or she should and should not behave is made aware that the play therapy setting differs from other settings.

Step two, establishing a permissive environment, means that children are permitted, within reason, to do as they wish in the playroom. Permissiveness is communicated verbally by telling each child that he or she may play with whatever toy he or she chooses and nonverbally by not interfering when the child tests the sincerity of the verbal statement. In some cases children are unresponsive and unwilling to play with any of the toys. The therapist must avoid insisting that the child do something. If the child sits quietly, the therapist should sit quietly as well. In other cases, children deliberately engage in the behaviors that usually draw adult criticism, such as spilling water or making noise. In a permissive environment the therapist permits much behavior of this type, drawing the line when the child's activity is judged to be dangerous, abusive, or destructive. For example, the child who chooses to jump up and down while screaming may not be interrupted by the therapist, but the child who begins banging his or her head against the wall, destroying toys, abusing other children, or punching the therapist is stopped. The issue of setting appropriate limits in a permissive environment will be discussed later in this section.

An extension of a permissive environment is one devoid of probing questions. The child must be permitted to bring forth important information after he or she has developed a feeling of trust in the therapist. To establish this level of interaction the therapist must avoid prematurely imposing thoughts and ideas on the child. For example, the child who begins smashing the mother doll against the floor is not queried as to his or her reasons. The therapist does not probe by asking: "Do you feel angry with the mother doll?" Such questions are intrusions into the child's private world. When the child feels comfortable with the therapist or when he or she is prepared to deal with the emotions underlying this behavior he or she will offer reasons for the actions.

Step three, the ability to recognize and reflect feeling, is another extension of the permissive interaction between the child and the therapist. The play therapist is alert to the child's utterances and play activities for a significant remark or behavior. Significant activities are those that appear to pertain to the child's problem. For example, a child may spend a long period of time pouring water from one bucket to another—an activity that is probably nonsignificant. Finally, he or she dumps a bucket of water over the head of the mother doll and says: "This mother doll is mean." The actions and remarks are significant representations of his or her feelings, and the therapist must react to them. The type of reaction is very important. The nondirective therapist does not seek to interpret behavior. In other words, she or he does not attempt to comment on the reasons for the child's behavior regardless of how obvious they appear to be. The therapist's task is to reflect back the child's behavior or remarks. When the child says: "This mother doll is mean," the therapist follows with "You think the mother doll is mean," not "You think your mother is mean." Thus, the therapist recognizes the child's feelings without attempting to elicit an admission the child may not be able to make or accept.

The therapeutic attitude that avoids criticism, praise, and the temptation to interpret the child's remarks, demonstrates step four, the therapist's confidence that the child has the ability to solve his or her own problems. The child can be trusted to broach sensitive subjects when ready to deal with them emotionally. If the therapist has trust the child will move toward self-improvement.

When the child is ready to talk about the subject, he or she will make comments such as: "This doll is my mother. She doesn't like me." The therapist again reacts only to the information that the child is willing to offer by remarking: "You feel your mother doesn't like you." Again there is no attempt to probe. Just as the child has come to the point where he or she can recognize and discuss feelings about mother, he or she will eventually be able to discuss problems in greater detail.

Step five evokes more controversy than all the other steps together. Therapists differ on the limitations they set in the playroom. Some, like

Axline, provide only those limits necessary for safety, whereas others provide much more structure. According to Ginott (1961), the variations in techniques regarding behavioral limits reflect different therapeutic definitions of permissiveness. Nondirective therapists like Axline define permissiveness to mean acceptance of all behavior as it appears in therapy, whereas analytically oriented persons like Ginott define it as acceptance of all "symbolic" behavior such as feelings, thoughts, dreams, and wishes, as opposed to direct acting-out behaviors. Directive therapists set more rigorous limits on children's overt actions. For example, they might not permit swearing, screaming, water throwing, and other such activities. They would permit and presumably encourage symbolic expressions of hostile feelings, such as puppetry, that depicted matricide, patricide, or mass mayhem.

It is also possible that the behavioral limits set by play therapists do not necessarily reflect their theoretical orientations, but rather indicate their unique sensitivities about the behaviors they are willing to tolerate. The therapist who feels that it is inappropriate for children to swear in therapy may not be able to function properly unless she or he limits swearing. Another therapist may have no difficulty permitting swearing but may need to draw the line at other behaviors. Obviously, the therapist is not a machine. His or her particular value system must influence the manner in which play therapy is implemented.

Regardless of the factors that determine the setting of therapeutic limits, all therapists agree *first* that the necessary limits should be established immediately and enforced consistently. For example, the therapist who cannot abide swearing must limit it immediately. *Second,* limits should be delineated clearly so that there is no confusion over acceptable and unacceptable behavior. For instance, if punching the therapist is unacceptable, so is slapping. *Third,* the establishment of limits should be done in as nonpunitive a manner as possible. The child may be told that he or she must stop jumping on the furniture in a calm, firm manner without conveying anger. The therapist might say: "I know you want to jump on the furniture but it is against the rules." If the child persists he or she should be taken out of the playroom until willing to return without jumping on the furniture. At no time should the therapist voice anger with the child.

Finally, the child's disappointment or frustration when behavior is limited should be recognized and accepted by the therapist. The therapist should say: "I know you are angry because you can't jump on the furniture, but that is the rule." The therapist must never personalize the child's anger by responding as though his or her behavior was a personal insult. Disturbed children are expected to test limits. If the therapist responds to these events with calm enforcement of the limits without projecting anger or annoyance, the child will eventually learn that, although he or she is not permitted to engage in certain behaviors, he or she is still held in high regard by the therapist.

PHYSICAL PLANT AND EQUIPMENT

Opinion varies over the type of room and materials necessary to conduct play therapy. Axline (1947b) notes that although a separate playroom is desirable, it is not necessary. She reports the successful use of play techniques in a corner of a regular classroom. Other therapists (Slavson, 1952, Ginott, 1961) attribute far more importance to providing an appropriate physical setting. They recommend a private room of 300 to 400 square feet that is well lighted, windowless, and sturdily constructed. The floors and walls should be easily cleaned, a sink should be built in, and the furniture should be functional and substantial. Several tables, one long and low to be used for puppet and dollhouse activities, and the others round to be used for finger painting, clay play, and so on, should be included.

There is no agreement on the type of materials that are necessary for play therapy. Axline recommends that the toys selected be substantial and that games such as checkers as well as mechanical toys be avoided because they interfere with creative or expressive play. She believes that play therapy can be conducted with a suitcase of items such as a doll family, doll furniture, boxes or paints, drawing paper, crayons, puppets, toy guns, toy soldiers, and toy cars. If funds and space are available she recommends a large doll house, a stage furnished with child-sized furniture, and a sand box. Axline goes on to say that the materials should be kept in an orderly manner lest the child be overwhelmed by a wildly disorganized profusion of scattered objects.

Maisner (1950) disputes the necessity for a wide variety of toys, suggesting that a box of modeling clay may be as effective as a variety of other materials. Fraiberg (1954) agrees that few toys are necessary.

Ginott (1961) has developed several criteria for the selection of appropriate toys. First, the toys selected must be those that most clearly convey the child's message to the therapist. The therapist may find it relatively easy to understand the meaning of the child's play about family interactions if representative dolls are available for use. The child might portray these family relationships with marbles or blocks, but the meaning of the play is difficult for the therapist to interpret.

Second, the materials selected must be appropriate for each particular group. For example, hyperactive children may be overstimulated by materials such as finger paints, whereas highly inhibited children may benefit greatly by indulging in such smearing, dirtying behavior without fear of reprimand.

Third, materials should be varied so that children are presented with new challenges. For instance, providing one highly desirable toy to be shared among three children forces social interactions and provides an opportunity for them to learn techniques of cooperation.

EDUCATIONAL APPLICATIONS

A direct application of play-therapy techniques in the schools may be undertaken by teachers who are interested in (1) helping mildly maladjusted children release maladaptive behaviors, (2) helping children maintain good states of mental health, and (3) acting as a model for children by demonstrating a tolerant, accepting attitude toward others.

To accomplish these goals, teachers may schedule weekly play-therapy sessions in their classrooms after school for children requiring an outlet for their feelings or an opportunity to learn more constructive affective behavior. For instance, fearful children who lack the confidence to work independently or to interact openly with their classmates in the large-class setting might be grouped with a confident, outgoing child in play sessions. The confident child serves as a model for the fearful children. Also, the relatively unstructured small-group setting is devoid of pressures for achievement. Consequently, fearful, dependent children may have the opportunity to relax and enjoy a school experience.

Highly active or aggressive children might be scheduled for play sessions on an individual basis. Thus the child has the opportunity to relate to the teacher in a situation where he or she is far less likely to break rules or violate limits.

In proceeding with play-group activities the teacher need only apply several rules. First, seriously disturbed children shoud not be involved in school sessions. A child who is too disturbed to observe behavioral limits might harm other children and destroy the teacher's program.

Second, the teacher should structure play sessions to observe major school standards for behavior. Although play therapy demands a permissive environment, the teacher will achieve greater success if she or he adopts a more directive, conservative position in setting behavioral limits. In other words, the teacher should set rules that ensure that the children maintain sufficient control of their behavior. Without doing so, it is doubtful if either parents or school administrators would support school-based group sessions.

Also, the teacher is accustomed to providing a great deal of direction in the usual classroom instruction situation. Although play sessions require far less direction, the teacher must provide enough structure to ensure that she or he functions efficiently in the leadership role. Finally, it is easier for the teacher to wear two hats—that of academic instructor and that of play therapist if there is some consistency in behavioral standards.

These cautions are not meant to imply that the play sessions should replicate typical classroom settings. The notion of the permissive environment is the foremost requirement for successful play therapy. The teacher must never forget that the child involved in the play session selects activities and pursues them as he or she wishes. The limits are imposed to deal with excess.

Third, the teacher should treat the play-therapy sessions as a portion of the instructional program. She or he should make clear to children, administrators, parents, and fellow teachers that such sessions are provided for the general affective growth and development of her or his students. Just as she or he teaches addition to children who haven't mastered it, she or he teaches improved social skills to children who require additional assistance. Such assurance clarifies the teacher's goals. It removes the implication that the teacher is encroaching on the territory of professional mental health specialists.

Fourth, the teacher should use a minimal amount of resources to establish the play-therapy sessions. Axline's idea of adapting a corner of the classroom as the play area is well-founded. The fewer demands the teacher makes for resources, the more likely she or he is to be permitted to undertake the program. Toys such as dolls and a doll house may be borrowed from the kindergarten teacher. More prosaic items such as crayons, finger paints, hand puppets, and clay, are usually readily available in most schools.

Fifth, the teacher should provide opportunities for every child in the class to be part of a play session at some point throughout the school year. She or he might create subgroups within the class who engage in creative play activities such as art projects or puppetry shows, as a matter of course, once a week during the school day. In these sessions the teacher's goal is to provide opportunities for cooperative group efforts rather than to help specific children overcome problems. The general use of play-therapy sessions not only pleases and benefits the children but also prevents the activities from becoming associated exclusively with problem children.

Sixth, the teacher should gear play materials and opportunities to the chronological age of her or his class. Obviously, play therapy is designed for young primary-grade children who have not obtained the level of cognitive and linguistic development necessary to conduct verbal, discussion therapy. These children are quite comfortable using toys such as dolls and guns to symbolize their life situations. Play therapy for more mature children must employ techniques such as drawing, story writing, drama, and puppetry, which are appropriate for their level of interest. Each of those techniques is discussed elsewhere in this book.

EFFICACY RESEARCH

Several problems exist in attempting to formulate any conclusive opinions regarding the effectiveness of play therapy from an examination of the existing literature. First, the main body of studies were conducted during the 1950's and early 1960's. Apparently the notion of play therapy for children was in its heyday during that period and a great deal of investigation was undertaken. Relatively few studies that pertain exclusively to play therapy have been conducted since 1970.

Second, the available studies are fraught with methodological weaknesses, for example, no control for maturation or regression effect, samples too small, inappropriate sampling techniques, and so forth. Unfortunately, the conclusions formulated from these studies, both pro and con, cannot be accepted with confidence.

Third, it is difficult to generalize from the results of even the best studies. Play therapy is a relatively general term for various types of therapeutic activities conducted with children. Information about the effectiveness of one approach does not reflect on other approaches.

For those reasons, no attempt will be made to report the results of specific research studies in this text. The interested reader can find a thorough discussion of the research done before 1961 in Ginott. Also, Scheidlinger and Rauch (1972) have reviewed research done in the 1960's. Essentially, the reader is left to draw his or her own conclusions about the efficacy of play-therapy techniques from the marvelous case studies presented by Axline (1947b), Baruch (1953), and Moustakas (1959). Such studies suggest that these techniques work when they are used by certain therapists with certain children, and perhaps that is enough justification for their continued use.

The reader might also decide to implement play therapy, keep careful records of student progress, and formulate his or her own conclusions about the value of this method. Such conclusions might not be valid in that the child might improve or fail to improve for other reasons. However, they would be no more speculative than the results of the existing efficacy research.

If one were to engage in speculation, however, it seems most likely that play therapy is not the panacea that advocates like Axline think it is. It certainly is not the best means of remediating serious reading or speech problems, as she has indicated. However, if the teacher's goals for the use of play therapy pertain to helping children develop increasingly mature and adaptive social skills, establishing a nonthreatening relationship with children who are difficult to reach, and/or providing opportunities for disturbed children to model better adjusted peers, it may prove to be a helpful technique.

STUDY QUESTIONS—CHAPTER 10

1. Discuss Axline's five steps that establish a nondirective therapeutic relationship.
2. Discuss therapeutic permissiveness. How can such a principle be used in a school setting?
3. Discuss how children's play gives clues about their emotional well being.
4. Discuss the therapeutic model that provides the basis for Axline's ideas about play therapy.
5. Develop a list of realistic goals that might be obtained by establishing play-therapy sessions in the classroom.

REFERENCES

Axline, V. Nondirective therapy for poor readers. *Journal of Consulting Psychology*, 1947a, *11*, 61–69.

Axline, V. *Play therapy*. Boston: Houghton Mifflin, 1947b.

Axline, V. Play therapy: a way of understanding and helping reading problems. *Childhood Education*, 1949, *26*, 156–161.

Baruch, D. *How to live with your teen-ager*. New York: McGraw-Hill, 1953.

Buhler, C. *Values in psychotherapy*. New York: Free Press of Glencoe, 1962.

Dorfman, E. Play therapy. In C. Rogers (ed.). *Client-centered therapy*. Boston: Houghton Mifflin, 1951.

Fraiberg, S. *Psychoanalytic principles in casework with children*. New York: Family Service Association of America, 1954.

Freud, A. *Normality and pathology in childhood: Assessments of development.* New York: International Universities, 1965.

Ginott, H. *Group psychotherapy with children*. New York: McGraw-Hill, 1961.

Hobbs, N. Client-centered psychotherapy. In J. L. McCary (ed.). *Six approaches to psychotherapy*. New York: Dryden, 1955.

Lebo, D. Age and suitability for non-directive play therapy. *Journal of Genetic Psychology*, 1956, *89*, 231–238.

Lippman, E. *Treatment of the child in emotional conflict*. New York: McGraw-Hill, 1956.

Maisner, E. Contributions of play therapy techniques to total rehabilitative design in an institution for high-grade mentally deficient and borderline children. *American Journal of Mental Deficiency*, 1950, *55*, 235–250.

Moustakas, C. *Psychotherapy with children*. New York: Harper, 1959.

Newman, R. Groups: how they grew and what they're all about. In N. Long, W. Morse, and R. Newman (eds.). *Conflict in the classroom*. Belmont, Cal.: Wadsworth, 1971.

Scheidlinger, S., and Rauch, E. Group psychotherapy with children and adolescents. In B. Wolman (ed.). *Handbook of child psychoanalysis*. New York: Van Nostrand Reinhold, 1972.

Segal, H. Melanie Klein's technique of child analysis. In B. Wolman (ed.). *Handbook of child psychoanalysis*. New York: Van Nostrand Reinhold, 1972.

Slavson, S. *Child psychotherapy*. New York: Columbia University Press, 1952.

Slavson, S. Criteria for selection and rejection of patients for various types of group psychotherapy. *International Journal of Group Psychotherapy*, 1955, *5*, 3–30.

11
Drama Therapy

Drama therapy is based on the assumption that an individual may gain greater understanding of the dynamics influencing his or her behavior if he or she is permitted to act out various aspects of his or her life. In effect, an individual may create a drama that represents important life situations and role play himself or herself as he or she interacts with other key figures in the environment.

The principles underlying drama therapy stem directly from the work of Dr. J. L. Moreno, a Vienna-born psychiatrist. Moreno, who began his clinical study of personality disorders early in the 1900's, innovated a form of psychotherapy that thrust patients into representative interactions with persons whom they perceived as contributing to their problems. Moreno's theories were, in part, a reaction against Freudian principles. He was disenchanted with the Freudian emphasis on the patient's past history. He believed that the disturbed person must deal in the here and now with emotionally charged situations. He also objected to the relatively pessimistic Freudian view of human beings as will-less puppets, directed by instinctual and unconscious forces. Although he, like Freud, developed a dynamic, tension-reduction theory of personality, he integrated concepts common to the humanist and existential frames of reference. Essentially, he perceived human beings as basically good, capable of striving for and achieving self-improvement. He noted that whatever the causes of personal problems, human beings must ultimately assume responsibility for their own behavior. Personality maladjustment frequently results from the pressures of integrating self with the world at large. Problem solution depends on the reduction of inner tension through the development of new insights about behavior. Such insights can evolve only when human beings are encouraged to actively demonstrate attitudes, beliefs, and perceptions as though they are the leading character in a play. They must act out their thoughts and feelings, as they would in real-life situations. Moreno coined the terms *psychodrama* and *sociodrama* to describe his therapeutic approach.

Psychodrama and sociodrama are similar techniques. They are forms of group therapy that provide the opportunity for individuals to act out events that have an important bearing on their lives. A selected person assumes the role of protagonist or star, while various group members act the roles of other influential figures in the drama. The remainder of the group constitutes the audience. The therapist is the director.

The differences between psychodrama and sociodrama lie in their purpose. In the former, the emphasis is on solving the protagonist's personal problems. Consequently the actors represent important persons in his or her life. Sociodrama deals with much broader sociological problems such as racial or ethnic stereotypes. Actors are literally group symbols. Because Moreno's concepts and techniques, particularly as they relate to psychodrama, are the essence of drama therapy, they will be discussed in detail.

PRINCIPLES OF PSYCHODRAMA

Moreno (1964) identified six key concepts as components of psychodrama: spontaneity, situation, encounter, tele, catharsis, and insight. *Spontaneity* is the force behind creativity, the spark generated by psychological health. Disturbed persons typically lack spontaneity, they react to their environment with rigid, preconceived responses. Individuals must be encouraged to abandon static response patterns and to demonstrate less inhibited or restrictive actions. The opportunity for spontaneous behaviors is present in the psychodrama situation.

In psychodrama, the *situation* may encompass any part of the disturbed person's life. Barriers of time and space are removed, thus past and future events are portrayed as present occurrences. Actors may assume the roles of persons not actually present in the protagonist's physical life space. In this way old unresolved conflicts, such as those experienced with parents or siblings, may be re-created and faced by the protagonist. Also, fears of future happenings may be portrayed. The emphasis on bringing all possible problems into the present is predicated on the belief that the disturbed person's perceptions of reality are a critical determinant of his or her mental health. An old problem, such as a traumatic relationship with a parent, cannot remain buried. It must be acted out as though it were presently occurring, because it is still important to the protagonist. Often such interactions take the form of an encounter.

The *encounter* occurs when the protagonist confronts himself or herself and important people in his or her life in the psychodrama. The confrontation is always in the here and now, although it may depict past or future events. In effect, the individual is forced to face other people's views of himself or herself even though they may be contradictory to his or her self-perceptions. He or she also must examine his or her thoughts and emotions toward others.

. *Tele* is a state that emerges from the encounter. It refers to the exchange of empathy and understanding between the persons involved in the psychodramatic situation. Moreno borrowed the term from the Greek word for "far" and sums up the notion in this oft-repeated quote from his book *Psychodrama* (1964).

> A meeting of two: eye to eye, face to face. And when you are near I will tear your eyes out and place them instead of mine, and you will tear my eyes out and place them instead of yours, and then I will look at you with your eyes and you will look at me with mine. (p. 127)

Catharsis is an emotional release that occurs after a psychodramatic session. This cleansing discharge of emotion is due to the spontaneous action involved in the drama. Catharsis produces *insight,* the sudden awareness or understanding not previously experienced by the individual. When the protagonist experiences insight he or she suddenly "sees" or "perceives" the situation in a new light. Moreno described insight as a new understanding of the perceptual field.

THE "WARM-UP" AND DRAMATIC TECHNIQUES

Moreno and his disciples have developed a wide variety of methods and techniques for psychodrama. They are the tools with which the director develops and maintains the dramatic situation. Certain methods pertain to the *warm-up,* that is, the means by which the director prepares the group for the drama. The dramatic techniques provide the means for maintaining the flow of dramatic action. Both the warm-up and the dramatic techniques will be discussed in detail.

The Warm-Up

The warm-up is a very important aspect of psychodrama. Through the warm-up the director sets the stage for the drama by fostering communication among the participants and establishing goals for the session. There are three warm-up methods, nondirective, semidirective and directive, all involving general group discussion. The discussion may range from a rather open-ended assessment of group concerns or opinions about potential dramatic topics to a highly structured attempt to promote group interest in a specific, preselected topic. The type of discussion conducted reflects the director's warm-up method. In some instances the director may choose to hold a nondirective warm-up. This method places the responsibility for the selection of the drama topic and the choice of actors on the group. The director makes only the most general remarks, usually to stimulate group reaction and discussion. In the semidirective method, the director has a particular drama topic in mind and calls it to the group's attention. He or she may also suggest that a certain protagonist be selected. He or she remains responsive to group opinion, however, and alters the drama plan in accordance with their wishes.

In the directive warm-up, the director has selected a topic and a protagonist. He or she may even have decided who will play alternate roles. The warm-up session may be used to share these plans with the group and to discuss their roles in the drama. In some instances the director may use the warm-up to question the protagonist, in the manner of a psychiatric interview. The purpose is to acquaint the group with the nature of the problem and to suggest the types of roles they will play.

Enneis (1974) has categorized three types of warm-up procedures including: (1) cluster, (2) chain of association, and (3) directed. To use a cluster warm-up the director instructs the group to discuss topics for drama among themselves. Each suggested topic draws a cluster of persons interested in the discussion. On some occasions these clusters interact and a dominant theme emerges and becomes the topic for the drama. On other occasions two dominant clusters emerge and a compromise topic is chosen. This is a nondirective format, as the topic of the drama is selected by the group. The protagonist also emerges from the group discussion and is usually either the person who suggested the accepted topic or the person who may most clearly demonstrate the topic behaviors. Enneis notes that it is not unusual for the emotions generated in this type of warm-up to range from boisterous joviality to harsh unpleasantness, and cautions the director to be prepared for any contingency.

The chain-of-association warm-up occurs when the group spontaneously discusses a topic of interest. One comment triggers another until the group responds enthusiastically to some particular suggestion. The director's role is to keep the chain of ideas flowing by interjecting occasional suggestions. This type of warm-up is also nondirective, although the director may lead the group toward an important topic with subtle suggestions. The emotional tone of chain-of-association warm-ups is usually pleasant.

The directed warm-up is controlled by the group director. The director selects the topic of the drama and presents it to the group. The group may discuss the topic at great length but they understand that it will serve as the focal point of the drama. The director encourages discussion to interest the group in the topic. When the group appears to be sufficiently motivated, the director selects the actors, choosing those individuals who will benefit most from the acting-out experience. In an alternate version of the directed warm-up, the director selects a group member in advance to present his or her problems to the group and to act as the protagonist of the drama.

Moreno emphasizes the importance of the warm-up. It is the director's first responsibility in assuring a successful drama. The group must be brought to a state of readiness for the drama and, more importantly, the director must ensure that each group member benefits from the drama. The benefits the group accrues from the drama depends, to a large extent, on the skill with which individuals are assigned to important roles. The director must monitor actor selections made by the group to ensure that each individual is ready and able to play key roles. Actors should be selected on the basis of their own personal needs. Since the goal of drama therapy is to provide a learning experience for all participants, each part is important. In instances where the group is a cohesive unit, experienced in drama techniques, they may have no difficulty selecting members for roles. In other cases, however, the director must play a dominant role in cast selection.

On some occasions, roles are played by the therapist or therapeutic aides. These occasions occur when the protagonist requires interaction with an individual who thoroughly understands the dynamics of a particular relationship. In no instance does the selection of actors depend on the physical characteristics of the group members. Actors are selected on the basis of their psychological needs, not their physical appearance. Thus, a tall, young male may play the role of a small, elderly woman, or vice versa.

Dramatic Techniques

Obviously, the responsibility of the director does not end with the warm-up. He or she is also charged with controlling the flow of the drama. In other words, the director must call for increases and decreases of emotional involvement, change scenes as new points are made, and, most importantly, protect the protagonist from generating more emotion than he or she can handle. To do so, the director must be capable of using a variety of dramatic techniques. Moreno and his disciples have generated a large number of techniques to ensure spontaneity in the drama. The most popular include role reversal, soliloquy, double, mirror, behind-the-back, high chair, empty chair, magic shop, and the ideal other (Greenberg, 1974).

In *role reversal*, the protagonist changes roles with one of the actors. For instance, a child may take the role of its father while the father actor takes the child's role. Through role reversal the protagonist learns to appreciate another person's perspective of a situation. In effect, he or she sees himself or herself as others see him or her.

In *soliloquy*, the protagonist is instructed to make a spontaneous speech that represents an expression of his or her innermost feelings and thoughts. These single-person speeches may be outbursts of anger or just pronouncements of general feelings. Such verbalizations are considered essential for catharsis and the development of insight.

Double is a technique used when the protagonist is overwhelmed by the other actors. Another group member stands with the protagonist and shares his or her identity. The double may remain silent and provide moral support for the protagonist, or he or she may speak as he or she perceives the protagonist would speak.

For withdrawn or noncommunicative persons, the *mirror* technique is used. It requires that an actor assume the role of the protagonist. The latter joins the audience and watches the drama. Theoretically, the mirror technique allows the protagonist to see his or her behavior from another person's point of view.

The *behind-the-back* technique also exposes the protagonist to the views of others. With this technique, however, the drama stops and the protagonist sits on a chair with his or her back to the audience. The director and audience discuss the protagonist, literally behind his or her back, speaking freely about their perceptions of the protagonist's behavior.

For protagonists who have difficulty asserting themselves or coping with threatening situations, the *high chair* technique is used. A chair is elevated in some way so that the protagonist is higher than anyone else on the stage. Presumably the added height conveys a feeling of superiority and power to the patient, which in turn enables him or her to deal more effectively with persons who may dominate him or her.

The *empty chair* technique also provides an opportunity for inadequate or unassertive persons to ventilate their feelings. The protagonist is directed to imagine his or her antagonist seated in an empty chair and to interact with him or her. Theoretically, the absence of an actual person reduces the protagonist's fears and inhibitions. He or she is able to give a more fluid expression of feeling. This technique is also employed to permit the protagonist to demonstrate his or her ideas about how key people regard him or her. The protagonist may reverse roles with the phantom person and interact with an imaginary self. In other words, the protagonist becomes the antagonist in the empty chair and interacts with a phantom of himself or herself.

Two additional techniques used in psychodrama are *magic shop* and *ideal other*. The magic shop is a method for generating thought about life goals. The protagonist is offered anything he or she wants, success or happiness, for example, in return for something he or she has, such as health, or honor. The resulting dilemma forces the protagonist to reconsider aspirations and desires in light of current assets.

The ideal other is used as a tension-reducing ploy at the end of therapy. The protagonist lists the ideal characteristics of an important person in his or her life space. An actor assumes the role of the other person and behaves in the ideal manner suggested by the protagonist. Presumably, the protagonist enjoys experiencing a relationship that is free of strife or conflict.

These are a few of the procedures used in psychodrama. The object is to stimulate the protagonist as well as the other members of the group to ventilate feelings and to develop a new state of awareness reflecting the recognition of those feelings. The drama is designed to benefit all participants, not just the protagonist, but also the actors and the audience. All group members are charged by the director with the responsibility of reflecting on the behavior displayed in the drama. The audience not only must help the protagonist learn by analyzing his or her behaviors, but also must share incidents from their own experiences that may be similar to those demonstrated in the drama. Consequently, all members of the group share in the learning experience. Understanding of self and others is promoted.

PSYCHODRAMA AS A UNIQUE FORM OF THERAPY

This brief synopsis of the theories, methods, and techniques that constitute psychodrama illustrates its uniqueness as a therapeutic methodology. Indeed, Moreno (1964) suggests that, although psychodrama is a form of group therapy, for a variety of reasons it is unlike any other type of group therapy.

The emphasis on creativity and spontaneity, two forces Moreno deems necessary for true expression of feeling, are not duplicated in other approaches. The notion of encounter, which has been adopted in other forms of group therapy (Perls, 1969; Berne, 1965), is uniquely represented in psychodrama. In the course of the drama the individual must confront himself or herself and others in his or her life. Even when unable to face the emotions engendered by these confrontations, the group forces the encounter. The individual cannot avoid dealing with the issues that contribute to his or her emotional disorder.

Also, the concepts of role and role reversal that provide the foundation for many psychosocial theories of personality are developed to the limits of practical significance in psychodrama. Moreno illustrates the importance of the role concept to his theory in volume 1 of *Psychodrama* (1964, p. 4) where he defines role as "the functioning form the individual assumes in the specific moment he reacts to a specific situation in which other persons or objects are involved." He goes on to explain that people assume many roles and develop many role relationships with others. The self is a combination of roles. To understand self implies knowledge of particular roles and role relationships. The technique of role reversal contributes greatly to this understanding. Although role playing may be used in other group therapies, none use it as effectively as psychodrama.

Psychodrama differs most critically from other forms of psychotherapy because it emphasizes actions that represent feelings. Other therapeutic methods depend almost exclusively on patient verbalizations. They are based on the premise that the individual will eventually talk through his or her conscious defenses and gain insight about the source of his or her problems. Moreno insists that role playing thrusts the individual directly into the problem-evoking situations and therefore is a much more efficient means of discovering the underlying kernels of personality disorders.

Regardless of the correctness of Moreno's opinions about the efficiency of psychodrama as a therapeutic approach, the dramatic technique would appear to be particularly applicable with individuals who may lack the verbal fluency necessary to talk about their problems. Obviously, children often rank among such individuals. Thus, the methods and techniques associated with psychodrama appear to be useful in school situations. It is equally obvious that the application of these principles with children must be done with care. The remainder of this chapter will present the means by which certain of the principles of psychodrama may be adapted for use by the teacher in the form of drama therapy.

APPLICATIONS IN THE SCHOOL

Teachers desiring to apply the principles of drama therapy in an educational setting must develop a comprehensive plan that incorporates the following components. First, the goal or purpose of the drama must be stated. Second, each step in the dramatic arrangement, that is, the choice of topic, the type of warm-up, the choice of actors, and the amount of role structure, must be planned. Third, the techniques employed to maintain the dramatic action must be considered. Fourth, the physical arrangements such as the location for the drama must be selected. Each of these components will be discussed in detail. Following that discussion, the benefits and cautions associated with the application of drama therapy will be presented. Finally, alternate application of dramatic techniques, specifically puppetry and story telling will be discussed.

Goals of Drama Therapy

Drama therapy may be used in school settings to serve a variety of purposes. They include (1) solving individual social and/or emotional problems, (2) conducting general affective educational programs, (3) solving common childhood problems, (4) exploring social and cultural issues, (5) developing group camaraderie, and (6) providing recreation.

The application of drama therapy to solve individual social and/or emotional problems most closely resembles Moreno's use of psychodrama. Although it is legitimate for teachers to apply dramatic procedures for this purpose, they must do so with extreme caution. As noted, psychodrama is an intense psychotherapeutic technique designed to be used in clinical settings with severely disturbed individuals. Obviously teachers, even those trained to work with emotionally disturbed children, are not equipped to act as therapists with psychotic or neurotic individuals. Such treatment is the province of either clinical psychologists or psychiatrists who are trained to understand the dynamics of personality.

Teachers may use drama therapy with individuals who demonstrate relatively mild adjustment problems. The children included in this group are those who, for the most part, appear to be in control of their behaviors, but who experience difficulty in particular situations. They might be best described as "their own worst enemies," since they invariably engage in behavior that causes them problems despite their good intentions. For example, such children might behave relatively well in structured situations such as the classroom, but have stormy interpersonal conflicts in less structured settings like the playground. Their playground problems occur despite their conscious intent to get along and avoid trouble.

Other children may experience no difficulties whatsoever in any setting other than the classroom. In that environment, however, they may underachieve and/or demonstrate a variety of other maladaptive behaviors such as wasting time and disrupting others, being quarrelsome and aggressive, acting fearful and overly dependent on teacher support, being withdrawn and unable to relate easily with classmates, cheating, tattling, lying, and stealing.

Many typical classrooms have a substantial proportion of such children. Obviously, they are not necessarily considered emotionally disturbed, although some, particularly the more aggressive children, might bear that label. In any event, the teacher may choose to help a child understand and consequently modify such behaviors through the use of drama therapy. For example, the teacher may use role reversal or mirror techniques to help a physically aggressive but verbally noncommunicative child learn how his or her behaviors are viewed by others. Presumably, the opportunity to act out situations that often culminate in physical aggression will increase the child's ability to understand feelings that he or she may be unable to articulate. Specific examples of the applications of dramatic techniques with children will be provided later in the chapter.

The second purpose for which dramatic therapy may be applied in the schools, that of *teaching children about feelings or emotions*, conceivably could become an integral part of the teacher's instructional program. Many teachers are aware that their educational responsibility to their students involves instruction in both affective and cognitive realms. However, their actual instructional program often pertains exclusively to cognitive areas, usually because they lack the methods to explore the affective domain. Through the use of drama, the teacher may help children learn about emotions and the importance of nonrational events on behavior. For example, the teacher may choose to have the class enact a drama about fear. They might explore themes such as fear of the dark, fear of animals, fear of school, and so forth. Discussions surrounding the drama should convey the fact that fear is a common emotion experienced by all people. The children learn that fears can be overcome more easily when they are shared with others.

The third goal of drama therapy involves *helping children overcome common problems.* There are many stumbling blocks on the road to adulthood that most children encounter. For example, test taking may traumatize many. Dating and its related social pressures constitute another obvious problem for most. In specific instances, particularly those involving such handicapped children as mental retardates or the emotionally disturbed, daily living events might evoke extreme concern. The stressful emotions associated with activities like these might be explored through drama therapy. The opportunity for the group members to act out these types of situations and to share their feelings should reduce the threat of the real-life experiences.

The fourth goal involves the *exploration of social and cultural issues.* This use, which is akin to Moreno's sociodrama, involves raising the group consciousness to the point where they understand the extent to which the prevailing social and cultural mores shape their attitudes on such critical issues as sex, race, and ethnicity. In essence the teacher has her or his children walk in another's shoes. For example, the teacher may wish to demonstrate the impact of social pressures on a particular minority group by casting various children in the role of minority persons and having them experience the frustrations of discrimination in dramatic situations.

The fifth goal that can be accomplished with drama therapy, the *development of group camaraderie,* has a great deal of practical value. Drama provides the teacher with an excellent method for shaping his or her class into a cohesive unit. As each individual member of the class is given the opportunity to help plan and act in a drama that is a class project, a sense of group identity is developed. In other words, each child feels like a member of a unit and, as such, is likely to experience increased feelings of personal well being. A cooperative rather than a competitive spirit is promoted within the class. With this in mind, the teacher might choose to use drama to break the ice at the beginning of a new school year, or to integrate a new child into an established class.

The sixth goal of drama therapy, that of *recreation,* is more important than it may at first appear. It is not uncommon throughout the course of a long school year for both teachers and their students to become stale and less interested in their school activities. As motivation decreases so does productivity and there is usually a corresponding increase in class-management problems. At such times the class requires recreational activities that are designed to reduce tension and to raise spirits. Drama therapy is an excellent technique for such a purpose because it provides the participants with an emotional outlet. The children create and enact a drama for the sheer fun of it. They may explore their fantasies or act out their wishes. The teacher may choose to participate as an actor and to permit various members of the class to act as the director.

An additional benefit of this use of drama therapy is to familiarize the children with the technique. Experience of this sort prepares them to participate in dramatic situations that may be directed toward more serious goals such as teaching social values or solving personal problems.

Steps in the Dramatic Arrangement

The dramatic arrangement is actually the preperformance plan for the drama. It includes the warm-up strategy, the topic selection, the cast selection, and the role structure. In developing these plans, the degree of control exerted by the teacher may range from nondirective to directive. The extent to which the teacher controls the dramatic arrangements depends on the goal of the drama. If she or he wants to use drama as a form of affective instruction, she or he may choose a general topic area and permit the group to develop the specific plan. For instance, the teacher might suggest a drama that deals with the subject of tolerance. A nondirective warm-up permits the group to develop the idea and to depict tolerance through actual situations. The choice of actors is also a group decision and there is little preperformance role structure provided by the teacher.

On the other hand, the teacher might wish to use drama to deal with a conflict between two classmates. In this instance she or he introduces the specific topic of interest, that is the types of conflicts that develop among people. Since the teacher is concerned with two children in particular she or he, and not the group, chooses to cast them in the important roles. The teacher may even brief them on the types of parts they are to play since she or he wants to ensure that certain behaviors are demonstrated. In short, the dramatic arrangement is highly structured or directive. The teacher uses the warm up only to generate class interest.

As a general rule, highly directive drama requires increased teacher sensitivity to the group's attitudes and feelings. The warm-up period provides the teacher with the opportunity to tap these feelings. Since a successful drama depends on the group's enthusiasm for the activity, the teacher must ensure their open acceptance of the drama topic. She or he may do this by

1. Permitting the class a full opportunity to explore the topic in the warm-up,
2. Being alert to the feelings of the children she or he would like to cast in the drama,
3. Resisting the temptation to overstructure certain key roles.

A full class discussion of the teacher's suggested topic is one that ideally will involve all class members. The teacher must take care to elicit opinions from reluctant speakers and to involve youngsters who otherwise might not participate. Although the topic for a highly directive drama is relatively specific, the teacher should introduce it in general terms and permit the children to evolve the specific issues through discussion. Their discussion serves to clarify their views and increases their level of understanding. Should the children fail to reach the specific topic that is of interest to the teacher, she or he can supply it during the course of the discussion. For example, the teacher concerned with the topic of a conflict between two class members might introduce a general discussion about the conflicts that occur among people. When the group discusses the type of conflict that is disturbing the teacher, she or he can suggest that it serve as the main subject for the drama. Generally, the more completely and thoroughly the class participates in the warm-up discussion, the greater the chances for a fruitful drama. In fact, a full discussion is so important that the teacher may wish to allot more than one warm-up session for its accomplishment.

When attempting to involve certain children in roles, the teacher must carefully elicit their enthusiastic cooperation. Obviously, a child who is reluctant to play a role cannot be forced or coerced into doing so. Since the drama is intended to instruct all group members, not just the actors, its impact is not lost on children who are not ready to become active participants. The actual role-playing involvement of many children may be accomplished only after extensive warm-up efforts, or, in some instances, only after the group has engaged in several dramas.

When planning the types of roles to be played in the drama the teacher must recognize the importance of role spontaneity. Even the most tightly structured drama is rendered useless if the actors are not permitted to react honestly, in accordance with their own views of the situation. Drama therapy differs from drama in the usual sense of the term in that the participants are acting out their feelings and thoughts, not reciting lines prepared by another person. This difference is essential to the use of drama as a therapeutic tool since only the spontaneous portrayal of feelings generates new insights into behavior. Thus, the teacher may suggest a general type of role and give the actor certain dimensions for the characterization, but should not interfere with the ongoing action. In fact, the director's major concern is to aid the flow of the drama, not to stifle it. The problem of maintaining productive action in the drama requires the use of dramatic techniques.

Dramatic Techniques

The teacher who wishes to use drama therapy must be able to apply many of Moreno's techniques to control the flow of the drama. The following discussion will demonstrate these procedures as they can be used in a school situation.

To begin the drama, the teacher acting as director may want to focus attention on the protagonist or star since that role provides the impetus for all ensuing events. The soliloquy technique is an efficient means of doing so. The star is directed to enact a scene where he or she typically experiences difficulty. As the star begins he or she is directed to discuss his or her thoughts or feelings. In effect, think out loud. For instance, a young boy, Alan, who fights on the playground is instructed to role play leaving the classroom for recess. As he enacts walking outside with his classmates, he is directed to say what is on his mind. Alan might say: "I hope there is no trouble today. Yesterday the teacher said I would have to stay in for a week if I fight again today. I don't know why they don't like me and let me play kickball. They hog the ball—especially Michael and his friends. I can beat him up any time I feel like fighting with him."

Alan's soliloquy has served two purposes. His fellow actors have gained information that will permit them to play their roles in the drama. Also, both the actors and the audience have been exposed to several unique dimensions of Alan's problem. Whereas previously they might have explained his behavior by assuming that he was a bad person who enjoyed causing trouble, they now realize the inadequacy of that explanation. Alan has informed them that he thinks he is disliked and that he really would like to be included in their games. His further statements of his attitude toward Michael and his propensity toward fighting arouse the group's interest and emotion and the drama is ready to proceed. For example, the audience and other actors might be thinking: "If he wants to play, why does he always ruin the game by keeping the ball away from everyone else. That's why Michael tries to take the ball away from him." In the course of the drama the children's feelings will be conveyed to Alan. He in turn will feel and demonstrate the uncooperative behavior that he typically displays during the game. Eventually he should learn why the children wish to exclude him from their activities and how he must behave to avoid exclusion.

Once the drama is underway it is often necessary for the director to highlight critical feelings that might be present in the ongoing events

Again soliloquy is a technique that may be employed. In this instance it can take the form of an aside to the audience. To use the example introduced above, Alan and Michael may be exchanging conversation about the kickball game. The star says: "Today I want you to let me have a shot at the ball instead of keeping it yourself or passing it to your friends." Michael answers: "You're the one who won't share, that's why we don't like you to play." An impasse between the actors has been reached. To prevent an ongoing exchange of accusations, the teacher directs Alan to soliloquize. He must report what he thinks or feels about Michael's remark. He says: "You think you are smart because you get better grades than I do. I am better at kickball than you are. I don't know why the other kids always listen to you." Several interesting points are conveyed in Alan's dramatic aside. The feelings that contribute to his unruly behavior are closely related to his desire to compete with Michael and to play a leadership role as Michael does. The drama may now proceed to incorporate this information.

As the drama progresses the actors may have difficulty sustaining their roles and be unable to generate significant actions and dialogue. At such times the director may use the *double* technique. This technique involves appointing another child to join the star and play his or her alter ego. The star's double stands beside him or her, behaves as the star does, and speaks for the star. For example, Alan's double might say: "I really want you to be my friend Michael. I wish you liked me." Thus, Alan is forced to move away from his more superficial remarks about Michael's responsibility for his playground problems and deal with his feelings toward Michael. Although he may reject his double's statement he is confronted with the issue.

In some instances the drama may falter because the protagonist is unable to portray himself or herself realistically. He or she may not recognize the behaviors that lead him or her to difficulty, or the protagonist may be so defensive that he or she deliberately alters his or her behavior when role playing. In these cases the director may use the *mirror technique* to expedite matters. This technique involves returning the star to the audience and appointing another actor to play his or her role. This actor uses the star's name and represents him or her in interactions with others. Thus, the star is confronted by himself or herself as other's view him or her. To use our example once again, Alan is unable to portray himself as he typically behaves at recess. In his role he politely interacts with the other children and carefully avoids conflict. Alan is instructed to join the audience while a classmate assumes his role and gives a more accurate portrayal of his playground behavior. The other actors react accordingly. The audience concurs that, indeed, Alan behaves in the manner being depicted. Alan is faced with the realization that his peers see him as a belligerent trouble maker. No matter how convinced he has been of his innocence, he must acknowledge the weight of opinion to the contrary.

Possibly the most important technique used in the drama is *role reversal*. Role reversal, or the exchange of roles, permits the actors to recognize the distortions in their perceptions of each other. In our sample drama, Alan takes Michael's part while Michael becomes Alan. Now the protagonist is forced to see himself through Michael's eyes. He must be Michael and defend the group against Alan's (as portrayed by Michael) disruptive play. On the other hand, Michael, as Alan, can be brought to realize how it feels to be excluded from a desired activity. Both boys share an invaluable experience, that of appreciating another person's point of view. The notion of absolute right and wrong that most children hold becomes less pronounced and begins to be replaced with greater understanding of the subtle interactions that contribute to interpersonal problems.

If the teacher believes that a particular problem is too sensitive for an initial encounter between the central figure and the group, *the treatment at a distance* technique may be used. With this approach, the central character is not present in the drama. His role is portrayed by another child. For instance, the teacher might choose to involve the group in a drama pertaining to fighting on the playground on a day when Alan is absent. The goal is to develop group understanding of the problem and to plan strategies for diminishing the likelihood of recurring conflicts.

Finally, the teacher may want to provide a troubled child with the opportunity to improve his or her self-concept. A dramatic technique that aids in this goal is called *wish fulfillment*. The child is instructed to plan a drama representing the attainment of a wish. He or she may create ideal conditions for the roles played by himself or herself and others. Let us assume that Alan's ideal desire is to be popular with others. He instructs the players to treat him as though they liked and respected him. He treats them in similar fashion. The drama permits Alan to experience the fruits of pleasant interaction and shows him that he can behave according to his ideals. Others begin to view Alan as capable of responding to kindness. He learns that it is possible to fulfill certain wishes.

To end the drama the director instructs the actors to return to the audience. The group, as a whole, discusses the events that occurred on the stage. Thus the nonperforming members of the group are not excluded from the experience. In fact, it is expected that they will gain many of the same benefits as the actors. Perhaps because they were not required to generate dialogue while role playing the audience may offer the most penetrating and perceptive remarks about the events that took place. This final technique is called the *wrap-up*.

These techniques are but a few that can be used to stimulate interactions among individuals. The examples given thus far depicted the social problems of one child. As noted, however, these techniques may be used for purposes other than the resolution of individual social and/or emotional problems. In fact, one of the most prevalent uses of dramatic reenactments in schools involves increasing children's awareness of global social problems. The following examples will illustrate the utilization of drama therapy for the purpose of social instruction.

The *treatment at a distance technique* is particularly useful in schools that mainstream handicapped children. Since handicapped children often experience social rejection from nonhandicapped classmates, a drama held either in advance of the handicapped child's enrollment or on a day when the child is absent may help the class behave in a friendlier fashion. The teacher may instruct various children to assume the role of a handicapped person. The other actors and the audience might be encouraged to act out their opinions and attitudes toward the handicapped. Presumably, the children will become more aware of how it feels to be viewed as different from others. They will become more cognizant of how their behavior may generate feelings of isolation in others.

A similar technique is called *representative protagonist*. This technique does not require that a specific protagonist be associated directly with the group. The protagonist is representative of a minority subgroup within the society. For example, the director may want to depict the treatment given to the American Indians by the white settlers. The roles of the Indians may represent actual historical figures such as Geronimo or Joseph, or they may be symbolic of all Indians. In such an enactment, the director must remain aware that the drama is not designed to depict past history, as might be done in a children's play about the life of Geronimo. The dramatic action must occur spontaneously, in the here and now. The goal is to increase the children's understanding about the treatment given to a particular minority within the society. To accomplish that goal, the children must feel the way the Indians felt.

Possibly the most useful technique to demonstrate important social issues is *role reversal*. Racial, sexual, and ethnic biases may be explored by having the children assume a variety of alternate roles. For instance, a black child might play a white child, a boy might play a girl, and so forth. The success of this type of drama is extremely dependent on the director's skill. Although the director must control the progress of the drama, she or he must be extremely careful not to force opinions on the actors that they do not share. For example, in a drama depicting sexual bias, the children must be permitted to express their true feelings, however hostile or rejecting they may be. The director must avoid interfering and censuring these expressions. The goal of drama therapy is to induce a spontaneous production of true feelings, opinions, and attitudes. If the director supresses remarks that run contrary to her or his own ideas about a particular issue, spontaneity would be seriously impaired. The drama would become nothing more than a social farce—the recitation of lines that are generally perceived as being what should be said. With the demise of spontaniety and the inhibition of true feelings, the opportunity for communication, catharsis, and insight that may lead to a genuine change in attitude is destroyed.

Obviously, other techniques may be used for the purpose of demonstrating important social issues. For instance, in a situation similar to that discussed regarding sexual bias, the teacher might want to use the mirror or double techniques to assist the children in understanding the importance of equality for the sexes. It is quite possible that one drama will generate a variety of ideas for succeeding dramas. The teacher may decide to use drama therapy on a somewhat regular basis. In effect, the dramatic method may become part of the instructional curriculum.

Physical Arrangements

From the most practical point of view, an important blessing of drama therapy is that it makes optimal use of imagination. The group or class need only pretend that they are in a certain place and, for the purposes of the drama, it becomes reality. The only necessity for staging a drama is enough space to rearrange furniture. Any room where the chairs can be arranged in a semicircle, to provide room for a makeshift stage at the front of the class, is adequate for drama therapy. In most cases the children's regular classroom should serve nicely.

In rare instances, the teacher may decide to hold a drama in a private room or office. She or he may want to settle an issue that involves a subgroup of children from the class, and see no purpose in revealing the matter to the entire group. Obviously, the aims of the drama should determine where it should be held.

The time necessary to stage a drama will vary depending on the teacher's aims and the children's experience and maturity. Less mature children may have difficulty sustaining the flow of action for periods in excess of a half-hour. When working with such children the director must avoid attempting to depict too many important points in one dramatic session. Older or more experienced children may be perfectly capable of sustaining interest and action for an hour or more. This is particularly true when they are exploring relatively complex issues. Ideally, the course of the drama should make the best time to terminate clear to the director. When the group's attention wanders or its action stagnates, the time for wrap up is at hand. Also, it is time to terminate when the basic goal of the drama has been accomplished, when the children have thoroughly considered the topic and further action would be superfluous. The ensuing wrap-up discussion should help clarify any points that remain vague, as well as delineate topics for future dramas.

BENEFITS OF DRAMA THERAPY

The advocates of drama therapy (Allport, 1955; Corsini, 1952; Osherson, 1968) make the following points regarding its advantages. First, it places the responsibility for growth and resolution of problems squarely on the shoulders of the individual involved. Although people, particularly those who face a dilemma, often seek advice and direction from an authoritative source, in the end it is usually to no avail. To make lasting adjustments in personality the individual must think for himself or herself. The individual must learn to evaluate himself or herself critically but not harshly, to be objective about his or her behaviors and, most importantly, to take responsibility for his or her conduct. From this perspective, it is impossible for external manipulation of behavior such as those practiced in behavior therapy to make a lasting impact on the individual. External behavioral changes are caused by internal motivation for change.

Second, drama therapy places emphasis on the development of social consciousness. Individual growth is intrinsically related to the development of a philosophy of life. Such a philosophy incorporates the individual's attitudes and convictions toward others and recognizes the notion of the individual's responsibility to the group.

The third benefit of drama therapy is its emphasis on the individual's future. This technique is designed to help the individual leave behind the concerns or cares of the past so that she or he might move creatively into new activities.

The fourth and most practical benefit of this approach is its efficiency. Moreno notes that these dramatic techniques bring the individual to the point of examining underlying emotions much faster than the more traditional forms of psychotherapy. The opportunity to reexperience important events in life rapidly generates insight.

The benefits attributed to psychodrama also may be applied to the application of drama techniques in school settings. In addition, the teacher has the added advantages of providing opportunities for the emotional and social development of children who are not seriously disturbed and creating a novel and enjoyable learning experience for children.

CAUTIONS

As noted, drama therapy has obvious appeal for children of all ages. For the most part, children enjoy play acting. They tend to lose inhibitions more quickly than adults and they bring a great deal of spontaneity to the dramatic situation. Thus, the proper application of drama therapy in the classroom not only can provide a marvelous instructional format for affective growth, but also can be a thoroughly enjoyable activity. However, both outcomes depend on the teacher's scrupulous observation of certain guidelines.

First, *the dramatic situations must be devoid of criticism.* The teacher and the class members may make suggestions regarding certain roles and they may offer comments about the course of the drama. However, demeaning or accusatory remarks are strictly prohibited.

Second, *the children who participate in drama must do so voluntarily.* Dramatic therapy is designed to promote affective growth. To be effective the children must be motivated to learn or improve. Children who are apprehensive, embarrassed, or defensive are not in a position to learn efficiently. They should not be teased or coerced into active role playing. They will learn far more as members of the audience.

Third, *the use of confrontation in the course of the drama must be regulated carefully.* A child should never be cast in a drama that will confront him or her with personal problems unless she or he has agreed in advance to act out the situations that cause trouble. Also, the teacher must ensure that such a child completely understands the events that will occur and is prepared to have the other group members speak frankly about his or her behavior. Even under these circumstances, the teacher must establish clear limits about the type and tone of permissible confronting remarks.

For the most part, confronting remarks should pertain to the child's behavior, "you fight a lot," rather than to general character traits, "you're a nasty person." The tone of the remarks must reflect constructive interest in helping to solve a problem rather than disgust or displeasure with the individual. For example, "you fight a lot," may be offered as a statement of an opinion, not as a harsh accusation.

Clearly, children require a great deal of practice if they are to understand these distinctions. Direct confrontation should never be staged until these limits are understood by the children.

ALTERNATIVE DRAMATIC TECHNIQUES

The applications of drama therapy in school settings discussed thus far pertained exclusively to the physical enactment of drama by the children. There are certain advantages to conducting drama on that scale. It exploits children's natural predilections to act out their feelings. Thus, it is relatively unique in school settings where physical demonstrations of emotion are usually restricted. Also, the children's active involvement in the drama usually ensures their interest and attention.

In some instances, however, the teacher might wish to employ dramatic techniques without resorting to active drama. Two such techniques are *puppetry* and *storytelling*. Puppetry, a familiar method of entertaining children, for many years has been used as a method of helping them resolve emotional problems. Woltmann (1951) writes of the therapeutic use of puppets from a psychoanalytic frame of reference. From this perspective, puppets are selected to fulfill key roles in the children's lives. The cast of characters typically includes a hero puppet who represents the child's idealized ego, an animal puppet such as a monkey who is the id, four parent puppets who represent the good and bad aspects of superego control, a menacing animal puppet such as an alligator or crocodile who represents oral aggression, and other assorted puppets such as a bad boy who is the negative side of the hero puppet.

Theoretically, children identify with the hero puppet as it struggles with various forces in the environment. The hero is reality oriented and tries to cope with events in a rational way. The other puppets create conflicts. The monkey puppet is pleasure oriented and totally concerned with the gratification of its impulses. The monkey does as it pleases without regard for rules or regulations. The bad mother puppet may be represented as a witch. She punishes the hero puppet by forcing it to do unpleasant jobs, denying it food, and so forth. The good mother is a puppet who reacts affectionately to the hero. The bad father puppet may be a giant, a policeman, a magician, or any dominating figure capable of outwitting or overpowering the hero. Good father is a protective and helpful puppet. The alligator puppet is an aggressive threat to the hero. The bad boy engages in all the behaviors the hero deplores. He is rude, negative, demanding, boastful, and so on. He serves as a clear contrast to the ideal behavior of the hero.

The drama enacted by the puppets is controlled by the puppeteer. It is designed to illustrate the threats and fears that may be disturbing the children. Strict adherence to reality is unusual. Fantasy is incorporated readily into the script and is accepted easily by the children. A puppet may be killed in one scene and resurrected in the next. They may levitate out of harms way, cast magical spells, and leap tall buildings in a single bound. The combined use of realistic and fantasy characters is deliberate. It emphasizes the make-believe aspect of the drama while enabling the child to identify with the hero.

Throughout the drama, the children are encouraged to interact with the puppets. The puppets address questions to the members of the audience, ask the children for advice or assistance, make remarks that draw the audience's attention to an event, and so forth. Usually, the children become closely involved with the puppet drama and their behavior may be observed for clues to personal problems. For instance, the type of life situation that they find upsetting or their feelings toward authority figures might be conveyed in their reaction to the puppets.

Obviously, puppetry need not adhere to a psychoanalytic model. A nondirective use of puppetry can be achieved by permitting the children to develop and enact the drama. The children may take responsibility for the choice of topic, puppets, roles, and persons to act as puppeteers. The actual parts may be created spontaneously by the children as they enact the drama. From the nondirective perspective the teacher has two major responsibilities, the warm-up and the sum-up.

In the warm-up the teacher suggests the idea of staging a puppet drama to the entire group and arouses their interest. If they are enthusiastic, she or he can offer them supportive suggestions as they discuss the project, such as possible topics, roles, or puppeteers. She or he also can suggest that the group establish certain rules to provide structure for the drama, for example, *time limits*, to ensure that the entire performance can be presented, *action limits*, to ensure that all group members have an opportunity to participate, and *behavioral limits*, to prohibit disruptive behaviors such as excessive aggression, profanity, or the like. Although the group should be permitted to make the ultimate decisions about these issues, the warm-up period is the teacher's best opportunity to ensure that the puppet drama has the structure necessary to make it a constructive learning experience. The children must appreciate that they are not playing with puppets, but are enacting dramatic roles. Generally, the age of the children and their experience with puppet drama will determine the amount of suggestion that the teacher must offer.

During the puppet show the teacher becomes a member of the audience. She or he sets an example for active audience participation by responding enthusiastically to the action, verbally interacting with the puppets, and so forth.

After the puppet drama, the teacher leads the group in the sum-up. The group is encouraged to discuss what they have seen. The teacher's purpose during this session is to emphasize and clarify the affective messages conveyed in the drama. Questions such as "How did the hero feel?", "What caused the problem?", or "What would you have done to help?", all stimulate the group to recognize and discuss affective lessons they otherwise might overlook.

Obviously, there are other ways the teacher might use puppetry. She or he might act as puppeteer to create and perform dramas about social values, interpersonal relationships, classroom problems, and so forth. Should the teacher be reluctant to create puppetry drama, she or he might wish to order commercial affective teaching materials such as Developing Understanding of Self and Others (DUSO). DUSO's star performer is a dolphin puppet who may be used in role-playing activities and as a leader of group discussions. This kit may be obtained from the American Guidance Service, Circle Pines, Minnesota.

There are advantages to the use of puppetry in the schools which the teacher should recognize. First, puppets are regarded by parents and administrators as innocuous, pleasure-evoking toys that belong in school.

The teacher should encounter little resistance to staging puppet dramas in the classroom. Second, puppets are easily acquired. They consist only of a head and a material costume. They can be constructed by the children or purchased inexpensively. Third, puppet shows require little space. A simple stage consisting of a square wooden frame and a curtain, set on a table, is all that is necessary to conduct them. Fourth, children love puppets. For the most part, they enter into puppet dramas without self-consciousness or inhibition. Fifth, the portrayal of feelings indirectly, through puppets, rather than by direct acting, ensures that no individual will be embarrassed or upset by dramatic action that probes too deeply in sensitive areas.

Storytelling in the therapeutic sense involves more than the simple recitation of a previously learned tale. The idea behind the technique is for children to create an original story that they will tell to the group. For example, the children might be requested to create a story about an Indian girl who moves from her reservation to take a job in a large city. The emphasis in the story must be upon the characters' feelings rather than upon their activities.

The storytelling project may be implemented by dividing the class into small groups of three to five children. The teacher's role is to confer with each group as the stories are being developed. She or he must encourage the children to cast themselves in the place of the story characters and to explore how they would feel in such a situation. During this period, the teacher's manner must be positive and supportive. Suggestions for story development may be offered, but the children's efforts are never criticized.

The actual storytelling may be done by one or all members of the groups. The children may dramatize various roles in the story and present it like a play, or they may tell the story without dramatic effect. After the story has been presented, the teacher attempts to emphasize the characters' feelings and to lead the group in forming generalizations from the story theme that relate to the development of social values.

A variation of the storytelling technique involves the open-ended story. The teacher tells a story that incorporates issues about social or personal values, or which depicts social or emotional problems, but leaves it unfinished. She or he may provide several alternatives for ending the story and ask the children to select one, or she or he may ask the children to develop an ending. For example, the teacher may create a story that presents a child in conflict with his or her parents, and instruct the children to decide how the story character may best deal with the situation.

Story endings may be developed by each child, then discussed by the entire class, or they may be developed and debated by the class as a whole. The teacher's principle purpose for using the technique is to elicit alternate views of the ending and to stimulate class discussion about the implications of each alternate ending.

STUDY QUESTIONS

1. Discuss the philosophic principles that underlie psychodrama.
2. Discuss the dramatic techniques associated with psychodrama. Then indicate how those techniques can be used by the teacher in a classroom situation.
3. Cite the advantages and potential dangers associated with the use of drama therapy in school.
4. Think of five different topics that could be introduced to your class or any group of children with puppets.

REFERENCES

Allport, G. *Becoming: Basic considerations for a psycholgy of personality.* New Haven, Yale University Press, 1955.

Berne, E. *Games people play.* New York: Grove Press, 1965.

Corsini, R. Immediate therapy. *Group Psychotherapy,* 1952, 9, 322–330.

Enneis, J. The dynamics of group and action processes in therapy: an analysis of the warm-up in Psychodrama. In I. A. Greenberg (ed.). *Psychodrama: theory and therapy.* New York: Behavioral Publications, 1974.

Greenberg, I. *Psychodrama: theory and therapy.* New York: Behavioral Publications, 1974.

Moreno, J. L. *Psychodrama,* vol. 1 and 2. Beacon, New York: Beacon House, 1964.

Osherson, S. Self acceptance through psychodrama. *Group Psychotherapy,* 1968, 20, 12–19.

Perls, F. *Gestalt therapy verbatim.* Lafayette, Cal.: Real People Press, 1969.

Woltmann, A. The use of puppetry as a projective method in therapy. In H. Anderson and G. Anderson (eds.). *An introduction to projective techniques.* Englewood Cliffs, N.J.: Prentice-Hall, 1951.

12
Art and Music Therapy[*]

Art and music therapy are distinct therapeutic tools that share the goal of producing desirable changes in an individual through media. Both artistic techniques provide a unique adjunct to the therapeutic milieu as nonverbal forms of communication. Although a certain mystical reverence for the healing effects of the arts has existed since primitive times, artistic and musical expression were not recognized and widely used as specific forms of therapy until the latter half of this century. In the period immediately following World War II, art and music served as forms of occupational and recreational therapy for injured, hospitalized veterans. Currently, they serve primarily as adjuncts or ancillary components of comprehensive treatments for the emotionally disturbed.

To varying degrees, both art and music therapy reflect a psychoanalytic orientation. They are often regarded as projective techniques through which an individual may express the unconscious forces that motivate his or her behavior. Theoretically, they enable an individual to creatively and spontaneously act out feelings.

In addition to sharing psychodynamic foundations, both art and music therapy lay claim to similar therapeutic advantages. First, they are nonverbal means of communication. This advantage is especially significant for young children with limited verbal competence who cannot participate in the verbal exchanges necessary for other types of therapy. It is also useful for reaching extremely withdrawn or psychotic children.

A second advantage is that the symbolic expressions of art and music may precipitate verbal expression. Naumburg (1966) points out that in art therapy, the visual art form often stimulates verbal communication

---

* This chapter was co-authored by Deborah David and Phyllis L. Newcomer.

when the child attempts to explain or describe his or her production. A third advantage is that art and music therapy provide opportunities for children to experience success and gain self-confidence. This aspect is important not only for the withdrawn and nonverbal child, but also for the academic underachiever or any other child lacking self-confidence. The fact that art and music activities are not restricted to emotionally disturbed children, but are normal activities for all children, makes them nonthreatening experiences and enhances their therapeutic value.

A fourth advantage is the use of art or music can build interpersonal relationships. Group projects such as painting a wall mural or playing an orchestral piece help children learn cooperation. In addition to developing social skills, children have the opportunity to express their feelings freely, a fifth advantage. Some emotionally disturbed children, particularly overly inhibited ones, need opportunities to express emotion without fear of violating social norms. Similarly, a sixth advantage of art and music therapy is that they are both stimulating and relaxing. Thus, these techniques may be used to calm overly excited or hyperactive children and to stimulate or arouse withdrawn, passive children. A seventh advantage is that music and art techniques help children improve their fine-motor coordination. A final, albeit indirect advantage of art and music therapy is that it might have a positive effect on academic achievement. A child who accrues the other seven advantages cannot help but be in a better position to undertake academic tasks. This statement does not imply that art or music therapy causes better academic achievement. It simply means that children who feel better about themselves might learn more efficiently.

The advantages attributed to both art and music therapy will be explored more fully in discussions of each therapeutic method. These discussions will include background information, including the traditional role of the therapist and the specific therapeutic techniques associated with each approach, educational applications, including candidates for each type of therapy, the physical arrangements required, and the teacher's role in the implementation of each approach.

ART THERAPY: THEORETICAL BACKGROUND

Art therapy has its roots in psychoanalytic theory. In fact, according to Kramer (1971), art therapy has mirrored psychoanalysis in its progressive development from early emphasis directed exclusively toward the interpretation of unconscious forces to a latter-day emphasis on ego functions. Initially, spontaneous artistic expression was used as a projective technique, that is, as a reflection of an individual's inner psychic conflicts and desires, much as dreams were interpreted as being representative of such forces. The art therapist was primarily a psychotherapist, and the techniques usually were practiced in clinics or hospital settings with persons suffering from severe emotional disorders. Freud himself (1963) cited the advantage of visual art as an expression of inner experience. Naumburg (1966) also noted that art therapy provided a more direct expression for dreams, fantasies, and fears than verbal exchange. Art expression was viewed as a more natural way to describe what so often occurred pictorially, and, therefore, as an important tool for psychoanalysis.

The characteristics of art therapy altered somewhat after World War II. During that period, art was used therapeutically in hospitals with wounded veterans as a component of recreational or occupational therapy. In the most basic sense, art activities provided physically and mentally traumatized patients with something to do. However, in some instances, the classical use of art to unlock the unconscious components of personality was retained.

Today, art therapy remains neo-Freudian in its theoretical orientation. Naumburg (1966) writes of "releasing unconscious conflicts, fantasies, and dreams," through artistic expression. Similarly, Kramer (1971, 1973) describes art therapy as a "means of supporting the ego," and the artist as one who has resolved the conflict between "the demands of his impulses and the demands of his superego, between reality and fantasy." The Freudian concept of sublimation, the transformation of socially unacceptable impulses into socially acceptable artistic products, remains a key premise of art therapy.

The current practice of art therapy departs from the traditional psychoanalytic approach in three respects. First, it focuses on present situations and feelings rather than on past conflicts. Second, the art therapist uses nondirective techniques, acting only to facilitate the child's production. Contrary to typical Freudian methods, the child rather than the therapist makes all interpretations of the artistic product. Third, greater emphasis is placed on the caliber of the artistic products, as opposed to their therapeutic value. Ulman (1977) remarks that "anything that is called art therapy must genuinely partake of both art and therapy."

Role of The Art Therapist

The third point cited above appears to be critical in defining the role of the art therapist today. The question of how much weight should be assigned to behaving as a psychoanalytical therapist as opposed to acting as an artist and teacher appears to divide the field. This division can be traced to the positions adapted by the two central figures in the field of art therapy, Margaret Naumburg and Edith Kramer.

According to Ulman (1977), Naumburg is considered the pioneer of art therapy in this country. She began her work in the early 1940's while participating in a research program with behavior problem children in the

New York Psychiatric Institute; she later worked with schizophrenic adults, and in 1958, established the first art therapy training program at New York University.

Naumburg's (1966) work reflects her belief that the art therapist should be well-trained in psychoanalytical principles. The art therapist's primary function is to use artistic expression as a projective technique— to uncover unconscious forces in the personality. The therapist need not have artistic talent, but only a sympathetic interest in the creative arts. Clearly, Naumburg's position is closely aligned to the traditional conceptualizations of the art therapist's role.

In contrast, Kramer conceives of the art therapist as a well-balanced combination of artist, teacher, and therapist. Her contribution to the field stems from her work in the 1950's with emotionally disturbed boys in the Wiltwyck School for Boys, and is presented in *Art Therapy is a Children's Community* (1973). She writes of the art therapist (1973, p. 5): "He is no psychotherapist, and it is not his function to interpret deep unconscious content to his students." Also, "The basic aim of the art therapist is to make available to disturbed persons the pleasures and satisfaction which creative work can give, and by his insight and therapeutic skill to make such experiences meaningful and valuable to the total personality" (pp. 5–6).

Kramer recognizes the need for the art therapist to have an understanding of psychodynamic processes. She agrees that it is unlikely that the products of art therapy can be considered art. However, whereas Naumburg considers creativity as secondary to the development of symbolic communication through the arts, Kramer stresses that the creative work is of primary importance. She believes that the creative process is healing, and that the quality of the creative work can serve as a measure of therapeutic success.

Ulman (1977) points out that although Naumburg and Kramer present what seem to be opposing points of view, in actual practice the conflict is not absolute. Indeed, they agree on the two basic principles that define the role of the art therapist. One of the principles is *total acceptance of creative works that constitute a sincere effort.* The art therapist must make no esthetic judgment on the quality or simplicity of the product. This acceptance conveys respect for each child's individuality, and creates a noncompetitive atmosphere for the art therapy session.

The second principle is that the *art therapist must be nondirective.* In a nondirective environment, the child may be permitted to choose the place, time, and frequency of the therapy. He or she also has a free choice of both the medium to use and the subject matter. Most importantly, the child interprets the product. The therapist plays a supportive role, giving assistance when necessary, eliciting the child's interpretations with open-ended questions, and offering encouragement.

Techniques

The techniques of art therapy are those that stimulate artistic production. In the simplest sense, these involve giving the child access to art material and watching him or her create. However, some children are reluctant to try artistic activities unless they are provided with more structure. Consequently, certain techniques have been developed to stimulate participation. With the exception of the scribble technique provided by Kramer (1971), all of the following procedures are adapted from Denny (1977). They are listed here under the trait they are purported to encourage.

Exploration   Encourages spontaneous expression.
1. Scribble Technique—The individual first "draws" in the air; then he or she draws those movements on paper while keeping his or her eyes closed. Next the child looks at the scribble from all sides until he or she sees a form to elaborate on to produce a drawing.
2. Blob and Wet Paper Technique—The individual allows ink, paint, or watercolors to flow naturally on the paper. He or she may fold the paper to make the blots. He or she then develops the design created.
3. Media Exploration—The individual is given free choice of media to experiment with. He or she may choose to work in a single medium such as clay, or use mixed media such as crayons and paint. Artistic products are stimulated by the type of material chosen.
4. Color Exploration—The individual is encouraged to select the color(s) he or she likes most or least and to work with them in free composition. Colors may be chosen to represent moods or the world around the individual.

Rapport Building   Encourages interaction between participants.
1. Conversational Drawing—Partners sit across from one another and take turns adding lines, shapes, colors, and so on to a single drawing. When the drawing is completed, the partners discuss their product.
2. Cooperative Group Painting—A group member produces a painting that is elaborated on by other group members. For example, if the individual paints a picture of a person, group members might improve the work by adding detail. The group discusses all changes that are made in the picture.
3. Painting with an Observer—One child paints and the partner comments on the painting by saying anything that enters his or her mind. The painter responds to the commentary.

Expression of Inner Feelings   Encourages understanding of feelings.
1. Problems and Feelings—The individual paints his or her present mood or a recent or recurring problem.

2. Dreams and Fantasies—The individual paints dreams and fantasies, especially those that are repeated. He or she may depict entire dreams or just the parts that interest or trouble him or her most.

3. Affective Words—The individual paints in response to words that relate to psychological states, such as love, hate, beauty, freedom. He or she may also express contrasting word pairs, such as strength, weakness.

4. Three Wishes—The individual depicts his or her wishes. These are discussed, particularly their realistic and unrealistic aspects.

5. Music and Poetry—The individual may either paint in response to musical or poetic stimulation, or respond to completed paintings by creating music and/or poetry.

Self-Perception Encourages awareness of body image and personal needs.

1. Self-Portraits—The individual may depict himself or herself realistically or abstractly in any medium, including pastels, paint, clay, or collage.

2. Phenomenal, Ideal, and Real Self-Portraits—The individual is instructed first to draw any person he or she wishes to draw. Next, the individual is requested to draw himself or herself as he or she would like to look. Finally, the individual is to draw himself or herself as he or she really is.

3. Immediate States—The individual selects one or more of the following phrases to paint: "I am," "I feel," "I have," and "I do." Discussions of creations may follow.

Interpersonal Relations Encourages awareness of others.

1. Portraits of Group Members—Group members draw each other. The group discusses the drawings.

2. Portraits by Combined Effort—One member of a group creates a self-portrait. Each group member adds something to the portrait to make it more like the subject. When the drawing is finished, the subject may ask the others about their contributions. He or she may also change the portrait to fit his or her self-perception.

3. Pair Portraits Technique—Group members choose partners. Each member draws a self-portrait and a picture of his or her partner.

4. Group Mural—The group works cooperatively on a large surface, such as brown wrapping paper, a wall, the sidewalk. The subject matter may be determined prior to the course of painting.

5. Draw Your Family—The individual may draw his or her family or the family he or she wishes to have. The individual need not include himself or herself.

Environmental Relations   Encourages awareness of one's relationship to the environment.

1. House–Tree–Person—The individual relates a human figure to the common environmental features of tree and house in a single drawing or painting.
2. Elements Picture Series—The individual may paint the elements of air, earth, fire, and water in rapid sequence. Discussions following completion center on the individual's feelings toward the natural forces of the environment.
3. Collage and Assemblage—The individual creates a product with a combination of two- and three-dimensional materials, for example, magazine pictures, fabric, wood, or any other natural objects. He or she pastes or glues them together to portray any theme of interest to him or her.

APPLICATION OF ART THERAPY TO EDUCATIONAL SETTINGS

In recent years there has been an increasing interest in art therapy as an educational technique. However, at present there are relatively few art therapy programs in the schools, therefore the interested teacher must establish her or his own program. To do so she or he must consider likely candidates for the program; physical arrangements, such as place, time, and materials; and, most importantly, her or his role in implementing the program.

Candidates for Classroom Programs

According to its advocates, art therapy is appropriate for persons of all ages. Kramer (1971) points out that it is most useful when children have the capacity to produce original artistic products, and she sets the optimal age range from 3 to 13 years. Children within this age range have learned to distinguish between art and play. They understand what is expected of them and are willing to attempt artistic tasks voluntarily.

In addition, the use of art therapy techniques in schools need not be limited to children with severe emotional disorders. Although these techniques are useful for making contact with severely handicapped children who have few if any alternate avenues of communication, they also may be used with children whose emotional problems are mild or moderate. In fact, in school situations art therapy techniques are more likely to be used with less seriously disturbed children. In many of these situations, entire groups or classes can engage in art therapy activities.

Physical Arrangements

The freedom of choice given the client in classical art therapy is not usually possible in the classroom. The teacher's program must conform to realistic limitations in space, time, and materials. The teacher probably will not have a special room available for art therapy, but will need to find *space* within the classroom. Although this type of arrangement may appear to be less than ideal, it actually has several advantages. The teacher can permit some children to engage in art activities while she or he helps others perform other tasks. It is also convenient for the children, who can work on their art projects during their free time, as well as for the teacher, who need not transport students, materials, and other equipment from one room to another.

Most experts recommend that a specific classroom area be maintained exclusively for art activities. If desks, chairs, and materials remain in place, the children have easy access to them. Also, art activities can be quite messy and attempts to conduct them in an area used simultaneously for other activities usually create problems.

Running water and a sink are important components of any type of art program. When they are not available in the classroom the teacher must improvise. Plastic dishpans or metal tubs may be filled with water and kept in the art area. Pitchers or lipped cups should be provided to distribute water needed to mix paints or wet clay. Piles of paper towels and newspapers should be readily available. Selected places should be set aside to dry and store pictures.

Having established where to conduct art therapy techniques, the teacher must consider appropriate *timelines for the sessions.* Generally, sessions lasting approximately one hour are recommended. This amount of time is usually sufficient for children to set up, create, and clean up. As to the frequency of the sessions, Kramer (1971) suggests that two scheduled sessions per week are adequate for most children. However, children who are difficult to reach through other media, but who participate enthusiastically in art projects, may be permitted to spend additional time in such activities.

The *best materials* for art therapy are those that are simple, familiar, and easily manipulated. The three basic media recommended because of their simplicity and multiple uses are paint, clay, and crayon-like materials. All three are readily available in most schools. Tempera or poster paint is preferred to oils and watercolors because it is colorful, easy to use, control, and mix, quick to dry, and may be applied to wet or dry clay. Both oils and watercolors require greater skill to use. Although watercolors are available in convenient containers and dry quickly, they are difficult to control while painting. Oils are easier to apply but are very slow to dry.

Clay has the advantage of being the most directly manipulated of the art materials. Children inhibited by a paint brush or a crayon often find clay a suitable alternative. Also, it is easier to handle and manage than paint. The crayon-like materials recommended include crayons, craypas, chalk, pastels, and charcoal. Crayons and craypas should be used with young children and with older children who are still in the stage of primitive or line drawing. Both provide rich colors that are easily controlled. Chalks, pastels, and charcoal are recommended for older children and adolescents who are able to control them in the shading and blending of color.

Other materials that the teacher will need are different sizes and types of paper, different sizes of brushes, a large roll of brown wrapping paper, oil-cloth pads, sponges, cups or cans for water, popsicle sticks for stirring paint, and cardboard tubes to roll out clay. Each child should have his or her own set of materials. Individual equipment is especially important when working with disturbed children who might become extremely upset if desired materials are missing or misplaced. Each individual kit should contain two or three brushes, a set of crayon-like materials, a container for water, and a tray for mixing colors. Kramer (1971) suggests using muffin tins for mixing paint, while Pine (1977) opts for the less expensive bendable ice-cube trays.

There are several kinds of materials that are not recommended for use in schools. Fingerpaints, long considered a basic tool of classic art therapy because they permit a direct expression of inner feelings, are regarded as an inappropriate material in the classroom where the primary goal is a creative production. Commercially produced products such as coloring books and paint by number kits should never be used in art therapy, as they do not involve a creative process. Kramer (1977, p. 109) says the following about these devices: "The greatest objection against coloring books is their bad taste, saccharine sweetness, and insipid content"; and painting by numbers is "possibly the most destructive of all pseudo-arts" (p. 108). She suggests that if the situation calls for busy work rather than creative activity, crafts such as weaving or embroidery are preferable.[1]

The final component of the physical arrangements necessary to conduct art therapy within the classroom is the establishment of a highly structured set of rules for the use and maintenance of the art area. Before involving the children in creative art projects, the teacher must specify precisely what behaviors are permitted in the art area and the circumstances under which the area may be used, when, for how long, and for

---

[1] Art therapists differentiate between art and craft. Art is a creative activity culminating in an original product, whereas craft involves transforming raw material into something useful.

what reason. She or he must also designate where objects are stored, and must assign children responsibility for various chores. In short, she or he must ensure that the children do not become overly stimulated by the art materials and behave chaotically. Even when firm rules are provided, the teacher may find that certain children simply cannot use art techniques constructively and that they must be excluded from the activity.

The Teacher as Therapist

Obviously, the teacher's goal in using art therapy activities is not to delve into her or his student's unconscious minds. The teacher is not expected to use psychoanalytical principles with the children. The usefulness of art therapy techniques in classroom situations depends on the teacher's ability to follow certain practical operational guidelines and to establish a realistic set of goals.

The first guideline is that the teacher learn about a few basic art techniques and become familiar with the use of popular art materials. Clearly, she or he need not be a gifted artist, nor need be competent in a vast array of art techniques. Her or his expertise, though limited, should be sufficient to interest the children in artistic expression.

The second guideline is that, whenever possible, the teacher should adhere to the principles of acceptance and nondirectiveness. The goal is to help the children express themselves through art, not to have them produce a masterpiece. Therefore, each child's efforts should be positively reinforced—used as an avenue for increasing self-esteem and building a positive trusting relationship.

Teacher directiveness should be channeled toward the establishment and enforcement of behavioral rules, not the generation or interpretation of the artistic product. Exceptions to that general rule should be made only under the following circumstances. When a child lacks imagination and stares at a blank paper without attempting to participate, the teacher should stimulate him or her with suggestions of materials and topics. Materials with inherent structure such as fabric and clay are particularly useful. When a child who originally was interested and active in art sessions becomes unmotivated, the teacher should encourage him or her to try alternate materials. Kramer (1971) suggests that a child under 10 should concentrate on the basic media, paint, clay, and crayon-like materials. Children approaching adolescence (ages 11–13) need a broader choice of materials to avoid boredom. Finally, certain handicapped children require direction toward particular types of materials. Both Kramer (1971) and Pine (1977) recommend clay and other touchable material for hyperactive and brain-injured children. Similarly, blind children enjoy touchable materials. Pine also suggests that schizophrenic children not be required to make too many decisions. The teacher should have them decide only what to make and should select their materials.

The third guideline incorporates two major strategies of art therapy. The teacher's main strategy (Naumburg, 1973) is to convince each child that his or her feelings, thoughts, and experiences are worthwhile material for artistic expression. The child must understand that perfect duplication of existing material does not constitute creative art. The second strategy is to help each child set realistic goals for himself or herself. The child must learn to accept technical limitations and must be brought to realize that no mistakes in art are irreparable.

The teacher's goals for the art therapy program are more general than the program guidelines, but no less important. The first goal is to *foster individual growth*. Basically, all children benefit from additional outlets for their emotions, particularly when they feel free of the fear of failure or criticism. The second goal is to *promote interpersonal and group relationships*. Group art sessions help children learn to encourage and understand each other. The optimal group size to promote positive interrelationships varies with the children involved. It can consist of as few as two or as many as ten. The critical variable is that the teacher maintain a noncompetitive atmosphere. Pine (1977) suggests that the teacher remind the members of the group that they draw differently from one another, not necessarily better or worse.

The third goal of art therapy is to *establish communication through the creative process*. A good means of achieving this goal is to exhibit each child's work. Themal (1977, p. 105) writes: "Exhibition, besides giving the children a feeling of accomplishment, meets another need, perhaps the greatest need of all . . . to communicate."

MUSIC THERAPY: THEORETICAL BACKGROUND

The historical development of music therapy in this country has some resemblance to that of art therapy. It began as a tool of the occupational and recreational therapists in post-war years, then was used strictly as an adjunct to analytically oriented psychotherapy. Now, music therapy has come to be recognized as a unique therapeutic method.

Gaston (1968) traces the history of music therapy through three stages of development. In the first stage, music was regarded as an almost magical healing agent and the therapist's role was minimized. This period was followed by one featuring a zealous regard for the therapist's role and deemphasized the musical element. Finally, in stage three, the emphases of stages one and two were balanced so that the elements of music and therapy were considered mutually supportive ingredients in the music therapy process. In the decade that has passed since the delineation of these three stages, music therapy has undergone further changes that constitute a fourth stage of development. Music therapy now is represented as a methodology to promote behavioral change. Michel (1976) notes that therapy must seek to accomplish specific treatment goals by changing behavior from undesirable to desirable and that each treatment must be individualized.

The devotees of music therapy cite its advantages. First, music provides a universal means of communication. It can be adapted for use with persons of various ages, backgrounds, and intellectual and emotional levels. It can provide a full continuum of self-expression, from simple rhythm to complex harmony. It can be a passive listening activity or an active participation activity. It can be used with individuals or groups.

Second, music encourages self-subordination. It provides the opportunity for individuals to learn to cooperate. Third, music is a structured activity that encourages discipline and self-directed behavior. Fourth, music therapy may be used in conjunction with other therapies, that is, behavioral therapy or reality therapy (Michel, 1976). It may serve as a useful tool in establishing a trusting relationship between child and therapist.

Role of the Traditional Therapist

Unlike the art therapist, the music therapist is not bound closely to psychoanalytic theory. Instead, she or he is a generalist who uses music to change individual behaviors. In the role of generalist, the therapist is expected to remain flexible, that is, to identify each child's specific needs and, through *improvisation*, to spontaneously alter the therapeutic program to meet those needs. Thus, improvisation is basic to the therapist's role. Nordoff and Robbins, (1968, 1971a, b) describe their use of improvisation with young psychotic children. They searched out a region of contact with each child by improvising rhythms and melodies in therapy. As the child's response changed, so did his or her musical stimulation.

Obviously, the music therapist's goal is not to produce better musicians. In certain cases this result may occur incidently; however, the ultimate goal is "to enable the individual to function at his best in society" (Gaston, 1968, p. 27). Harbert (1974), Robison (1968), and Sears (1968) have evolved a list of more specific goals. They may be categorized as general, personal, social, and musical.

The general goals are

1. To promote emotional health and development.
2. To provide emotional release.
3. To provide physiological release.

The personal goals are

1. To build self-confidence and self-esteem.
2. To increase attention span.
3. To help the acceptance of personal limits.
4. To provide acceptable ways of expressing feelings.

The social goals are

1. To develop social awareness.
2. To stimulate communication.
3. To foster satisfactory interpersonal relationships.
4. To increase range and flexibility of behavior in social interactions.

The musical goals are

1. To introduce the beauty and joy of music.
2. To provide a release for creative self-expression.
3. To channel latent musical abilities.
4. To offer an opportunity to display skills and accomplishments.

Techniques

Alvin (1976) believes that all children can be reached by music if the presentation of techniques is appropriate. Music offers a variety of techniques that may be used with individuals or with groups.

Individual Therapeutic Techniques   Individual music therapy is most often used with severe cases of emotional disturbance such as autism or schizophrenia, usually in hospital or clinical settings. These sessions generally begin with improvisation. The therapist plays an instrument, usually the piano, seeking to evoke a musical response from the patient. The patient's response might be vocal or instrumental. If instruments are involved, drums or cymbals are the usual choices in initial sessions. If the child responds, the therapist attempts to accompany his or her musical effort. The goal is to use the music to heighten the child's contact with reality and to provide a method for communication to children who either have not developed or have lost the ability to express themselves verbally. Other individual therapy techniques are essentially adaptations of the techniques explained under group therapy procedures.

Group Therapeutic Techniques   In recent years, group application of music therapy techniques has gained popularity. Group therapy involves three basic techniques: listening, singing, and playing. *Listening* is the most passive of the group techniques and is often the precursor to involvement in singing or playing. At the most elementary level, the therapist simply plays music or recordings of music while the group listens. More active listening is stimulated by the use of several techniques:

1. *Telling a story to music.* The children are encouraged to listen to the music, then to make up a story to fit the music. They may tell the story orally, write it down, or draw a picture depicting it. Alvin (1976) suggests giving a title to the musical piece to stimulate the listener's imagination.
2. *Expressing feeling to music.* The children are instructed to listen, then

to tell how music makes them feel. They also may show their feelings in nonverbal ways such as dance, painting, poetry.

3. *Using music as a source of subject matter.* The musical pieces are used to promote intelligent discussion. Topics such as the period or type of music represented, the composer's life, or the instruments used in the recording might be discussed.

Singing, while not a nonverbal technique, can provide a form of communication that is less threatening than speech. Group singing also provides a social foundation for the development of interpersonal relations. Nordoff and Robbins (1971a) recommend that songs used in music therapy relate to the children's personal experiences. Alvin (1976) recommends that the songs relate to concrete situations and enjoyable experiences. Generally, the songs used in music therapy fall into four categories: happy songs—express various uplifting feelings in a stimulating manner, purposeful songs—express a set of actions, thoughtful songs—express material of a meditative nature, and lyrical songs—express feelings of tenderness and wonder.

A technique often used to open a singing session with young children is a greeting or name song. For example, the children's names can be sung as in "Hello Sally, Hello Sally, How Are You?" to the tune of "Frère Jacques." Other songs that enhance communication, develop awareness, and promote basic academic learning may involve spelling common words, counting, identifying colors, and singing the days of the week or months of the year.

Playing has the advantages of involving the children in the live production of music, teaching them new skills, and being completely nonverbal. Nordoff and Robbins (1971a) categorize the best instruments for playing in music therapy as those that are sturdy, attractive, produce a good sound, and have a variety of uses. For young children or older children who have no experience with complex instruments, they recommend the use of simple rhythm instruments such as resonator bells, drums, tambourines, rattles, shakers, maracas, bells, triangles, xylophones, and tone blocks. The therapist gives each child an instrument, demonstrates its use, and leads the group usually by playing a recording of a rhythmic composition.

Playing activities for older children may involve more complex instruments such as guitar, banjo, ukulele, and autoharp. The recorder is an excellent alternative for use with groups, as it is inexpensive and relatively easy to play. Obviously, the therapist using these instruments must have expertise as a musician. Also, the children must evidence a great interest in musical activities and be capable of learning to play such instruments. Under these circumstances, the children can be taught simple songs and can play together as a group after very little practice.

APPLICATIONS IN CLASSROOM SETTINGS

Michel (1976) suggests that the field of music therapy is in transition. He believes its future lies not in institutional settings, but in health-related services and educational programs. Similarly, the role of the music therapist is changing from clinical specialist to that of resource person within the schools. When such specialists are not available, however, music therapy still can be a valuable asset for the teacher of emotionally disturbed children. Essentially it can serve as an adjunct to the teacher's comprehensive program of remedial instruction and behavioral management. To use music therapy techniques the teacher must consider candidates for the program, physical arrangements such as space, time, and materials, and her or his role as therapist.

Candidates

As is true of art therapy, music therapy can be used with children of all ages. The primary requirement is that the child be capable of responding to music when he or she hears it. Musical techniques may also be used with children whose emotional disorders range from mild to severe. Nordoff and Robbins have applied music therapy with handicapped children. A discussion of their experiences and the techniques they used is available in their book *Therapy in Music for Handicapped Children* (1971b).

Physical Arrangements

The essential physical component for a music therapy program is space. Most classroom sessions will involve groups and will require a relatively large amount of space. However, unlike an art area, a music area need not remain static. It can be established when needed simply by rearranging the portable elements of the classroom. The single exception to this rule recommended by most experts is the establishment of a permanent listening corner. This small section of the classroom should be kept available for the children who may wish to spend free time listening to music, may require music as a calming influence, or may choose to listen to music as an earned reinforcement.

Musical activities are generally easy to schedule as part of the school day. Unlike art they require little time for set-up and clean-up. Nordoff and Robbins (1971a) suggest a time range of 20 to 60 minutes per session, depending on the age and interests of the children and the complexity of the instruments they are using.

The materials used in a classroom program probably will be those readily available to the teacher. In addition to using her or his own equipment, school-based resources are the music teacher, the library, and the children. If the teacher plans a program of listening activities she or he will require a record player or tape recorder, accompanying head phones (if available), and various musical recordings. The recordings should vary in type and include both popular and classical music. Two basic categories are music that sedates and music that stimulates. Sears (1968) identifies stimulating music as music that tends to increase physical activity and reduce mental activity, has a fast tempo, detached (staccato) lines, complex and dissonant harmonies, and abrupt dynamic changes. In contrast, sedating music tends to reduce physical activity and increase contemplation, has a slow tempo, smooth (legato) lines, simple harmonies, and little dynamic change. The teacher can refer to the following source to aid in the selection of pieces: *Music and Your Emotions: A Practical Guide to Music Selections Associated with Desired Emotional Responses,* Liveright Publishing Corporation, New York, 1952.

Singing activities require only a selection of songs and, if desired, a musical instrument for accompaniment. Song books typically used with children in regular education are suitable for therapeutic use. Another source is *Opening Doors Through Music: A Practical Guide for Teachers, Therapists, Students, and Parents* (Harbert, 1974). This book is useful primarily with young children. Materials for adolescents should include a variety of classical, popular, and folk tunes that may be sung chorally or as solo pieces.

The choice of accompaniment for singing activities depends on the teacher's ability to play a musical instrument. If he or she cannot play, accompaniment can be vocal. If he or she is not confident about his or her singing ability, the accompaniment can be produced with recordings.

The Teacher's Role

The teacher of emotionally disturbed children is not interested in music therapy as a total therapeutic intervention. Obviously, the role of teacher belies such emphasis. If the techniques and methods associated with this intervention are to be useful, they must be integrated into the total educational program. To a teacher who enjoys music, and it is logical to assume that no other teacher would be interested in using these techniques, they provide an opportunity to relate to the children in an atypical or nonstereotypical fashion. In a sense, the teacher can share a pleasure-giving experience with the children that supersedes the customary instructor–student relationship. The manner in which these methods are integrated into the teacher's program will vary with the needs and interests of the class. Several obvious uses are

1. To produce a relaxing atmosphere. Often emotionally disturbed children become overly stimulated by classroom events. In these situations the teacher may use recorded music to calm the group.

2. To provide an opportunity to be successful. Some children have the inherent aptitude to excel at vocal or instrumental musical activities. Since they may have many academic and social problems, the opportunity to develop and display their talent can be an important avenue to increasing self-esteem.
3. To reinforce children. Musical activities can serve as a reward for improved behavior, completion of work, and so on.
4. To provide an expressive outlet. Musical activities such as those associated with singing or playing in a rhythm band are good ways to "blow off steam." Often, permitting emotionally disturbed children to ventilate in this socially acceptable way prevents undesirable displays of emotion.
5. To encourage social interactions. Emotionally disturbed children benefit from opportunities to work cooperatively with each other. Music is an excellent resource to encourage such activity.

SUMMARY

The thrust of this chapter has been to provide suggestions for the utilization of art and music as therapeutic aids in the classroom. The intent clearly is not to promote either technique as a cure-all or substitute for comprehensive therapeutic intervention that must involve individualized instruction and verbal exchanges oriented toward problem solving and behavioral change. These methods simply increase the teacher's therapeutic arsenal by providing the means to expedite the emotional growth of some children and to reach others who might otherwise remain unreachable.

STUDY QUESTIONS

1. Trace the theoretical frame of reference that underlies art therapy.
2. Plan both an art and a music therapy project, adapted for regular students within the classroom.
3. Develop an integrated educational plan for emotionally disturbed children that combines either art or music techniques with either behavioral or rational–cognitive therapy.

REFERENCES

Alvin, J. *Music for the handicapped child.* 2nd ed. London: Oxford University Press, 1976.
Betensky, Mala. *Self discovery through self-expression: use of art in psycho-*

therapy with children and adolescents. Springfield, Ill. Charles C Thomas, 1973.

Denny, James M. Techniques for individual and group art therapy. In E. Ulman and P. Dachinger (eds.). *Art therapy in theory and practice.* New York: Schocken, 1977.

Freud, S. New introductory lectures on psychoanalysis. In J. Strachey (ed.). *Dreams.* Vol. II, London: Hogarth Press, 1963.

Gaston, E. Thayer. Man and music. In E. Thayer Gaston (ed.). *Music in therapy.* New York: Macmillan, 1968.

Harbert, Wilhelmina K. *Opening doors through music: a practical guide for teachers, therapists, students, parents.* Springfield, Ill. Charles C Thomas, 1974.

Kramer, Edith. Art and craft. In E. Ulman and P. Dachinger (eds.). *Art therapy in theory and practice.* New York: Schocken, 1977.

Kramer, Edith. *Art as therapy with children.* New York: Schocken, 1971.

Kramer, Edith. *Art therapy in a children's community.* Springfield, Ill. Charles C Thomas, 1973.

Michel, Donald E. *Music therapy: an introduction to therapy and special education through music.* Springfield, Ill. Charles C Thomas, 1976.

Music Research Foundation. *Music and your emotions: a practical guide to music selections associated with desired emotional responses.* New York: Liveright, 1952.

Naumburg, Margaret. *An introduction to art therapy: studies of the "free" art expression of behavior problem children and adolescents as a means of diagnosis and therapy.* New York: Teachers College Press, 1973.

Naumburg, Margaret. *Dynamically oriented art therapy: its principles and practices.* New York: Grune & Stratton, 1966.

Nordoff, Paul, and Robbins, Clive. Improvised music as therapy for autistic children. In E. Thayer Gaston (ed.). *Music in therapy.* New York: Macmillan, 1968.

Nordoff, Paul, and Robbins, Clive. *Music therapy in special education.* New York: John Day, 1971a.

Nordoff, Paul, and Robbins, Clive. *Therapy in music for handicapped children.* New York: St. Martin's, 1971b.

Pine, Sandra. Fostering growth through art education, art therapy, and art in psychotherapy. In E. Ulman and P. Dachinger (eds.). *Art therapy in theory and practice.* New York: Schocken, 1977.

Robison, Doris E. Music therapy in a children's home. In E. Thayer Gaston (ed.). *Music in therapy.* New York: Macmillan, 1968.

Sears, William W. Processes in music therapy. In E. Thayer Gaston (ed.). *Music in therapy.* New York: Macmillan, 1968.

Themal, Joachim. Children's work as art. In E. Ulman and P. Dachinger (eds.). *Art therapy in theory and practice.* New York: Schocken, 1977.

Ulman, Elinor. Art therapy: problems of definition. In E. Ulman and P. Dachinger (eds.). *Art therapy in theory and practice.* New York: Schocken, 1977.

13
General Guidelines for
Using Alternate Therapies

Nine types of therapeutic interventions have been discussed in the preceding chapters. They are presented in Table 13.1, which shows the comprehensiveness of each approach, the degree of therapist directiveness, the optimal age ranges, the underlying theoretical orientations, key individuals associated with each position, important therapeutic techniques, and the primary goal of each approach. This summary information provides a general perspective of each therapy that may serve as a convenient basis for comparison of alternate approaches. It also provides a basis for the development of an eclectic program that incorporates a variety of therapeutic techniques. A discussion of the characteristics included in Table 13.1 will be followed by the presentation of a case for eclecticism.

CHARACTERISTICS OF NINE THERAPIES

The first characteristic, *comprehensiveness*, is the extent to which a therapy may serve as a total methodology for planning and implementing an intervention program for disturbed children. Among the nine therapies discussed, five are designed as complete methodologies and may be used independently. These are group, behavioral, educational, rational–cognitive and milieu.

Group therapy is perhaps the most atypical of the total methodologies, since it does not reflect a particular philosophical orientation, but simply delineates the therapeutic procedures involved in working with more than one person simultaneously. As noted, any of the approaches presented in Chapters 6 through 12 can be applied to groups. Yet, there is a technology specifically associated with group proceedings, for example, leader behaviors or group interaction processes, that to a great extent

Table 13.1 *Characteristics of Nine Therapies*

Therapy	Comprehensiveness	Therapist Control	Optimal Ages	Theoretical Orientation
Group	Total	Varied	6–21+	Varied
Behavioral				
Behavior Modification	Total	Directive	3–14	Behavioral
Clinical–Behavioral	Total	Directive	3–21+	Behavioral
Educational	Total	Directive	6–21+	Behavioral/others
Rational–Cognitive	Total	Directive	12–21+	Cognitive
Milieu	Total	Nondirective	6–21+	Sociological
Play	Ancillary	Nondirective	3– 8	Phenomenological
Drama	Ancillary	Nondirective	6–21+	Psychoanalytical
Art	Ancillary	Nondirective	3–21+	Psychoanalytical
Music	Ancillary	Nondirective	3–21+	Psychoanalytical

transcends specific orientations and that marks group therapy as a distinct comprehensive methodology.

Behavioral, educational, rational–cognitive and milieu therapies involve classroom-management strategies as well as techniques for evoking specific behavioral changes. Any of these approaches could be implemented as a total intervention program for emotionally disturbed children.

The four remaining therapies, play, drama, art, and music, are presented as ancillary techniques that should be used in conjunction with any of the comprehensive methodologies. For example, art therapy sessions might be integrated into a behaviorally oriented classroom to establish communication with withdrawn, nonverbal children.

The second characteristic is the extent to which the *therapist directs* or controls the therapeutic proceedings. In group therapy, that characteristic varies with the philosophical orientation of the therapist. For example, if she or he adhered to a client-centered or Rogerian philosophy she would be nondirective, whereas she or he would be far more directive operating from a rational-emotive (Ellis) orientation. Among the other comprehensive methodologies, all except milieu therapy establish a relatively directive role for the therapist. In other words, the therapist acts to control the therapeutic events through procedures such as reinforcing desired responses (behavioral therapy), telling the child to examine self-

Influential Person	Important Techniques	Primary Goal
Varied	Group Dynamics	Group Interactions
Skinner	Reinforcement	Manage Behavior
Wolpe/Lazarus	Systematic Desensitization	Alter Behavior
Hewett/Haring/Lindsley/ Peter	Task Analysis/Behavioral Objectives/Structure	Provide Academic Success
Ellis/Glasser	Altering Self-Talk/Reality Interviewing	Alter Thought
Redl/Morse/Hobbs	Life-Space Interview/Crisis Intervention	Alter Environment
Axline/Ginott	Permissive Group Techniques	Expression of Emotion
Moreno	Role Playing	Expression of Emotion
Kramer/Naumburg	Creative Art	Expression of Emotion
Nordoff/Robbins/Alvin	Listening/Singing/Playing	Expression of Emotion

talk (rational–cognitive therapy), or sequencing the child's academic assignments so he or she will be able to achieve success (educational therapy). With the exception of Hobbs's Re-ED program, (which could be classified as an educational approach), the milieu procedures involve far less leader directiveness. This fact is particularly apparent in the thrust of Redl's and Morse's remarks about life-space interviewing and crisis intervention. The important nondirective, phenomenological notion of eliciting and accepting the child's perceptions of events (feelings, attitudes and opinions), as *reality* is the keystone of both these techniques.

The ancillary interventions, to varying degrees, also involve nondirective roles for the therapist. Play therapy, particularly Axline's perspective, is founded on the basic techniques of the nondirective school: unqualified acceptance of the child, reflection and clarification of the child's feelings, and no interpretation of underlying motivation. In fact, Axline studied with Carl Rogers, the founder of the nondirective, approach to psychotherapy. Art and music therapy also reflect nondirective principles to the extent that the therapist encourages the child's creative expression by neither telling him or her what to do, nor interpreting his or her product. Drama therapy possibly is the least nondirective of the ancillary approaches. Role-playing techniques may be used to simulate situations that evoke anxiety as part of desensitization procedures—a very directive approach. However, many of the dramatic techniques are designed to increase self-awareness and to indirectly cause behavioral change, a nondirective approach.

Although it was stated before, it is worth reiterating, that all therapeutic approaches are designed to alter behavior. Some therapies advocate more direct avenues toward change than others. Often, in practice, directive and nondirective techniques are integrated and used selectively depending on variables such as the child's attitude and the environmental situation. However, the therapist's goal for therapy, that is, what he or she wants to accomplish, reflects the extent to which a directive or nondirective role is taken on.

The third characteristic involves the *optimal ages* for the use of each approach. Those ages presented fall within the range of 3 to 21, when school services are mandated for exceptional children. These age ranges are not intended to represent absolute limits for the use of each approach. Thus, they should not lead to conclusions such as "behavior modification cannot be used with children over the age of 14." Obviously, with the exception of play therapy, any of these interventions can be used with persons of all ages. The age ranges presented are simply suggestions of age periods when specific interventions *may be most effective.*

Group techniques are probably most effective after children have developed sufficient social interaction skills. Thus, the age of 6 seems to be a realistic lower limit for group proceedings. The age range of 3 to 14 is suggested for behavior modification techniques, not to imply that they are not useful with older children, but to suggest that they must be supplemented with strategies to alter cognitive operations when they are used with older children. As children mature, appeals to their reasoning ability add to the efficiency of the therapeutic intervention. Seemingly, aspects of clinical–behavioral therapy, as opposed to the operant procedures associated with behavior modification, include a more pronounced cognitive thrust. Therefore, the age range for that technique includes older children.

Educational therapy is useful with children throughout their school careers, beginning with the time their chronological age marks them as ready for academic instruction. Since academic failure is a significant contributing factor to the problem of emotional disturbance, the earlier a child's achievement difficulties receive attention, the greater the probability of effecting lasting behavioral change.

The rational–cognitive approach, particularly Ellis's techniques, should work best when the child has the cognitive and linguistic skills to understand the abstract concept of self-talk, and to monitor his or her internal verbalizations. The child should have reached Piaget's cognitive level of formal operations to engage in the reasoning processes required for this approach. Therefore, the age of 12 appears to be a realistic lower limit.

The interviewing techniques that are so important in milieu therapy would appear to work best when the child possesses the developmental maturity to control impulses and discuss behavior. Since he or she need not engage in abstract discussions of thought, but must deal with concrete situations and events, the child probably could respond effectively at age 6. A similar lower age limit appears applicable to drama therapy, where verbal competence is an important requisite for role playing and other techniques.

Play therapy is basically a technique for young children, aged 3 to 8, although some applications through games and sports can be used to "break the ice," and to develop rapport with older children. Forms of art and music therapy apply to a broad age range of children. Obviously, the specific techniques used depends upon the ages of the children involved.

As noted, these age ranges are suggestions, based on reason, not hard-and-fast rules. Apparently, the age levels at which specific therapeutic interventions are most successful never have been established empirically. Probably, the truism that "early intervention is most effective," is applicable to the problem of emotional disturbance. Young children are more flexible and change more easily than adults. However, to be effective, early intervention obviously must be focused on the alteration of the environment, changing the forces that act on the child through some aspects of milieu, behavioral, and educational therapy. The child does not have the maturity, the linguistic or cognitive skills, for self-analysis or for involved verbal interchanges with others. Change in a young child is dependent on the behavior of those around him or her.

This dependence on external changes is less true of more mature children, although in the treatment of emotional disturbance, maturity is a double-edged sword. It brings with it the reasoning capacity and verbal competence to engage in elaborate analyses of behavior. Thus, the older child car use reason to solve problems. However, the same cognitive development contributes to the child's emotional maladjustment. Problems become more complex and more difficult to identify and to solve, as defenses such as rationalization and denial are strengthened by increased cognitive capacity. As the child ages he or she is increasingly less responsive to environmental influences, and maladaptive behaviors are far more likely to endure.

Clearly, as children age, treatments that ignore their cognitive capacity are likely to fail. Nonverbal techniques that might make a three-year-old child feel better, like symbolically drowning a mother doll by dropping it in water, will hardly produce the same relief in an older individual. Thus the therapy used must directly promote self-understanding and internal motivation to change by encouraging the child to think and act in his or her own behalf.

The fourth characteristic concerns the *theoretical orientations* underlying the therapies. Most of these orientations have been discussed previously in this book. Only the rational–cognitive approach, particularly Ellis's work, is difficult to categorize in the classification system that was presented in Chapter 2. It simply does not belong with any of the existing major perspectives of emotional disturbance. Possibly, cognitive therapy is the approach of the future and its greatest impact is yet to be felt. Cognitive psychology may follow in the footsteps of behavioral psychology and produce a body of theory and empirical evidence that applies specifically to the study of abnormal behavior. Certainly, current research in the area of problem solving (D'Zurilla and Goldfried, 1971) and other related investigations bode well for this outlook. For the present, Ellis remains an innovator who recognized the important relationship between cognition and affect during an era when most theorists (other than the behaviorists) regarded them as two separate domains.

The fifth, sixth, and seventh characteristics of the therapies are provided as a source for convenient referral. The names of *influential persons, the important techniques,* and *the primary goals* of each approach have been elaborated in detail in each chapter.

A CASE FOR ECLECTICISM

It already has been stated that the adjunct or ancillary therapies may be used in conjunction with any of the more comprehensive approaches. It also is true that the methodologies presented as total therapies need not be regarded as mutually exclusive approaches. Group therapy may be integrated with any of the alternate approaches. There are many parallel aspects of behavioral and educational therapy, the latter reflecting, for the most part, the application of the technology discussed in the former to classroom organization and instructional procedures. Additionally, the rational–cognitive approach may be integrated with behavioral procedures, and, in fact, a combination of these two perspectives reflects the most current emphasis in neo-behavioral interventions. Many behavioral therapists now believe that altering internal cognitive operations such as attitudes, feelings, and ideas is more important than manipulating overt behaviors.

Even aspects of milieu therapy, which is philosophically the most different from the other approaches, may be integrated into programs that incorporate components of behaviorial, educational, and rational–cognitive therapy. A basic principle of the milieu approach, that of encouraging the child to assume responsibility for his or her own welfare conforms to the current emphasis in all other approaches. For example, behavioral contracting (behavioral approach), and group problem-solving sessions (rational–cognitive approach) address the same goal by involving the child directly in the resolution of his or her problems.

Another principle of milieu therapy, that of using every aspect of the patient's life as a treatment resource, to some extent simply expands the range of many rational-behavioral-educational procedures. Constructive interventions practiced in the classroom are expanded and applied elsewhere within the school and the home.

The above statements are not meant to convey the impression that the therapies discussed thus far are the same candy in a different wrapper. As noted, most of them reflect different theoretical orientations and differ in emphasis over the most efficient way to influence or change human behavior. In fact, some advocates of specific approaches would resist the suggestion that there are similarities among respective treatments. They focus on the very real philosophic and pragmatic differences that exist and remain committed to the superiority of one particular methodology.

With due respect toward those with the honest reservations about the ability of most persons to competently apply techniques associated with one methodology, not to mention a variety of approaches, the teacher is encouraged to be eclectic, to draw from as many therapeutic sources as possible. With the exception of behavioral therapy, there is little empirical evidence of the efficacy of various approaches—thus teachers are justified in undertaking a certain degree of experimentation within the classroom. Also, the teacher, of necessity, is and is entitled to be, a pragmatist, interested far more in finding strategies that work in her or his unique situation with her or his particular children, than in adopting any specific approach to the solution of emotional problems. The more alternatives available, the stronger the teacher's position. Ultimately, there are three major categories of consideration that should influence the types of intervention strategies practiced. These encompass teacher, student, and environmental variables.

Teacher Variables

Included in this category are all the personal forces that affect behavior, values, feelings, ideas, and so on. Obviously, these forces largely determine what types of interventions will appeal to each individual. Often it is true that unless an individual accepts the validity of a particular intervention methodology she or he probably will not use it effectively or efficiently. Therefore, the teacher who does not believe in the effectiveness of crisis-intervention techniques, or who detests art activities, or who dislikes the whole idea of a token economy, may need to choose alternate procedures for her or his classroom program.

Before deciding to avoid or abandon a particular procedure, however, the teacher should understand all dimensions of the approach and, in some cases, that she or he has "given it an honest try" in the classroom. For example, the teacher may feel skeptical about conducting in-class group meetings, or using dramatic techniques, but on reading and thinking about these interventions, may begin to appreciate their value and may be willing to implement them. On implementing these procedures, the teacher may find that they are easier to use than expected and that they appear to benefit the children. Often a skeptical attitude can be the most valuable precursor to new learning. They key is that the teacher remain objective and make an honest effort to implement the procedure.

This type of teacher objectivity is particularly important when she or he must assume an unfamiliar role. New roles such as discussion-group facilitator, may be threatening or anxiety evoking. Elevated anxiety does not coexist with comfortable feelings, thus initial impressions about an unfamiliar technique might be negative. Obviously, time is needed to adjust to new activities, to gain valuable experience, and to learn to feel comfortable in a new role. However, if the teacher, after making an attempt to implement a particular intervention approach, continues to feel uncomfortable or dissatisfied with the technique or procedure, she or he should consider an alternate approach.

Student Variables

This category encompasses all relevant student characteristics from age and intelligence to academic achievement levels and type and severity of emotional problems. Clearly, age is an important determinant of selected interventions. For example, preschool children may benefit most from behavioral and play techniques that require limited verbalizations and little capacity for higher order abstract reasoning. In contrast, adolescents may require verbal problem-solving group sessions that emphasize rational–cognitive strategies as well as the general use of reinforcement principles. Generally, children above the age of 12 or 13 are more likely to respond to direct efforts to alter their disturbed thoughts. Children below that age are less likely to understand verbal premises but are more readily influenced by applied behavior techniques. Similarly, the child's intellectual level is important. Low-functioning children respond best to behavioral programs. The techniques must be highly structured and teacher directed if the children are to understand what is expected of them.

Children with academic achievement problems require educational therapy techniques. Academic failure may contribute extensively to their general emotional problems, and educational interventions may provide the entry point for more encompassing forms of therapy. Finally, the type and severity of the emotional condition is the most complex of all student variables. Among the severely disturbed, autistic children have made limited responses to opèrant techniques, as well as to art and music therapy. Obviously, verbal discussion is not often useful. Basically, the approaches used with severely disturbed or psychotic children must be highly structured and teacher directed.

When working with moderately and mildly disturbed children, the teacher has a greater selection of intervention techniques. She or he can place greater emphasis on encouraging the child to bear much of the responsibility for behavior changes. As a rule of thumb, mildly neurotic children respond favorably to many different interventions, including systematic desensitization, group discussions, and positive reinforcement schedules. They also may benefit from the freedom to pursue art and music expression. On the other hand, psychopathic or delinquent children are quite resistant to most interventions, with the possible exception of behavioral techniques.

These comments are general statements, as there is no intelligent way of specifying a particular therapeutic intervention for a type of child. Regardless of the label a child bears, he or she will respond to therapy as an individual. Techniques that work in one case may fail in another and vice versa.

Environmental Variables

This category includes school-related conditions such as school regulations, administrator attitudes, and teacher assignment, as well as home-related conditions such as parental attitude.

Some schools set clear limitations on the types of intervention programs that may be implemented. For example, some schools are committed exclusively to behavior modification programs. To successfully implement alternate programs the teacher probably will need to sell administrators on their value. Rather than try to replace one approach with another, the best procedure is to try to integrate new ideas into the old program. Thus, a behavioral program could be expanded to include life-space interviewing or crisis intervention. Art, music, and dramatic activities might be introduced as reinforcing activities.

It is also true that school administrators may be particularly biased against certain types of intervention techniques. Occasionally, the language used to describe the technique may cause them alarm. For example, the term *crisis teacher* was resisted by administrators who maintained that the children in their schools did not experience crises. Thus Morse altered the term to *helping teacher,* a much more acceptable label, and resistance faded. Teachers may want to avoid reference to the term *therapy* when discussing their intervention plans with others. Therapy connotes long, complex mental treatments, psychiatric clinics, and, to some, in-depth psychoanalysis. Supervisory and administrative personnel may have visions of teachers attempting tasks for which they are unqualified and creating more problems than they solve. It is far more informative and less threatening to discuss the specific activities of a classroom program, for example, hold group meetings to discuss class problems, use role playing to improve social interaction skills, and so on. Most administrators will not resist the introduction of new techniques if they are presented properly and if they involve no extensive costs.

The teacher's instructional assignment, whether resource teacher, self-contained teacher of the emotionally disturbed, or regular teacher of mainstreamed disturbed children, obviously will affect the types of intervention programs she or he chooses to implement. A resource teacher who sees children for brief periods of time each day probably is primarily concerned with educational therapy. Most emotionally disturbed children have such significant problems with academic achievement that the resolution of those problems usually takes precedence over alternate therapeutic approaches. The exception to this general rule might occur when the teacher works with secondary-level students who may benefit more from daily problem-solving group discussions than from remedial instruction. Also, some emotionally disturbed children do not have problems with academic achievement, and the resource teacher might arrange to provide them with alternate types of therapy on the same basis as she or he provides educational therapy to failing children.

Teachers of self-contained classes for emotionally disturbed children are not restricted by time limitations in the types of interventions they may use with their charges. Obviously, they must attend to educational needs, but they may use a variety of approaches designed to alter nonacademic behavior simultaneously. For example, they may use highly structured, goal-oriented procedures to conduct the class, but provide opportunities for self-expression and student direction in drama techniques or group meetings.

Regular educators may use many of the techniques for helping emotionally disturbed children as part of the basic affective educational curriculum. For example, role playing may help illustrate the prevalent social dilemmas that exist in the environment. Also, many techniques that benefit disturbed children are equally beneficial for nondisturbed children. For instance, the use of positive reinforcement to encourage greater productivity. As for dealing with disturbed children mainstreamed into the regular classroom, the teacher has a right to expect considerable support from special educators who presumably have a higher level of expertise in these matters. For example, the use of interviewing techniques as a means of crisis intervention or as an avenue for the solution of long-range problems probably remains in the domain of a special teacher, one who is not responsible for the education of 25 to 30 "normal" children, as well as for the emotionally disturbed children integrated into the group.

Parental influences are the final aspect of the environmental variables that bear on the choice of therapeutic techniques used in the classroom. Unless the student's parents understand and support the use of specific therapeutic techniques with their children, they may quickly adopt an adversary attitude toward the teacher's efforts. For example, a parent who learns through gossip that her child receives candy if she completes her assignments might decide that this constitutes bribery and become angry at school authorities. This type of misunderstanding can be avoided through frequent parent conferences during which all elements of the school program are explained to the parent. When, despite thorough explanations, parents remain insistent that certain techniques not be used with their children, the teacher should abide by their decision. Although they may be misguided, their opposition is bound to undermine the teacher's program and be detrimental to the child.

One final point regarding the choice of therapeutic interventions remains to be made. One of the apparent mysteries of effective therapy is the fact that, for some unknown reason, certain people respond to certain techniques as they are practiced by certain therapists. In other words, *therapy is an interactive triad—client × technique × therapist*. The resolution of emotional problems is the product of those three interactive forces. Therefore, by virtue of client differential, the resolution must differ in each specific case, even when the therapist and the technique are held constant. In cases where the product of the interaction is not the desired result, the teacher maintains the option of altering the technique component.

STUDY QUESTIONS

1. Plan an intervention program using any or all of the theories discussed in this book for:
   a. A self-contained class of "normal" sixth-grade students.
   b. A group of high-school students who have volunteered to stay one hour after school three days a week to talk about their problems.
   c. A self-contained class of mild and moderately emotionally disturbed children aged 10 to 13.
   d. A group of second- and third-grade children who are serious academic underachievers and who have been assigned to a resource room.
   e. A self-contained class of six psychotic children aged 7–10.
   f. A self-contained class of "normal" third-grade students.

REFERENCE

D'Zurilla, T., and Goldfried, M. Problem solving and behavior modification. *Journal of Abnormal Psychology*, 1971, 78, 107–126.

Appendix

Underlying Rationale And Basic Concepts Of Behavioral Psychology

The basic rationale of the behavioral approach is that all behavior, normal and abnormal, is learned according to the same principles and that all behavior can be modified or altered according to those principles. This emphasis on learning illustrates the importance of environmental factors in shaping behavior and suggests that alterations or adjustments of components in the environment will cause alterations in behavior. Thus, the behavior approach places primary emphasis on the *manipulation of environmental events* to provide the individual with learning experiences that promote adaptive behavior.

Behavioral theorists have formulated three major sets of principles to explain how behavior is learned: classical or respondent conditioning, instrumental or operant conditioning, and observation learning or modeling.

Classical Conditioning First illustrated by Ivan Pavlov (1848–1939), classical conditioning demonstrates how stimuli come to evoke reflex responses. These responses, termed *respondents,* are involuntary or autonomic, that is, they appear to be outside the individual's control or sphere of learning. For example, responses such as pupil constriction to the stimulus of light, or a startle reaction to a loud noise stimulus appear to occur without conscious effort. The light and sound are termed *unconditioned stimuli* (US) and the responses they trigger are *unconditioned responses* (UR). When an US is paired frequently with a neutral stimuli, that is, one that does not elicit a reflex response, that neutral stimuli (now referred to as a *conditioned stimuli,* CS) eventually will elicit the respondent behavior (now termed a *conditioned response,* CR). For example, if a neutral stimulus, a white rabbit, were presented to a child, and the introduction of the rabbit was followed by a loud noise (US) that evoked a startle reaction (UR), eventually the presentation of the rabbit would evoke the startle reaction. In effect, the child's response is dependent on the *arrangement of preceding stimuli*. With this type of experiment, Watson and Rayner (1920) conditioned an 11-month-old boy, Albert, to fear a white rat and appeared to prove that fears can be acquired through classical conditioning.

Operant Conditioning   A term introduced by Skinner (1953), operant conditioning refers to behavior that is not reflexive. Operants are responses performed because of the consequences that follow them. For instance, a child who utters "mama" and receives a great deal of parental attention, will be likely to utter "mama" again. The consequences of the behavior were such that the probability of the response reoccurring was increased. In operant conditioning, the events that follow behavior usually are termed *reinforcements*. The principles of reinforcement are relatively elaborate and will be discussed later in this section.

Before discussing observational learning it is necessary to note that the traditional distinctions between operant and classical conditioning presented above are becoming somewhat blurred. Current behavioral research has demonstrated that the differentiation between voluntary and involuntary responses is no longer a valid indicator of two distinct types of conditioning paradigms. Responses such as heart rate, blood pressure, galvanic skin responses, and so on, which were once considered involuntary, have been shown to be changeable through operant conditioning (Kimmel, 1967, 1974).

Also, in applied situations, it is often impossible to distinguish between respondent and operant behaviors. A child may demonstrate fear at the sight of a rabbit as a function of the association of the animal with a loud noise (respondent behavior) or may exhibit fear because parents react with increased attention (operant behavior). Finally, operant behaviors, usually conceived of as being influenced by events that follow the response may also be controlled by preceding stimuli. If a response has been reinforced in a given environmental situation, certain cues from that situation will increase the probability that the response will occur again. Thus, the child who utters "mama" because of the affectionate hug that follows the response is likely to utter "mama" at the sight of mother entering the room. The response is in no way involuntary; therefore, it cannot be construed as a classical response. Despite the theoretical overlap of these two conditioning paradigms, the behavioral literature often represents them as separate entities. Thus, the necessity for discussing them as such in this chapter.

Observational Learning or Modeling (Bandura and Walters, 1963)   This involves learning that is not dependent on performance. Simply stated, behaviors are learned through observation of a model who demonstrates those behaviors. The learner acquires the response cognitively (Bandura, 1971). Once learned, or internalized, the response may or may not be performed, depending on environmental circumstances. One circumstance is the consequences of performing the response. Bandura (1965) demonstrated that children who watched an adult demonstrate aggressive behavior such as striking a doll, performed aggressive behavior when the model either had been rewarded or ignored. They were less likely to behave aggressively when the adult had been punished. Bandura subsequently proved that all the children had learned the aggressive behavior by showing that they all behaved aggressively when given an incentive for aggressive behavior.

Another circumstance affecting performance is the characteristics of the models. Greater imitation usually occurs when models are high in prestige, status, or expertise, and when they are similar in appearance, race, and socioeconomic status to the learner. According to Bandura (1969) modeling encompasses both classical and operant responses and affects both the development of new responses and the frequency of performing previously learned responses.

These three major categories of learning provide the backbone of the behavioral position. Further elaboration of terminology will clarify the applied procedures which will be discussed later in the chapter.

Reinforcement As noted previously, this principle constitutes the basis of operant conditioning. Reinforcement involves the contingency of behavior—it *always increases* the frequency of a response. There are two types of reinforcement: positive and negative. *Positive reinforcement* is an event following behavior that increases the frequency of that behavior. In the example used previously, when the frequency of the child's utterance "mama" was increased by parental attention, the attention was positive reinforcement. A positive reinforcer is not necessarily a reward, although the two terms are often used as synonyms, and rewards often do act as positive reinforcers. The difference lies in the effect on behavior. A positive reinforcer must increase the frequency of the response it follows. Rewards, although appreciated by the recipient, often do not do so. For example, an individual rewarded for saving a drowning child may never demonstrate that behavior again. Also, an event that may appear subjectively to be unrewarding, such as criticism, may act as a positive reinforcer to the individual who, when criticized for a behavior, repeats it. In contrast, an event that subjectively appears to be rewarding, such as praise, may cause diminished responding in a child who is suspicious of praise. Therefore, in this instance, praise is not a positive reinforcer.

Generally, positive reinforcers are categorized in two ways: as *primary or unconditioned reinforcers,* or as *secondary or conditioned reinforcers.* Primary reinforcers are unlearned, natural events that diminish drive states. For example, food and water are automatically reinforcing to an individual who is thirsty and hungry. Their reinforcing value does not depend on previous learning. Of course, since primary reinforcers are associated with internal drive states, their reinforcing value alters as those drive states change. Thus, food is not a good reinforcer if an individual is not hungry.

Secondary reinforcers are events such as praise, money, tokens, grades, and so on, that are not automatically reinforcing, but whose reinforcement potential is learned. Originally, this type of reinforcer is neutral in value, but they acquire reinforcing properties because they have been paired with primary reinforcers or previously conditioned secondary reinforcers. For example, money becomes a reinforcer because it has been paired with a primary reinforcer such as food, or an alternate secondary reinforcer such as a toy. Similarly, tokens may become secondary reinforcers if they are paired with a conditioned secondary reinforcer such as money or a primary reinforcer such as food.

Money serves to illustrate another category of reinforcers referred to as *generalized conditioned reinforcers* (GCR). Generalized conditioned reinforcers are particularly effective in altering behavior because they have been paired with a wide variety of reinforcing events. For example, money may have been paired with items and events such as food, fun, relaxation, comfort, warmth, or status—all useful reinforcers. The reinforcing value of money is greater than any of these independent items, because it may be exchanged for any of them. Thus, the strength of GCR's is derived from the value of the reinforcers they have been associated with. Obviously, tokens are another example of generalized conditioned reinforcers. They may be used to secure a variety of alternate or backup reinforcers.

The types of reinforcement discussed thus far all have been stimuli presented after a response. An alternate and distinct reinforcement category involves reinforcing a response with another response. The Premack principle (1965) states that "Of any pair of responses or activities in which an individual engages, the most probable one will reinforce the less probable one." In other words, if the opportunity to perform a high-probability response is made contingent on performance of a low-probability response, the frequency of the low-probability response will increase. Thus, if eating chocolate cake (a high-probability response) were made contingent on finishing homework, the frequency of homework-completing behavior would increase. In applying this principle, it is important to ensure that a high-probability behavior is a preferred behavior and not simply one that occurs frequently. Taking out the trash might have a high frequency of occurrence, but probably is not a preferred behavior. Therefore, it would not serve as a reinforcer for finishing homework.

Negative reinforcement involves an aversive stimulus whose removal increases the probability of occurrence of the response it follows. For example, visiting a dentist is reinforced by the discontinuation of pain. A more contrived example might involve the presentation of a loud, unpleasant noise that is discontinued when the desired response is performed. Obviously, a negative reinforcer must be presented to an individual before the response so it can be removed when the response occurs.

Often negative reinforcement is confused with punishment. The difference lies in the fact that negative reinforcement always increases the probability of response occurrence, while punishment decreases it. In applied situations this distinction is often lost, and, in fact, many behaviorists refer to punishing stimuli as negative reinforcers, while others wisely avoid confusion by using the term negative contingency to include punishment and negative reinforcement. However, the distinction is useful since it shows how discontinuation of an unpleasant circumstance can reinforce behavior, and also provides a rationale for the old joke about the man who kept banging his head against the wall because it felt so good when he stopped.

As is true of positive reinforcement, there are primary and secondary negative reinforcers. Stimuli that are automatically aversive, such as shock or pain, are primary reinforcers. The aversive quality of secondary reinforcers is learned through association with primary reinforcers. For example, a parent's raised hand, associated previously with pain, may increase a child's attention to work.

Punishment is defined as "a reduction of the future probability of a specific response as a result of the immediate delivery of a stimulus for that response." (Azrin and Holz, 1966, p. 381). The key words in the definition are *reduction, future,* and *immediate.*

As was noted previously, a *reduction* or decrease in the response distinguishes punishment from negative reinforcement. In a more practical vein, the notion of reduction of behavior distinguishes the behavioral concept of punishment from the popular conception. For instance, it is commonly and subjectively assumed that a spanking is punishment. However, from the behavioral perspective, if the response that has elicited the spanking does not diminish, then the aversive stimulus, spanking, is not punishment. In fact, it might be reinforcing, as when a spanked child continues to exhibit a certain maladaptive behavior to secure adult attention. Similarly, a criminal is said to be punished for crime by imprisonment. If the aversive stimuli, imprisonment, does not lead to a decrease in criminal activity, it does not fit the behavioral definition of punishment.

The word *future* is important because it distinguishes between the immediate cessation of behavior, whereas an aversive stimuli, such as spanking, is being administered, and the long-term frequency of occurrence of the behavior. Azrin and Holz (1966) hold that response reduction during punishment is not a sufficient outcome and that punishment as an effective contingency requires future reduction in the frequency of a response.

According to Arzin and Holz, the *immediate* delivery of the aversive stimulus is of critical importance in determining the effectiveness of punishment. Delays between the maladaptive response and punishment should be avoided. Other determinants of effectiveness that they have discovered are that punishment be as intense as possible, continuous, and introduced at maximum strength rather than gradually. Also, extended periods of punishment should be avoided, motivation to emit the punished response should be reduced, and alternative reinforced responses should be available.

Craighead, Kazdin, and Mahoney (1976) elaborate further on the use of punishment. They believe that each occurrence of a maladaptive response should be punished, responses incompatible with the punished response should be reinforced, and a description of the punishment contingency should be given whenever possible. These authors also distinguish between two types of punishment, punishment by application and punishment by removal.

Punishment by application occurs when an aversive stimulus is applied after a response. Examples might be spanking, scolding, a traffic ticket, or a self-induced contingency such as illness caused by overeating. *Punishment by removal* involves the discontinuation of a positive reinforcer after a response. Examples are loss of permission to watch television because of poor grades, loss of dessert because of refusal to eat other food, or loss of tokens earned previously.

Despite what appears to be current evidence that punishment, when used correctly, is a valuable therapeutic device, it remains a touchy issue evoking much disagreement among behavioral therapists. For example, the possibility of negative side effects remains as a detriment to its use in applied situations. Craighead et al. (1976) list as possible side effects: increased emotional responding, avoidance of the punishing agent, and imitation of the use of punishment. They conclude that the use of extinction (to be discussed next) is often preferable, except in situations where the behavior is so dangerous to the child that it must be decreased quickly, such as head banging or fire setting.

Extinction   This concept refers to the decrease in response strength that follows cessation of reinforcement. A behavior that has increased in frequency because of positive reinforcement will decrease when that reinforcement is withheld. Thus a child whose tantrums have been reinforced by parental attention will cease the behavior when the attention is not given.

Craighead et al. (1976) point out that the term *extinction* is often used as a synonym for reduction of behavior brought about by a variety of interventions such as punishment. In fact, the term applies only to the reduction of a previously established bond between a response and its consequences. Its practical applications usually involve ignoring a response that had previously been reinforced, usually by attention. An example occurs when a teacher ignores a child who calls out answers without raising his or her hand, after having previously recognized him or her and reinforced that behavior. Often extinction results in a temporary increase in response rate before the subsequent decrease, as when the child calls out more consistently when ignored, before discontinuing the behavior.

Spontaneous Recovery   After a response has been extinguished and a rest period has occurred, the reintroduction of the conditioned stimuli will cause the response to reappear. For instance, a dog, originally trained to come when a whistle sounds, who has undergone extinction and no longer answers a whistle, will, after a period of time, once again respond to the whistle.

Spontaneous recovery also refers to increases in behavior that occur after cessation of punishment. Thus a behavior, such as calling out in class, that has been controlled through either withdrawal of privileges or application of aversive stimuli, may increase if the punishment is suspended.

Reacquisition   After spontaneous recovery, the conditioned response can be returned to maximum strength faster than the rate demonstrated during the initial training. It also reextinguishes faster when the reinforcement is withdrawn.

Stimulus Control   A response may be reinforced when it is associated with certain stimuli and may not be reinforced in the presence of other stimuli. When it is reinforced consistently, the eliciting stimuli signals that reinforcement is coming and is termed *discriminative stimuli* (SD). Therefore, the probability of a response occurring can be arranged through stimulus control, that is, presenting or removing SD.

Higher Order Conditioning   This procedure involves pairing a formerly neutral stimulus (light) that has become a CS after association with an US (food) with a second neutral stimulus (tone). The second stimulus, tone, becomes a CS exclusively through association with light. It is never associated with the US.

Habit-Family Hierarchy   This concept states that any given stimulus may be attached to a variety of possible responses, each having different habit strength. Habit strength refers to the probability of the response occurring. The greater the habit strength the more likely the response will appear first, that is, before those with lesser habit strength. If the response is not appropriate, in that it either is not reinforced or is punished, its strength declines. If habit strength drops below that of the second response in the hierarchy, then the second response will occur. For example, if a child's highest habit strength response to teacher's stimuli "Clean up your desk," is to make paper airplanes out of waste paper, that response will be demonstrated. Teacher nonreinforcement may drop the strength of that response and raise to the top of his or her hierarchy a more adaptive response.

Drive   This concept pertains to motivational forces that interact with habit strength to produce reaction potential. Reaction potential is simply the probability that the individual will perform a response.

Inhibition   This concept refers to the internal forces that mitigate against the repetition of a response. Hull (1943) hypothesized that inhibiting forces related to fatigue build up and interfere with response performance. These inhibiting factors explain the distinction between massed and spaced practice in motor learning. Spaced practice, with rest periods between trials, is significantly more effective than massed practice with no rest periods for learning motor tasks. Presumably, inhibition reduces learning when practice is massed, is dissipated by rest, and has no effect when practice is spaced.

Reinforcement Schedules   Reinforcement schedules are the arrangements used to control the contingencies of behavior. The simplest schedule, *continuous reinforcement*, requires that the response be reinforced each time it occurs. A schedule involving reinforcement of a response on an intermittent rather than consistent basis is called *intermittent reinforcement*. Research has demonstrated that continuous reinforcement is more effective in eliciting a higher rate of the desired responses during the initial period of learning. However, intermittent reinforcement is more efficient for response maintenance. Also, when intermittent reinforcement is used, the conditioned response is far more resistant to extinction once reinforcement is discontinued.

Schedules for intermittent reinforcement can be arranged according to the number of responses, *a ratio schedule*, or on the basis of the time interval between reinforcements, an *interval schedule*. In other words, a ratio schedule involves reinforcement following a given number of responses, whereas an interval schedule requires that the responses be reinforced after a specified period of time has elapsed.

With both ratio and interval schedules, the delivery of reinforcers can be unvarying or *fixed*, or can be *variable*. Therefore, four basic reinforcement schedules may be used: fixed ratio, variable ratio, fixed interval, and variable interval.

To use a *fixed-ratio schedule*, reinforcement is delivered after a certain previously established number of responses. For example, a child might be reinforced after every fourth demonstration of the desired response. The reinforcement schedule is Fixed-ratio: 4. A *variable-ratio schedule* also involves reinforcement after a previously established number of responses. However, the number of responses required for reinforcement is based on an average. Therefore, if an average number of four responses were required over eight trials, the number of responses per trial might be: 1, 4, 2, 7, 5, 6, 3, 4, which average to four responses per trial. Thus the child on a reinforcement schedule of Variable-ratio: 4, would, over the course of eight trials be required to demonstrate the same number of responses to earn reinforcement as his or her peer on a Fixed-ratio: 4 schedule. However, he or she would not be aware of the number of responses required for reinforcement, as is usually the case with a fixed-ratio schedule.

The unpredictability of the response schedule is one benefit to using variable-ratio schedules. They typically result in a consistent rate of response because the subject never knows when reinforcement will occur. In contrast, fixed schedules produce inconsistent response rates. Responses occur rapidly until reinforcement, then drop off for periods of time. The length of time during which the desired response is not performed is directly related to the largeness of the ratio necessary for reinforcement. Larger ratios produce longer pauses.

With a *fixed-interval schedule* an unvarying time period is established and the first response to occur after that interval passes is reinforced. Thus, if the schedule were Fixed-interval: 5, and the 5 referred to minutes, the first response after each 5-minute period elapsed is reinforced. Subsequent responses during that interval are not reinforced. A *variable-interval schedule*, like the variable-ratio schedule, is computed on an average. If the schedule were Variable-interval: 5 over ten trials, the time intervals in minutes necessary for reinforcement might be: 4, 9, 3, 7, 8, 2, 6, 5, 2, 4, which average 5. Obviously, the time interval selected need not reflect minutes, but can be constituted by any unit of time.

As was the case with ratio schedules, the fixed-interval schedules lead to inconsistent rates of responding. Pauses occur after reinforcement; however, in this case, they are extended until the end of the interval, when the individual anticipates reinforcement. Once again, the variable scheduling prevents this type of anticipation and results in more consistent performance and a higher rate of response.

A comparison of the two types of scheduling reveals that ratio scheduling usually produces a higher response rate. Obviously, an increased number of responses means more frequent reinforcement, whereas with interval schedules, the number of responses has no bearing on reinforcement.

The establishment of a comprehensive program of reinforcement might begin with continuous reinforcement. Once the level of performance reached a satisfactory rate, an intermittent reinforcement schedule that slowly and progressively established longer time intervals between reinforcers, might be used. Ultimately, the reinforcement would be discontinued and, because of the strength of the intermittent scheduling, the desired response will continue to occur, that is, be highly resistant to extinction.

Shaping   This technique involves breaking down a response into a series of sequenced steps and reinforcing each successive step until the terminal response is demonstrated. It is a useful procedure in instances where a desired behavior is not in the subject's repertoire, and therefore cannot be reinforced in toto. For example, a mute child who lacks the ability to say *boy* cannot be reinforced for that behavior. The verbal behavior must be shaped through reinforcement of successive approximations until *boy* is produced, and, from that point on, can be reinforced whenever it occurs. Successive approximations are the sequenced steps that lead the child closer to the production of the word *boy*. He might begin by imitating the sound /b/, then the sound /o/, and so on, in as many steps as necessary until the word is produced. Similarly, shaping is necessary to evoke the performance of tasks that are too complex for the child to produce in toto. For example, the high jump is dependent on the mastery of sequenced lower-order motor behaviors. In shaping behavior, each new step is introduced only after the preceding step has been firmly established and is displayed with high frequency. As learning occurs, the criterion for reinforcement is altered slightly so that the next response more closely resembles the final goal.

Chaining   A chain is a sequence of two or more behaviors. Generally, the successive responses in a chain are part of the individual's behavioral repertoire. The ordering or chaining of these behaviors culminates in a particular complex behavior. Direct reinforcement occurs when the final response in the chain is performed. Earlier behaviors in the sequence are maintained or reinforced by discriminative stimuli, that is, events that signal reinforcement for a particular response. An example of chaining can be seen in the behavior of a violinist who performs a difficult concert and is reinforced by critical acclaim, public applause, and a high salary. The chain of behaviors that culminated in the performance may have been initiated by an agreement with an agent to give a concert. Responses that followed may have included: selection of music, preparation of the violin, and practicing the music. (Obviously each of these steps could be reduced into smaller segments, but they should illustrate the point.) The ultimate response, the concert, which precedes direct reinforcement, acts as a discriminative stimulus, that is, it signals that reinforcement is coming. It also becomes a reinforcer in its own right for the previous link, practicing the music. Practicing in turn acts as a reinforcer for preparing the violin, and that behavior is a reinforcer for selecting the music. In other words, the chaining procedure is a sequence of backward reinforcement, with the last directly reinforced response precipitating the reinforcing properties of all preceding responses. In plain language, one might say "you can't earn the reinforcement if you don't give the concert, you can't give the concert if you don't practice, you can't practice if the instrument isn't ready, and you can't play the instrument if you have no music."

Prompts   Prompts are auxiliary stimuli or events such as verbal directions, gestures, or cues that help bring about a response. They are antecedent events in that they precede the response. If the prompt is used frequently to help produce a response, and the response is reinforced, it will eventually act as a discriminative stimulus and signal that reinforcement will follow the response. Usually prompts are faded or dropped from the antecedent stimuli as the desired response is more firmly established. For example, the teacher says "One and one are /tt/." The prompt /tt/ eventually is eliminated.

The terms defined above are fundamental to understanding behavior theory. There are many additional terms pertaining more directly to the practical applications of that theory. Those are introduced and defined in the body of Chapter 6, Behavioral Therapy. Also, all references for this appendix are incorporated in the references for Behavioral Therapy.

Author Index

433

Main, T., 318
Maisner, E., 362
Malmo, R., 219
Malmquist, C., 74
Mandell, A., 26
Mandell, D., 77
Mann, P., 247
Margaret, A., 73
Marks, I., 209
Martin, G., 202
Martin, R., 215, 216
Martyn, M., 86, 87
Maslow, A., 44–46, 158, 267
Mather, M., 220
Mattson, R., 204
Maultsby, M., 305, 306
Maurer, R., 199
May, R., 50, 148
Mayer, G., 182, 186, 187
McAllister, L., 200
McArthur, M., 196
McBride, G., 67–69
McClure, G., 115
McConnell, D., 200
McGlynn, F., 209
McGuiness, E., 86
McKay, G., 276
McKee, J., 216
McMenemy, R., 248
McNeil, D., 120
McNeil, T., 28, 72
McQueen, M., 202
Mead, G., 54
Mealiea, W., 209
Mednick, S., 28, 72
Mees, H., 197
Meichenbaum, D., 202, 219
Mendels, J., 75
Menninger, K., 66, 155
Menolascino, F., 28
Meyer, V., 208, 218, 220
Meyers, A., 202
Michel, D., 401, 402, 405
Migler, B., 211
Miller, N., 41, 161, 179
Milne, D., 213
Minskoff, E., 32
Minskoff, J., 32
Mogel, S., 212
Money, J., 29
Montenegro, H., 82
Moreno, J., 116, 118, 368, 373, 411

Morris, L., 68
Morrow, R., 234
Morse, W., 274, 278, 330–336, 345, 411
Moss, T., 212, 215
Moustakas, C., 355, 357
Mowrer, O., 41, 179, 218, 309
Mowrer, W., 218
Murphy, H., 75
Murphy, I., 221
Murray, H., 102
Myers, P., 77

National Institute of Mental Health, 65, 77
Naumburg, M., 391, 393, 394, 401, 411
Nawas, M., 209
Neale, D., 218
Neale, J., 180
Nelson, R., 217
Newcomer, P., 32, 100, 107, 108, 128, 213, 214
Newcomer, R., 107
Newman, R., 282, 283, 355
Newsweek, 82
Nolen, P., 204
Nordoff, P., 402, 404, 405, 411

O'Leary, K., 196, 199, 201, 202, 205
O'Leary, S., 199
Ornitz, E., 30
Osherson, S., 384
Osmond, H., 27
Otto, W., 248

Palomares, V., 279
Park, R., 53, 55
Parker, J., 77
Patterson, G., 212, 214, 216, 221
Paul, G., 73, 208, 211
Paul, J., 336
Pavenstedt, E., 67
Pavlov, I., 28, 39, 40, 179, 421
Peale, N., 300
Peck, H., 73
Pekich, J., 110
Perkins, D., 86
Perkins, W., 216
Perls, F., 159, 160, 373
Perrin, L., 86
Peter, L., 238, 411

Subject Index